MW01698930

SPRING 2007

PUBLIC AFFAIRS 599

CASE STUDIES IN BENEFIT COST ANALYSIS AND LEAST COST PLANNING

Richard O. Zerbe Jr.

Parrington 226
zerbe@u.washington.edu

This class considers case studies in Cost Benefit Analysis along with readings to explain cost –benefit concepts. The grades are based on class discussion and a paper, as follows:.

Grades	
Discussion	15%
Presentation of Case	15%
Paper	70%

The textbook is Richard Zerbe and allen Bellas, A Primer for Benefit-Cost Analysis (published by Edward Elgar) This can be purchased from the instructor for a reduced price. This course presupposes that you are familiar with a book such as the textbook or can learn or relearn as necessary the material contained there quickly.

PAPER

The paper can consists of a critique of one of the assigned CBA's or one that you and I pick by mutual agreement., plus the inclusion of such additional material as may help to illuminate the issues discussed. In exceptional cases, your own CBA can be used. The critique and your own analysis should follow a format in which at least the following questions or steps are covered and analyzed:

- Background

1. Set Out assumptions of analysis.

2. Determine who is the Client and from what perspective is the analysis performed?
   List Client

3. Who is to be given standing in the analysis? Who is denied standing? What sentiments are counted and not counted? Why?

List those parties or sentiments with and without standing

4. What are Alternative Projects?
   analyze these.

5. What are the emotional and physical consequences of the project?

6. Monetize these consequences where possible.

7. List the non-monetizable consequences.

8. Account for uncertainty and the non-monetized effects

9 Conclusions
   How robust are the conclusions?
   Recommendations

10. How useful did you find the CBA technique ?
    Explain
    Further Recommendations

CLASS SCHEDULE

DATE	READINGS AND TOPIC	DISCUSSION LEADER
27-Mar	Lecture: Introduction To BCA and CBA	Zerbe
29 Mar	Chapter 2 And 3 Zerbe & Bellas	Zerbe
3 April	T. McDaniels, R. Gregory and D. Fields," Democratizing Risk Management: Successful Public Involvement in Local Water Management Decisions", Risk Analysis, vol. 19, no. 5, 1999	
5-Apr	Paul Portney," Penny-wise and Pound Foolish, New Car Mileage Standards in the United States" Resources, Spring 2002, issue 147, p10f	
10-Apr	J. Rapport & C. Wilkerson, "What Are the Benefits of Hosting a Major League Sports Franchise?, Economic Review First Reserve Bank of Kansas City,, First Quarter, 2001	
12-Apr	Zerbe and Bellas, Chap 94	
17-Apr	"Hahn et al, Should You Be Allowed to Use	

	Your Cellular Phone while Driving:, Regulation, Volume 23, No. 3, p. 46f [Note,: the session leasder should check with AEI-Brookings to determine updates to this.	
19-Apr	I will giving a speech to the ABA in Washington D. C. (on predatory bidding in antitrust law and economics)	No Class
24-Apr	~~Charles Collins~~, on Least Cost Planning for Sound Transit ch 10	Collins problems set
26-Apr	Zerbe & Bellas, Chapter 10; G. Ginsberg and D. Silverberg, "A Cost-Benefit Analysis of Legislation for Bicycle Safety Helmets in Israel" American Journal of Public Health, April 1994, vol. 84, No. 4	zerbe outline for paper (outline w/ refs. 2-3p.)
1-May	P. Lansing, E. Vogel "Restoring the Lower Snake River. Report of the Oregon Natural Resources Council Fund, no date listed: see also Zerbe and Graham, "The Role of Rights in Benefit-Cost Methodologyu: The Example of Salmon Hydroelectirc Dams" Washington LR, vol 74, No. 3, 1999, p763f	
3-May	Stephane Hallegatte, "A Cost-Benefit Analysis of the New Orleans Flood Protection System" AEI-Brookings Joint Center for Regulatory Studies", 2006	
8-May	R. Haveman, 'The Chicago O'Hare Expansion: A Case-Study of Administrative Manipulation of Benefit-Cost Principles, forthcoming 2008 in Research in Law and Economics, (ed. by Zerbe) See also accompanying Material	
10-May	Zerbe & Bellas, Chap 11 Ethanol Deb	
15-May	R. Santerre and J. Vernon, "A Cost-Benefit Analysis of Drug Price Controls in the U. S." AEI-Brookings Joint Center for Regulatory Studies Oct. 2004	
17-May	R. Morimoto and Chris Hjope, "Applying a CBA Model to the Three Gorges Project in	

	China	
22-May	G. Chen, R. Warburton, "Do Speed Cameras Produce Net Benefits? Evidence from British Columbia, Canada" JPAM, vol. 25, no 3, 661-678, 2006	
24-May	E. Garces D. Thomas and J. Currie, "Longer-Term Effects of Head Start" American Economic Review, Sept 2002	
29-May	Student Presentations *	
31-May	Student Presentations	

papers due
June 4th

Risk Analysis, Vol. 19, No. 3, 1999

Democratizing Risk Management: Successful Public Involvement in Local Water Management Decisions

Timothy L. McDaniels,[1] Robin S. Gregory, and Daryl Fields

This paper discusses a successful public involvement effort that addressed and resolved several highly controversial water management issues involving environmental and flood risks associated with an electrical generation facility in British Columbia. It begins with a discussion of concepts for designing public involvement, summarizing research that indicates why individuals and groups may find it difficult to make complex choices. Reasons for public involvement, and the range of current practices are discussed. Next, four principles for designing group decision process are outlined, emphasizing decision-aiding concepts that include "value-focused thinking" and "adaptive management." The next sections discuss the Alouette River Stakeholder Committee process in terms of objectives, participation, process, methods for structuring values and creating alternatives, information sources, and results. Discussion and conclusions complete the paper.

1. INTRODUCTION

Two prestigious U.S. advisory panels, the Presidential/Congressional Commission on Risk Assessment (1997) and the National Research Council's Committee on Risk Assessment (1996), called for increased public involvement in setting policy for risk management questions. This directive has drawn responses from risk professionals ranging from wholehearted endorsement to deep skepticism. Such a range in responses is understandable. On one hand, it is clear that policy for risk management involves public resources and public values, so it is easy to argue that judgments by the public should be used to help guide such decisions. On the other hand, all concerned parties would agree that risk management decisions are enormously complex, replete with technical uncertainties and perplexing value tradeoffs. Making and implementing wise policy choices is difficult, even for those who have specialized in risk management efforts for decades. How then could members of the interested lay public hope to understand and play a meaningful role in making such complex, high stakes choices?

Perhaps wisely, neither of the panel reports spelled out in detail what it meant by public involvement and how it should be conducted.[2] Because there is a wide range of both motivations and processes for public involvement, greater clarity is needed urgently. Moreover, despite the existence of a voluminous literature discussing the pros and cons of various public involvement alternatives, documented success stories that provide insight about concepts and methods are in short supply.

This paper attempts to address that gap. It discusses a successful public involvement effort that ad-

[1] Address correspondence to Timothy L. McDaniels, Institute of Resources and Environment, School of Community and Regional Planning, 6333 Memorial Rd., Vancouver, BC, Canada V6T 1W5. email: timmcd@unixg.ubc.ca

[2] The Appendix of National Research Council, 1996, provides an example of a multiattribute value elicitation approach completed by John Lathrop for Florida Power that has conceptual links to the approach here.

0272-4332/99/0600-0497$16.00/1

dressed and resolved a highly controversial water management question involving an electrical generation facility in British Columbia. In late Fall 1995, two of us (Gregory and McDaniels) were asked by the provincial electrical utility, British Columbia Hydro and Power Authority (BC Hydro), to design and implement a process that would result in a new operating plan for managing water flows in the Alouette River in southwestern British Columbia. The intent was to help develop a water management plan to address ecological risks, power generation, and flood control for the river. The third author (Fields) coordinated the activities of BC Hydro on this project.

The paper begins with a discussion of concepts relevant for public involvement, then turns to the Alouette River experience, which was built on those concepts. Section 2 first considers several lessons from both descriptive and prescriptive decision research to inform public involvement efforts, focusing on the decision-aiding potential of concepts such as "value focused thinking" and "adaptive management." Section 3 turns to the Alouette River Management Committee process. It discusses the history of the issues, outlines initial steps, and summarizes the key activities that included structuring objectives, creating alternatives, characterizing impacts, clarifying tradeoffs, and seeking areas of agreement. Section 4 presents the results, including the consensus decisions reached on all major issues. Section 5 provides discussion and conclusions.

2. CONCEPTS FOR DESIGNING PUBLIC INVOLVEMENT

2.1. Individual and Group Behavioral Decision Research

Behavioral decision research with individuals has developed over the last three decades as a major theme in social psychology and a fundamental influence on social science applications in risk management. These research findings show consistently that, in experiments and real life situations, "humans are quite bad at making complex, unaided decisions" (Slovic, Fischhoff, and Lichtenstein, 1977). Individuals naturally respond to complex tasks by using their judgmental instincts to find an easy or adequate way through the problem at hand. They respond to probabilistic information or questions involving uncertainties with predictable biases that often ignore or misprocess important information (Kahneman, Slovic, and Tversky, 1982). They seem to have little instinctive ability to clarify objectives (March, 1978), create a wide variety of alternatives (Keeney, 1992), or structure decision tasks (Simon, 1990). When asked to consider value tradeoffs or select among alternatives, they may employ a number of heuristic reasoning processes that are susceptible to a variety of contextual or task-related influences (Payne, Bettman and Johnson, 1992). In short, there are many reasons to expect that, on their own, individuals (either lay or expert) will often not make informed, thoughtful choices about complex issues involving uncertainties and value tradeoffs.

Behavioral research regarding group decision processes is equally discouraging about the unaided ability to make wise choices about complex tasks. In general, groups can (at best) do about as well as the more deliberative or well-informed members would on their own in addressing complex judgment tasks. Groups can have improved performance over individuals because more perspectives may be put forward for consideration, and because the chances of having natural systematic thinkers involved is higher. On the other hand, the performance of unaided groups is susceptible to the tendency to establish entrenched positions, a tendency which makes discussion of compromise difficult. Groups also are subject to adopting a common perspective and ignoring contrary information, a tendency termed "group think" (Janis and Mann, 1977). As a result, a single forceful or cantankerous member can have a dramatic effect on a group's activities.

These findings should not be taken as a condemnation of public involvement on the grounds of cognitive shortcomings. They relate to *unaided* efforts at judgment tasks, not to situations in which individuals or groups are aided within structured decision processes. Thus, these findings (intentionally) ignore the crucial role played by those who help participants structure, understand and grapple with the required decision tasks.[3]

The views of two eminent decision scientists help

[3] One reviewer was concerned that the remarks in Sections 2.1 to 2.3 displayed a condescending attitude toward the competence of citizens to make collective decisions, and that the specific paragraph aggrandized the role of experts. Although we can understand these sensitivities, we must disagree with their substance. We think the findings of behavioral decision research are clear and well established. We think the ability of structured processes to improve on unaided decision making is becoming more established (Keeney, 1992), and is a major reason why society has interest in the role of citizen participation.

clarify what is needed to assist individuals and groups to address complex risk management questions. James March draws attention to the need for help with identifying and defining goals by observing that "human beings have unstable, inconsistent, incompletely evolved and imprecise goals at least in part because human abilities limit preference orderliness" (March, 1978, p. 598). Herbert Simon emphasizes the need for an effective decision structure and workable tasks: "[h]uman rational behavior is shaped by a scissors whose two blades are the structure of task environments and the computational capabilities of the actor" (Simon, 1990, p. 7). The implication is that efforts to assist public involvement processes in making defensible choices should stress methods for clarifying fundamental individual or social objectives and for structuring the decision tasks so they are meaningful, and within the capabilities of those involved. At the same time, the goals and tasks must be useful for making responsible choices in the given decision context.

2.2. Reasons for Public Involvement

Public involvement, in various forms, has been a feature of the North American political landscape for decades. An early paper by Arnstein (1969) provided a taxonomy for public involvement based on the role of the participants within the process. At the bottom rung of Arnstein's public involvement ladder, the interested parties are only "informed" of policy issues; at the top rung, the public "makes the decision." Arnstein's choice of metaphors may have had a detrimental effect on expectations for public involvement practice. By implying that letting the public make the decision is the "highest" form of public involvement, that paper may indirectly have contributed to heightened expectations. Virtually all public involvement efforts with group processes have to address the question of whether the participants are empowered to set policy, and then explain why not. Yet, given representative governments and the complexity of the issues involved, there are formidable reasons to assert that one should never allow public involvement processes to actually set policy. Presumably that role should be reserved for legitimate government agencies or elected representatives, who are empowered by institutions to make public choices. At most, the objective of public involvement should be to provide insight that will foster widely supported policy choices reflecting public values, and to build lasting support for those choices.[4] Another taxonomy, similar to Arnstein's but cast from the viewpoint of the process proponent, could be based on the ends (objectives) the public involvement activities are intended to achieve. These ends range from simply informing publics (to obtain their approval for selected actions) to meaningfully involving the public (in order to make choices that reflect public values). The means (techniques or methods) to conduct public involvement efforts to achieve these ends have been discussed at length elsewhere (Creighton *et al.,* 1982). Of course, the methods selected for a given public involvement effort should be selected on the basis of the ends to be achieved. Although this seems like basic advice, in our view, it has been overlooked in a surprisingly large share of public involvement efforts we have observed.

A third taxonomy, provided by Fiorino (1990), outlines three rationales for public involvement in risk decisions: normative, substantive, and instrumental. The normative rationale "derives from the principle that government should obtain the consent of the governed," and consequently "citizens have rights to participate meaningfully in public decision making." The substantive rationale is that "relevant wisdom is not limited to scientific specialists," whereas instrumental reflects the understanding that successful implementation is far more likely with broad public support (National Research Council, 1996, pp. 23–24).

2.3. The Extremes of Current Public Involvement Practice

One could characterize much of public involvement practice in North America by dividing it into two extremes on a continuum of "stakeholder control" of involvement activities. One extreme involves group processes, relying on consensus among participants as the decision rule. The most extreme form of this approach, and one that has wide endorsement, argues that the decision process a particular group should adopt should be entirely designed by the group itself. For example, consider a set of principles developed by the Canada National Round Table on

[4] The exception might be public involvement with official referenda, which have problems of their own (Magleby, 1984), and decision structuring processes that have been proposed to address them (McDaniels, 1996).

the Environment and the Economy (1993) intended to encourage improved decisionmaking to achieve a sustainable future for Canada. The principles call explicitly for "consensus" in "self-designed process" involving "all parties with a significant interest" as the prescription for improved decisionmaking. While we can understand the political reasons for offering such guidelines, we believe they will often be unworkable in practice. In particular, we think relying on lay participants to self-design decision processes for complex risk management questions could be a recipe for disaster, precisely for reasons outlined in Section 2.1.[5]

The other camp, polar opposite from consensus processes, allows public participation only in the form of specific, formally structured value judgments. For example, members of the public may only provide judgments about specific nonmarket value tradeoffs cast in terms of willingness-to-pay in dollar terms (Mitchell and Carson, 1989). Remaining aspects of the decision process—such as the range of objectives considered, the nature of the alternatives proposed, and the characterization of the impacts of alternatives—may be influenced by the values of focus groups or media reviews but are presented in a distilled form based on judgments made by the analyst or project proponent. This extreme approach is standard practice for social benefit/cost analysis based on welfare economics. It too has obvious shortcomings that have led to extensive criticisms (Kelman, 1981; Gregory, Lichtenstein, and Slovic, 1993).

The approach in this paper adopts a middle course between these two extremes. It employs a group process, with substantial responsibility placed on group participants to provide judgments, to assimilate information, and to provide views on the acceptability of alternatives. Yet it also adopts a clear structure for the decision process, requiring both formal and informal benefit/cost comparisons. The general outlines of this structure are established by the group leaders, and although participants have the ability to fine-tune, the scope of their role falls well short of a license to redesign the process.

[5] Note that in making this statement, we are not discrediting the wisdom or abilities of lay participants to contribute to defining the decisions to be made, clarify values important for the decision from their viewpoint, or contribute technical information about risk management choices (National Research Council, 1996). Rather, we are relying on the findings of behavioral decision research (and our own experience) which demonstrates that structuring a complex decision process is not instinctive or straightforward, and can often benefit from practical advice.

2.4. Concepts for Designing Group Decision Processes

We believe four concepts are particularly important for group decision processes for complex risk management choices. All involve the pragmatic application of formal decision analytic concepts.

2.4.1. Value-Focused Thinking

Keeney (1992) describes "value-focused thinking" in simplest terms as "deciding what is important and how to achieve it." Value-focused thinking emphasizes the preeminent role of values in all decisionmaking. It involves value-structuring approaches drawn from multiattribute utility theory. It uses these judgments to create more attractive alternatives that stand a better chance of wide support, determine the information needed to characterize impacts of alternatives, and, formally or informally, evaluate alternatives. Value-focused thinking was the key to designing and implementing the public-involvement process described in this paper.

2.4.2. Adaptive Management

Holling (1978), Walters (1986), and others developed "adaptive management" as a means of coping with profound uncertainties in managing complex natural resource systems involving predator–prey relationships such as fisheries. Since then, it has been applied to a wide range of resource management issues as well as strategy design and other management contexts (McDaniels, Healey, and Paisley, 1994). In simple terms, adaptive management could be characterized as follows: When faced with profound uncertainties, take a purposeful step forward, monitor the consequences, learn from the results, and avoid costly failures. It sees decision making as an iterative process rather than a one-time exercise, and emphasize the role of learning from successive management choices. While adaptive management could be applied in a formal experimental design (Walters, 1986), it is also helpful as an informal impetus to seek opportunities for learning over time in any iterative decision context.

2.4.3. A Structured Decision Process

The basic steps of decision analysis (Keeney, 1992; von Winterfeldt and Edwards, 1986), which are essentially the steps of any structured planning or decision framework, provide a responsible, informative and complete structure for a decision process. For the purposes of designing public involvement with groups of stakeholders, these steps can be cast in terms of a series of questions:

- What ends (objectives) are important to achieve in selecting a management alternative for the question at hand?
- What alternatives can be constructed to achieve these objectives?
- What information is needed to characterize the impacts of these alternatives, in terms of measures for the stated objectives?
- What tradeoffs arise in selecting among the alternatives?
- What alternatives can the participants support?

2.4.4. An "Informative" Decision Rule

The last question raises the issue of the appropriate decision rule for group public involvement processes directed towards recommending risk management alternatives.[6] Perhaps the most common is a consensus rule, in which every participant effectively has a veto over the decisions of the group (and often over every step of the process). In our view, a far more useful and informative decision rule is to ask participants what alternative(s) each can support. By "informative" we mean a decision rule that fosters learning about the process, the alternatives, and the values of participants (which should be important for public involvement). Greater insight occurs throughout the process because less time is spent dealing with objections that might occur with a veto-based consensus rule, and as a result every step is more straightforward.

An informative decision rule is akin to approval voting (Brams and Fishburn, 1983) as opposed to unanimous agreement. However, the group does not make its ultimate recommendations based on majority or plurality voting, because typically the number of participants and the groups they represent is not rigorously structured as a legislative body with a representative structure. Instead, the decision rule is simply to report to the elected or appointed decisionmakers who are seeking input through the process what alternatives the various stakeholders can support. This approach is in keeping with the role of decision analytic approaches with multiple stakeholders, where utility functions for various groups could be used to inform the decisionmaker on preferences of constituents (von Winterfeldt and Edwards, 1986).[7]

[6] The National Research Council (1996) report stresses the need for decision rule in "Achieving Closure" (pp. 129–131). It outlines variants of veto-based decision rules, but does not mention the "approval" rule outlined here.

3. THE ALOUETTE RIVER STAKEHOLDER INVOLVEMENT PROCESS

3.1. Project Objectives

An operating plan provides a set of working guidelines for a hydroelectric generating facility. In this case, it identifies operational procedures to be followed by BC Hydro system staff for the Alouette hydroelectric facility, in the light of stakeholder interests and values as well as natural conditions (e.g., rainfall). The Alouette hydroelectric facility includes a reservoir and dam on the South Alouette River, a tributary of the Fraser River in southwestern British Columbia, and a tunnel to two other hydroelectric facilities that generate power from South Alouette River water.

From the viewpoint of BC Hydro, which sponsored the work, the immediate regulatory objective was to meet the directive of the British Columbia Water Comptroller (the provincial regulator of water use). As one condition of relicensing another nearby facility, the comptroller instructed the utility to "consult" with specific groups of stakeholders in developing a water management plan for the South Alouette River. The broader objective of the utility was to meaningfully address concerns over fisheries and flood control issues that had been sources of controversy on the South Alouette for decades.

The authors' principal responsibilities on this project were to structure and facilitate discussions of

[7] The stakeholder-based multiattribute utility theory approach, often discussed but rarely practiced, is to elicit utility functions for each stakeholder group, and then use these to score various alternatives (Hobbs and Horn, 1997). The results clarify areas of agreement and disagreement and can be used to help create win–win alternatives. Yet, the cognitive effort, time requirements and possible annoyance or confusion to stakeholders are substantial costs of this approach. Moreover, it does not meet Simon's criterion of "workable decision tasks" for most stakeholders. How the tradeoffs are combined with technical performance scores would not be transparent to most participants.

the Alouette Stakeholder Committee (ASC), which included technical guidance on clarifying members' objectives, using these values to create operating plan alternatives, fostering understanding by committee members of the pros and cons of selected alternatives, and leading the group toward making specific decisions about its recommendations.

3.2. Membership of Stakeholder Committee

The stakeholder committee had 17 official members drawn from a wide array of interested groups and organizations. Members of the ASC were selected on the basis of several criteria. First, the participation of certain key agency representatives and community groups was specified by the directive of the Provincial Water Controller. Second, invited individuals were considered to represent a group with an interest (a "stake") in the outcomes of discussions concerning BC Hydro's operating plans on the river. These groups included local citizens, municipal staff members, provincial and federal government agencies, First Nations, BC Hydro, and other key user groups. Third, selected individuals were considered to be good candidates for an open, participatory process that would rely heavily on skills of articulation, listening, learning, and mutual cooperation.

Two rules were also adopted by the ASC to aid in the stakeholder involvement process. First, if a member was unable to attend one meeting due to a scheduling conflict, it was agreed that a designated alternate could take their place at the table. Second, if other people wanted to observe a meeting of the ASC, it was agreed that they could listen and watch providing they did not sit at the ASC table and providing they did not speak or otherwise disrupt the committee's deliberations. Some observers provided information when asked for input from the ASC.

3.3. Stakeholder Committee Meetings and Reporting

Meetings of the ASC generally were held at a high school in Maple Ridge, a community of about 20,000 people, about 60 km east of Vancouver. A total of 15 official meetings, averaging about three hours each, occurred over a 6-month period from January to July, 1996. The committee meetings were structured on the basis of the five fundamental questions noted in Section 2.4 as comprising a structured decision process.

The meetings typically began with a status report by the consultants, followed by brief discussions of member concerns. The main agenda items in most meetings included presentations, either by the consultants or by invited speakers, to address gaps in the information base that were considered by ASC members to be critical for informed decision making. These gaps ranged from questions about the system operating procedures employed by BC Hydro engineers to the status of work being conducted on the Alouette River by a multiagency Fish Flow Study Team. After each meeting, a set of minutes was prepared and circulated to document progress. These minutes, combined with the many brief reports prepared to summarize and present information at meetings, provided an ongoing record of activities. As the process drew near conclusion, ASC discussions were summarized in a draft consultant's report, which was circulated to all members of the committee. After two more meetings, a final report was submitted by the consultants to all ASC members and to BC Hydro. This document was made available to interested members of the public and it served as the basis for BC Hydro's submission of a water management plan to the provincial water comptroller.

3.4. Process Considerations

The intent of the consultants was to provide a respectful, open forum for discussion of issues relevant to determining a preferred operating plan, or set of plans, for the Alouette system. Members of the ASC were reminded that their role was not to write the operating plan proposal for the water comptroller. Instead, they were charged with providing advice to BC Hydro concerning the key elements of an operating plan preferred by stakeholders. Final decisions regarding the content of the application would be made by BC Hydro. However, it was acknowledged that any elements of an operating plan that were agreed to unanimously by ASC members would carry a substantial significance. If any deviations from the eventual ASC recommendations were to be sought by BC Hydro, these were to be identified and explained.

It is one thing to say that the desired process should be open; it is another thing to make sure that desired standards of transparency and comfort are achieved. This was particularly true in light of the legacy of mistrust and adversity that was inherited from the history of Alouette system operating concerns. As a result, the consultants made several explicit decisions:

1. Share all information, by distributing copies of key data to all ASC members;
2. Seek flexibility, by acknowledging the precedent-setting nature of the discussions;
3. Develop information in response to ASC members' questions, through modelling and computer simulations;
4. Bring in speakers and presenters, as requested by ASC members;
5. Have ASC members participate in decisions regarding evaluation strategies;
6. Maintain close ties with other relevant community and provincial activities; and
7. Acknowledge the emotional content of the issues under consideration.[8]

It was also acknowledged that close communication should be maintained with the citizenry of Maple Ridge through several independent, parallel processes. For example, an open house was held midway through the stakeholder involvement process. It provided an opportunity for informal comments and input from local residents. Discussions within the ASC, coupled with related initiatives outside the ASC, led to a special public meeting with riparian residents to discuss concerns of community residents who might be affected particularly by changes in flood-control policies. Additional periodic reports were made by ASC members to key decision makers, including the mayor of Maple Ridge and senior management at BC Hydro.

The most crucial process considerations were those relating to points raised in Section 2.4 regarding the structured decision process and decision rule. The consultants presented the set of basic questions to guide the process, and the proposed decision rule, to the group. Both were confirmed by committee members as a reasonable basis for structuring the group's activities.

Another key decision was how tradeoffs would be considered and articulated by the committee. The consultants summarized three possible approaches: (1) all tradeoffs could be considered in dollar terms, based on willingness-to-pay concepts; (2) all tradeoffs could be considered in terms of multiattribute utility measures; or (3) tradeoffs could be considered, by determining the (qualitative or quantitative) pros and cons of alternatives and then letting participants select and provide a reasoned explanation for the alternatives they prefer. After some discussion, the committee selected the third approach, recognizing that the background research and thoughtful introspection required for (3) were also first steps for responsibly completing (1) or (2) as well, so (3) could be followed by (1) or (2) if desired.

3.5. Identifying Stakeholder Values

The starting place for the ASC activities was to define and understand participants' values for the decisions at hand. The values of committee members indicated "what mattered" and served as the basis for design of a recommended operating plan. The approach for clarifying values as a basis for structuring objectives followed the concepts of multiattribute value characterization (Keeney, 1992). Initial information suggesting possible objectives for Alouette facility water management came from a series of interviews with more than 20 key informants, including community leaders as well as with individuals in government agencies.

Drawing on these interviews, a preliminary set of objectives (in no particular order) for an operating plan was developed:

- avoid adverse effects from flooding;
- promote recreational activities;
- promote the health and biological productivity of the South Alouette River and Alouette Lake (including fisheries); and
- avoid cost increases to provincial residents.

Discussions of these objectives revealed that something was missing. ASC members were concerned about the level of uncertainty in our current knowledge of fisheries ecology and management on the Alouette River. It was acknowledged that additional studies, to be conducted over a period of time (perhaps 1 year, perhaps 10 years), were needed to deepen our understanding of the fundamental relationships between water flow and velocity, aquatic and riparian habitat, and fisheries productivity. As a result, a fifth objective was added to the list:

- promote flexibility, learning and adaptive management for the Alouette system.

Table I presents this set of structured objectives.

[8] For a related discussion of process issues, see Fisher and Forester, 1993; Renn, Webler, and Wiederman, 1995; or Majone, 1989.

how measure pub. sup.? #1?

Table I. Objectives and Measures for ASC Water Management Planning Activities

Overall Objective: Select the best possible operating plan for the Alouette River.

Objective	Measure
1. Avoid adverse effects of flooding —on people —on private property —on public property —on cultural resources —on perceptions	• Frequency of floods, of a size equal to or greater than the flood of November, 1995 (3,200 cfs daily average flow at Alouette Dam)
2. Promote the ecological health and productivity of South Alouette River and Alouette Lake —for fish (salmonids and others) —for other species (plants and animals)	• Hectares of high quality fish habitat in Alouette River • Quality of fish habitat in Alouette Lake • Shape of river hydrograph
3. Avoid cost increases for provincial electrical supply —costs of electrical energy —other financial costs —costs of environmental impacts of replacement generation	• Annual dollar costs of generation to be replaced, in 1996 dollars • Environmental costs associated with incremental generation, in 1996 dollars
4. Promote recreational opportunities associated with Alouette Lake and South Alouette River —for the river and its environment, including boating, swimming, fishing, hiking, viewing, and horseback riding —for the lake and its environment, including boating, swimming, fishing, hiking, viewing, and camping	• Number and quality of recreation opportunities affected
5. Promote flexibility, learning and adaptive management regarding impacts of water flows on ecology of South Alouette River and Alouette Lake —flexibility for ease of changes in management —learning about ecology —adaptive management for incorporating learning and flexibility	• Learning opportunities and flexibility resulting from management structure

The overall objective is to: "Select the best management plan for the Alouette facility." The subobjectives specify the characteristics of the "best" plan, assuming there were no constraints or limits on what could be achieved. In practice, it is unlikely that any single alternative could fully achieve all these objectives because several of them conflict, as is natural in public policy issues. Thus, tradeoffs among the objectives must be considered to clarify what the best possible alternative would entail.

Measures to indicate how well the objectives are achieved are also shown in Table I. The choice of measures necessarily reflects the available data, what the objectives mean, and specific choices by the ASC. Two key measurement issues were resolved during the early ASC meetings.

1. Whether flooding should be measured in terms of the magnitude of losses (to people and property) or in terms of the frequency of severe floods (i.e., those requiring protective actions). It was also acknowledged that the ASC needed to address the question of what would be defined as a "flood." A flood event was determined to equal or exceed flows that occurred during a damaging flood in November 1995, that averaged approximately 3200 cfs released from the dam for the peak day. That definition was selected because the impacts associated with a flood of that level were still fresh in the minds of local participants. The best measure for flood control, given available information, was determined to be based on the frequency of floods of the November, 1995 flood (or greater). The current level of protection, determined from the operating system models, was calculated to be about 1-in-12 (i.e., if the system were operated strictly according to the then extant rules, a flood event equal to or exceeding 3200 cfs would be predicted to occur once every 12 years, on average).
2. Whether biological productivity of the South

Alouette River should be measured in terms of broad indicators of ecosystem health, the numbers of various species, the numbers of salmonids, or the area of high-quality habitat available for salmonids. After discussion, it was decided that the area of high-quality salmonid habitat would serve as the best indicator of the biological health of the Alouette River. It was noted that one possible exception to this choice is the effects of changes in flow regimes on bird populations of adjacent terrestrial areas. It was agreed that this topic could be considered in the future. Additional discussions of the effects of releases on fish populations stressed the importance of flow velocity as well as water depths, as shown by preliminary results from the Alouette River Fish Flow Study Team.

3.6. Information Requirements and Sources

Several kinds of information were required to understand the impacts of operational alternatives for the Alouette electrical facilities. The ASC meetings devoted considerable time to identifying key issues regarding the various kinds of impacts and to receiving presentations from technical specialists who provided important information about impacts. Table II summarizes various questions about impacts that were discussed during the meetings.

Technical specialists conducted substantial research and modelling efforts to provide information for the ASC planning activities. For example, BC Hydro staff conducted extensive simulation modelling about flood control and power production, considering a wide range of possible operating scenarios. This modelling focused on alternative "operating rules" for three key elements of the Alouette system: the Alouette spillway, the "adit" (a tunnel) from Alouette to nearby Stave Lake, and releases through the Alouette low-level outlet. Parts of several meetings of the ASC were devoted to ensuring that committee members understood and were comfortable with the approach taken on simulation modelling for flood control and power production. The committee asked for and received substantial information on the accuracy or "calibration" of the modelling efforts, leading to agreement that the results were useful and relevant for comparative analysis.

The issue of obtaining defensible fisheries information proved difficult, because the work of the Alouette River Fish Flow Study Team (an interagency effort) was occurring simultaneously to the work of the stakeholder committee. Although some early information was available regarding the study process being followed by the Fish Flow Study Team, no results were available until near the end of the ASC deliberations. In fact, the schedule for the ASC was extended to allow more time for the Fish Flow Study Team to complete its initial research. Even at the time of a presentation by fish flow team members to the ASC, substantial issues remained unresolved. The most notable was the uncertainty over the relationship between changes in river flows and quality of salmonid habitat for the South Alouette River. Two competing predictions for this relationship, based on different data sets, were considered and extensive discussions occurred regarding the differences in estimates. The ASC also recognized the need for adaptive management procedures to foster learning in a scientifically defensible manner.

3.7. Creating Operating Plan Alternatives

Several alternatives were identified as possible ways to achieve each objective. It was recognized that these alternatives would necessarily involve tradeoffs with other objectives, such as costs. The approach was to identify a range of possible alternatives, involving different levels of tradeoffs, so the ASC could understand how the tradeoffs changed from one alternative to another. In general, the approach was also to consider alternatives (and their costs) to achieve each objective separately, and then to examine how these separate alternatives could be combined into various plans. Information about the impacts of the alternatives was communicated using "objectives by alternatives" matrices. For a specific decision, this approach involves constructing a matrix with the relevant objectives (and measures) shown along one side and the relevant alternatives shown along the other side. The cells in the matrix then contain information that characterizes how well a given alternative performs in terms of a given objective. As discussed below, several technical issues influenced the alternatives considered for each objective.

3.7.1. Fisheries and Ecological Health

Fisheries and ecological health can be affected by "flushing" flows, regular flows, and fish habitat enhancement works. Flushing flows are significant flows (e.g. 1000 cfs or greater) lasting a short period of time (e.g., 2–3 days) that remove silt from the river, thereby improving benthic and substrate habitat for salmon spawning. Operations at that time did not include flushing flows. Regular flows into the river, usually expressed as *minimum* flows, affect the amount of habitat available for fisheries spawning and rearing. Historic operations allowed for a minimum of 20 cfs to be released through a low level outlet at the Alouette dam; since September 1995, the flow had been set at 70 cfs as part of an interim agreement until the operating plan review was completed. The low level outlet of the Alouette dam can release a maximum of 105 cfs, depending on the water level in the reservoir. Fish habitat enhancement can occur by opening side channels, or spawning channels. These are natural gravel areas adjacent to the river, through which river water is diverted to make larger areas of quality gravel available for spawning.

3.7.2. Flood Control

Flood control can be affected by flow-related and non-flow related activities. Flow related actions involve use of the Alouette facilities to reduce the probability of floods on the South Alouette River. Flood protection efforts could rely on the judgement of facility operators as to when the adit and spillway should be opened, or on explicit operating rules about when these facilities should be opened, or on a combination of these approaches. Nonflow related flood control actions could entail improved communication and warnings, efforts to reduce or end development in the flood plain, or improved forecasting.

3.7.3. Recreation Activities

Recreation activities are largely affected by flows in the South Alouette River. In summer, flows below 70 cfs and over 105 cfs at the dam could be expected to adversely affect some kinds of family-oriented recreation opportunities. Winter recreation is closely tied to steelhead angling, for which higher flows (over 70 cfs) improve angling opportunities by increasing the quality of the fishing experience (i.e., improvements in "fishability").

3.7.4. Power Production

Power production is affected by flows into the South Alouette River either through the low level outlet or the spillway, because that water is not available for power generation. Power production is also affected by flows through the adit to nearby Stave Lake, but to a much lesser degree. Diverting water through the adit only entails a loss of about one-third the available power from a given amount of water, because it can still generate power at the other facilities downstream.

3.7.5. Learning and Adaptive Management

Learning and adaptive management is shaped by management practices for river flows that affect fisheries issues. In part, the management practices that occur would be influenced by which organizations hold water licenses on the river, or which have an explicit role in management decisions, or both.

4. RESULTS

The operating plan alternatives considered by ASC members were constructed on the basis of the five key objectives outlined in Table I. In each case, the ASC worked to select alternatives and achieve consensus on a single component of the plan option that would achieve the desired outcome for the objective under consideration while recognizing effects on other aspects of the plan. When agreement among ASC members was not possible, participants were asked to designate their favored component of a plan from among a small set of alternatives, and to discuss their reasons for this choice based on their values and knowledge of the pros and cons of the options.

The basis of comparison in evaluating alternatives generally focused on whether the benefits from nonpower objectives justified the potential reduction in power output (and increases in cost) associated with adopting a plan that does not maximize electrical generation from the facilities.[9] The ASC discussion

[9] Considerable modeling and analysis was conducted to identify the incremental costs of each alternative for each objective. Tradeoffs between cost and each of the other objectives were thus addressed quantitatively in terms of cost increases to achieve performance improvements on another objective. Then the aggregate costs of the package of accepted policy choices (Table III) were carefully considered.

Table II. Key Factual Questions Regarding Issues Associated with Alouette Facility Operating Alternatives

Issues	Key questions
Recreation	• What types of recreation activities are important in the area? • Where on the river/lake do activities take place? • How are activities and key sites affected by different flow levels? • How are levels of recreation use likely to change in the future?
Flood protection	• How big a flood is a concern? • What can be done to avoid adverse impacts of flooding? • How effective are various measures in decreasing frequency of floods? • How often would floods occur if there were no dam?
Costs	• How big are the power benefits at issue? • How should the power benefits be valued in dollar terms? • How significant is "certainty" of power output at BCH? • How are mitigation costs accounted for? • How would the power be replaced?
Fisheries and ecological health	• What is the relationship between flows and the suitability of habitat for various fish species? • How much quality habitat, in hectares, results from various flows, by month? • What would be the consequences of "flushing" flows to improve substrate habitat?
Water licenses/flexibility and adaptive management	• What are the specific rights held by BC Hydro under its current water licenses? • What are the controls on license holders? • What does the water comptroller want to see as recommendations from the committee?
First Nations rights and interests	• How do First Nations and the courts view their rights? • What are the implications of forthcoming treaty-making activities?

recognized the importance of maintaining an assured supply of electrical power to provincial residents. However, the ASC also discussed that this security should be consistent with the multiple uses of water from the Alouette system and must recognize requirements of the federal Fisheries Act as well as future treaty agreements with First Nations. In addition, it was recognized that all elements of a proposed operating plan should be evaluated as part of a package that includes nonmonetary benefits and costs (e.g., the recreational benefits of improved steelhead angling opportunities) as well as monetary benefits and costs (e.g., the foregone power costs of flushing flows).

After 15 meetings, the ASC reached complete consensus on all major issues it was asked to address. Table III summarizes the set of specific decisions agreed to by all participants, along with a consensus recommendation to either "reject" or "adopt" the proposed action.

In addition to these direct results of the stakeholder involvement process, a longer term result has been the initiation of several changes in practice, both by BC Hydro and by the Office of the Water Controller, regarding water management and planning in British Columbia. Before the ASC process, the utility had been given water licenses with minimal restrictions, addressing only extreme operating parameters for the facilities. The ASC was the first attempt to create a more detailed water management plan for a hydroelectric facility with extensive public input. Some months after the ASC process was completed, BC Hydro and the Province of British Columbia announced the intent to develop water management plans for all hydroelectric systems in the province. The replanning processes are to adopt the same basic principles as developed by the ASC, as summarized earlier.

5. DISCUSSION

The title of this paper asserts this is a "successful" public involvement effort. What criteria are appropriate to judge success in an undertaking of this kind (cf Moore, 1996; Renn, Webler, and Wiedermann, 1995)?

The obvious criterion is that a consensus agreement was achieved among a group of diverse representative stakeholders. This agreement has held over the past year, with all concerned parties generally satisfied with the results. Yet, achieving consensus is at best a partial criterion for success in such efforts. As outlined here, the objective of public

Table III. Summary of Stakeholder Committee Decisions

Objective/Measure	Decision: Benefits	Decision: Cost	Decision: Recommendation
1. Promote ecological health			
• Should flushing flows be implemented?	Substantial improvement in quality of substrate habitat	$50–75k yearly, with preset timing	Reject
		$2–30k yearly, with flexibility in timing	Adopt
• Should base water flow (year round) be increased to full capacity of current facility?	Substantial improvements in fisheries habitat and aesthetics	$270–440k/year	Adopt
2. Avoid adverse flooding effects			
• Change operating rules for generating facility to improve protection from major flooding event	Increase protection from major flood from current 1-in-12 year to 1-in-32 year	$30k/year	Adopt
3. Promote recreational activities			
• Improve angling opportunities via higher water flows • Maintain quality of non-angling recreation	Key consideration to local stakeholders	Minimal	Adopt
4. Avoid cost increases			
• Should water flows be increased beyond capacity of current facility?	Maximum fisheries production potential	Annual costs: 700–1055k Capital costs: $3–6 million Some adverse effects on recreation	Reject
5. Promote learning and flexibility			
• Establish ongoing management committee with stakeholder representation • Fund monitoring and adaptive management studies	Provides ongoing basis for stakeholder involvement and improvements in fisheries base	Approximately $50k/year	Adopt

involvement is to provide insight to decisionmakers, *not to resolve* a dispute. One could imagine a group of stakeholders achieving a negotiated agreement on a policy decision and yet knowing remarkably little about the relevant objectives, range of alternatives, or the impacts and tradeoffs they involve. In fact, we suspect this may be a common state of affairs in self-designed consensus-based public involvement with a dispute resolution emphasis. Hence, consensus alone is only a partial measure of success.

Another criterion, more in keeping with the orientation of this paper, judges success by the way the steps of the process were addressed. As seen in Section 3, a set of clear objectives was structured and written down, with specific measures for each objective (Table I). A wide range of alternatives was articulated, designed to address the various objectives (Table III). Considerable modeling, data collection and expert judgment were employed to characterize the impacts of these alternatives in ways understandable to the participants and that addressed their key factual questions (Table II). The tradeoffs involved in selecting one alternative over another, and the rationales for preferring one set of actions over another, were explicitly considered by the participants. The tasks the participants were asked to complete, by selecting the alternatives they could support, were made as clear and straightforward as possible.

We believe these steps comprise the elements of a "quality" decision process, and thus are why this public involvement effort can be termed a success. In making this statement we are explicitly adding to the definition of "decision quality." Early work defined decision quality as the result of involving "the right people and the right information." More recently, decision quality has been defined in terms of the right decision framework, as well as the right people and right information (Matheson and Matheson, 1998). We would suggest that the selection of a decision framework is a critical first step in deciding who the right people are and in identifying the necessary type and quality of information. We also believe the four concepts outlined in Section 2.4 are elements of the right decision frame for stakeholder involvement for risk management.

Another criterion for the success of this public involvement effort is in the nature of the alternative recommended by the process. In essence, the participants created a recommended alternative that was highly effective in meeting all the objectives established for the decision. In the parlance of the economist, the selected alternative moved up the cost curve for "improving ecological health" by increasing water releases, to the maximum possible given the existing facilities, to the point where further water releases would entail a substantial jump in capital costs. The level of flood control was selected by setting the expected annual cost of flooding equal to the incremental cost of flood control incurred. Finally, the management committee structure allows for adaptive learning over time to reduce uncertainties.

Still another criterion for judging success involves comparing the costs and benefits of the process itself. Excluding the costs of fisheries studies, which were undertaken for other purposes, the total costs of the ASC process amounted to about $700,000 Cdn ($500,000 US), including costs for consultants as well as BC Hydro staff time. The benefits included obtaining useful public input (and endorsement) for a water management plan that was a prerequisite for obtaining a new operating license for another nearby hydroelectric facility. In addition, BC Hydro managed to address and resolve issues of the appropriate water flow in the river, questions that had been a sore point in the community and with resource management agencies since the 1930s. Finally it obtained an agreement on a new flood control regime in a location where it had experienced a highly controversial flood the previous year. In essence, the utility resolved some of the most pressing regulatory, resource management, flood control, and public image concerns it faced in recent years. These are substantial benefits compared to the costs.

6. CONCLUSION

In our view, risk management decision processes can be made more "democratic," as the title of this piece suggests, but only with a clear structure and a decision framework focusing on values, meaningful technical information, tradeoffs, and insight. Public involvement could take many forms, ranging from surveys to short small-group meetings to the extensive deliberative process outlined here. All these types of activities could, in our opinion, benefit from attention to the four concepts outlined in Section 2.4. On the other hand, employing these concepts will be no panacea for complex risk management choices involving difficult tradeoffs. The best one can hope for is that by combining value judgments and technical information in a structured framework involving workable decision tasks, participants will gain more insight and thus provide better informed recommendations. Anything more than this—such as the consensus agreement achieved in the case of the Alouette River—is a bonus.

ACKNOWLEDGEMENTS

The authors wish to acknowledge B.C. Hydro, the Social Sciences and Humanities Research Council of Canada, and the U.S. National Science Foundation (Award SBR 95-25582) for their financial support in the completion of this paper. McDaniels' efforts in preparation of this manuscript were also supported by a grant from the U.S. National Science Foundation (SBR 95-21914) to the Center for Integrated Study of the Human Dimensions of Global Change at Carnegie Mellon University.

REFERENCES

S. R. Arnstein (1969). "A Ladder of Citizen Participation." *Journal of the American Planning Association.* **35,** 216–224.

S. Brams and P. Fishburn (1983). *Approval Voting.* Boston: Birkhauser.

Canadian National Round Table on the Environment and the Economy (1993). *Building Consensus for a Sustainable Future.* Ottawa.

J. D. Creighton, J. Priscoli, and C. M. Dunning (1982). *Public Involvement Techniques: A Reader of Ten Years of Experience at the Institute for Water Resources.* IWR Research Report 82-R1, Institute for Water Resources, Ft Belvoir, Virginia.

D. J. Fiorino, "Citizen Participation and Environmental Risk: A Survey of Institutional Mechanisms," *Science, Technology, & Human Values.* **15**(2), 226–243 (1990).

F. Fisher and J. Forester (1993). *The Argumentative Turn in Policy Analysis and Planning.* Durhan: Duke U. Press.

R. Gregory, S. Lichtenstein, and P. Slovic (1993). Valuing Environmental Resources: A Constructive Approach. *Journal of Risk and Uncertainty.* **7,** 177–197.

R. Gregory, and R. Keeney, (1994). Creating Policy Alternatives with Stakeholder Values. *Management Science.* **40,** 1035–1048.

B. Hobbs and G. Horn (1997). "Building Confidence in Energy Planning: A Multimethod MCDM Approach to Demand-Side Planning at BC Gas" *Energy Policy,* **25**(3), 357–375.

C. S. Holling, (1978). *Adaptive Environmental Assessment and Management.* New York: John Wiley and Sons.

I. Janis and L. Mann (1977). *Decision Making: A Psychological Analysis of Conflict, Choice, and Commitment.* New York: The Free Press.

D. Kahneman, P. Slovic, and A. Tversky (1982). *Judgment Under Uncertainty: Heuristics and Biases.* New York: Cambridge University Press.

R. Keeney (1992). *Value-Focused Thinking: A Path to Creative Decisionmaking.* Cambridge, Mass.: Harvard University Press.

S. Kelman (1981). "Cost–Benefit Analysis: An Ethical Critique." *Regulation,* **5**(1), 33–40.

D. Magleby (1984). *Direct Legislation: Voting on Ballot Propositions in the United States.* Johns Hopkins University.

G. Majone (1989). *Evidence, Argument and Persuasion in the Policy Process.* New Haven: Yale.

J. March (1978). Bounded Rationality, Ambiguity, and the Engineering of Choice. *Bell Journal of Economics,* 587–608.

D. Matheson and J. Matheson (1998). *The "Smart" Organization: Creating Value Through Strategic R & D,* publisher.

T. McDaniels (1996). The Structured Value Referendum: Eliciting Preferences for Environmental Policy Alternatives. *Journal of Policy Analysis and Management,* **15**, 227–251.

T. McDaniels, M. Healey, and R. Paisley (1994). "Cooperative Fisheries Management Involving First Nations in British Columbia: An Adaptive Approach to Strategy Design." *Canadian Journal of Fisheries and Aquatic Science,* **51**(9), 2115–2125.

R. Mitchell and R. Carson (1989). *Using Surveys to Value Public Goods: The Contingent Valuation Method.* Washington, D.C.: Resources for the Future.

S. A. Moore (1996). "Defining 'Successful' Environmental Dispute Resolution: Case Studies from Public Land Planning in the United States and Australia." *Environmental Impact Assessment Review,* **10**, 151–169.

National Research Council (1996). *Understanding Risk: Informing Decisions in a Democratic Society.* Washington, D.C.: National Academy Press.

J. Payne, J. Bettman, and E. Johnson (1992). Behavioural Decision Research: A Constructive Processing Perspective. *Annual Review of Psychology,* **43**, 87–132.

O. Renn, T. Webler, and P. Wiedemann (eds.) (1995). *Fairness and Competence in Public Participation: Evaluating Models for Environmental Discourse.* Dordrecht: Kluwer Academic Press.

Presidential/Congressional Commission on Risk Assessment and Risk Management (1997). Framework for environmental health risk management, Final Report, Vol. 1. Washington, D.C.

H. Simon (1990). "Invariants of Human Behaviour." *Annual Review of Psychology,* **41**, 1–19.

P. Slovic, B. Fischhoff, and S. Lichtenstein (1977). "Behavioural Decision Theory." *Annual Review of Psychology,* **28**, 1–39.

D. Von Winterfeldt and W. Edwards (1986). *Decision Analysis and Behavioral Research,* Cambridge University Press, Cambridge.

C. Walters (1986). Adaptive Management of Renewable Resources. Wiley: New York.

PENNY-WISE AND POUND-FUELISH?

New Car Mileage Standards in the United States

Paul R. Portney

The debate over domestic energy policy has one side shouting "produce more" while the other side shouts "use less." Not surprisingly, the Corporate Average Fuel Economy (CAFE) standards were fought over during hearings on the Senate energy bill. The chairman of the NRC's CAFE Committee offers his perspective on where to go from here.

Our seemingly endless debate about energy policy in the United States has been especially sharp since May 2001 when the Bush administration announced its new national energy policy. If anything, that debate has been much sharper still since the terrorist attacks of September 11, 2001, reminded us of the perils of using as much oil as we do in the United States.

Most of us remember the tiresome beer commercial in which seemingly normal people debated whether a particular brand was better because it "tasted great" or was "less filling." At the risk of only some exaggeration, we have our own version of this debate over domestic energy policy, with half the protagonists shouting "produce more" while their opponents shout "use less." The former look especially fondly at the Arctic National Wildlife Refuge (ANWR) as a possible source of additional oil, while the latter focus on improved fuel economy standards for new cars as the way to slake America's unquenchable thirst for petroleum. Both sides suffered at least temporary losses when the Senate—in the space of a few short days—recently rejected efforts to open ANWR for oil exploration and to tighten the Corporate Average Fuel Economy (or CAFE) standards for all new light-duty vehicles produced in the United States.

Paul R. Portney is a senior fellow and the president of RFF.

Last year, I had the pleasure of chairing a committee assembled by the National Research Council (the study arm of the National Academy of Sciences) to examine the past and possible future effects of the CAFE standards (hereafter referred to as the CAFE Committee). The committee's final report, *Effectiveness and Impact of Corporate Average Fuel Economy (CAFE) Standards*, was published last summer. Accordingly, I watched the debate over fuel economy standards quite closely. Here I report on the findings of that study and offer some suggestions on the way readers might think about the CAFE program. Let's begin with a bit of history regarding the fuel economy standards and what we know (and don't know) about their early effects.

LOOKING BACK

Because of several disruptions in world oil markets during the 1970s, the price of oil went from less than $20/barrel in 1970 to more than $80/barrel in 1981 (converted to year 2000 dollars). Even before the end of that decade, Congress passed legislation requiring all new passenger cars and light-duty trucks (in other words, pickup trucks, minivans, and the now-ubiquitous sport utility vehicles, or SUVs) to meet federal mileage standards. Cars were required by Congress directly to meet a fleet average of 27.5 miles per gallon (mpg) by 1985, and the National Highway Traffic Safety Administration mandated that light-duty truck fleets were to average no less than 20.7 mpg. Since new cars were averaging only about 16 mpg in 1977, the year before the CAFE requirements begin to ramp up, and new trucks about 13 mpg, these required increases were quite significant.

What effects did the new standards have? Perhaps surprisingly, this is a harder question to answer than one might think. The principal confounding factor is that the price of gasoline had been going up since well before the CAFE standards were established. This created a strong demand on the part of new car buyers for more fuel-efficient cars, as well as an incentive for automakers to produce them. The CAFE Committee found that these two forces working together—higher gasoline prices and federally mandated fuel economy standards—resulted in a greater than 50% improvement in new car and light-duty truck fuel economy between 1978 and 1985. As a result, the country enjoyed significant reductions in oil consumption and also emissions of carbon dioxide, a greenhouse gas.

In fact, the CAFE Committee estimated that by the year 2000, improved fuel economy was reducing oil consumption by 2.8 million barrels per day (or about 14% of the current total) and reducing annual emissions of carbon in the United States by about 100 million metric tons (or 6% of current annual emissions). The committee could not determine how much of these improvements were due to the price effect (which subsided rather dramatically beginning in 1981 when oil prices began their fall back to about $20/barrel in year 2000 prices) and how much was due to the effects of the CAFE standards. Since 1981, it is highly likely that fuel economy remained where it did solely because of the federal standards.

There is another, less happy consequence to the rapid improvement in fuel economy between 1978 and 1985, however. Because automakers were being forced both by consumer demand for more fuel-efficient cars (for a time, at least) and by government regulations, they had little choice as to the way they could improve fuel economy so rapidly. The result was an almost decade-long cohort of new cars and light-duty trucks that were smaller and lighter than their predecessors. According to all but two dissenting members of the CAFE Committee, the rapid downsizing and "downweighting" of new vehicles that began in 1978 was responsible by 1993 for about 2,000 more fatalities annually than would have been observed had vehicles remained as large as they were prior to 1978. As we shall soon see, this does not necessarily mean that further enhanced fuel economy must come at the cost of highway safety, but the rapid improvements of the late 1970s and early 1980s most likely did.

LOOKING AHEAD

Given the improvements of the past, why the continuing concern about future fuel economy? Despite the fact that both passenger car and light-duty truck fleets continue to meet their respective standards, the average fuel economy of the combined new car fleet has declined about 8% since 1986. "How can this be?" you might reasonably ask. Actually, the answer is quite simple, as Figure 1 illustrates. In 1975, when the law establishing the CAFE program was passed, light-duty trucks (once again, this category comprises pickups, minivans, and SUVs) accounted for about 2 million of the 10 million total vehicles sold that year in the United States. By 2001, however, light-duty truck sales accounted for 51% of the 17 million-plus new vehicles sold. Since these light-duty trucks are only required to average 20.7 mpg, as opposed to 27.5 mpg for passenger cars, their growing share of all new-vehicle sales is gradually pulling down the combined new vehicle fuel economy average. Along with robust growth in the number of miles that all cars are being driven, this shift in the new-car mix is a major reason why oil use and imports are growing steadily.

FIGURE 1

HISTORIC VEHICLE SALES

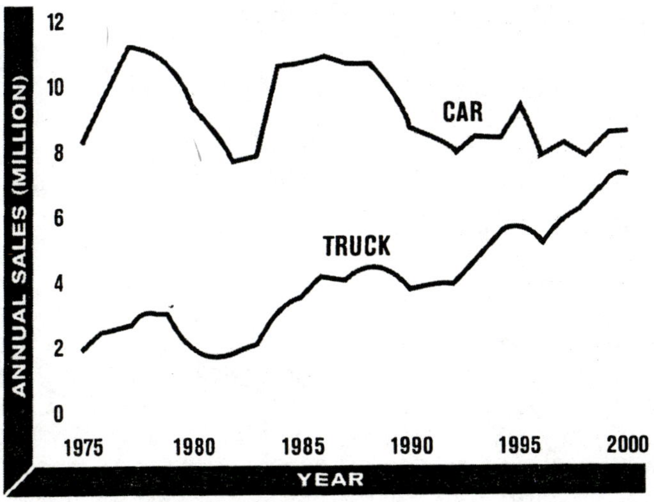

Notes:
1. Source: Friedman et al. (2001) (see For More Information for details).
2. Trucks include vehicles under 8,500 pound gross vehicle weight (GVW) that are not classified as passenger cars.

What can and should be done about this? The former is much easier to answer than the latter. Regarding possible future fuel economy improvements, the CAFE Committee thoroughly investigated the technological potential for short-, medium- and long-term gains. According to the committee report, "Technologies exist that, if applied to passenger cars and light-duty trucks, would significantly reduce fuel consumption within 15 years."

I cannot even begin here to identify all the technologies the committee considered, but they include mostly things that are already in limited use for some parts of the new vehicle fleet rather than technologies for which dramatic breakthroughs are required. Examples are such things as variable valve timing, intake valve throttling, variable-compression ratio engines, continuously variable transmissions, friction reductions, 42-volt electrical systems, and reduced aerodynamic drag and rolling resistance.

So what if the technological potential exists for fuel economy improvements? It is almost always possible to do better technologically than we are currently doing—whether from an automotive, computing, medical, or agricultural standpoint. The really important questions are how much will these improvements cost and what benefits will we derive from them?

The committee provided at least some information along these lines. Beginning with technologies that could improve fuel economy rather inexpensively, and moving successively to those that could do so but at greater expense, the committee first sketched out what economists would recognize as a marginal cost curve for fuel economy improvement. This was done on the assumption that the automakers would have at least 10 and as many as 15 years to make these changes—an extraordinarily important assumption, as we shall later see. By combining these cost estimates with estimates of the discounted value of the fuel that would be saved, the committee summarized part of its work in a table like that in Table 1.

As the table indicates, through the application of the technologies the committee identified, it would be possible in 10 to 15 years to improve the fuel economy of a mid-sized passenger car (for example, a Buick Regal, C-class Mercedes, or Honda Accord) from the current mpg average of 27.1 to 32.6 (a gain of 20%). This would add an estimated $791 to the purchase price of the car but would be more than offset by the $1,140 in discounted (at 12%) fuel economy savings over the assumed 14-year life of the car. Additional fuel-saving technologies could be applied, but according to the committee these technologies would add more to the purchase price of the car than they would save in discounted fuel costs. The larger the car, the greater the savings: the fuel economy of a mid-size SUV (such as a Ford Explorer or a Toyota Highlander) could be improved from its current 21 mpg to 28 mpg (33%). This would add $1,254 to its purchase price but would result in more than $2,000 in discounted fuel savings over its lifetime.

One question immediately arises: would these estimated improvements in fuel economy adversely affect safety? No, according to the committee. In fact, the committee found that neither passenger safety nor vehicle performance (acceleration and towing capacity, for example) would suffer when measured against today's standards so long as the technologies the committee identified were introduced throughout the fleets. The committee even figured into its calculations a slight increase in the weight of vehicles because of safety requirements likely to be imposed over the next 15 years. (It is possible, even likely, however, that performance would suffer in comparison to what it might be in 10 to 15 years were automakers not required to improve fuel economy.)

TABLE 1

Vehicle Class	Base mpg	Enhanced mpg (% Improvement)	Purchase Price Increase ($)	Lifetime Fuel Savings ($)
CARS				
Subcompact	31.3	35.1 (12)	502	694
Compact	30.1	34.3 (14)	561	788
Midsize	27.1	32.6 (20)	791	1,140
Large	24.8	31.4 (27)	985	1,494
LIGHT TRUCKS				
Small SUVs	24.1	30.0 (25)	959	1,460
Mid SUVs	21.0	28.0 (33)	1,254	2,057
Large SUVs	17.2	24.5 (42)	1,629	2,910
Mini Vans	23.0	29.7 (29)	1,079	1,703
Small Pickups	23.2	29.9 (29)	1,067	1,688
Large Pickups	18.5	25.5 (38)	1,450	2,531

Source: Adapted from NRC CAFE report (see For More Information for details).

THINKING MORE DEEPLY

Does all this mean that it's a good idea to impose more stringent fuel economy standards on automakers? Possibly, but not necessarily. First, one could argue, most people already know full well they could get better fuel economy by purchasing a different car. After all, no one buys a large SUV thinking it will stretch his or her gasoline dollar. Rather, at gasoline prices that typically range between $1.25 and $1.75 per gallon, there simply isn't very great demand among the American public for "fuel-sippers." Although I take strong issue with several of the arguments put forward by automakers during the recent Senate debate on CAFE, they are dead right on at least one count. CAFE standards require them to produce more fuel-efficient cars than large segments of the public appear to want—at least at current gasoline prices.

Second, if the government does require better new-car fuel economy, or if automakers provide it voluntarily, then the cost of driving a given distance falls (you'll use less gas per mile driven). This means the number of miles traveled will increase—about 1 to 2% for each 10% reduction in the cost of driving, according to research. This "rebound" effect—andits possible contribution to air pollution, increased congestion, and accident risks—has to be factored into CAFE policymaking.

Third, if people are much more sensitive to the upfront cost of buying a new car than to the fuel savings they will enjoy over its life, tighter CAFE standards could slow down the retirement of older vehicles on the road. ("We can't afford a new car, so we'd better keep ol' Bessie for a while.") We have observed this effect (called "new source bias") in decisions regarding the construction of new coal-fired power plants, certainly (see the article by Gruenspecht and Stavins in this issue), and it could keep gas-guzzlers on the road longer than we expect.

Fourth and finally, suppose CAFE standards are made more stringent. Although the CAFE Committee argued that this need not adversely affect safety or performance so long as automakers adopt the technologies identified by the committee, there certainly would be no requirement that they do so. If they chose to meet tighter standards by, once again, making cars smaller and lighter, drivers and passengers could be put at greater accident risk. Of course, consumer insistence on vehicle safety could force automakers down the technological route to enhanced fuel economy.

Given these possible shortcomings, CAFE standards must be weighed against the benefits of improving fuel economy. It is clearly worth something to reduce emissions of carbon dioxide and there are benefits as well to lessening our dependence on oil and, hence, our vulnerability to oil price shocks.

Suppose that a ton of carbon reduced is valued at $50, the figure used by the CAFE Committee (admittedly at the high end of the current range of estimated benefits of carbon abatement). Suppose further that the external benefits of each barrel of reduced oil consumption are valued at $5 (again, at the high end of estimated values). Together, these are equivalent to a $0.25 premium on the price of a gallon of gasoline. For this premium to be larger, either additional benefits of fuel economy improvements have to be identified or larger values justified for carbon reduction and/or oil consumption reductions.

A BOTTOM LINE

By far, the hardest question for any policy analyst to answer is this one: What would you do if the decision were yours to make? First, recognize that CAFE standards are distinctly inferior to higher gasoline taxes (and thus prices) as a way of dealing with both climate change and oil market externalities, a key finding in the CAFE Committee report. Higher gasoline prices would motivate new car buyers to demand better fuel economy; accordingly, automakers would be more willing to produce such vehicles since the demand would be there. Much more importantly, higher gasoline prices would also create an incentive for those driving the 200 million plus vehicles already on the road in the United States to drive less, carpool (or take public transport) more, and keep their cars in better tune. By working only on the new-car margin, CAFE is an incredibly slow way to deal with climate change and oil consumption. Thus, in my world of worlds, I would gradually increase gasoline taxes (along with taxes on all other carbon-based fuels), while rebating the tax revenues to the public by reducing other taxes so as not to exert drag on the economy.

But what if our elected officials continue to lack the wisdom or, more likely, the will to increase the taxes on gasoline and other carbon-based fuels? Is the CAFE program an acceptable, second-best alternative? Yes, I reluctantly conclude, but only if it is modified in ways the committee recommended.

I would support gradual increases in the required fuel economy targets automakers face, beginning in model year 2007 and extending through 2017. By that time, the passenger car fleet ought to be averaging 35 mpg and the light-duty truck fleet, 28 mpg. However, manufacturers whose fleets fall short of these targets must be able to purchase fuel economy "credits" from companies whose cars or light-duty trucks exceed the goals.

There is no reason why an automaker wishing to specialize in heavy-duty pickups or large SUVs should have to produce smaller vehicles to offset its fleet impact so long as it can pay another manufacturer to make "gasoline misers." Moreover, if fuel economy improvements are harder to come by technologically than the CAFE Committee believed (so that safety might be compromised), the government should offer to sell extra fuel economy credits to automakers at some predetermined price—a "safety valve," if you will, to ensure that the fuel economy program does not become more expensive than it should.

There are no easy calls regarding fuel economy. Now you have mine.

For More Information:

Committee on the Effectiveness and Impact of Corporate Average Fuel Economy (CAFE) Standards, Board on Energy and Environmental Systems, Transportation Research Board, National Research Council. 2001. *Effectiveness and Impact of Corporate Average Fuel Economy (CAFE) Standards.* Available from the National Academy Press at http://www.nap.edu/catalog/10172.html (accessed May 13, 2002).

Friedman, David, Jason Mark, Patricia Monahan, Carl Nash, and Clarence Ditlow. 2001. *Drilling in Detroit: Tapping Automaker Ingenuity to Build Safe and Efficient Automobiles.* Cambridge, MA: Union of Concerned Scientists.

Stelzer, Irwin. 2002. Oil's Well That Ends Well. *Weekly Standard,* May 13: 24–28.

Union of Concerned Scientists' Clean Vehicles website at http://www.ucsusa.org/index.html (accessed May 13, 2002).

What Are the Benefits of Hosting a Major League Sports Franchise?

By Jordan Rappaport and Chad Wilkerson

Over the last few decades the number of U.S. metropolitan areas large enough to host a franchise from one of the four major professional sports leagues has soared. Even as the National Football League, Major League Baseball, the National Basketball Association, and the National Hockey League have expanded to include more franchises, demand by metro areas continues to exceed supply. As a result, metro areas have been forced to compete with each other to retain and attract franchises.

Large public expenditures on the construction of new sports facilities have been the main form of this competition. Sports stadiums and arenas are extremely expensive. A new football or baseball stadium costs approximately $325 million; a new basketball or hockey arena costs approximately $200 million. The public's share of these costs has averaged $200 million and $100 million, respectively. During the 1990s more than $6 billion in public funds was spent on construction of sports stadiums and arenas. Almost $4 billion has already been allocated toward new facilities scheduled to open by the end of 2004.

The large public spending on sports facilities has been controversial. Usually these costly projects are justified by claims that hosting a sports franchise spurs local economic development by creating numerous new jobs and boosting local tax revenue. However, independent economic studies suggest that taxpayers may not be getting such a good deal. In

*Jordan Rappaport is an economist at the Federal Reserve Bank of Kansas City. Chad Wilkerson is an associate economist at the bank. This article is on the bank's web site at **www.kc.frb.org**.*

seeking to quantify the job creation and tax revenue benefits produced by a sports franchise, these studies overwhelmingly find that the benefits are much smaller than the outlay of public funds.

Does this mean that public funding of sports franchises is not justified? Perhaps not. An important element missing in the debate is the impact of a sports franchise on a metro area's quality of life. While difficult to measure, the contribution of a sports franchise to quality of life may exceed more traditional job creation and tax revenue benefits. If so, when quality-of-life benefits are included in the calculation, public spending may not appear to be such a bad investment for some metro areas.

The first section of this article reviews the current rush by metro areas to build sports facilities and lays out the arguments both in favor of and against using public funds to do so. The second section shows why the job creation and tax revenue benefits from hosting a major league franchise fall far short of typical public outlays on constructing a new sports facility. The third section argues that the large quality-of-life benefits associated with hosting a major league team may justify the public outlays.

I. THE DEBATE ON PUBLIC FINANCING FOR SPORTS STADIUMS

More than half the U.S. population lives in one of the 38 metro areas that host one or more teams from the four major professional sports leagues. And millions more live in rapidly growing metro areas with populations large enough to make them a potentially attractive place to locate a team. With demand for hosting major league teams exceeding supply, both current and potential host metro areas have been forced to compete to retain and attract franchises. Doing so almost always requires allocating large public expenditures to the construction of sports stadiums and arenas.

This section documents the scope and magnitude of public spending on professional sports franchises. It then summarizes the claims made to justify such spending as well as the critique of these claims by independent economists.

Table 1

STADIUM AND ARENA OPENINGS, 1994–2004

	Number of facilities	Avg. cost ($mil)	Avg. public cost ($mil)	Public cost as percent of total
1994-2000 new				
MLB/NFL	17	286	188	66
NBA/NHL	19	185	84	45
1994-2000 major renovations*				
MLB/NFL	6	110	88	82
NBA/NHL	2	114	98	86
2001-04 new†				
MLB/NFL	15	366	230	63
NBA/NHL	3	225	114	51

* Renovation of at least $60 million

† Facilities approved by January 1, 2001

Source: Sports Facility Reports (National Sports Law Institute)

The scope and magnitude of public financing for sports stadiums

The National Football League (NFL), Major League Baseball (MLB), the National Basketball Association (NBA), and the National Hockey League (NHL) are the four most widely followed professional sports leagues in the United States. Of the 121 teams in these four leagues, 111 play in 92 stadiums and arenas in 38 U.S. metro areas (Appendix 1). The remaining ten teams play in eight stadiums in six different Canadian metro areas.

Since 1994, more than $8 billion has been spent constructing new stadiums to host major league teams. Another $1 billion has been spent on major renovations of existing stadiums. While a few of the stadiums were financed privately, most received large contributions from local and state governments. Public spending on these new and renovated stadiums has totaled $5.4 billion. An additional $3.7 billion in public funds has already been allocated toward the construction of stadiums and arenas scheduled to open by the end of 2004. As a result of all this spending, by 2004 more than two-thirds of the 111 major league teams in the United States will be playing in venues that either opened or were heavily renovated in the previous ten years.

Sports stadiums and arenas are expensive. For the 17 football and baseball stadiums built since 1994, the average public contribution has been $188 million, or 66 percent of the total cost (Table 1). For the 19 basketball and hockey arenas built during the same period, the average public share has been $84 million, or 45 percent of the total. The average public contribution toward stadiums and arenas currently under construction is even higher: $230 million for baseball and football stadiums (63 percent of the total), and $114 million for basketball and hockey arenas (51 percent of the total). Appendix 2 shows public contributions for individual stadium and arena projects.

To finance their contributions toward stadium and arena projects, local and state governments issue bonds. Such bonds are usually paid off through various sorts of taxes enacted especially for this purpose. Sales taxes directed at tourists (for example, on hotel rooms, rental cars, and convention space) have been an especially popular method used to repay stadium bonds. Also common are general sales taxes that can apply across multiple counties or only in the county or municipality where the stadium is located. Other means of repaying stadium bonds in recent years have included gate taxes (surcharges on tickets to events at the sports facilities), state lottery proceeds, taxes on businesses in specially designated districts, and local and state government general funds.

Justifying public spending on sports facilities

Supporters of using public expenditures to finance the construction of sports facilities argue that hosting a major league franchise helps spur economic development. Impact studies commissioned by stadium proponents attempt to quantify how hosting a team affects a variety of local economic indicators such as output, personal income, jobs, and tax revenue. Stadium advocates suggest that increases in these indicators justify the large public outlays on sports facilities.

Table 2 contains a representative sample of benefit claims made in recent stadium impact studies. A 1996 study, for instance, argued that the NFL Seahawks in their former stadium increased total Seattle annual output by $69 million, increased total Seattle annual personal income by $41 million, created 1,264 Seattle jobs, and raised $3.3 million in state and local taxes per year. Impact studies also often label the expenditures and jobs associated with the construction phase of stadium projects as economic benefits. For instance, a 1996 study supporting the public financing of separate new sports stadiums for Cincinnati's NFL Bengals and MLB Reds suggests that the construction of these two sta-

Table 2

CLAIMED BENEFITS BY PRO-STADIUM IMPACT STUDIES

Year of study	Metro area	Team (league)	Annual economic impact ($mil)	Annual personal earnings ($mil)	Permanent jobs created	State/local taxes ($mil)	Total impact of construction ($mil)	Construction jobs created
1996	Seattle	Seahawks (NFL)*	69	41	1,264	3.3	–	–
1996	Cincinnati	Bengals (NFL)—current stadium*	77	24	1,785	1.4††	–	–
		Bengals (NFL)—new stadium*	92	28	2,134	1.8††	1,100‡	18,461‡
		Reds (MLB)—current stadium*	158	50	3,742	3.0††	–	–
		Reds (MLB)—new stadium*	192	59	4,474	3.7††	1,100‡	18,461‡
1998	Phoenix	Diamondbacks (MLB)	319	–	4,110	14.9	694	4,626
1998	Hartford	Patriots (NFL)†	171	71	2,757	15.6	–	–
1999	Boston	Red Sox (MLB)—current stadium*	120	–	1,597	–	–	–
		Red Sox (MLB)—new stadium*	186	–	2,629	–	492	4,769
1999	Wash/Balt	Ravens (NFL)	202	96	2,772	11.6	–	–
1999	San Antonio	Spurs (NBA)	77	43	–	3.3††	372	–
2000	Green Bay	Packers (NFL)	144	89	1,620	9.6	–	–
2000	Houston	Rockets (NBA)	187	91	2,400	13.0	–	–
2001	Kansas City	Chiefs (NFL) & Royals (MLB)	328	218	4,418	19.8	–	–

* Impacts due only to spending from out-of-area residents

† The Patriots play in the Boston MSA, but proposed moving to Hartford in 1998. Impacts are projections for 2001

†† Local tax revenues only

‡ Total for both Cincinnati stadiums

Sources: Team impact studies

diums would generate $1.1 billion in economic activity for the Cincinnati metro area and create 18,461 temporary jobs.

These impact studies that justify stadium projects can be subject to a number of criticisms. Many of the studies look at only the positive effects of hosting a major league franchise. Taking account of negative effects such as offsetting job losses, however, would produce much lower estimates of the net impact on local economic development. Moreover, the impact studies almost always fail to measure benefits in a form that can be compared with public outlays. While increases in output, increases in personal income, and job creation all measure increases in underlying economic activity, how should a metro area value these increases?

In response to the shortcomings of such impact studies, independent economists have attempted to measure the effect of professional sports teams on metro areas in a number of ways. One method is to compare growth rates of metro areas with and without professional teams, after controlling for other variables. For example, in a study of the growth of per capita personal income in 48 metro areas from 1958 to 1987, Baade (1994) found no significant difference between metro areas with major league teams and those without. In a study of 46 metro areas from 1990 to 1994, Walden actually found a negative relationship between economic activity and the presence of a sports team.

A second way of measuring the impact of teams is to examine the subsequent growth of cities that acquire new teams. Baade and Sanderson did this for ten metro areas that obtained new franchises between 1958 and 1993 and found no significant increases in employment or output. Results from Coates and Humphreys showed that per capita income fell when metro areas added teams.

Still another approach to measuring the impact of professional sports teams is to analyze the specific economic activity generated by specific teams in specific locations. For example, Hamilton and Kahn measured the annual returns to Maryland residents from Baltimore's NFL Ravens at approximately $1 million, compared to a $14 million annual public cost for their new stadium. Similarly, Baade (1997) measured the annual returns to Washington state residents from Seattle's MLB Mariners at between $3.8 and $5.1 million, compared to a $28 million annual public cost for their new stadium.

Regardless of method, none of the academic studies has so far been able to find significant economic development benefits sufficient to justify the large public outlays. As Siegfried and Zimbalist concluded in a recent survey of the economics of sports facilities,

> Few fields of empirical economic research offer virtual unanimity of findings. Yet, independent work on the economic impact of stadiums and arenas has uniformly found that there is no statistically significant positive correlation between sports facility construction and economic development.

Similarly, Noll and Zimbalist introduced a collection of 14 essays on the economics of sports stadiums by stating, "The overriding conclusion of this discussion is that the economic case for publicly financed stadiums cannot credibly rest on the benefits to local business, as measured by jobs, income, and investment."

So which view is correct? Do sports teams promote economic development as claimed by the impact studies? Or are such economic development benefits illusory as suggested by the independent economists? The next section examines whether the economic development benefits from hosting a major league franchise justify typical public outlays on sports stadiums and arenas.

II. MEASURING JOB CREATION AND TAX REVENUE BENEFITS

To measure the benefits associated with hosting a professional sports team, both stadium proponents and their critics focus on the increased economic activity and additional tax revenue that may be generated by a team's presence. The most common measure of economic activity is the creation of new jobs. Correctly measuring the benefit from job creation requires both accurately accounting for the net number of new jobs associated with a team's presence along with valuing the benefit of these jobs to the host metro area. Increased tax revenue resulting from the presence of the professional sports team arises from sales taxes and income taxes. Estimates of the combined benefits from net job creation and increased tax revenue fall considerably short of typical public outlays on new sports stadiums and arenas.

Measuring job creation benefits

Net job creation is a relatively good measure of the possible increase in economic activity associated with hosting a professional sports team. Estimated net job creation can be explicitly valued in terms of its benefit to a metro area's existing residents. Such an approach provides an estimate of benefits that can be directly compared with the public outlay costs while avoiding double counting that may arise from other methods. A possible limitation of this approach is that an increase in economic activity may benefit a metro area's existing residents even without any net job creation—for instance, if hosting a team causes everyone's wages to increase. However, the findings in numerous independent studies suggest that using net job creation to measure economic activity does not miss any large benefits.

Estimating net job creation. To estimate the number of jobs created from hosting a professional sports team, it is necessary to distinguish between gross and net job creation. Gross job creation is the number of jobs that can be observably linked to the presence of a sports team. Such observable jobs are created mainly within the stadium itself and at nearby businesses catering to people who attend sports events. But the presence of a professional sports team also creates job losses, because individuals who spend money to attend sports events have less to spend at businesses elsewhere in the host metro area. Less spending results in job losses. And benefits generally arise only from a net increase in jobs.[1]

Gross jobs created at a sports stadium include the players and other team employees; stadium management, maintenance, and support staff; and the various vendors selling goods at stadium events. Gross jobs created at nearby stadium businesses arise from the before-game and after-game spending of people attending sports events. Depending on the specific design and location of a sports stadium, such spending may support a number of local businesses, such as parking lots, restaurants, nightclubs, and souvenir shops. Some additional tourism-related jobs that can be linked to the presence of a sports team may also be created further away from stadiums. These arise from the spending of people who visit a host metro area to attend a sports event—for instance, at hotels and restaurants located throughout the metro area.[2]

Both stadium and nearby-stadium job creation may be offset by job losses throughout a host metro area. Such job losses must be subtracted from the above job gains to obtain an estimate of net job creation. In particular, economic research shows that people's total spending on entertainment is not affected by the presence of a professional sports team. For example, the more people spend on attending sports events, the less they may spend on movies and restaurants (Baade and Sanderson). Similarly, the more people spend at restaurants and nightclubs located near a stadium, the less they may spend at restaurants and nightclubs located elsewhere. Because the job losses from lower spending are spread across a large number of businesses and a wide geographic area, they usually cannot be observably linked to the presence of a sports team.

In addition to observable gross jobs, hosting a professional sports team also creates unobservable "local multiplier" jobs. These jobs arise from changes in local spending due to gross job creation and the offsetting job losses. For example, local spending by team players supports jobs across a range of local service industries, including at restaurants, nightclubs, and retail stores. Hence the total number of jobs created in a host metro area is some multiple of the observable number of jobs created. Similarly, the reduced local spending of people who lose jobs causes additional, again unobservable, job losses. Hence the total number of jobs lost is some multiple of the "initial" (also unobservable) number of jobs lost.[3]

Because local multiplier jobs cannot be easily linked to a sports team's presence, the size of the local multiplier is controversial. Estimates of total job creation in the stadium impact studies use local multipliers as high as 2.5. In other words, these studies assume that 2.5 total jobs are created for each initial observable job created from hosting a sports team. In contrast, the independent economic studies suggest that the appropriate local multiplier to apply to the gross jobs created from hosting a sports team is probably no more than 1.25 (Hamilton and Kahn; Siegfried and Zimbalist). The lower local multipliers used by the independent studies appear more reasonable because a large portion of local spending goes to purchase goods and services produced outside the host metro area. In addition, many professional sports players reside outside the metro area in which they play, either during the off-season or following retirement.

Taking explicit account of job losses and using estimates of the local multiplier from independent studies suggest that the net number of jobs created from hosting a professional sports team is quite low. It is almost certainly less than 1,000 and likely to be much closer to zero. For example, the methodology and numbers reported in Hamilton and Kahn suggest that Baltimore's hosting of the Orioles baseball team has created just 770 jobs in the Baltimore metro area. Statistical analysis reported in Baade and Sanderson found evidence of positive net job creation in only three of ten metro areas examined; their highest estimate of the number of net jobs created from hosting a sports team was 356 (associated with the Kansas City Royals). Surveying the economics literature, Siegfried and Zimbalist concluded that hosting a sports team might actually be associated with net job destruction rather than net job creation.[4]

Valuing the benefits from net job creation. To measure the benefit from increased economic activity, it is not enough just to estimate the net number of jobs created. It is also necessary to value explicitly the benefit of these jobs to the metro area.

It is important to realize that a metro area's existing residents may not benefit at all from net job creation. Consider the case of metro area residents who already have high paying jobs which they enjoy. How do they benefit from more jobs in a metro area? On the positive side, property prices are likely to rise and local governments may be able to raise revenues from a larger tax base, in turn allowing for lower tax rates. On the negative side, a rise in property prices could make housing less affordable, and traffic and other sorts of congestion may increase. For some existing residents, the net result may be that they are hurt rather than helped by net job creation.[5]

Whether and how much a metro area benefits from net job creation is an empirical question that a number of economists have attempted to answer. In particular, statistical techniques have been used to look at the correlations across metro areas among population, employment, wages, and house values. For a given increase in population and employment, benefits accrue through associated rises in wages or house values. For people who do not own their homes, net benefits are likely be negligible as any rise in wages is offset by the higher cost of housing. But for residents who already own a home, there is no offset and so benefits may be positive.

Using such techniques, economists have estimated metro area benefits to range from $0 to $1,500 per net job created (Rosen; Roback; Gyourko and Tracy; and Hamilton and Kahn).[6] At one extreme, if the benefit per net job created is indeed zero, metro areas will not benefit at all from any possible net job creation from hosting a professional sports team. At the other extreme, even if the benefit per net job created is at its upper bound estimate of $1,500, the total benefit to a metro area from any net jobs created will be far smaller than the total of the associated salaries.

Table 3
ESTIMATES OF NET JOB CREATION
FROM HOSTING A PROFESSIONAL SPORTS TEAM

Number of net jobs created	0 to 1,000
Benefit per net job created	\$0 to \$1,500
Baseline annual benefit (500 jobs x \$750 benefit per job)	\$375,000

Sources: Authors' calculations based on estimates from Hamilton and Kahn, Baade and Sanderson, Gyourko and Tracy, Rosen, and Roback

Valuing the net job creation benefit from a team requires combining the above estimates of the number of net jobs created with the value of these jobs to the host metro area (Table 3). Using the lower and upper bound estimates, respectively, values the net job creation benefit at \$0 and \$1.5 million per year. Using the midpoints from each of these ranges as a baseline values the net job creation benefit at \$375,000 per year (500 jobs times \$750 per job).

Measuring tax revenue benefits

The second main source of benefits on which both stadium advocates and independent economists focus is the increased tax revenues that may arise from hosting a team. Fans' spending before, during, and after games is likely to be subject to local and state sales taxes. And the income accruing to any net increase in jobs is often subject to local and state income taxes.

Estimating imported sales tax revenue. The main way in which increased sales tax revenue benefits a host metro area is if it is paid by nonlocal residents. Nonlocal sports fans visiting to attend games pay sales taxes on all local purchases before, during, and after games. Such spending "imports" tax revenue, which in the absence of a professional sports team would have accrued to governments outside the host metro area. Imported sales tax revenue benefits the host metro area by reducing the amount of taxes that need to be raised from local residents.[7]

Estimating the imported sales tax revenues associated with hosting a team is straightforward. To do so, first the number of nonlocal fans who visit to attend sports games must be estimated. This estimate is then multiplied by the fans' estimated average spending before, during, and after games. Finally, this latter result must be multiplied by the relevant local sales tax rate. The difficult part, of course, is estimating the number of visitors and how much they spend on average. Among the four major professional sports leagues, specifics such as ticket prices, average attendance, and the number of home games per season vary enough to require separate estimates. And regardless of league, it is necessary to distinguish nonlocal sports fans who visit for the purpose of attending a game from nonlocal visitors who happen to attend a game.

Table 4 derives the estimated imported sales tax benefit from hosting a team from each of the four major sports leagues. The listed percentages of nonlocal visiting fans are toward the high end of estimates from a number of impact and economic studies.[8] For calculating the imported sales tax revenue benefit attributable to hosting a sports team, what matters is not the number of nonlocal residents who attend games but rather the number of nonlocal residents whose visits are explicitly motivated by the presence of a team. The distinction is crucial. Nonlocal residents who attend games may be visiting the host metro area for non-game-related reasons such as business or family. If so, their spending at games most likely represents a shifting away from spending on other forms of local entertainment and hence the associated imported tax revenues should not be attributed to the presence of the sports team.[9]

Average spending by visiting sports fans is estimated to range from $63 for MLB games to $99 for NBA games. The concession portion of average spending is based on the purchase of a representative bundle of food, merchandise, and parking at the average 2000 season price in the respective league (FOXSports.com). The out-of-stadium portion of average spending is based on a survey of fans attending Baltimore Orioles games in 1992, converted to 2000 dollars (Hamilton and Kahn).

The imported tax revenue from a given amount of visitors' spending obviously depends on the applicable rate of sales tax. Assuming an extremely high local sales tax rate of 5 percent suggests that hosting a sports team imports from $696,000 per year for an NHL team to $1,537,000 per year for an MLB team. At a more typical local sales tax rate of 2 percent, imported sales tax revenues for the four types of teams range from just $278,400 per year for an NHL team to $614,800 per year for an MLB team.[10]

Estimating income tax revenue. Many of the localities in which professional sports teams play levy local income taxes. If so, the income tax revenue on salaries due to any net job creation is imported in the sense that in the absence of a professional sports team, it would be paid to

Table 4

ESTIMATES OF IMPORTED SALES TAX REVENUE PER TEAM, 2000 SEASON

	NFL	MLB	NBA	NHL
Number of home games (including preseason)	10	81	44	44
Average attendance (based on all teams for 2000 season)	66,100	30,125	16,800	16,300
Nonlocal fans	35%	20%	20%	20%
Number of nonlocal fans per season	*231,350*	*488,025*	*147,840*	*143,440*
Average ticket price	$46	$15	$48	$46
Average concessions/parking	$19	$15	$18	$18
Average out-of-stadium spending by non-MSA visiting fans	$33	$33	$33	$33
Average per visit spending by non-MSA fans	*$98*	*$63*	*$99*	*$97*
Total annual spending by visiting non-MSA fans	*$22,672,000*	*$30,746,000*	*$14,636,000*	*$13,914,000*
Annual sales tax revenues with a 5% local sales tax rate	**$1,134,000**	**$1,537,000**	**$732,000**	**$696,000**

Sources: FOXSports.com; authors' calculations based on estimates from impact and independent economic studies

other localities. Such imported income tax revenue does not necessarily benefit the host metro area since at least in part it goes to cover any additional costs in providing municipal services to accommodate the growth in employment and population.[11]

Nevertheless, because player salaries are extremely high, the associated income taxes are likely to far exceed the marginal cost of any municipal services used by players. This is especially so since many players reside outside the host metro area for a significant portion of the year. Moreover, because they tend to be young, few players have children in local public schools. Income taxes on the relatively high salaries of a team's general manager and head coach are also likely to exceed the marginal cost of the additional municipal services these individuals use.

Table 5 derives the estimated imported income tax benefit from hosting a team from each of the four major sports leagues. Applying a 2 percent income tax rate to the estimated team payrolls suggests that increased local income taxes range from $868,000 per year for NHL teams to $1.4 million per year for NFL teams. The assumed 2 percent local income tax rate is toward the high end of the rate at which local governments tax income. Indeed, many professional teams play in metro areas whose local governments do not levy income taxes. On the other hand, many state governments tax income at higher than a 2 percent rate. Using the highest combined state and local income tax rate from the metro areas that host teams (10.6 percent for New York City) establishes an upper bound on the imported annual income tax benefit ranging from $4.6 million for an NHL team to $7.5 million for an NFL team.

Comparing job creation and tax revenue benefits to public outlays

How do benefits of estimated job creation and tax revenue compare with typical public outlays on sports facilities? Adding together the annual estimated benefit values of the net job creation, imported sales taxes, and increased income taxes yields baseline estimates of the value of hosting a franchise ranging from $1.9 million per year for an NHL team to $2.9 million per year for an NFL team (Table 6).

A last necessary step toward the goal of comparing benefits and costs is to convert benefits quantified on an annual basis into benefits quantified on a net present value basis. The question is, how much should a metro area be willing to spend for each dollar of *annual* benefits associated with hosting a franchise? Calculating the answer is straightforward. Assuming that metro areas can borrow (by issuing municipal bonds) at a 6 percent interest rate and that the proceeds are used to purchase an annual stream of benefits starting one year in the future and lasting for 30 years (a reasonable estimate for the life of a sports stadium), it follows that each $1 of annual benefits is worth $13.76 to the metro area.[12]

On a net present value basis, the estimated value of the combined jobs and tax benefits from a franchise range from $26.7 million for an NHL team to $40.3 million for an NFL team (Table 6). Such values fall far short of typical public outlays on sports facilities. The average public outlay on new baseball and football stadiums completed between 1994 and 2000 was $188 million. Thus, for most sports stadium projects, costs exceeded the above estimated benefits by well over $100 million. The average public outlay on new basketball and hockey arenas completed over the same period was $84 million. Thus, for most sports

Table 5

ESTIMATES OF INCOME TAX REVENUE PER TEAM, 2000 SEASON

	NFL	MLB	NBA	NHL
Number of players on rosters	53	25	15	23
Average salary, in millions of dollars	1.3	1.9	3.2	1.8
Head coach + general manager	2	2	2	2
Average salary, in millions of dollars	1	1	1	1
Total player, head coach, and general manager payroll, in millions of dollars	*70.9*	*49.5*	*50.0*	*43.4*
Annual income tax revenues with a 2% local income tax, in millions of dollars	1.4	1.0	1.0	.9

Source: FOXSports.com; authors' calculations

Table 6

ESTIMATES OF JOBS AND TAX BENEFITS, 2000 SEASON

	NFL	MLB	NBA	NHL
Baseline annual benefit value (% of total job + tax benefit):				
Net job creation benefit	$375,000 (12.8%)	$375,000 (12.9%)	$375,000 (17.8%)	$375,000 (19.3%)
Imported sales taxes benefit	$1,134,000 (38.7%)	$1,537,000 (53.0%)	$732,000 (34.7%)	$696,000 (35.9%)
Increased income taxes benefit	$1,418,000 (48.4%)	$990,000 (34.1%)	$1,000,000 (47.5%)	$868,000 (44.8%)
Total annual benefit value	*$2,927,000*	*$2,902,000*	*$2,107,000*	*$1,939,000*
Net present value of jobs and tax benefits from hosting a team for 30 years using 6% interest rate (annual benefit times 13.76)	$40,275,520	$39,931,520	$28,992,320	$26,680,640

Source: Authors' calculations

arena projects, costs exceeded the above estimated benefits by well over $50 million. The amount by which public costs exceed estimated jobs and tax benefits is even higher for the sports stadiums and arenas currently under construction.

If anything, the baseline values estimated above likely overstate rather than understate the benefits they measure. As discussed, there is much doubt that hosting a professional sports team creates any jobs. Moreover, many host metro areas tax spending at a rate lower than the assumed 5 percent baseline. And, many do not tax income at all. As a result, it is reasonable to believe that the net present value of the jobs and tax benefits may be no more than $5 million from hosting an NBA or NHL team and no more than $10 million from hosting an NFL or MLB team. Even using the upper-bound estimates from the analysis above suggests that the public outlays on current sports facility projects far exceed any associated jobs and tax benefits.

The bottom line, then, is that the benefit to a host metro area from increased economic activity as measured by net job creation and increased tax revenues appears to fall far short of the public outlays typically needed to retain and attract professional sports teams. Nevertheless, metro areas continue to approve ever-larger public outlays on new sports facility construction. If such public outlays represent good investments, there must be some other large benefit from hosting a team that the above analysis is not measuring. The next section explores whether a professional sports team's contribution to a host area's quality of life may be exactly such a benefit.

III. QUALITY-OF-LIFE BENEFITS FROM HOSTING A MAJOR LEAGUE FRANCHISE

The presence of a major league sports franchise can help make a metro area an attractive place to live. Nearly all analyses of the benefits from hosting professional sports teams recognize this contribution to a metro area's quality of life. But because quality-of-life benefits are difficult to quantify, stadium proponents and critics usually pay them little attention beyond such acknowledgment.

The term "quality of life" used in this article is meant to capture the satisfaction, or happiness, residents derive from shared metro area attributes. Examples of shared attributes include pleasant weather, scenic vistas, and natural recreational opportunities. Of course, residents' happiness also depends on their individual circumstances, such as having a good job and living in a nice house.

This section discusses how the presence of a major league franchise contributes to the quality of life of a host metro area's residents. Three possible ways of valuing this benefit are presented. Together they suggest that hosting a major league franchise contributes substantially to quality of life and perhaps justifies public outlays on sports stadiums and arenas.

How hosting a professional sports team contributes to quality of life

Professional sports teams contribute to a metro area's quality of life primarily by increasing the happiness of sports fans. The most visible source of fan happiness comes from attending home games. However, only part of this happiness actually counts as a quality-of-life benefit attributable to hosting a team. This is because fans must pay to attend games. In the absence of a professional sports team, fans could instead use what they paid for game admissions on other sources of happiness, such as watching a movie or traveling to a different metro area to attend a game.

Formally, the quality-of-life benefit to a particular fan who attends a sports game is the amount above the admission price they would have been willing to spend to attend the game. For instance, if someone is willing to spend $30 to attend a game that only costs $20, they receive a $10 quality-of-life benefit. Adding up the individual quality-of-life benefits of all residents who attend games yields the total metro area's quality-of-life benefit from game attendance.[13]

A second source of happiness for fans comes from rooting for a team more generally, independent of actually attending games in person. Fans watch games on television, listen to them on the radio, and read about them in local newspapers. Games serve as an occasion for parties and barbecues. Teams' performance is the subject of long discussions among friends. And second-guessing team decisions is the subject of nearly continuous banter on local talk radio.

It is also possible that hosting a franchise increases the happiness of all metro area residents, regardless of their being sports fans. Home games and rooting for a sports team provide for shared community experiences. And hosting a sports team may increase civic pride—for instance, by contributing to a sense that one lives in a "world class" city.

On the other hand, hosting a team may also decrease the happiness of some metro area residents. Home games impose traffic and congestion in the vicinity of sports facilities. And television viewers face interruption of their favorite syndicated shows by local game broadcasts.

Such possible negative contributions must be subtracted from positive contributions in valuing the net contribution to quality of life from hosting a team.

Valuing quality-of-life benefits

Valuing the happiness metro area residents derive from the presence of a major league team is extremely difficult. A person's happiness from attending a game or from watching one on television is not observable. Nevertheless, there are several possible approaches to valuing quality-of-life benefits. A first approach is to ask a sample of metro area residents how much they would be willing to pay to retain or attract a team. A second approach uses variations in metro area wages and house prices to implicitly value quality-of-life attributes that may be similar in magnitude to hosting a major league franchise. A third approach looks at the actions of metro areas that have lost sports franchises and so may have the best information on the quality-of-life benefits from hosting a team.

Surveying residents. The most direct approach to valuing the quality-of-life benefits from hosting a team is to ask local residents how much they would be willing to pay to keep their team from moving.

In the only major study of this kind, Pittsburgh metro area residents were asked during the winter of 2000, "What is the most you would be willing to pay out of your own household budget each year in higher city taxes to keep the Penguins in Pittsburgh?" (Johnson, Groothuis, and Whitehead). The responses implicitly valued the quality-of-life benefits from hosting the NHL Penguins at somewhere between $0.83 to $2.30 per Pittsburgh metro area resident per year. Given metro Pittsburgh's population of 2.4 million and converting to a net present value basis using a 6 percent interest rate, as described in the previous section, the value of hosting the Penguins for 30 years is estimated to fall somewhere in the range of $26.9 million to $74.7 million.

Note that the lower-bound estimate of the quality-of-life value of hosting the Penguins is nearly the same as the baseline estimate of the job creation and tax benefit value of doing so. The upper-bound estimate of the quality-of-life value of hosting the Penguins begins to approach the $84 million average public contribution to NBA/NHL sports arenas completed between 1994 and 2000.

Moreover, there are several reasons to believe that the quality-of-life benefits to Pittsburgh from hosting the Penguins may be low relative to such benefits associated with other major league teams. First, the quality-of-life benefits from hosting an NHL team are probably the lowest of the four leagues considered in this article. For instance, only 15 of the 24 NHL teams currently have local network television contracts. And when NHL games are broadcast, their ratings tend to be less than half those for MLB games (*SportsBusiness Journal*). Second, Pittsburgh also hosts the NFL Steelers and the MLB Pirates. So even if it were to lose the Penguins, Pittsburgh would still host two major league teams. Economic theory argues that the additional benefit of something decreases the more you have of it. Third, at the time the survey was conducted, the Penguins organization was in Chapter 11 bankruptcy proceedings. Whatever problems caused the Penguins' financial difficulties may also have lowered the team's contribution to Pittsburgh's quality of life. Fourth, as will be argued below, it may be that only by losing a team do metro area residents come to accurately value the team's contribution to quality of life.[14]

Comparing to quality-of-life valuations of other attributes. The second approach to valuing the quality-of-life contribution from hosting a team considers the valuations of other attributes that also contribute to quality of life. For instance, the quality-of-life net present value associated with one extra day per year of pleasant weather for 30 years turns out to be similar in magnitude to many of the recent public outlays on stadium projects. So if the contribution to quality of life from hosting a major league team is at least as great as the contribution from one extra day per year of pleasant weather, then the public outlays on sports stadiums and arenas may be justified.

The quality-of-life benefits of certain attributes that naturally differ across metro areas, such as the weather, can be measured by variations in wages and house prices. All else equal, metro areas with attributes that positively contribute to residents' happiness attract population inflows. This puts downward pressure on local wages and upward pressure on local house prices as people who move in try to find jobs and housing. The lower wages and higher house prices serve as negative "compensation" for the high quality of life. Conversely, metro areas that offer low levels of happiness lose population, putting upward pressure on local wages and downward pressure on local house prices as firms try to retain workers and the people who move out vacate housing. The higher wages and lower house prices serve as positive "compensation" for the low quality of life.[15]

Using data on a large number of individuals and households living in more than 100 different metro areas, statistical techniques can measure the variations in wages and house prices that are due to each of several metro area attributes. The quality-of-life value of a given metro area attribute can then be calculated as the sum of the lower wages individuals are willing to accept and the higher house prices they are willing to pay to live in an area with such an attribute.[16] Table 7 summarizes a few results from research that estimates such "compensating differentials."

The quantitative benefits from quality of life are found to be quite large. For instance, the estimates suggest that the annual value to a metro area of one extra sunny day per year is between $7 to $12 per person. So a metro area with two million people should be willing to pay between $14 million and $24 million per year for the extra annual sunny day (or roughly between $193 million and $330 million up front for an average extra sunny day over each of the subsequent 30 years). Quantitatively similar valuations are estimated for the quality-of-life benefits of one less rainy day per year and one inch less snow per year.

Unfortunately, this second approach cannot be used directly to value the quality of life from hosting a major league team. The reason is that nearly all teams choose to locate in metro areas with high levels of population and employment. This makes it impossible to distinguish between the variations in wages and house prices that are due to the presence of a sports team and those that are due to the high population and employment.

Nevertheless, the high valuations of the quality-of-life benefits that flow from geographic attributes such as pleasant weather serve as a useful benchmark for the quality-of-life benefits from hosting a major league team. In particular, large public outlays to attract and retain a major league team may make sense if the team's contribution to the area's quality of life is similar in magnitude to that of one extra sunny day per year (or one less rainy day per year or one inch less snow per year). Fan willingness to endure extreme weather to attend games at outdoor stadiums suggests that the positive contribution to happiness from hosting a professional sports team may exceed such a threshold.

The experience of metro areas that lost teams. A third approach to valuing quality-of-life benefits points to the actions of metro areas that hosted a major league team that then moved elsewhere. These metro areas should be among those with the best information on the quality-of-life benefits from hosting a team since they can compare happiness

Table 7

ESTIMATE OF ANNUAL PER PERSON CONTRIBUTION TO QUALITY OF LIFE

Attribute	Annual per person value, 1999$	Source
Weather: 1 less rainy day per year	$12+	Rosen
Weather: 1 extra sunny day per year	$ 7 $12	Gyourko and Tracy Blomquist et al
Weather: 1 inch less snow per year	$11	Roback
Pollution: 10 fewer micrograms suspended particulates per cubic meter air	$ 3 $24	Blomquist et al Gyourko and Tracy
Pollution: 1 less Superfund site per county	$93	Blomquist et al
Violent crime: 100 fewer violent crimes per year per 100,000 population	$ 91 $114	Blomquist et al Gyourko and Tracy

both with and without a team. Subsequent to losing a team, many of these metro areas were willing to significantly increase the size of their public outlays on constructing new sports facilities. This willingness suggests that residents revised upward their estimates of a major league team's contribution to their happiness. The resulting success of such metro areas in attracting replacement teams indicates that quality-of-life benefits may indeed justify the large public outlays.

Since 1980, only 12 U.S. metro areas have lost major league teams.[17] Six of these lost National Football League teams: Oakland (1983), Baltimore (1984), St. Louis (1988), Los Angeles (two teams in 1995), Cleveland (1997), and Houston (1997). Four metro areas lost National Hockey League teams: Atlanta (1980), Denver (1982), Minneapolis/St. Paul (1993) and Hartford (1997). And two metro areas lost National Basketball Association teams: Kansas City (1984) and San Diego (1984).

Losing a football team seems clearly to have caused metro area residents to revise upward their estimates of the associated quality-of-life benefits.[18] Of the metro areas that lost NFL teams, all but Los Angeles subsequently allocated considerably more public financing to attract a new NFL team than it would have cost to keep their old team. For example, St. Louis' NFL Cardinals departed in 1987 after the city refused to allocate $120 million toward the construction of a new football stadium (Quirk and Fort). Less than three years later, St. Louis voters approved $280 million in public funds for a new football stadium—even before they had a team to play in it.[19] And two years following the departure of the NFL Browns, Cleveland allocated $214 million toward construction of a football stadium for a newly awarded expansion team. The owner of the former Cleveland Browns commented, "The only regret I have, to be honest with you, is that if they gave me half of what they're doing now, I'd still be in Cleveland" (Meyer). Similarly, Oakland, Baltimore, and Houston each increased by at least one-third the amount of public funds they were willing to spend on building new football stadiums.[20]

The experience of metro areas that lost NHL and NBA teams has been more mixed. Minneapolis-St. Paul would probably have needed to spend only about $17 million to prevent the 1993 departure of its NHL team (Bremner). But in 1999 it decided to allocate $130 million to attract a new NHL team. At the same time, Atlanta and Denver managed to endure the loss of their NHL teams for 19 and 13 years, respectively. They were eventually able to attract replacement NHL teams at what is probably a lower public cost than what would have been required to prevent the original losses. Hartford has been more aggressive in attempting to attract an NFL team rather than a replacement for its departed NHL team. And neither Kansas City nor San Diego has made an extensive effort to replace their NBA teams.[21]

Taking account of quality-of-life benefits

The previous section's discussion of the job creation and tax revenue benefits from hosting a major league franchise suggested that such benefits fall far short of typical public outlays on the construction of new sports facilities. Can quality-of-life benefits make up the difference?

Based on results of a survey asking Pittsburgh metro area residents how much they would be willing to be taxed to keep the NHL Penguins, the answer may be yes. However, caution warns against generalizing the results from a single survey.

Alternatively, results of economic studies of compensating differentials provide a benchmark in assessing quality-of-life benefits. For instance, if the contribution to metro area residents' happiness from hosting a major league sports franchise is similar in magnitude to that from an additional day of pleasant weather per year, the net present value quality-of-life benefit may indeed approach the magnitude of recent public outlays on sports facility construction.

Finally, the aggressive bids by metro areas to replace teams that have departed further supports the view that the overall value to a metro area from hosting a professional sports team may exceed the associated large public expenditures. Of course, this will not always be the case as is illustrated by the metro areas that have not made extensive efforts to reattract lost teams. But for those metro areas that have bid aggressively, this would almost certainly have to be due to a large contribution to residents' quality of life.

IV. SUMMARY AND CONCLUSIONS

U.S. metro areas have had to compete with each other to retain and attract major league sports franchises. The resulting large public outlays to finance the construction of sports facilities have been quite controversial. Proponents of using public funds to finance stadium construction argue that the benefits from increased economic activity and increased tax revenue collection exceed the public outlays. But independent economic studies universally find such benefits to be much smaller than claimed.

So does it makes sense for metro areas to use public funds to attract and retain major league sports franchises? The answer is definitely not if benefits are limited to increases in economic activity and tax revenue collection. A strong case can be made, however, that the quality-of-life benefits from hosting a major league team can sometimes justify the large public outlays associated with doing so.[22]

Quality-of-life benefits are rarely explicitly included in the debate on using public funds to attract and retain a major league sports franchise. Acknowledging that the main benefit from hosting a team comes from improved metro-area quality of life should help to value this contribution. Doing so does not require impact studies. Residents and elected officials who understand that the benefits of a sports team are the same sort that flow from parks, zoos, museums, and theater can decide on their own how much hosting a major league team is worth.

Appendix 1

LARGEST U.S. METRO AREAS AND THEIR MAJOR LEAGUE TEAMS

Size	Metro area	Pop 2000	MLB	NFL	NBA	NHL	Teams	Venues	Pop/team
1	New York	21,199,865	2	2	2	3	9	6	2,355,541
2	Los Angeles	16,373,645	2	–	2	2	6	4	2,728,941
3	Chicago	9,157,540	2	1	1	1	5	4	1,831,508
4	Washington/Baltimore	7,608,070	1	2	1	1	5	4	1,521,614
5	SF/Oakland/San Jose	7,039,362	2	2	1	1	6	5	1,173,227
6	Philadelphia	6,188,463	1	1	1	1	4	2	1,547,116
7	Boston	5,819,100	1	1	1	1	4	3	1,454,775
8	Detroit	5,456,428	1	1	1	1	4	4	1,364,107
9	Dallas/Fort Worth	5,221,801	1	1	1	1	4	3	1,305,450
10	Houston	4,669,571	1	1	1	–	3	3	1,556,524
11	Atlanta	4,112,198	1	1	1	1	4	3	1,028,050
12	Miami	3,876,380	1	1	1	1	4	3	969,095
13	Seattle	3,554,760	1	1	1	–	3	3	1,184,920
14	Phoenix	3,251,876	1	1	1	1	4	3	812,969
15	Minneapolis/St. Paul	2,968,806	1	1	1	1	4	3	742,202
16	Cleveland	2,945,831	1	1	1	–	3	3	981,944
17	San Diego	2,813,833	1	1	–	–	2	1	1,406,917
18	St. Louis	2,603,607	1	1	–	1	3	3	867,869
19	Denver	2,581,506	1	1	1	1	4	3	645,377
20	Tampa	2,395,997	1	1	–	1	3	3	798,666
21	Pittsburgh	2,358,695	1	1	–	1	3	3	786,232
22	Portland	2,265,223	–	–	1	–	1	1	2,265,223
23	Cincinnati	1,979,202	1	1	–	–	2	1	989,601
24	Sacramento	1,796,857	–	–	1	–	1	1	1,796,857
25	Kansas City	1,776,062	1	1	–	–	2	2	888,031
26	Milwaukee	1,689,572	1	–	1	–	2	2	844,786
27	Orlando	1,644,561	–	–	1	–	1	1	1,644,561
28	Indianapolis	1,607,486	–	1	1	–	2	2	803,743
29	San Antonio	1,592,383	–	–	1	–	1	1	1,592,383
30	*Norfolk/Va. Beach*	*1,569,541*	–	–	–	–	–	–	–
31	*Las Vegas*	*1,563,282*	–	–	–	–	–	–	–
32	Columbus	1,540,157	–	–	–	1	1	1	1,540,157
33	Charlotte	1,499,293	–	1	1	–	2	2	749,647
34	New Orleans	1,337,726	–	1	–	–	1	1	1,337,726
35	Salt Lake City	1,333,914	–	–	1	–	1	1	1,333,914
36	*Greenboro/Win-Salem*	*1,251,509*	–	–	–	–	–	–	–
37	*Austin*	*1,249,763*	–	–	–	–	–	–	–
38	Nashville	1,231,311	–	1	–	1	2	2	615,656
39	*Providence*	*1,188,613*	–	–	–	–	–	–	–
40	Raleigh/Durham	1,187,941	–	–	–	1	1	1	1,187,941
41	*Hartford*	*1,183,110*	–	–	–	–	–	–	–
42	Buffalo	1,170,111	–	1	–	1	2	2	585,056
43	*Memphis*	*1,135,614*	–	–	–	–	–	–	–
44	*West Palm Beach*	*1,131,184*	–	–	–	–	–	–	–
45	Jacksonville	1,100,491	–	1	–	–	1	1	1,100,491
155	Green Bay	226,778	–	1	–	–	1	1	226,778
U.S. metro areas with pro sports		147,176,402	28	32	27	24	111	92	1,325,914
Total United States		281,421,906	28	32	27	24	111	92	2,535,332

Appendix 2

FINANCING OF NEW SPORTS FACILITIES AND MAJOR RENOVATIONS, 1994–2004

Metro area, Facility (League)	Total cost ($mil)	Public cost ($mil)	Source of public funding	Type of tax used to repay bonds or other means of public financing
1994–2000 new				
Atlanta Turner Field (MLB)	235	0	–	n/a
Atlanta Philips Arena (NBA/NHL)	214	173	County	Gate/concession, Hotel/rental-car
Boston Fleet Center (NBA/NHL)	160	0	–	n/a
Buffalo HSBC Arena (NHL)	123	54	State,County,City	Gate/concession
Charlotte Ericcson Stadium (NFL)	298	10	City	General fund
Chicago United Center (NBA/NHL)	150	11	City	General fund
Cincinnati Paul Brown Stadium (NFL)	452	452	State,County,City	Sales
Cleveland Jacobs Field (MLB)	173	152	County	Alcohol/tobacco, Gate/concession
Cleveland Gund Arena (NBA)	152	73	State,County	Alcohol/tobacco, Capital improvement fund
Cleveland Cleveland Browns Stadium (NFL)	309	216	County	Alcohol/tobacco
Columbus Nationwide Arena (NHL)	150	0	–	n/a
Dallas/Fort Worth Ballpark at Arlington (MLB)	191	153	City	Sales, General fund
Denver Coors Field (MLB)	215	161	Multi-county	Sales
Denver Pepsi Center (NBA/NHL)	165	5	County	General fund
Detroit Comerica Park (MLB)	290	145	County	Hotel/rental-car, casino revenues
Houston Enron Field (MLB)	266	180	County	Hotel/rental-car
Indianapolis Conseco Fieldhouse (NBA)	175	72	City	Sales, Capital improvement fund
Los Angeles Staples Center (NBA/NHL)	321	71	City	
Miami National Car Rental Arena (NHL)	212	184	City	Hotel/rental-car
Miami American Airlines Arena (NBA)	241	142	City	Hotel/rental-car
Minneapolis/St. Paul Xcel Energy Center (NHL)	130	130	State,City	Sales
Nashville Gaylord Entertainment Center (NHL)	144	144	City	General fund
Nashville Adelphia Coliseum (NFL)	292	292	State,City	Hotel/rental-car, Gate/concession, General fund
Philadelphia First Union Center (NBA/NHL)	206	23	State,City	General fund
Phoenix BankOne Ballpark (MLB)	355	270	County	Sales, Gate/concession
Portland Rose Garden (NBA)	262	200	City	Gate/concession, General fund
Raleigh Raleigh Entertainment/ Sports Arena (NHL)	160	139	State,County	Hotel/rental-car, General fund
Seattle Safeco Field (MLB)	517	393	State,County	Sales, Hotel/rental-car, Gate/concession
SF/Oakland/San Jose Pacific Bell Park (MLB)	306	15	City	Special financing district
St. Louis Savvis Center (NHL)	160	24	City	General fund
St. Louis TWA Dome (NFL)	300	300	State,County,City	
Tampa Ice Palace (NHL)	139	86	State,County,City	General fund

Appendix 2 continues on following page

Appendix 2, continued

Metro area, Facility (League)	Total cost ($mil)	Public cost ($mil)	Source of public funding	Type of tax used to repay bonds or other means of public financing
Tampa Raymond James Stadium (NFL)	190	190	City	Sales
Washington/Baltimore FedEx Field (NFL)	251	70	State,City	General fund
Washington/Baltimore MCI Center (NBA/NHL)	260	60	State,City	General fund
Washington/Baltimore PSINet Stadium (NFL)	229	200	State	General fund, Lottery proceeds
1994–2000 renovations				
Buffalo Ralph Wilson Stadium (NFL)	63	63	State	General fund
Jacksonville Alltel Stadium (NFL)	135	122	State,City	General fund, Hotel/rental-car, Gate/concession
Los Angeles Edison International Field (MLB)	117	30	City	Gate/concession, Hotel/rental-car, General fund
San Diego Qualcomm Field (MLB/NFL)	78	60	City	General fund
Seattle Key Arena (NBA)	107	75	City	General fund
SF/Oak/SJ Network Associates (MLB/NFL)	200	200	County,City	General fund
SF/Oak/SJ Oakland Arena (NBA)	121	121	County,City	General fund
Tampa Tropicana Field (MLB)	65	51	State,City	Hotel/rental-car, Gate/concession, General fund
2001–2004 new*				
Boston New Patriots stadium (NFL)	325	70	State	General fund
Chicago New Bears stadium (NFL)	587	387	City	Hotel/rental-car
Cincinnati Great American Ballpark (MLB)	297	224	County	Sales
Dallas/FW American Airlines Arena (NBA/NHL)	325	125	City	Hotel/rental-car
Denver Invesco Field (NFL)	360	270	Multi-county	Sales
Detroit Ford Field (NFL)	245	125	County	Hotel/rental-car, General fund
Green Bay New Lambeau Field (NFL)	295	169	County	Sales
Houston Reliant Stadium (NFL)	402	287	County	Hotel/rental-car
Houston New Rockets arena (NBA)	175	70	County	Hotel/rental-car, General fund
Milwaukee Miller Park (MLB)	322	232	State,County,City	Sales, General fund
Philadelphia New Eagles stadium (NFL)	642	304	State,City	General fund, Gate/concession
Philadelphia New Phillies stadium (MLB)	367	170	State,City	General fund, Gate/concession
Phoenix New Cardinals stadium (NFL)	331	229	County	Hotel/rental-car, Player income
Pittsburgh PNC Park (MLB)	233	193	State,County,City	Gate/concession, General fund
Pittsburgh New Steelers stadium (NFL)	244	177	State,County	General fund, Sales
San Antonio SBC Arena (NBA)	175	147	County	Hotel/rental-car
San Diego New Padres stadium (MLB)	411	296	City	Hotel/rental-car, General fund
Seattle New Seahawks stadium (NFL)	430	323	County	Sales, Gate/concession, Hotel/rental-car, Lottery proceeds

* Facilities approved by January 1, 2001

Sources: Sports Facility Reports, ballparks.com, newspaper reports

ENDNOTES

[1] Benefits may also arise when high-paying jobs replace low-paying ones.

[2] Impact studies usually attribute to the presence of a professional sports team gross job creation due to all local spending by nonlocal residents who attend a sports game. But some of this spending is likely to have occurred anyway, as many of the nonlocal residents who attend a game may be visiting the metro area for other reasons (e.g., to visit family or for business).

[3] Equivalently, local multiplier jobs can be thought of as implying that total net job creation will be some multiple of observable jobs created less unobserved jobs lost.

[4] Many impact studies also claim large benefits from the actual construction jobs associated with building stadiums. But such jobs are unlikely to produce large metro area benefits. Except in the depths of a recession, any very large construction project must either hire workers from elsewhere who temporarily relocate into a metro area or else hire local workers away from other local construction projects. In both cases, wages for local construction workers should rise, which for them is certainly a benefit. But the remaining residents of the metro area will temporarily face higher costs for doing any construction. Even if the former benefit exceeds the latter cost, the one-time nature of construction implies that any net benefit will be small in magnitude (i.e., it is already on a net present value basis and so is not scaled up as is the permanent job creation annual benefit).

[5] The ambiguity of whether a metro area benefits from net job creation sharply contrasts with the common perception that local net job creation is a benefit in and of itself. The perception is easy to understand given that net job creation usually reflects beneficial underlying metro area fundamentals. For instance, Denver has seen explosive employment and population growth during the late 1990s. Many firms and individuals cite the natural beauty and recreational opportunities afforded by the nearby Rocky Mountains as key reasons for choosing to locate in Denver. It is this natural beauty and recreational opportunity which benefit Denver's residents, both long-time and newly arrived. The job growth just reflects such benefits.

[6] To the extent that such statistical techniques fail to control for underlying fundamentals that cause simultaneous increases in jobs, wages, and property values, they will overestimate the benefits associated with increases in employment. For instance, statistical analysis will tend to attribute Denver's rapidly rising wages and house values to its explosive population and employment growth. But as argued in note 5 above, probably the growth of all three should be attributed to individuals' increasing desire to enjoy the natural beauty and recreational opportunities afforded by the nearby Rocky Mountains. Rappaport (2000) shows how an increase in either quality of life or productivity lends to simultaneous changes in population, employment, wages, and home values.

[7] A second way that increased sales tax revenue benefits a host metro area is if it is due to local residents' spending a greater proportion of their entertainment dollars within the host metro area rather than elsewhere. For example, in the absence of a local professional sports team, local sports fans may travel to other metro areas to watch games. If their total expenditures on entertainment are to remain unchanged, such fans will end up spending less in their home metro area and hence contribute less to local sales tax revenue. By spending money in other tax jurisdictions, these fans are exporting sales tax revenue. From the perspective of local residents, the recovery of exported sales tax revenue by the shifting of their spending

from outside to a home tax jurisdiction is definitely a benefit. After all, if they are going to pay sales taxes, they should prefer to do so to their own local government rather than the local government of someone else. Local residents nevertheless implicitly may choose to export tax revenue if the things they wish to purchase are not available locally (or if they are more expensive locally). For local sports fans, hosting a team makes available locally something they formerly had to travel to purchase. However, it is not actually clear that hosting a professional sports team recovers exported sales tax revenue. No good estimates exist on the magnitude of exported sales tax revenues due to a metro area's not hosting a professional sports team. In addition, it is possible that host metro area fans' traveling to attend away games of their home team may export as much sales tax revenue as is recovered by fans' not traveling to attend "home" games in the absence of a local team.

Hosting a professional sports team may also increase local sales tax revenue if local residents' spending on admissions and concessions at sports games is subject to higher than average sales taxes. However, any such increase in local tax revenue represents a cost rather than a benefit to the host metro area. To see this, consider that the host metro area could also increase its sales tax revenue simply by raising the sales tax rates which apply to all local spending (with the caveat that the higher rates are not more than offset by lower spending). Local residents' willingness to pay the higher local sales tax on stadium admissions and concessions shows that they perceive an attached benefit (that such taxes support the presence of a sports team). But all else equal, locally residing fans should certainly prefer not to be taxed at a higher than average rate.

[8] Of course, depending on particular circumstances, visits by non-MSA fans may vary tremendously. For instance, a study of fans attending Baltimore Orioles games in 1992 concluded that 46 percent were from outside the Baltimore metro area and 31 percent were from outside the state of Maryland. A likely factor contributing to such a high percentage of nonlocal fans is Baltimore's location less than a one-hour drive from Washington D.C., a metro area that lacks a baseball team. In addition, 1992 was the first year the Orioles played in the new Camden Yards stadium which also might have contributed to above-average nonlocal attendance (Hamilton and Kahn).

[9] However, any revenue due to such visitors' spending at games being taxed at higher than average rates does count as a benefit attributable to hosting a sports team.

[10] On the other hand, 5 percent is not an uncommon state sales tax rate. But for states, imported tax revenue accrues only from visits by out-of-state sports fans, which is likely to be a smaller percentage than for non-metro sports fans.

[11] To the extent that any increased income tax revenue from net job creation does exceed the marginal cost of providing any associated increased municipal services, the resulting benefit is largely what underlies the explanation of how net job creation benefits a metro area's existing residents. To include it again as an imported income tax benefit would be to double count. Hence Table 5 excludes assistant coaches along with the approximately 100 people team organizations employ in "front office" positions, for instance managing business operations, selling advertising, and maintaining physical facilities.

[12] Using a 5 percent interest rate instead implies that each dollar of annual benefits is worth $15.37. Using a 7 percent interest rate implies that each dollar of annual benefits is worth $12.41.

13 This aggregate quality-of-life benefit is known as "consumer surplus." Estimates of consumer surplus from major league game attendance range from $2 million to $54 million per team per year (Alexander et al, Irani).

14 On the other hand, many economists argue that people overestimate their willingness to pay for things when answering surveys (Diamond and Hausman).

15 Population inflows drawn to high quality of life may also result in large-scale job creation. The straightforward intuition is that firms desire to locate where they can affordably hire good workers. High quality of life is commonly cited as a reason for rapid job growth in a number of U.S. states including Arizona, California, Colorado, Florida, and Nevada. Looking across U.S. counties at the relationship between weather and 1990 employment levels, statistical analysis suggests that a one degree Celsius higher mean January temperature is associated with a 3 percent increase in employment. For a medium-sized metro area with 2 million residents, such an increase is more than 30 times the size of even the most optimistic estimates of the observable job creation from hosting a professional sports team.

Because all else is not equal, metro areas with high quality of life may be observed to have high rather than low average wages. First, individuals who can earn a high income regardless of where they live may be more likely to choose to do so in high quality-of-life metro areas. Hence, measuring the effect of metro area attributes on metro area wages requires taking account of individual-specific characteristics such as education and occupation. Second, attributes that contribute positively to a metro area's quality of life may also contribute positively to its productivity and so raise wages. For instance, location on an ocean coast provides both recreational opportunities and access to low-cost seaborne transport (Rappaport and Sachs). Indeed, the unobservable job creation due to high quality of life may itself be a source of high productivity by bringing external economies of scale to a metro area's firms.

16 More specifically, individuals' wages are regressed on individual-specific characteristics and metro area characteristics. Negative coefficients on the metro area characteristics measure positive contributions to quality of life. House prices are regressed on house-specific characteristics and metro area characteristics. Positive coefficients on the metro area characteristics measure positive contributions to quality of life.

17 In addition, two relatively small Canadian metro areas, Quebec and Winnipeg, lost NHL teams in the mid-1990s.

18 It could also be that the metro areas revised upward their estimates of the job creation and tax revenue benefits. But this seems unlikely given economists' unanimous inability to find evidence of any large such benefits.

19 Additional incentives were later added to lure the NFL Rams in 1995.

20 Los Angeles, as well, committed to a $100 million public outlay in a bid to win an NFL expansion team that was awarded in 1999. Given the large quantity and variety of alternative entertainment venues in the Los Angeles metro area (e.g., four major league teams, two top college athletic programs, four major amusement/theme parks, beaches, nearby mountains), it is not surprising that the quality-of-life benefits from hosting an additional team may be lower to Los Angeles than they are to other metro areas.

21 One reason that Kansas City and San Diego may not have done so is that both cities already host both an MLB and an NFL team. As was argued above with regard to the NHL Pittsburgh Penguins, the additional quality-of-life benefit from a third team may be much smaller than the benefit from a first or second team. In

addition, both of the departing NBA teams had losing records in the several seasons prior to leaving, which also may have lowered their contributions to quality of life.

22 A conceptually different question is whether metro areas would be better off if all public contributions to the building of sports stadiums were prohibited. On the one hand, the competition among metro areas for sports teams transfers benefits from metro area residents to team owners and players. On the other hand, competition for teams should cause the teams to locate in metro areas where total benefits will be greatest.

REFERENCES

Alexander, Donald L., William Kern, and Jon Neill. 2000. "Valuing the Consumption Benefits from Professional Sports Franchises," *Journal of Urban Economics*, September.

Baade, Robert A. 1997. "Mariner Economic Analysis," prepared for Citizens for Leaders with Ethics and Accountability Now, March.

________. 1994. "Stadiums, Professional Sports, and Economic Development: Assessing the Reality," Heartland Institute Policy Study, No. 62.

Baade, Robert A., and Allen R. Sanderson. 1997. "The Employment Effect of Teams and Sports Facilities," in Roger G. Noll and Andrew Zimbalist, eds., *Sports, Jobs, and Taxes: The Economic Impact of Sports Teams and Stadiums*. Washington: Brookings Institution Press.

Blomquist, Glenn C., Mark C. Berger, and John P. Hoehn. 1988. "New Estimates of Quality of Life in Urban Areas," *American Economic Review*, March.

Bremner, B. 1990. "Ice Folly in Minneapolis," *Business Week*, February 26.

CSL International. 2000a. "Green Bay Packers Impact Analysis," prepared for the Green Bay Packers.

__________. 2000b. "Houston Rockets Impact Analysis," prepared for Central Houston, Inc.

Center for Economic Education, University of Cincinnati. 1996. "The Effects of the Construction, Operation, and Financing of New Sports Stadia on Cincinnati Economic Growth," prepared for the Hamilton County Administrator, January.

Coates, Dennis, and Brad R. Humphreys. 2000. "The Stadium Gambit and Local Economic Development," *Regulation*, no. 2.

Conway, Dick, and Associates. 1996. "Seattle Seahawks Economic Impact," prepared for HOK Sport and King County, March.

Diamond, Peter A., and Jerry A. Hausman. 1994. "Contingent Valuation: Is Some Number Better Than No Number?" *Journal of Economic Perspectives*, Fall.

Gyourko, Joseph, and Joseph Tracy. 1991. "The Structure of Local Public Finance and the Quality of Life," *Journal of Political Economy*, August.

Hamilton, Bruce W., and Peter Kahn. 1997. "Baltimore's Camden Yards Ballparks," in Roger G. Noll and Andrew Zimbalist, eds., *Sports, Jobs, and Taxes: The Economic Impact of Sports Teams and Stadiums*. Washington: Brookings Institution Press.

Irani, Daraius. 1997. "Public Subsidies to Stadiums: Do the Costs Outweigh the Benefits?" *Public Finance Review*, March.

Johnson, Bruce K., Peter A. Groothuis, and John C. Whitehead. 2001. "The Value of Public Goods Generated By a Major League Sports Team: The CVM Approach," *Journal of Sports Economics*, February.

Johnson, C.H., Consulting, Inc. 1999. "Economic Impact Analysis of the Proposed Ballpark for the Boston Red Sox," prepared for Greater Boston Convention and Visitors Bureau and Greater Boston Chamber of Commerce, June.

KPMG. 1998. "Economic and Fiscal Impact Analysis for a Proposed New Stadium to Host the New England Patriots in Hartford, Connecticut," prepared for State of Connecticut, November.

Meyer, Ed. 1997. "Cleveland Sells NFL on Its Abilities," *Akron Beacon Journal*, January 22.

Mid-America Regional Council. 2001. Update to "Economic Impact of the Kansas City Chiefs and Kansas City Royals on the State of Missouri," prepared for Jackson County Executive, January.

National Sports Law Institute of Marquette University Law School. 2000. *Sports Facility Reports*, vol. 1, no. 2.

Noll, Roger G., and Andrew Zimbalist, eds. 1997. *Sports, Jobs, and Taxes: The Economic Impact of Sports Teams and Stadiums*. Washington: Brookings Institution Press.

Office of Business and Economic Research, Maryland Department of Business and Economic Development. 1999. "Impact of the Baltimore Ravens Pro Football Team on the Maryland Economy: 1999 Update," October.

Pollack, Elliott D., and Company. 1998. "Economic and Fiscal Impact of BankOne Ballpark and the Arizona Diamondbacks," prepared for Downtown Phoenix Partnership, September.

Quirk, James, and Rodney Fort. 1992. *Pay Dirt: The Business of Professional Team Sports*. Princeton: Princeton University Press.

Rappaport, Jordan. 2000. "Why Are Population Flows So Persistent?" Federal Reserve Bank of Kansas City, working paper no. 99-13, August.

__________, and Jeffrey Sachs. Forthcoming. "The U.S. as a Coastal Nation," Federal Reserve Bank of Kansas City, working paper.

Roback, Jennifer. 1982. "Wages, Rents, and the Quality of Life," *Journal of Political Economy*, December.

Rosen, Sherwin. 1979. "Wage-Based Indexes of Urban Quality of Life," in Miezkowski and Straszheim, eds., *Current Issues in Urban Economics*. Baltimore: Johns Hopkins University Press.

Siegfried, John, and Andrew Zimbalist. 2000. "The Economics of Sports Facilities and Their Communities," *Journal of Economic Perspectives*, Summer.

Street and Smith's SportsBusiness Journal. 2000. "Special Report: Broadcast Media," April 17-23.

Texas Perspectives, Inc. 1999. "The Role of the Spurs in the San Antonio Economy," prepared for City of San Antonio.

Walden, Michael. 1997. "Don't Play Ball," *Carolina Journal*, October/November.

Regulating cellular phone use: too little benefit for too much cost

Should You Be Allowed To Use Your Cellular Phone While Driving?

BY ROBERT W. HAHN, PAUL C. TETLOCK, AND JASON K. BURNETT

During the past few years, consumers, politicians, academics, and interest groups have expressed growing concern about the safety of using cellular phones in cars and trucks. The increasing use of cellular phones in vehicles is part of a larger trend related to the introduction of technologies that could divert attention from driving. A recently published National Highway Traffic Safety Administration (NHTSA) survey reports that 44 percent of drivers have a phone with them when they drive, 7 percent have e-mail access, and 3 percent have facsimile capabilities. Those numbers are likely to increase. Other technologies that increase possible distractions will also be added to new vehicles, such as easily accessing the Internet, getting directions electronically, and receiving real-time information on traffic patterns.

With mounting concern among the public about such distracting devices in vehicles, we think it is appropriate to undertake a careful analysis of their advantages and disadvantages. This paper focuses on cellular phone use in vehicles because it is currently the most common of the new technologies. We believe, however, that the methodology developed in this paper could be helpful in assessing how best to address the use of other distracting technologies in vehicles.

Cellular phone subscribership in the United States has grown dramatically in recent years, from 92,000 people in 1985 to more than 77,000,000 in 1999. Cellular phones in cars provide important conveniences, including the ability to check on children, get help in an emergency, and coordinate schedules. In addition, drivers sometimes use cellular phones to report accidents and alert police and firefighters to problems that need to be addressed.

Unfortunately, cellular phones can also impose costs on society. One of the potentially significant costs of cellular phone usage while driving is the increased risk of vehicle accidents, some leading to serious injury or death. We estimate that several hundred people die each year in the United States as a consequence of collisions related to cellular phone use. While small in comparison to the 41,000 people who die in all vehicle accidents each year in the United States, municipalities, states, and even some countries have proposed a large array of restrictions on the use of cellular phones. Although only a few American municipalities have implemented a ban on people's use of hand-held cellular phones while driving, several foreign countries have enacted laws, including limited and total bans.

In this article we provide an economic evaluation of cellular phone regulatory options. Our primary conclusion is that banning cellular phone usage by drivers is a bad idea. A ban in the United States is estimated to result in annual economic welfare losses of about $20 billion. (All numbers are adjusted to 1999 dollars by using the consumer price index. Calculations are generally rounded to two significant digits.)

Less intrusive regulation, such as requiring the use of a hands-free device that would allow a driver to use both

Robert W. Hahn is director of the AEI-Brookings Joint Center for Regulatory Studies, a resident scholar at the American Enterprise Institute, and a research associate at Harvard University. **Paul C. Tetlock** was a researcher at the AEI-Brookings Joint Center for Regulatory Studies and is a graduate student at Harvard University. **Jason K. Burnett** is a researcher at the AEI-Brookings Joint Center for Regulatory Studies.

hands for steering is probably not economically justified. Instead of direct regulation, we argue that the government should focus on gathering additional information to determine the extent of the problem and also consider providing information to the public on the relative risk of cellular phone use in vehicles.

CELLULAR PHONE REGULATION IN VEHICLES

ON MARCH 22, 1999, BROOKLYN, OHIO, BECAME THE FIRST city in the United States to ban hand-held cellular phone use in vehicles. Brooklyn's ordinance bans the use of cellular phones while driving unless drivers keep both hands on the steering wheel. While the city has been enforcing that ordinance aggressively, offenses are punishable only by a $3 fine. Because Brooklyn was also the first city to mandate the use of seatbelts, media speculation surrounding the Brooklyn ordinance has focused on its potential national repercussions. Following Brooklyn's lead, other cities have implemented similar laws. For example, Conshohocken, Hilltown Township, and Lebanon in Pennsylvania and Marlboro Township, New Jersey, have hands-free mandates similar to Brooklyn's ordinance, while New York City bans taxi and limo drivers from using cellular phones.

No state has taken as aggressive a position as those cities. As Table 1 shows, even the strictest state laws simply provide guidelines for the use of cellular phones in vehicles. This table also shows, however, that several states have legislative proposals that would ban some or all uses of cellular phones while driving. These proposals, like the existing city ordinances, allow drivers to place emergency calls. States did not begin to address specific concerns about cellular phones until 1987, and most state legislative proposals have been introduced in the past two years. The table shows that a total of 88 proposals have been introduced at the state level in the past year. Great variation exists across states in terms both of laws and proposed legislation.

States have enacted either very modest measures aimed at regulating cellular phones or no measures at all. Most existing state legislation focuses on gathering data and educating drivers who use cellular phones. Massachusetts has the most stringent law of all the states, requiring drivers to keep at least one hand on the wheel while talking on their cellular phones. California's law orders rental car dealers to provide customers with instructions for the safe use of a cellular phone in all rental cars with installed phones. Florida prohibits the use of certain headset devices in conjunction with a cellular phone because such devices impair a driver's ability to hear surrounding sounds of the road.

All states have laws designed to prevent inattentive driving. These laws aim to curtail a driver's irresponsible habits, but the laws are often vague, open to legal interpretation, and poorly enforced. The concerns about cellular phone use while driving may lead many states to adopt stricter inattentive-driving laws. Five states—Delaware, Idaho, New Mexico, Ohio, and Wisconsin—recently specified unacceptable practices. It is unclear whether additional efforts to strengthen these laws will affect driving habits.

BENEFIT-COST ANALYSIS

OUR BASIC FINDING IS THAT THE ECONOMIC COSTS OF A ban on cellular phone use in vehicles far outweigh the benefits. Therefore, we argue against a ban. The reason is simple—cellular phone use in vehicles provides substantial benefits to users but does not appear to contribute to a large number of serious accidents. Next, we make calculations addressing a more difficult issue—whether particular regulations mandating cellular phone innovations would represent a relatively low-cost way of reducing accidents. As an example, we consider the case of mandating a hands-free device that is similar to a phone headset used in office environments. While the results are not as clear-cut as a ban, they suggest that such regulation is probably not warranted on benefit-cost grounds. Next, we develop a calculation that shows a break-even incremental cost for the regulation of cellular phones, which could be useful to regulators who are thinking about necessary conditions for intervening in this technologically dynamic market. Finally, we review some important limitations of our benefit-cost analysis and we highlight key insights.

Costs of a Ban The benefit-cost analysis of a ban requires estimating the cost to cellular phone users, the cost to producers, and the monetized benefits associated with a reduction in accidents. If cellular phone service is produced at constant marginal costs, the costs of a ban to cellular phone users is the welfare loss to consumers. Industrywide demand functions for cellular phone service allow economists to approximate the economic loss to consumers from a general ban. We estimate the amount of money that would be necessary to compensate cellular phone users so they would be indifferent to a ban.

Our analysis begins with an estimate by Hausman of industrywide demand for cellular phone services and then uses that measure to approximate the loss to consumers from a ban on using cellular phones in vehicles. Hausman finds that the price elasticity of cellular phone demand is –0.51, meaning that a 10 percent reduction in cellular service pricing would increase demand by 5.1 percent. This result is consistent with our own unpublished analysis using 1999 data. Based on Hausman's calculations that use 1994 data, we estimate that consumers in the United States would need to receive at least $27 billion a year to be indifferent to a ban. Using a linear approximation, we find that this number would now exceed $41 billion, employing 1999 price and subscribership figures.

The proportion of total cellular phone revenues arising from calls occurring in vehicles multiplied by the total amount that consumers would have to be compensated yields an estimate of the cost to consumers of prohibiting cellular phone use by drivers. This estimate assumes that cellular phone demand by drivers resembles the total cellular demand analyzed by Hausman. Using an industry market-

Table 1

Finalized and Recently Proposed Cellular Phone Legislation[a]

State	Mandated Data Collection	Guidelines for Cell Phone Use	Heightened User Penalties in Contributing to an Accident	Ban on All Hand-Held Devices	Total Ban on All Cell Phone Use[b]	Total Number of Proposals since 1999
Arizona	P				P	1
California		F[c] (1987)				0
Colorado				P		1
Connecticut		P		P		4
Delaware	P					1
Florida		F[d] (1992)				0
Georgia		P	P	P	P	7
Hawaii	P			P		3
Illinois				P		2
Indiana					P	1
Iowa		P				2
Kansas				P		1
Kentucky					P	2
Louisiana	P	P				2
Maine				P		1
Maryland				P	P	2
Massachusetts		F[e] (1990), P			P[f]	2
Michigan		P	P	P		3
Minnesota	F[g] (1991)					0
Missouri					P	1
Nebraska			P			1
Nevada					P	1
New Hampshire		P			P	2
New Jersey	P	P			P	6
New York	P	P		P	P	19
Ohio	P				P	1
Oklahoma	F[h] (1992)					0
Oregon	P			P	P	3
Pennsylvania	P	P		P	P	8
Rhode Island	P			P		4
South Carolina				P		1
Texas					P	1
Virginia					P[i]	1
Washington	P		P			2
West Virginia			P			1
Wyoming				P		1

Note: P = Proposed Legislation F = Finalized Legislation

[a]Proposed state legislation in this table dates back to January 1, 1999. Finalized legislation, however, spans the entire history of this legislative issue.

[b]Most proposed legislation banning the use of cellular phones permits emergency calls and allows a one- or two-minute grace period for pulling off to the side of the road.

[c]In California, rental cars with cellular telephone equipment must include written operating instructions concerning its safe use.

[d]Cellular phone use in Florida is permitted as long as the device provides sound through one ear and allows surrounding sound to be heard with the other ear.

[e]Cellular phone use in Massachusetts is permitted as long as it does not interfere with the operation of the vehicle and one hand remains on the steering wheel at all times.

[f]This piece of legislation only applies to school bus drivers.

[g]This statute requires police officers to indicate on motor vehicle accident reports whether or not cellular phone use played a part in the accident.

[h]This statute requires police officers to indicate on motor vehicle accident reports whether or not cellular phone use played a part in the accident.

[i]This piece of legislation only applies to school bus drivers.

Sources: "Cell Phones and Driving: 1999 State Legislative Update." NCSL, 1999. Environment, Energy, and Transportation Program. <http://www.ncsl.org/programs/esnr/celphone.htm>.

Legislative Tracking Database provided by the National Highway and Transportation Safety Board in conjunction with the National Conference of State Legislatures. <http://www.nhtsa.dot.gov/ncsl> (Legislative year: 2000. View Available Records: Cell Phone Issue).

National Highway Traffic Safety Administration, 1997, State Net search through Lexis Nexis.

Personal communication with ComCARE Alliance (1999).

"Spring 2000, Telecommunications Report." StateScape. June 30, 2000: 59.

Allyson Vaughn. "Missouri: Jail Time for Car-Phone Use?" Wireless Week, February 7, 2000. <http://www.wirelessweek.com/news/feb00/ftwo27.htm>.

Allyson Vaughn. "Driving, Talking Targeted Again." Wireless Week, April 3, 2000. <http://www.wirelessweek.com/News/safety/in43.htm>.

ing survey conducted by the Yankee Group, we estimate that consumers spend 60 percent of their cellular phone time while driving. This estimate would imply that, for consumers to remain indifferent between a ban and no ban, they would need to be paid about $25 billion if they were not allowed to use their cellular phones while driving.

Benefits of a Ban Economists can measure the costs of cellular phone use by drivers in terms of the *lost* lives, property damage, and injury costs of accidents associated with driver use. Collisions are caused by several contributing factors, so it is difficult to attribute all the costs to a single factor, such as the use of a cellular phone. In our cost estimates, we assumed that drivers using cellular phones did not take into account any of the accident risks. If drivers did take account of some or all of these risks, the demand curve would reflect that. Counting them again would bias our benefit-cost analysis in favor of a ban.

The best estimate of accidents and fatalities was based primarily on the available data from actual accident reports and narratives at the state and national level. We also used an influential epidemiological study by Redelmeier and Tibshirani. We chose to construct our best estimate based on a careful, subjective weighting of these two data sources.

We relied more on the actual data because we felt that they were likely to yield a more reliable measure of the impact of cellular phones on vehicle accidents and fatalities. Our upper bound is generated by using an estimate of risk of driving from the epidemiological study.

We used state and national accident data to generate four different estimates of the number of accidents associated with cellular phones. For the purposes of this analysis, we will assume that those accidents are actually caused by drivers' use of cellular phones. The lowest estimate is that fewer than 3 in every 10,000 accidents were related to driver cellular phone use in 1999. The highest estimate from state data is that cellular phones were associated with 1 in every 1,000 vehicle accidents. Weighting the four estimates equally–two from state data and two from national data–yields an estimate that 2 out of every 1,000 accidents were associated with driver cellular phone use. The state and national data imply that about 80 fatalities out of 41,000 national fatalities each year are associated with cellular phone use in cars. If only 3 in every 10,000 accidents are related to driver cellular phone use, then only 10 fatalities a year are associated with cellular phone use in cars. We will use that estimate as our lower bound.

Redelmeier and Tibshirani estimated the relative risk of talking on a cellular phone while driving was 4.3 for accidents not involving injuries. It is not clear that the same risk factor holds for more serious accidents. Assuming that it does, the probability of having an accident while using a cellular phone is 4.3 times the probability of having an accident when not using a cellular phone.

It may not be appropriate to use that risk factor to extrapolate to an estimate of cellular phone accidents nationally. Cellular phone users may not be representative of the general driving population and may not use their phones for the same proportion of time during all driving conditions. If cellular phone users are safer than average drivers or if they use their phones during relatively safe periods, then a direct extrapolation using the risk factor of 4.3 would overestimate the number of accidents. In addition, drivers may be willing to take small risks of getting in minor accidents as Redelmeier and Tibshirani have shown. This finding does not necessarily imply that these same drivers would take a comparable risk if the consequences were death. We also believe that those who use cellular phones while driving are likely to be better educated and have higher incomes, on average, than other drivers. Such characteristics may make them more careful than average drivers to avoid fatal accidents. Because of these potential biases, we treat the risk factor of 4.3 as an upper bound.

Using that risk factor, we developed an upper bound estimate of fatalities related to cellular phone use. Using survey data, we estimate that 0.7 percent of driving time is spent on a cellular phone. Assuming drivers using cellular phones are as safe as average drivers and drive under similar conditions, we estimate that 3 percent (0.7 times 4.3) of accidents occur while a driver is talking on a phone. Subtracting the general risks from traveling in a vehicle implies that about 2.3 percent of accidents are attributable to the use of a cellular phone while driving. This percentage implies that about 1,000 out of 41,000 driving-related fatalities annually are caused by cellular phones.

If we assume that cellular phones increase the risk of minor accidents, injury accidents, and fatal accidents equally, our estimates suggest between 10 and 1,000 fatalities are associated with or caused by cellular phones. After considering the concerns about the two estimates, we decided to calculate our best estimate by taking a weighted average of our estimates from crash data and the epidemiological study. We used 300 as our best estimate of the number of fatalities caused by cellular phones. We used the estimate based on the relative risk as our upper bound. In summary, we estimated cellular phone use in vehicles causes 300 fatalities per year, with a range of 10 to 1,000 fatalities. Assuming the same percentage of accidents as fatalities yields a best estimate of 38,000 accidents involving injuries, with a range of 1,300 to 130,000.

We then placed a dollar value on those estimates of accidents. Our analysis draws heavily on a study by NHTSA (1994), which monetizes the economic costs of motor vehicle accidents. The study found that traffic accidents result in annual losses of about $170 billion. By chance, the total numbers of crashes and fatalities in 1994 were almost exactly the same as projections for 1999. Thus, the 1994 data offer a reasonable approximation of economic costs of accidents in 1999. The $170 billion figure represents the present value of lifetime economic costs for 41,000 fatalities, 5.2 million nonfatal injuries, 3.7 million uninjured occupants, and 27 million damaged vehicles. These accidents include both police-reported and unreported accidents. Most of the $170 billion in NHTSA's calculation stems from lost productivity in the workplace and direct medical expenses.

NHTSA's measures of costs take account of only direct costs but do not consider what an individual would be willing to pay to reduce mortality and morbidity risks. If we use Viscusi's 1993 willingness-to-pay estimate of $5 million per statistical life, adjusted to $6.6 million to account for inflation, NHTSA's estimate would increase from $170 billion to $410 billion. If willingness to pay to prevent injuries (morbidity) were taken into account, NHTSA's estimate would increase to $630 billion. That amount is our best estimate of the total annual cost of motor vehicle accidents.

Estimating that cellular phone use contributes to just under 0.74 percent of total accidents, we calculated the costs of drivers' cellular phone use to be $4.6 billion per year (0.0074 times $630 billion). About half of this $4.6 billion is attributable to the 300 estimated fatalities associated with driver use of cellular phones, while the other half represents the costs associated with more minor accidents in which cellular phones were a contributing factor.

Net Benefits of a Ban On the basis of the preceding cost and benefit estimates, national legislation banning cellular phone use by drivers would impose annual net costs of about $20 billion ($25 billion in costs minus $4.6 billion in benefits). Indeed, the costs of a ban are more than five times greater than the benefits. These results are summarized in the first part of Table 2 as our best estimate.

A great deal of uncertainty exists in many of the parameter values used in our model. To account for key uncertainties, we considered a wide range of parameter values for the number of lives saved, the amount of time drivers spend using a cellular phone, and the price elasticity of demand. A range of 10 to 1,000 is used for lives saved, based on a lower bound from NHTSA's study of North Carolina crash narratives and an upper bound from an extrapolation from Redelmeier and Tibshirani's estimate of relative risk. Hausman's estimate for price elasticity applies to all cellular phones, not only phones in vehicles. To account for that additional source of uncertainty, we used a range of –0.17 to –0.84 for price elasticity, based on two of Hausman's standard error estimates. A range of 40 percent to 70 percent was used for the percentage of time cellular phones are used by drivers. The lower-bound estimate assumes passengers use cellular phones proportionally to drivers while our best estimate assumes that passengers rarely use phones.

The qualitative nature of our ranges does not allow us to provide precise confidence intervals. To present this uncertainty, we first calculated the minimum and maximum costs, benefits, and net benefits by choosing the most extreme values for all parameters simultaneously. The results are presented in the last column of Table 2. For example, the benefits of a ban range from at least zero to $21 billion, which primarily reflects the large uncertainty in the number of fatalities associated with cellular phone use. This approach creates the largest plausible ranges, although it is unlikely that the costs, benefits, or net benefits are near the ends of those ranges. Such a result would require unlikely values for all our estimates simultaneously. For that reason, the ranges presented in Table 2 overstate the uncertainty in our results.

Another approach to illustrating the sensitivity of the results is shown in Figure 1, which shows the effect of varying one parameter at a time. By varying each parameter, we are able to determine the most important uncertainties. We use a plausible range for each key variable and calculate the corresponding range of net benefits. Varying the price elasticity of demand yields net cost estimates ranging from $14 billion to $73 billion. Varying fatality and injury estimates also generates a large range for net costs, but even if cellular phones cause 1,000 fatalities a year, a ban would still result in net costs of $9 billion annually. Only when extremely conservative estimates are used for both the number of fatalities and the price elasticity of demand do we calculate positive net benefits. Because that result requires extreme assumptions for two variables simultaneously, we feel that it is extremely unlikely for the benefits of a ban to exceed the costs. We found that for most plausible ranges for parameter values, a ban on cellular phones while driving cannot be justified for the United States on narrow grounds of economic efficiency.

Table 2

Benefits and Costs of Policies Regulating Cellular Phones in Vehicles (in millions of dollars)

Ban on the Use of Cellular Phones While Driving

	Best Estimate	Range [a]
Benefits	$4,600	$110 to $21,000
Costs	$25,000	$10,000 to $87,000
Net Benefits [b,c]	($20,000)	($87,000) to $6,800 [d]

Mandate for Hands-Free Devices

	Plausible Estimate	Range [a]
Benefits	$690	$0 to $6,300
Costs	$1400	$100 to $7600
Net Benefits	($710)	($7600) to $6,200

Sources: Hausman (1997), NHTSA (1996, 1997, 1998, 1999).

[a] Ranges are determined by taking maximum and minimum values of key parameters.

[b] Numbers in parentheses are negative.

[d] The upper bound on benefits and the lower bound on costs cannot occur at the same time because they assume different levels of penetration. The $6,800 figure represents the maximum net benefits when the penetration rate in the cost and benefit calculation is the same.

Hands-Free Mandate Despite that strong evidence that a ban would not pass a benefit-cost test, less draconian policies could still be justified. For example, a policy that mandates the use of a hands-free device in conjunction with a conventional cellular phone would allow consumers to reap many of the benefits of using phones while driving, albeit at some additional cost. At the same time, such a mandate could reduce the number of accidents by freeing a driver's hands. Other approaches, such as a policy requiring voice-activated dialing or one restricting who may use a phone or under what conditions, may also be justified but we did not make those calculations because of a dearth of data.

We analyze the economics of a hands-free mandate and assume that drivers using cellular phones would purchase the least expensive hands-free technology. We define the least expensive device as the one that provides the lowest net cost to consumers after they have already taken into account the convenience of the device and the time it takes to shop for it. The least expensive hands-free device, ignoring convenience benefits and shopping costs, has a price of $20 to $60, depending on the model of phone. A hands-free mandate would force people who currently own a phone to make an extra trip to purchase the hands-free device. After a hands-free mandate is in place, people would presumably purchase the hands-free device concurrently with their new phone purchase and thereby save time, but in this example we include the additional search costs. We assume that the opportunity cost of time for cellular phone users is $20 per hour. Each person who uses a hand-held phone in a vehicle is assumed to spend 30 minutes shopping for a hands-free device; thus, the search cost is $10. Adding the search cost to the price of the phones produces a range of $30 to $70 for the full cost of the device with an average price of $50. If we assume that consumers do not incur losses in

Figure 1

Sensitivity of Best Estimate to Key Variables

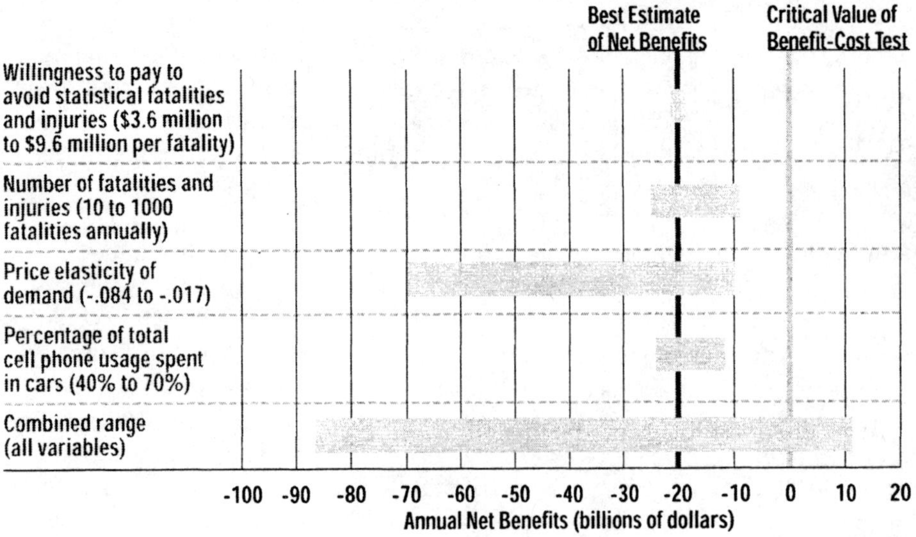

Sources: Hausman (1997), NHTSA (1997), Viscusi (1993), and author's calculations.

convenience for having that device in their car, we can place an upper bound of the net costs of such a device at $50. Those users have not purchased that device on their own, so their revealed preference suggests that the lower bound on the net costs is slightly more than zero. We take the average of those two extremes as our best estimate of the net costs of obtaining such a device. Assuming the device lasts for three years, we calculate an amortized cost of purchasing the device to be $9 annually.

After individuals purchase their devices, the hands-free mandate would also require them to use the device for every phone call that they make while driving. Drivers had the option to do so without that requirement, however. Such a requirement therefore will not make drivers better off and may be inconvenient. It is difficult to calculate the costs of that possible inconvenience but we offer the following example of how it might be done. If one assumes that the average person drives two times a day, prepares the cellular phone for use in the vehicle, and that it takes 15 seconds to plug the device into the phone and install the earpiece, the user would spend 3 hours a year connecting and disconnecting the device. At $20 per hour, this example suggests that the annual inconvenience costs could be on the order of $60. We do not believe that the inconvenience would necessarily be close to $60 annually for the average user, due to offsetting utility gains from using the device. For purposes of this calculation, we use $15 annually as our best estimate of the inconvenience cost.

Adding the $9 purchase cost and the $15 inconvenience cost produces a plausible estimate of $24 for those individuals using cellular phone in cars who do not currently own a hands-free device. We call this a plausible estimate to reflect the large uncertainty in our calculation.

This estimate ignores some other potentially important costs. For example, people may simply dislike using the hands-free device. Moreover, attaching the device while driving could actually increase risks. Unfortunately, we do not have any data or reasonable ways of bounding such costs.

Net Benefits of a Hands-Free Mandate

Multiplying the 60 million affected cellular phone users (23 percent of the 77 million cellular phone users do not operate hand-held phones while driving) by the net cost of about $24 per user yields our plausible estimate that a hands-free mandate would cost $1.4 billion. Using this estimate and our best estimates for all risk variables, we find that hands-free regulation would fail a benefit-cost test unless it resulted in roughly a 25 percent reduction in accidents related to cellular phone use.

According to evidence from accident data in Japan and North Carolina, about 15 percent of cellular-related collisions could have been avoided if the drivers had been using hands-free devices. This estimate is very uncertain because the studies on which they are based suffered from a lack of data and did not focus particular attention on the safety of hands-free devices.

A 25 percent reduction in accidents from hands-free regulation seems unlikely, so proposals to ban hand-held phones fail our benefit-cost test unless consumers receive larger convenience and safety benefits from hands-free devices than we assume in our example. The conclusion is dependent on the number of fatalities attributable to cellular phones. If evidence reveals that cellular phones cause significantly more fatalities than our best estimate of 300, a hands-free mandate would pass our benefit-cost test.

The second part of Table 2 presents best estimates and ranges for the benefits and costs of a hands-free device mandate in the United States. The benefit of this mandate is equal to the benefit of a ban times the percentage of accidents reduced. Our illustrative estimate is that a hands-free mandate would cost users $23 per year, which implies a total cost of $1.4 billion annually. If we assume a 15 percent accident reduction, the benefits would be roughly $700 million, suggesting net costs of $700 million. Our estimated net benefits range between $6.2 billion and negative $7.6 billion. The range of net benefits is very large because of the large uncertainty in the number of fatalities and injuries reduced by a hands-free mandate.

While it is possible future information will reveal that a hands-free mandate is cost-effective, we would be reluctant to recommend a mandate at this point. We believe a mandate would not be warranted because the data on the effectiveness of these devices are very uncertain and our analysis suggests that a mandate would not pass a benefit-cost test. Moreover, the introduction of other technologies, such as voice activation, could reduce the need for hands-free devices. The key policy point is that we should be wary about mandating a technology whose efficacy is questionable and which may be superseded or complemented by new technologies that are safer.

A FRAMEWORK FOR POLICY EVALUATION

GIVEN THE LIMITED DATA, WE HAVE BEEN ABLE TO EVALUate quantitatively only two options for regulating cellular phones while driving—a ban and a mandate of hands-free devices. Because the cellular phone industry is so dynamic, a framework for analyzing future technological developments could assist regulators in making informed decisions. Figure 2 provides such a framework. It presents a graph of the tradeoff between accident reduction and the cost of regulation to cellular phone subscribers which was obtained from our model. The positive slope of the line illustrates that as a technology or policy increases in cost, it needs to be more effective in reducing risks for it to pass a benefit-cost test or a cost-effectiveness test. A proposal lying above the line in the graph is not cost effective in the sense that it fails to reduce accidents sufficiently to justify its expense. For the case of mandating hands-free devices, analyzed earlier, the figure shows that the area corresponding to the plausible range of accident reduction and cost per subscriber falls almost entirely outside the cost-effective region. This result suggests that a hands-free mandate is not likely to be economically justified.

To illustrate the power of this framework, consider the following example. Assume that built-in, voice-activated technology on cellular phones prevents half of all accidents related to cellular phone use and that consumers derive no utility from the technology. From Figure 2, we see that a technology that reduces accidents by 50 percent would pass a benefit-cost test if it costs no more than about $30 per subscriber annually.

The framework underlying Figure 2 can also accommodate changes in a variety of key assumptions. For example, a critical concern is how accidents could be affected by increases in drivers' cellular phone use in vehicles. Some would argue that the risks will increase more than proportionally if the number of drivers using cellular phones increases. Current data do not support that view, however. Predictions of fatalities from driver cellular phone use that are based on linear extrapolations from previous years overestimate today's observed fatalities. The important point for analysis is that both views can easily be accommodated in Figure 2 by simply adjusting the slope of the line to reflect particular cases of interest.

We emphasize that this framework provides a useful tool for examining different policy options. However, we think that it is not definitive because there are many uncertainties and biases not addressed in our analysis and because other factors may be important in the design of policy. For example, if society values accident reductions to average citizens at a premium relative to its valuation of the welfare gains that drivers using cellular phones receive, then the slope of the line in Figure 2 would increase.

Figure 2

Framework for Identifying Cost-Effective Policies

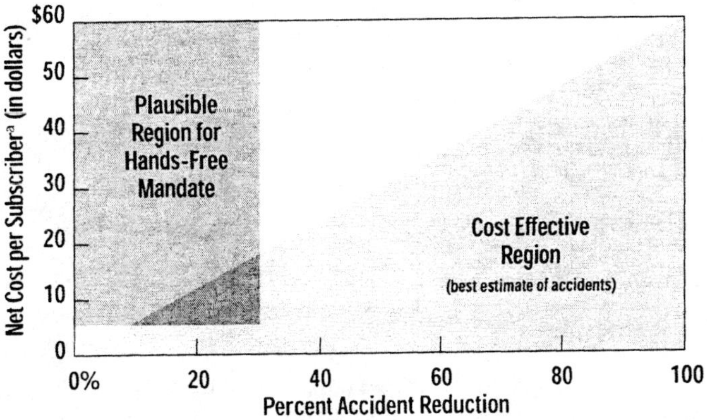

Sources: Hausman (1997), NHTSA (1996, 1997, 1998).
[a]Net cost is the cost in excess of offsetting utility gains

POSSIBLE CRITIQUES OF OUR ANALYSIS

THE PRECEDING ANALYSIS LEAVES OUT AT LEAST THREE important factors that could alter our policy conclusions: our demand elasticity estimates; the possibility of substitution to other risky behavior; and how policies are actually enforced.

Demand Elasticity The demand curve used in our analysis describes the cellular service industry as a whole. It does not explicitly consider the ease with which consumers can switch between using cellular phones in vehicles and cellular phones in other places, such as at the office or on the street. Our demand curve considers only the ease of switching cellular phone calls with other types of communication methods like pager calls and traditional landline calls. This demand curve is not valid if replacing in-vehicle calls from cellular phones with out-of-vehicle cellular phone calls (i.e., if the driver pulls to the side of the road before calling) is easier for consumers than replacing in-vehicle calls from cellular phones with landline calls (the demand curve for cellular phones while driving would be more elastic than the one Hausman estimates for the entire industry). In that case, our estimate of the cost of a policy intervention limiting cellular phone use while driving is likely to be overstated.

It is unlikely, however that the price elasticity will be sufficiently high to change our ultimate conclusions with respect to a ban. For a ban to pass a benefit-cost test, the absolute value of the price elasticity required is at least three. Thus, if a 3 percent reduction in cellular calls made while driving results from a 1 percent increase in the price of calls from vehicles, then a ban might increase economic welfare. Because many businesspeople place a high value on their time, however, calls made while commuting to work are unlikely to be dramatically affected by a 1-percent increase in this price.

The bias is also not very likely to affect the qualitative conclusion on net benefits for a hands-free technology mandate. The decision to implement hands-free technology is insensitive to elasticity changes unless a substantial number of consumers would choose to forgo vehicle calls altogether when confronted with hands-free regulation, a situation we consider unlikely.

Substitution Effects A second potential source of bias in our results lies in the driver response to hands-free regulation or an outright ban. The analysis implicitly assumes that the driver will not engage in other risky driving behaviors as a result of that policy intervention. If drivers instead respond to regulation by performing other distracting tasks in place of using the phone, the gross accident figures from NHTSA data systematically overstate the extent to which a ban would help. In fact, we do not know whether a driver would be likely to engage in more or less risky behavior. It is highly unlikely, however, that the intervention would result in changes in driving behavior that are riskless.

In an extreme scenario, one could imagine a driver's performing a task more distracting than talking on a phone under a ban. More than half of all cellular phone users have used their phones to call for directions according to a 1995 Cellular Telecommunications Industry Association survey. Drivers who value their time may need directions to a destination. With access to phones, they may elect to call from their vehicle for directions. Without access to phones, they may attempt to read a map while they are driving. According to the Transportation Research Institute, reading a map is actually more distracting than talking on a phone. In this example, a ban would increase the risk a driver imposes on others.

While we are not arguing that overall risks would increase, we are arguing that the gross number of accidents and fatalities associated with cellular phones is likely to overstate the actual risk that is reduced from a policy intervention perhaps by a large amount. Drivers, especially those who are as time-conscious as the drivers using cellular phones, will increase the amount of time they spend on other distracting tasks if they are not permitted to use their cellular phones while driving. If cellular phone use in vehicles were banned, we would not be surprised to see additional fatalities resulting from such tasks as eating, tuning a radio, talking to a passenger, or surfing the Web . Indeed, NHTSA estimates that fatalities associated with accidents from such inattentive driving activities number 4,000 annually, compared with a best estimate of 300 resulting from cellular phones.

Another important factor that could lead to overestimation of net fatalities is the impact a ban would have on reporting potential problems to authorities. Although most of the proposed regulations would exempt cellular phone use in an emergency, a ban on nonemergency use would tend to decrease the instances of people's carrying phones in their cars. The safety-enhancing effect of ubiquitous cellular phones is a byproduct of having the phones available for other uses. Thus, some of the positive social impacts of cellular phones, like the quicker reporting of accidents, for example, would be reduced.

The effect of overestimating accidents and fatalities on our results would be to make the proposed ban and the mandate to use hands-free devices look less attractive from an economic point of view. Because they already are unlikely to pass a benefit-cost test, that effect is unlikely to change our qualitative results.

Enforcement A final key issue that needs to be addressed is how a policy is actually enforced. Our calculations have assumed that policies are perfectly enforced. We know that in many countries these policies are either not enforced or that enforcement is far from perfect. Moreover, some of the policies may be quite costly and difficult to enforce. Imagine, for example, trying to enforce a total ban in the United States. Drivers who use cellular phones could respond by putting tinted glass in their vehicles, which would make phone use harder to detect. Many cab drivers in New York City use hands-free devices, possibly, in part, to avoid detection.

Less than perfect enforcement is likely to reduce both the costs and the benefits of the two policies considered here. A plausible assumption is that the costs and the benefits will be reduced proportionally. If benefits and costs are reduced proportionally when a policy is imperfectly enforced, then the qualitative relationship between benefits and costs is not likely to change.

The proportionality assumption may not be realistic, however. Suppose, for example, that those users who benefit most from cellular service would be the ones willing to risk getting caught. Under such circumstances, the cost of regulation would decrease dramatically if the law were poorly enforced. The people getting the most surplus from cellular service would be the people who break the law. But if the citizens receiving the greatest surplus from cellular phones are also the citizens who are most likely to abide by the law, a ban would have relatively greater costs. Without more detailed information, it is difficult to know how imperfect enforcement will affect costs and benefits.

Another important issue related to enforcement arises if the police have a fixed amount of resources. If some resources were devoted to enforcing driver cellular phone regulations, then some benefits would presumably be forgone elsewhere because other policies would be enforced with less vigilance. Without more information, it is difficult to know whether that issue is important empirically.

Our basic conclusion is that the enforcement considerations could be important determinants of the total level of net benefits achieved from the policies considered here. At the same time, they are not very likely to change the qualitative results.

POLICY RECOMMENDATIONS AND CONCLUSIONS

REGULATION OF THE USE OF CELLULAR PHONES BY DRIVERS is now commonplace outside the United States and has been proposed in a number of jurisdictions in the United States. On benefit-cost grounds alone, a proposed ban and a mandate to use hands-free devices are not likely to be justified in the United States. We are less sure whether such policies are justified elsewhere because of an absence of data, nor does our analysis consider the effect of a ban or hands-free mandate on particularly accident-prone subpopulations.

We doubt that the net benefits from a ban on drivers' use of cellular phones would be significant for three reasons. First, the results of our quantitative benefit-cost analysis suggest that costs are likely to exceed benefits under a range of assumptions. Second, our best estimates of accident and fatality reductions do not take into account how drivers would alter their behavior in response to regulation. If regulations were enforced, drivers might simply switch to other risky behaviors. Thus, the net reductions in accidents and fatalities are likely to be overstated, which means that the benefits of regulatory interventions could be quite small. Third, the technology is already moving in the direction of voice-activated cellular calls, which could reduce risks.

The economic analysis of mandating drivers' use of hands-free devices is less conclusive. Our benefit-cost analysis suggests that such devices may be justified, but the uncertainties on both the benefits and costs are large. Without stronger data supporting the view that such devices actually reduce accidents and fatalities, we would be reluctant to recommend requiring their introduction.

It is likely that the market will more effectively address risks associated with cellular phone usage than would highly regulatory government intervention. As an example, several cellular phone makers and service providers have recently introduced voice-recognition technology.

If the problem with using cellular phones while driving becomes severe enough, vehicle insurance companies may begin to classify drivers who use cellular phones in higher-risk groups and charge those drivers commensurately higher insurance premiums. Because an insurance company bears the burden of reimbursing injured parties for their losses, a rational company would consider charging drivers who use cellular phones higher premiums to compensate for any increased risk that cellular phone use forces the company to assume. Insurance companies are not likely to introduce such pricing schemes if the transaction costs of doing so exceed the private benefits to the company.

Instead of regulating now, the government should carefully monitor the problem and improve the information base for making regulatory decisions. It is possible that fatalities are significantly underestimated now. Moreover, an argument can be made that accidents will increase more than linearly as more drivers use cellular phones. Finally, technologies could emerge that the government should encourage. To address those issues, the federal government and the states should collect more systematic information on the possible relationship between cellular phone use while driving and accidents.

The government should also assess the benefits and costs of mandating the use of promising new technologies, such as voice activation, as well as older ones, such as hands-free devices. More research on the effectiveness of hands-free devices in countries and municipalities that have required their use could help determine whether these devices should be encouraged. There is also a need for research on the extent to which cellular phones increase net accidents and fatalities, while taking into account the potential positive impacts that cellular phones could have on the reporting of hazards and accidents.

Simple improvements in information collection could help reduce uncertainty. If all states included a statistic in their accident reports describing whether the driver was using a cellular phone at the time of a collision, the resulting national data would be much more reliable. Similar additions to the Fatality Analysis Reporting System, endorsed by NHTSA, could substantially improve the federal database. More Info Needed (fault/cause)

Government may also have a role in providing easily accessible information to consumers on the risks of different kinds of cellular phone usage. A number of parties currently supply such information, including newspapers, companies, and interest groups, so the government needs to be careful not to duplicate their efforts.

A useful role the government could play is to help sort out high risks from low risks. For example, some gas stations have banned the use of cellular phones while refueling. We think the risks of serious accidents in this situation are likely to be minimal, and the government could play a useful role here by providing information that could reduce "cell-phone phobia" in areas where it is not justified.

The general lesson we take from this analysis is that the mere existence of a problem does not, by itself, warrant government intervention. Our review of the available data suggests that drivers' cellular phone usage does lead to an increase in accidents and fatalities. It is not obvious, however, that feasible government policies would significantly reduce the size of the problem. Moreover, for government intervention to be warranted, a strong case needs to be made that the likely economic benefits exceed the costs by a significant amount. Our analysis suggests that the case has yet to be made for regulating drivers who use cellular phones; however, a more tempered response, in which government continues to assess the size of the problem, provide useful information, and fund research, is warranted.

The problem of regulating potentially risky technologies in vehicles is not likely to go away. Many technologies other than cellular phones have the potential to distract drivers and increase the risk of our roads. The U.S. government has chosen not to regulate some of these technologies; car radios are an example. Others, such as e-mail, Web browsing, fax machines, or cellular phones, may be regulated. We strongly encourage governments to consider the economics of such choices before implementing a potentially costly regulation.

readings

- Battelle. *Lexington Area Travel Data Collection Test*. Final Report to Federal Highway Administration, 1997 (available at *www.fhwa.dot.gov/ohim/lextrav.pdf*).
- William J. Baumol and Wallace E. Oates. *The Theory of Environmental Policy*. Cambridge, Mass.: Cambridge University Press, 1975.
- Cellular Telecommunications Industry Association (CTIA). *CTIA Survey*. Washington, D.C.: World of Wireless Communications, 1996 (available at *www.wow-com.com*).
- CTIA. *Semi-Annual Wireless Survey*. World of Wireless Communications, 1999 (available at *www.wow-com.com*).
- Council of Economic Advisers. *Economic Report of the President 1999*. Washington, D.C.: U.S. Government Printing Office, 1999.
- S. H. Fairclough. "Voice Communication in Vehicles," In *Driving Future Vehicles*, edited by S. Franzer and A. Parkes. London: Taylor and Francis, 1993.
- John D. Graham and Jonathan B. Wiener. *Risk Versus Risk: Tradeoffs in Protecting Health and the Environment*. Cambridge and London: Harvard University Press, 1995.
- Scott E. Harrington. *Insurance Deregulation and the Public Interest*. Washington, D.C.: AEI-Brookings Joint Center for Regulatory Studies, January 2000.
- Jerry A. Hausman. "Valuing the Effect of Regulation on New Services in Telecommunications." *Brookings Papers on Economic Activity, Microeconomics*, 1997: 1.
- M.S. Horswill and F.P. McKenna. "The Effect of Interference on Dynamic Risk-taking Judgements. *British Journal of Psychology* 90 (1999): 189.
- Japanese National Police Agency. "Study of Inquiry Producing Crashes during June 1996." *Daily Automobile Newspaper*, August 17, 1996.
- Lester B. Lave. The Strategy of Social Regulation: *Decision Frameworks for Policy*. Washington, D.C.: Brookings Institution, 1981.
- Randall Lutter, John F. Morrall III, and W. Kip Viscusi. "The Cost per Life Saved Cutoff for Safety-Enhancing Regulations." *Economic Inquiry* (forthcoming).
- James McKnight and A. Scott McKnight. "The Effect of Cellular Phone Use upon Driver Attention." *Accident Analysis and Prevention* 25 (1993): 259.
- Minnesota Department of Public Safety, Office of Traffic Safety. *Minnesota Motor Vehicle Crash Facts*, 1998. St. Paul, Minn.: Department of Public Safety, 1998.
- Steven A. Morrison, Tara Watson, and Clifford Winston. "Fundamental Flaws of Social Regulation: The Case of Airline Noise." *Journal of Law and Economics* 42 (1999): 723.
- National Highway Transportation Safety Administration, Federal Highway Administration (NHTSA/FHA). "Motor Vehicle Accident Costs—Technical Advisory." Washington, D.C.: National Highway Transportation Safety Administration, 1994.
- NHTSA/FHA. 1996 *Traffic Safety Facts*. Washington, D.C.: National Highway Transportation Safety Administration, 1996.
- NHTSA/FHA. *An Investigation of the Safety Implications of Wireless Communications in Vehicles*. Washington, D.C.: National Highway Transportation Safety Administration, 1997.
- NHTSA/FHA. *1998 Traffic Safety Facts*. Washington, D.C.: National Highway Transportation Safety Administration, 1998.
- NHTSA/FHA. *Early Assessment of 1998 Crashes, Injuries, and Fatalities*. NHTSA/NCSA. Washington, D.C.: National Highway Transportation Safety Administration, 1999 (available at *www.nhtsa.dot.gov/people/ncsa/Reports.html*).
- L. Nilsson. "Behavioral Research in an Advanced Driving Simulator: Experiences of the VTI System," *In Proceedings of the Human Factors and Ergonomics Society 37th Annual Meeting*, 1993:612.
- Oklahoma Department of Public Safety, Highway Safety Office. 1997 *Oklahoma Traffic Crash Facts*. Oklahoma City: Department of Public Safety, 1997.
- Philip M. Parker and Lars-Hendrik Röller. "Collusive Conduct in Duopolies: Multimarket Contact and Cross-Ownership in the Mobile Telephone Industry." *RAND Journal of Economics* 28 (1997): 304.
- A. M. Parkes "Drivers' Business Decision-Making Ability Whilst Using Carphones." In *Contemporary Ergonomics, Proceedings of the Ergonomic Society Annual Conference*, edited by E. Lovessey. London: Taylor and Francis, 1991.
- Sam Peltzman. "The Effects of Automobile Safety Regulation." *Journal of Political Economy* 83 (1975): 677.
- Personal Communications Industry Association (PCIA). *Wireless Users and Safety: A Survey of Usage and Attitudes Towards Safety and Regulation*. Washington, D.C.: Personal Communications Industry Association, 1999.
- PCIA. *Market Demand Forecast for Terrestrial 3rd Generation (IMT-2000) Services for the PCIA*, 1998 (available at *www.pcia.com/wireres/3gstudy.htm*).
- Donald A. Redelmeier. "Car Phones and Car Crashes: an Ecologic Analysis." *Canadian Journal of Public Health* 89 (1998): 157.
- Donald A. Redelmeier and R.J. Tibshirani. "Association Between Cellular Telephone Calls and Motor Vehicle Collisions." *New England Journal of Medicine* 336 (1997): 453.
- Donald A. Redelmeier and Milton Weinstein. "Cost-Effectiveness of Regulations Against Using a Cellular Telephone While Driving." *Medical Decision Making* 19 (1999): 1.
- J.M. Violanti and J.R. Marshall. "Cellular Phones and Traffic Accidents: An Epidemiological Approach." *Accident Analysis and Prevention* 28 (1996): 265.
- W. Kip Viscusi. "The Value of Risks to Life and Health." *Journal of Economic Literature* 31 (1993): 1912.
- Clifford Winston and Chad Shirley. *Alternative Route: Toward Efficient Urban Transportation*. Washington, D.C.: Brookings Institution Press, 1998.
- Yankee Group. *1999 Mobile Users Survey*. Boston, Mass.: Yankee Group, 1999.

7

A Cost–Benefit Analysis of Legislation for Bicycle Safety Helmets in Israel

Gary M. Ginsberg, DrPH, MSc, and Don S. Silverberg, MD

ABSTRACT

Legislation requiring bicyclists to wear helmets in Israel will, over a helmet's 5-year duration (assuming 85% compliancy, 83.2% helmet efficiency for morbidity, and 70% helmet efficiency for mortality), save approximately 57 lives and result in approximately 2544 fewer hospitalizations; 13 355 and 26 634 fewer emergency room and ambulatory visits, respectively; and 832 and 115 fewer short-term and long-term rehabilitation cases, respectively. Total benefits ($60.7 million) from reductions in health service use ($44.2 million), work absences ($7.5 million), and mortality ($8.9 million) would exceed program costs ($20.1 million), resulting in a benefit–cost ratio of 3.01:1. (*Am J Public Health.* 1994;84:653–656)

Introduction

Almost all bicycle accident mortality results from head and brain damage,[1–5] and nonfatal head injuries sometimes result in victims requiring expensive, lifelong care for their disabilities.[6–11] Between 70.9% and 95.5% of head injuries and about 70% of fatalities involving head injuries could be prevented through the use of crash helmets.[12–21] Fewer than 2% of Israel's estimated 833 000 cyclists[22] currently use such helmets.[11,23]

During the period from 1967 to 1991,[24] accidents to bicyclists accounted for annual mortality, hospitalization,[23] and emergency room visitation rates of 5.02, 228.5, and 2262.4 per million, respectively,[24] after adjustment for the estimated 88.9% (95% confidence interval [CI] = 87.7%, 90.1%) underreporting of emergency room cases.[23,25] Hospitalization rates were stable throughout this period, while mortality rates decreased between 1975 and 1980 and then stabilized. Persons under 20 years old accounted for 57.0% of hospitalizations, and older individuals had higher case fatality rates[24] (Table 1).

This paper estimates the costs and benefits from expected reductions in mortality and morbidity if mandatory bicycle helmet use legislation were enacted in Israel.

Methods

Direct (i.e., including only health service benefits) and total (direct, work, and mortality) or societal benefit–cost ratios based on the parameters in Table 2 were calculated on a spreadsheet; a 5% per annum discount rate was used. Lifetime costs of premature mortality, institutional care, and special education were discounted and attributed to the year in which the accident occurred.

The 85% compliancy rate (see Table 2) is based on Israelis' 90% compliancy with car seat belt laws,[26] only 6% less than the 96% achieved for bicycle helmet use after legislation in Melbourne, Australia.[21]

The gross national product per capita method of valuing life,[27] which assigns an equal value to each member of society equivalent to the annual per-capita gross national product of the population ($10 728 in 1990), was used to estimate mortality costs. These costs were based on discounting the value of the deceased's expected years of life lost.

Results

In 1994, bicycle-related injuries will account for approximately 26.5 deaths, 1203 hospitalizations, and 11 913 persons requiring emergency room treatment.

The cost of crash helmets (current retail price: $23.40) for Israel's 833 000 cyclists would be $19.5 million. An additional $607 000 would be required over 5 years for health education purposes.

Legislation for bicycle helmet use in Israel would, over a helmet's 5-year duration,[28] prevent approximately 57 deaths. Also, it would result in 2544 fewer hospitalizations, 13 355 fewer emergency room visits, 26 634 fewer ambulatory visits, and 832 and 115 fewer short- and long-term rehabilitation cases (including 45 children needing special education), respectively (Table 3).

The direct benefit ($44.20 million) to cost ($20.14 million) ratio is 2.19:1. When benefits from reductions in work absences ($7.55 million) are included, the benefit–cost ratio rises to 2.57:1. After adding benefits from reductions in mortality ($8.94 million), the total benefit–cost ratio to society rises to 3.01:1 (Table 3).

Sensitivity analyses available upon request from the authors show the benefit–cost ratio to be sensitive to

Gary M. Ginsberg is with the Department of Data Analysis, Division of Computing and Information, Ministry of Health, Jerusalem, Israel. Don S. Silverberg is with the Department of Public Health, Tel Aviv, Israel.

Requests for reprints should be sent to Gary M. Ginsberg, DrPH, MSc, Reuven 25/2, Baka, Jerusalem, 93510, Israel.

This paper was accepted July 14, 1993.

TABLE 1—Deaths, Hospitalizations, and Light Injuries from Bicycle Injuries, by Age: 1979 through 1990, Israel

Age, y	Deaths (n = 184), %	Hospitalizations (n = 2177), %	Light Injuries (n = 9071), %
0–4	0.5	1.0	0.9
5–9	9.2	12.6	8.0
10–14	14.7	25.6	22.1
15–19	12.0	17.8	19.7
20–24	2.7	6.3	7.6
25–34	8.2	7.1	10.5
35–44	7.6	5.5	7.5
45–54	10.9	7.4	7.2
55–64	12.5	7.1	7.9
65+	21.7	9.5	8.7
Total	100.0	100.0	100.0

TABLE 2—Parameters Used in Cost-Benefit Analysis

	Parameter	Source
Israeli population (1992)	5 266 000	(Reference no). 42
Per capita gross national product, $	10 728	43
Average annual wage costs, $	14 338	43
Average income of person in bicycle accident, $	5 519	Calculations on ref 24
Unemployment (1992), %	12.0	42
Male accident victims, %	87.0	24
Helmet cost, $	23.40	Retailers
Health education costs (5 years), $	607 000	Ministry of Health
Bicycle ownership rate, %	8.55	22
Riders per bike	1.85	22
Duration of helmet life, y	5	28
Initial compliancy, %	2.00	6
Final compliancy, %	85.00	5% less than refs 14, 21
Mortality		
Deaths due to head injuries, %	74.05	Midpoint range, refs 1–4, 14, 20, 44–46
Helmet efficiency, %	70.00	1
Dead on arrival at hospital, %	67.06	1
Average survival time, d	11	1
Cost of intensive care per day, $	1 057	47, 48
Average age at death, y	38.2	24
Life expectancy at 38.2 yrs.	38.3	43
Value of life at 38.2 years, $	181 449	Gross national product method
Value of life per deceased, $	170 519	Human capital method
Hospitalizations		
Helmet efficiency, %	83.20	Midpoint range, refs 12–16, 21, 49, 50
Serious head injuries, %	70.00	15, 26, 44, 46, 51–54
Average length of stay, d	9.7	Neurology department, ref 10
Cost of neurology department per day, $	446	55
Head injuries with other diagnoses, %	12.50	6
Average length of stay, d	4.5	6
Internal/orthopedic department cost per day, $	238	56
Emergency room		
Helmet efficiency, %	83.20	Midpoint range, refs 12–16, 21, 49, 50
Facial trauma alone, %	20.00	17, 57
Mild head trauma, %	24.36	4, 51–53, 58, 59
Severe head trauma, %	8.11	4, 51–53, 58, 59
Average cost per visit, $	117.50	Half of full day's hospitalization
Males, %	87.0	24

(continued)

changes in the discount rate, duration of helmet life, compliancy rate, and helmet effectiveness and cost.

Direct benefit breakeven points (where direct benefits are equal to costs) are met if compliancy falls below 40%, helmets last only 25 months, the helmet effectiveness rate is 37.8%, helmets cost $52.29, or there are more than 4.15 riders per bike. Breakeven points to society are met if compliancy falls below 29.6%, helmets last only 18 months, the helmet effectiveness rate is 17.8%, helmets cost $72.08, or there are more than 5.68 riders per bike.

Changes in the percentage of emergency room visits, unemployment, head injury death, and bike ownership rates, as well as use of the human capital method to value life, had little effect on the benefit to cost ratios.

Discussion

If compulsory bicycle crash helmet legislation were enacted in Israel, considerable reductions in mortality, morbidity, and residual disablement would occur, resulting in net savings of $43.3 million to society over a 5-year period. In almost all of the sensitivity analysis scenarios, both direct and total benefits exceeded program costs.

The benefit–cost ratios are biased downward since our conservative model did not consider reduced pain, worry, grief, work losses for ambulatory visits, or even time off from housework as a result of bicycle injuries. Nor did we consider the intangible benefit of the lessening of anxiety concerning crashes by cyclists or by their friends and relatives. Our calculations excluded revenues from possible fines as a consequence of the legislation, since payments of fines represent simply transfer payments that result in neither a net gain nor a net loss to society.

Another conservative assumption was that helmets would not reduce severe facial injuries, since recent experience revealed a reduction in severe upper facial injuries of approximately 73% as a result of helmet use.[17] Including benefits from decreased upper facial injuries only slightly increased the direct and total benefit–cost ratios to 2.27:1 and 3.13:1, respectively.

Those who object to bicycle helmet legislation argue that legislation infringes on the freedom of the individual. However, there is a legal precedent created by the fact that already-established legislation for motorcycle helmets in Israel has resulted in reduced morbidity and mortality.[24] Studies conducted in the United States have shown huge health service cost savings as a result of motorcycle crash helmet legislation.[29-34]

Health education campaigns alone (even with bicycle helmet subsidies) have achieved only low compliancy rates ranging from 7.2% to 32.2%.[14,21,35-39] However, when legislation was added to a health education campaign in Victoria, Australia, compliancy rates rose from 30% to 90% in under a year.[14,21] Similar legislation for children under 16 years of age in Howard County, Maryland, increased compliancy to 47% relative to 19% from a community education program alone in a neighboring county.[40]

The imposition of legislation, backed by the threat of fines, is a powerful and preferred means of raising helmet wearing compliancy. The monetary benefits are sufficiently large to warrant the government ministries and/or the major health insurance funds to consider subsidizing[41] the costs of providing helmets to Israeli bicyclists. □

TABLE 2—Parameters Used in Cost-Benefit Analysis (*Continued*)

	Parameter	Source
Emergency room *(continued)*		
Workdays lost	5.56	23
Average wages lost per cohort member per day, $	21.39	43
Ambulatory visits		
Visits per emergency room survivor	2.00	Panel of doctors
Time of visit, min	15	Panel of doctors
Physician cost per year, $	32 640	60
Physician cost per hour, $	16	60
Short-term disabilities		
Emergency room visits with temporary cognitive disability, %	0.68	2, 61
Cost of rehabilitation care per day, $	7 250	55
Average length of stay, d	89.1	62
Long-term disabilities		
Emergency room visits with permanent cognitive disability, %	0.0028	2, 10, 11
Average age, y	27.0	51
Cost of institutional care per day, $	40.45	Ministry of Labor and Social Welfare
Average length of stay, y	40	51
Lifetime care costs, $	253 000	Discounted
Employable, %	15	Panel of doctors
Working years lost	38	30
Special education		
Extra cost per year, $	7 841	Ref 30, Ministry of Education
Average years needed	5.9	51

TABLE 3—Benefits of Crash Helmet Legislation for Bicyclists for 5 Years[a]

	Before	After	Reduction	Benefits, $	Benefit to Cost Ratio
Deaths	132	75	57	188 773	
Hospitalizations	6 016	3 471	2 544	10 549 317	
Emergency room visits	59 562	46 206	13 355	1 358 673	
Ambulatory care	118 946	92 312	26 634	92 249	
Rehabilitation	1 205	373	832	5 223 610	
Total health service benefits				17 412 622	0.86
Long-term care	167	52	115	25 263 243	
Special education	65.4	20.2	45	1 527 131	
Total direct care benefits				44 202 996	2.19
Mortality benefits				8 939 979	0.44
Work benefits[b]				7 545 779	0.37
Total benefits to society				60 688 755	3.01
Costs				20 143 985	
Total resource savings				43 276 133	

[a]Based on 5.0% discount rate, 85% final compliancy rate, 2% baseline compliancy, 12% unemployment rate, 8.55% bicycle ownership rate, 1.85 riders per bike, helmet effectiveness rates of 83.2% (injuries) and 70% (deaths), 5-year duration of helmet costing $23.40, 70% of deaths and 32.47% of emergency room cases from head injuries, 11.07% of emergency room visits reported, and 0% reduction in facial injuries.

[b]$6 198 569 from reduction in permanent disabilities and $1 347 210 from reduction in emergency room visits.

References

1. Fife D, Davis J, Tate L, Wells JK, Mohan D, Williams A. Fatal injuries to bicyclists: the experience in Dade County, Florida. *J Trauma.* 1983;23:745–755.
2. McDermott FT, Klug GL. Head injury predominance: pedal cyclists vs motor cyclists. *Med J Aust.* 1985;143:232–234.
3. Nixon J, Clacher R, Pearn J, Corcoran A. Bicycle accidents in childhood. *Br Med J.* 1987;294:1267–1269.
4. Sacks JJ, Holmgreen P, Smith SM, Sosin DM. Bicycle-associated head injuries and deaths in the United States from 1984 through 1988. *JAMA.* 1991;266:3016–3018.
5. Schmidt P, Haarhoff K, Bonte W. Fatal bicycle accidents in Dusseldorf 1980–1989. Analysis of autopsy cases. *J Traffic Med.* 1991;19:113–118.
6. Rimel RW, Giordani B, Barth JT, Boll TJ, Jane JA. Disability caused by minor head injury. *Neurosurgery.* 1981;9:221–228.
7. Lundar T, Nestvold K. Pediatric head injuries caused by traffic accidents: a prospective study with 5-year follow-up. *Child Nerv Syst.* 1985;1:24–28.
8. Kraus JF, Fife D, Couray C. Incidence, severity and outcomes of brain injuries involving bicycles. *Am J Public Health.* 1987;77:76–78.
9. Nakayama DK, Gardner MJ, Rogers KD. Disability from bicycle-related injuries in children. *J Trauma.* 1990;30:1390–1394.
10. Levi L, Lynn S, Gilbourt I, Feinsod M. Head and brain trauma as a result of bicycle accidents [in Hebrew]. *Harefuah.* 1990;118:575–576.
11. Silverberg D, Meer A, Silvinger E, Gross M, Feldman S. Head injuries after serious bicycle accidents. *Eur J Epidemiol.* 1992;8:826–831.
12. Dorch MM, Woodward AJ, Somers RL. Do bicycle safety helmets reduce severity of head injury in real crashes? *Accident Analysis Prev.* 1987;19:183–190.

13. Wasserman RC, Waller JA, Monty MJ, Emery AB, Robinson DR. Bicyclists, helmets and head injuries: a rider-based study of helmet use and effectiveness. *Am J Public Health.* 1988;78:1220–1221.
14. Wood T, Milne P. Head injuries to pedal cyclists and the promotion of helmet use in Victoria, Australia. *Accident Analysis Prev.* 1988:20:177–185.
15. Thompson RS, Rivara FP, Thompson DC. A case control study of bicycle safety helmets. *N Engl J Med.* 1989;320:1361–1367.
16. Wasserman RC, Buccini RV. Helmet protection from head injuries among recreational bicyclists. *Am J Sports Med.* 1990;18:96–97.
17. Thompson DC, Thompson RS, Rivara FP, Wolf ME. A case control study of the effectiveness of bicycle safety helmets in preventing facial injury. *Am J Public Health.* 1990;80:1471–1474.
18. Runyan CW, Earp JAL, Reese RP. Helmet use among competitive cyclists. *Am J Prev Med.* 1991;7:232–236.
19. Williams M. The protective performance of bicyclist's helmets in accidents. *Accident Analysis Prev.* 1991;23:119–131.
20. Spaite DW, Murphy M, Criss EA, Valenzuela TD, Meislin HW. A prospective analysis of injury severity among helmeted and nonhelmeted bicyclists involved in collisions with motor vehicles. *J Trauma.* 1991;31:1510–1516.
21. Vulcan AP, Cameron MH, Watson WL. Mandatory bicycle helmet use, experience in Victoria, Australia. *World J Surg.* 1992;16:389–397.
22. Katz A. Some characteristics of bicycle travel and accidents in towns. *Transportation Res Rec Transportation Res Board.* 1978;683:25–33.
23. Avitsur M. *Traffic Injuries, Causes, Methods of Transportation and Results.* Jerusalem, Israel: Department of Community Medicine, School of Public Health and Social Medicine, Hebrew University; 1992.
24. *Road Accidents with Casualties—1967 to 1991.* Jerusalem, Israel: Central Bureau of Statistics; 1968–1992.
25. Gofin R, Palti H, Adler B, Edet E. Childhood injuries: a population based study of emergency room visits in Jerusalem. *Paediatr Perinatol Epidemiol.* 1989;3:174–178.
26. Zedar A, Mokous D, Hakert S, et al. *Seat Belt Use in Cities, Analysis of Utilization and Evaluation of Safety.* Haifa, Israel: Transportation Research Institute, Technion-Israel Institute of Technology; 1989. Research Report No. 145.
27. Ginsberg GM. Cost-effectiveness analysis, cost-benefit analysis and the value of life. In: Laaser U, Roccella EJ, Rosenfeld JB, Wenzel H, eds. *Costs and Benefits in Health Care and Prevention.* Berlin: Springer-Verlag; 1990:6–19.
28. Wilson MH, Baker SP, Teret SP, Shock S, Garbarino J. *Saving Children—A Guide to Injury Prevention.* New York, NY: Oxford University Press; 1991:78.
29. Shankar BS, Ramzy AI, Soderstrom CA, Discinger PC, Clark CC. Helmet use, patterns of injury, medical outcome, and costs among motorcycle drivers in Maryland. *Accident Analysis Prev.* 1992;24:385–396.
30. Offner PJ, Rivara FP, Maier RV. The impact of motorcycle helmet use. *J. Trauma.* 1992;32:636–641.
31. Braddock M, Schwartz R, Lapidus G, Banco L, Jacobs L. A population-based study of motorcycle injury and costs. *Ann Emerg Med.* 1992;21:273–278.
32. Muelleman RL, Mlinek EJ, Collicott PE. Motorcycle crash injuries and costs: effect of a reenacted comprehensive helmet use law. *Ann Emerg Med.* 1992;21:266–272.
33. Kelly P, Sanson T, Strange G, Orsay E. A prospective study of the impact of helmet usage on motorcycle trauma. *Ann Emerg Med.* 1991;20:852–856.
34. McSwain NE, Belles A. Motorcycle helmets—medical costs and the law. *J Trauma.* 1990;30:1189–1197.
35. Pendergast RA, Seymore-Ashworth C, Durant RH, Litaker M. Correlates of children's bicycle helmet use and short-term failure of school-level interventions. *Pediatrics.* 1992;90:354–358.
36. Weiss BD. Trends in bicycle helmet use by children: 1985 to 1990. *Pediatrics.* 1992;89:78–80.
37. Cushman R, James W, Waclawik H. Physicians promoting bicycle helmets for children: a randomized trial. *Am J Public Health.* 1991;81:1044–1046.
38. Cushman R, Down J, MacMillan N, Waclawik H. Helmet promotion in the emergency room following a bicycle injury: a randomized trial. *Pediatrics.* 1991; 88:43–47.
39. Bergman AB, Rivara FP, Richards DO, Rogers LW. The Seattle children's bicycle helmet campaign. *Am J Dis Child.* 1990;144:727–731.
40. Cote TR, Sacks JJ, Lambert-Huber DA, et al. Bicycle use among Maryland children: effect of legislation and education. *Pediatrics.* 1992;89:1216–1220.
41. Capron AM. Bicycle safety helmets. *N Engl J Med.* 1989;321:1194. Letter.
42. *Monthly Bulletin of Statistics.* Jerusalem, Israel: Central Bureau of Statistics; December 1992;43:12.
43. *Statistical Abstract of Israel 1991.* Jerusalem, Israel: Central Bureau of Statistics; 1991.
44. Reynolds R, Cohen D. Children, bicycles and head injuries. *Med J Aust.* 1987;146: 615–619.
45. Guichon DMP, Myles ST. Bicycle injuries: one year sample in Calgary. *J Trauma.* 1975;15:504–506.
46. Bouvier R. Bicycle accidents in childhood: social and preventive aspects. *Aust Fam Physician.* 1984;13:287–289.
47. Ginsberg GM, Shouval D. Cost-benefit analysis of a nationwide neonatal inoculation programme against hepatitis B in an area of intermediate endemicity. *J Epidemiol Community Health.* 1992;46:587–594.
48. *Hospitalization Prices from 1.1.92.* Jerusalem, Israel: Ministry of Health; 1991.
49. Thompson RS, Rivara FP, Thompson DC. Bicycle safety helmets. *N Engl J Med.* 1989;321:1195–1196. Letter.
50. Thompson DC, Thompson RS, Rivara FP. Incidence of bicycle-related injuries in a defined population. *Am J Public Health.* 1990;80:1388–1389.
51. Siebst SM, Alexander D, Ruddy R. Bicycle related injuries. *Am J Dis Child.* 1987;141:140–144.
52. Bjornstig V, Naslund K. Pedal cycling accidents—mechanisms and consequences. *Acta Chir Scand.* 1984;150:350–359.
53. McKenna PJ, Welsh DJ, Martin LW. Pediatric bicycle trauma. *J Trauma.* 1991; 31:392–394.
54. Arinson CJ, Pollard CW. Child cyclist injuries: a prospective study. *Med J Aust.* 1986;144:144–146.
55. *Departmental Costing of Ezrat Nashim Hospital 1987.* Jerusalem, Israel: Health Economics Consultants; 1988.
56. Ginsberg GM, Penchas S, Israeli A. Alternative methods of hospital remuneration in Israel. *Isr J Med Sci.* 1991;27: 583–589.
57. Hodgson VR. *Impact, Skid and Retention Tests on a Representative Group of Bicycle Helmets to Determine Their Head-Neck Protective Characteristics.* Detroit, Mich: Wayne State University, Department of Neurosurgery; 1990.
58. Centers for Disease Control. Bicycle-related injuries; data from the National Electronic Injury Surveillance System. *MMWR.* 1987;86:269–271.
59. *Accident Facts, National Safety Council.* Chicago, Ill: National Safety Council; 1982:45–91.
60. Ginsberg GM, Tulchinsky TH. Costs and benefits of a second measles inoculation of children in Israel, the West Bank and Gaza. *J Epidemiol Community Health.* 1990;44:274–280.
61. Kraus JF, Rock A, Hemyar P. Brain injuries among infants, children, adolescents and young adults. *Am J Dis Child.* 1990;144:684–691.
62. *Hospitals and Day Care Units in Israel. Statistical Information on Patient Movements by Institution and Department 1990.* Jerusalem, Israel: Ministry of Health, 1991.

RESTORING THE LOWER SNAKE RIVER

SAVING SNAKE RIVER SALMON AND SAVING MONEY

RESTORING THE LOWER SNAKE RIVER

SAVING SNAKE RIVER SALMON AND SAVING MONEY

ECONOMIC ANALYSIS BY PHILIP S. LANSING, ANALYTICA
ADDITIONAL TEXT BY EVE VOGEL

Give brief background of ONRC

THIS REPORT IS A PROJECT OF THE
[OREGON NATURAL RESOURCES COUNCIL FUND]

5825 North Greeley
Portland, Oregon 97217
(503) 283-6343

environmental groups

AND IS SPONSORED BY THE FOLLOWING GROUPS:

Antioch Living Systems Collective
Boulder-White Clouds Council
Coalition for Salmon-Steelhead Habitat
EarthJustice Legal Defense Fund
Federation of Fly Fishers Steelhead Committee
Friends of the Earth
Hells Canyon Preservation Council
Idaho Conservation League
Idaho Rivers United
Idaho Steelhead & Salmon Unlimited
Idaho Wildlife Federation
Inland Empire Public Lands Council
Institute for Fisheries Resources
North Cascades Conservation Council
Northwest Ecosystem Alliance
Northwest Environmental Defense Center
Oregon Natural Desert Association
Oregon Wildlife Federation
Pacific Coast Federation of Fishermen's Associations
Rivers Council of Washington
Sawtooth Wildlife Council
Taxpayers for Common Sense
Washington Wilderness Coalition
Willamette Riverkeeper

This report is made possible through the grant support of **The Pew Charitable Trusts** and **Patagonia, Inc.**
Special thanks to Pat Ford and other staff of Save Our Wild Salmon. Layout and design by Vicki Moser/CopperMoon Design

TABLE OF CONTENTS

Saving Snake River Salmon and Saving Money
Executive Summary

Snake River salmon once swam in the millions, travelling up to 1,000 miles inland to remote Idaho, Washington, Oregon and Montana streams. Until the 1960s Snake River Chinook, sockeye, coho and steelhead provided a living resource that supported ancient cultures, a vibrant fishing industry and diverse inland ecosystems.

Today, we have almost lost this natural treasure. Snake River coho are extinct and returning Snake River sockeye can be counted on a few fingers. Snake River Chinook and steelhead are listed under the Endangered Species Act, and are only slightly further from the brink of extinction.

> **Restoring the Lower Snake River would save approximately $87 million each year.**

The people of the Pacific Northwest and the United States care about salmon. We care enough that in the past 20 years we have spent, even by modest estimates, $1.7 billion trying to bring salmon back to healthy population levels - more than has ever been spent on any other endangered species. A 1997 poll from the Northwest's largest newspaper *The Oregonian* showed that salmon protection is the number one environmental concern in the state; 86 percent of Oregonians want to preserve salmon runs in the Columbia and Snake Rivers. In Washington, over 70 percent of people believe protecting wild salmon is important.

Up until now, the money we have spent has not worked to save Snake River salmon. We have paid to transport salmon for hundreds of miles in trucks or barges just to get them past dams. We have built million-dollar dam by-pass systems, and supported hatcheries just so a few young salmon will survive the gauntlet of dams. We have released water from upstream dams, foregoing some power production, to increase flows as salmon migrate through the dam-impounded reservoirs.

We have been poor stewards: our fish are still dying. It is time to stop treating the symptoms and address the root cause of their decline.

Dams kill salmon. Fish die going through turbines, or become traumatized, disoriented and easy prey as they come out of dam by-pass systems, trucks and barges. Spilled over dams, young salmon smolts survive better, but when spills are managed poorly, the smolts may become afflicted with gas bubble disease, a salmon version of the bends.

Perhaps even more significantly, dams destroy rivers, and salmon need rivers. What used to be the Lower Snake River is now a series of slow-moving reservoirs. Young migrating salmon take weeks or months longer than before dam construction to find their way to the ocean. On their slow journey, they can find few places to feed in the drowned river reaches.

The dams that the Snake River salmon cannot survive are the four Lower Snake dams: Ice Harbor, Lower Monumental, Little Goose and Lower Granite. Before these dams were built, the Snake River salmon survived - albeit at reduced numbers - the hurdles of the Lower Columbia dams. Since the last of the four Lower Snake dams, Lower Granite, was built in 1975, every Snake River salmon species has been listed under the Endangered Species Act.

The four Lower Snake dams were built to provide hydroelectric power, river transportation to Lewiston, Idaho, and inexpensive irrigation. Today, they provide about 5 percent of the Pacific Northwest's electricity, allow shipment of about 3.5 million tons of grains each year, and reduce irrigation costs for thirteen large farms. These economic benefits are dwarfed by the money we have spent unsuccessfully to reduce the dams' impact on salmon.

We need to stop throwing money at failing efforts to help Snake River salmon survive the Lower Snake dams and reservoirs. We need to restore the Lower Snake River and restore the Snake River salmon.

Saving Snake River Salmon by Restoring the Snake River

Some of the largest areas of pristine salmon spawning and rearing habitat in the Northwest are in Idaho, on tributaries of the Snake River. If enough salmon can survive the trip down the Snake and Columbia Rivers and return to Idaho habitat as adults, populations can become sustainable. Scientists from the State and Tribal Fisheries Agencies' Analytical Team have predicted that if the Lower Snake River is restored, salmon populations can recover. They predict an 80 to 100 percent probability of returning spring and summer Chinook salmon populations to the levels of the 1960s within 24 years. Recovery to those levels would allow removal of these runs from the Endangered Species list, and prevent the need for expensive restoration efforts.

RESTORING A RIVER

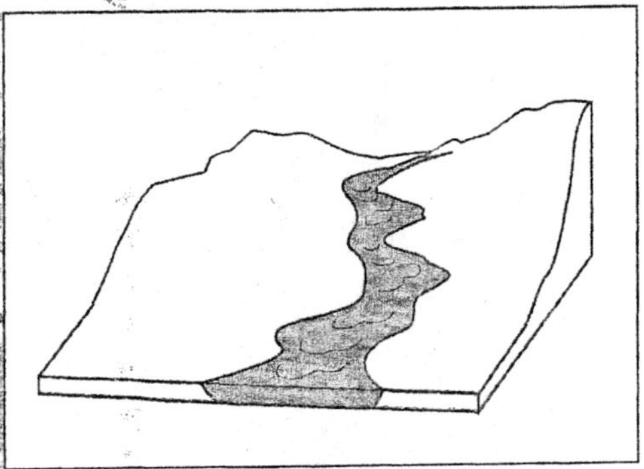

Before the dams were built, the Lower Snake River flowed freely, sustaining millions of salmon.

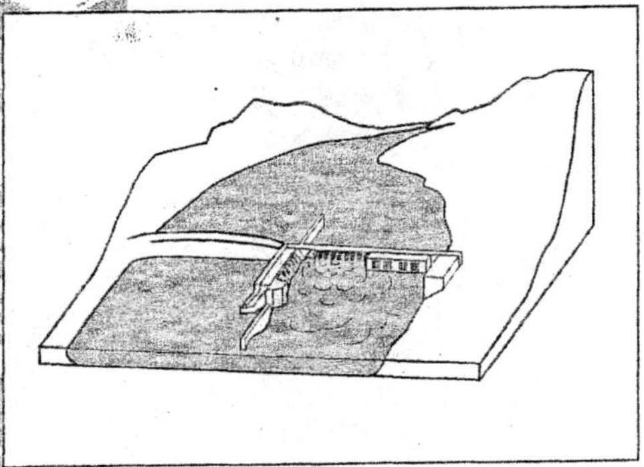

Currently the four dams create a series of long, slow reservoirs. Salmon die both in the reservoirs and at the dams.

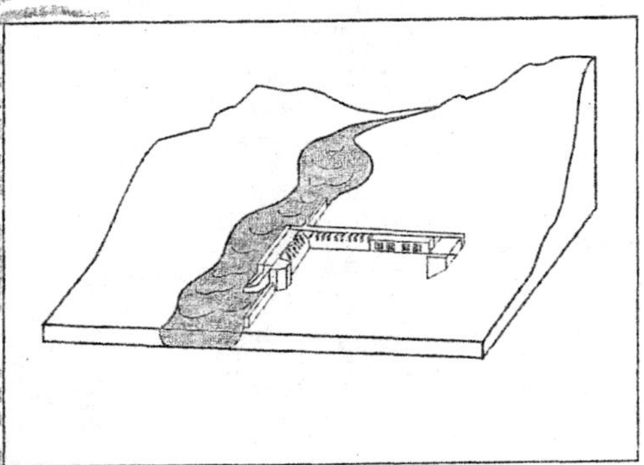

River restoration would require breaching the earthen portion of the dams and allowing the river to flow freely past the concrete structures.

Until recently, it was politically unthinkable to consider removing or retiring large dams, no matter what their ecological or economic damage. Now the Army Corps of Engineers, the very agency that built and operates the Lower Snake dams, is seriously considering removing the earthen portions of the four dams to return the Lower Snake to a natural river and hence restore the salmon. Their findings are expected in an Environmental Impact Statement in 1999.

Economic Concerns and the Purpose of this Report

The proposal to restore the Lower Snake River has raised alarm in some quarters. Opponents argue that we cannot afford the economic losses that would result from losing the Lower Snake dams. The electric power, river transportation, and inexpensive irrigation they provide are seen as essential to the Northwest economy.

Given how much has already been spent to reduce the impact of the dams, it is reasonable to ask how much more it would now cost to retire the dams and restore the Snake River.

This paper addresses this question:
Would restoring the Lower Snake River to free-flowing conditions cost or save money?

This question is a bit more complex than simply adding up annual spending on keeping the dams in place and comparing it with the costs of restoring the river. What is required is a comparison of the actual net economic benefit provided by the dams at present with the net benefit that would result from river restoration.

In other words,

Which is greater: Net economic benefit of Lower Snake dams and reservoirs or net economic benefit of restored Lower Snake River?

Net economic benefit is a technical term meaning economic return to society after all costs are accounted. Net benefit is typically a positive amount, but it can be negative when hidden costs are included in the reckoning. For the Snake River dams, the benefit is negative.

Net economic benefit is very different from economic impact. An impact study might focus, for example, on the impact of a proposed course of action on a local community. There will be many different impacts in different areas if the Lower Snake River is restored, some positive and some negative. Our benefits analysis does not address local impacts. Instead, it takes a broader view and focuses on changes in overall economic wealth.

Comparing Net Economic Benefits: Dams and Reservoirs vs. Restored River

The following table summarizes the costs and benefits provided by the Lower Snake dams and reservoirs, and by a restored Lower Snake River.

ECONOMIC BENEFITS AND COSTS OF LOWER SNAKE DAMS AND RESERVOIRS	ECONOMIC BENEFITS AND COSTS OF RESTORED LOWER SNAKE RIVER
BENEFITS	BENEFITS
▪ Hydroelectric power generation	▪ End expensive, failing salmon restoration
▪ River transportation	▪ End dam operations and maintenance
▪ Greater returns to farmers who use inexpensive irrigation water pumping	▪ End navigation and irrigation supports
	▪ Restored fishery
COSTS	COSTS
▪ Operations and maintenance	▪ Removing earthen dam, re-routing roads, etc.
▪ Salmon restoration spending	▪ Replace power
▪ Support for river transportation and irrigation	▪ Replace transportation
	▪ Irrigator buyout or additional support

This report details calculations of net benefits for both sides of this table. The results of this analysis are significant.

KEY FINDINGS (RELEVANT REPORT SECTIONS IN PARENTHESES):

- The Lower Snake dams and reservoirs require the Bonneville Power Administration to spend $194.4 million every year on salmon restoration. (Section 1, p. 13, and Appendix for Section 1, pp. 26-29.)
- Taxpayers and electric ratepayers subsidize electric power production, river transportation and irrigation from the Lower Snake dams and reservoirs. With all costs accounted, these three Lower Snake dam "benefits" actually produce a net benefit loss to the economy of $114 million every year. (Section 3, p. 25.)
- Electric power from the Lower Snake dams is not competitive. It costs 2.44 cents per kilowatt-hour. If we restore the Lower Snake River and purchase power elsewhere, we could provide energy for 1.87 cents per kilowatt-hour. (Section 2, pp. 17-18 and Appendix for Section 2, p. 29.)
- River transportation on the Lower Snake is expensive and heavily subsidized. Although river shippers pay only $1.23 per ton to go from Lewiston, Idaho to Kennewick, Washington, taxpayers and electric ratepayers pay an additional $12.66. The total cost to ship one ton of goods on the Lower Snake is $13.89. In comparison, rail costs only $1.26. (Section 2, p. 19-21 and Appendix for Section 2, pp. 30-32.)
- Thirteen agribusinesses pump water from the Ice Harbor reservoir. Together, these farms earn a net $1.9 million per year. But taxpayers and electric ratepayers subsidize these farms with $11.2 million. If the farms paid their full costs, they would lose $9.3 million every year. It would be cheaper to buy these farms outright and end their production altogether. (Section 2, pp. 22-24 and Appendix for Section 2, pp. 32-34.)

We make two major assumptions in calculating net benefits. First, we assume ALL power generation constraints adopted to restore Snake River salmon under the Endangered Species Act will be removed if salmon are restored and thus removed from Endangered Species Act protection. Second, we assume there are benefits from restored Snake River fisheries but their calculations are beyond the purview of this paper. The first assumption increases our calculated economic benefit with river restoration and the second assumption decreases it.

Restoring the River: Summary of Net Yearly Costs and Benefits

The following tables summarize the money lost to the economy because of the Lower Snake dams and reservoirs and the economic losses caused by a restored Lower Snake River. The difference is the savings that would result each year from retiring the four Lower Snake dams and restoring the Lower Snake River.

Restoring the Lower Snake River would save $87 million every year.

Conclusion

Restoring the Lower Snake River would produce an economic benefit of $87 million each year. This includes the costs of replacing Snake River hydropower, ending the barge transportation system, and buying out the thirteen farms that use Lower Snake water for irrigation.

comparing costs of both projects:

COSTS WITH DAMS:

Managing dams and reservoirs.

The Snake River dams and reservoirs require on-going operations and maintenance. They also cause damage to the Snake River salmon. Government agencies and society pay for this damage when we haul salmon, flush water for fish instead of electric power turbines and otherwise attempt to make the dams and reservoirs less lethal to fish.

Providing hydropower, river transportation and irrigation.

Transportation and irrigation as provided by the dam-reservoir system are heavily subsidized by taxpayers and electricity ratepayers. U.S. taxpayers subsidize production of crops that are irrigated by water pumped with subsidized electricity. Local taxpayers support the ports necessary for river transportation. Water consumed by irrigation and river transportation cannot be used to produce power; electricity ratepayers' costs are higher because of this foregone power.

In addition, grain shippers pay a fee to ship goods; this private cost is an additional cost of river transportation.

ANNUAL COSTS WITH DAMS:

	$ (MILLIONS)
Managing dams and reservoirs	
Operations and maintenance	$33.6
Salmon restoration spending	$194.4
Providing hydropower, river transportation and irrigation	
Transportation costs	$6.4
Irrigation costs	$1.8
TOTAL ANNUAL COSTS WITH DAMS	$236.2

doesn't address benefits yet: this analysis seems a bit worthless without comparing benefits.

COSTS WITH RESTORED RIVER

Restoring and managing a restored Lower Snake River.

Restoring the Lower Snake River would require physically removing the earthen portion of the dams and re-routing infrastructure like roads and bridges. Operations, maintenance and salmon restoration spending would be unnecessary in a natural river.

Providing electric power and river transportation.

We assume that if the Snake River is restored, hydroelectric power and river transportation may need to be replaced with other sources of power and shipping.

Loss of irrigation.

Although irrigation pump in-takes could be extended to natural river level to make irrigation possible even with the Lower Snake River restored, it is an expensive proposition and one whose full economic effects are unknown. We calculate benefit assuming that irrigated lands are purchased outright and their farm production is lost.

ANNUAL COSTS WITH RESTORED RIVER:

	$ (MILLIONS)
Restoring and Managing restored Lower Snake River	
Restoration (How did they get this?)	$25.6
Operations, maintenance and Snake River salmon restoration	$0.0
Providing electric power and river transportation	
Replacement power	$115.6
Alternative transportation	$4.4
Loss of irrigation	
Purchasing lands	$2.0
Loss of net crop returns	$1.9 (w/ subsidies)
TOTAL ANNUAL COSTS WITH RESTORED RIVER:	$149.5

FOREWARD

History: The Lower Snake River Project

BY KEITH PETERSEN

To understand why we have four dams along the Lower Snake River, one must first understand Lewiston, Idaho's long love affair with inland navigation.

The gold rush of the early 1860s established Lewiston as the queen city of north central Idaho. Even after the short gold rush boom was over, though, it seemed to Lewiston boosters that the new city was extraordinarily well situated, if it could only take advantage of the Snake River that flowed nearby.

Sternwheelers had already provided a transportation network viable enough to haul more than 60,000 people to the Idaho gold fields between 1861 and 1863. But the Snake was a wild and unpredictable river. At many times of the year even a fearless riverboat captain could not get through. The Lower Snake had more than thirty rapids that steamers had to negotiate. Lewiston residents in the early 1860s began what would become a more than 100-year campaign to seek federal assistance in creating a year-round navigable waterway between that Idaho town and the Pacific Ocean.

Heeding the demands of Lewiston residents and others along the Lower Snake and Columbia, in 1876 Congress authorized the Army Corps of Engineers to construct Cascade Locks around the boiling rapids of the Columbia downstream from The Dalles. Once completed, the locks proved their value; steamers carrying thousands of tons of materials now slipped easily past the Cascades.

Merchants and farmers lobbied for more navigational aids to allow steamers to pass all the way to Lewiston. The next obvious obstruction was Celilo Falls, upstream from The Dalles. Congress again authorized the Corps to construct a passageway, which it completed in 1915.

Yet hardly had Celilo Canal opened when Columbia and Snake River steamboating collapsed. Sternwheelers had become outmoded, unable to compete with the speed, efficiency and greater carrying capacity of trains. Once tracks crossed into the wheat regions, the boats had no hope of seriously threatening railroad dominance. Railways simply lowered their rates until steamers lost their freight trade.

But by the 1930s marine technology had changed. Now powerful tug boats and barges could compete with railroads, and once again lobbyists clamored for an open river from Lewiston to the sea. No one proved more tireless at making those demands than Herbert G. West of Walla Walla, executive secretary of the Inland Empire Waterways Association (IEWA). For decades West badgered Congress about the need for a reliable navigation system to Lewiston.

In 1945 Congress finally authorized the Army Corps of Engineers to construct a series of dams on the Lower Snake River. There, between 1955 and 1975 the Engineers built Ice Harbor, Lower Monumental (which backs up a reservoir appropriately named after Herbert G. West), Little Goose, and Lower Granite. Together with the Corps' four dams on the Lower Columbia, these massive structures transformed an entire region. Prior to the dam-building era of the 1930s to 1970s, the Northwest was a sparsely populated region with an economy based upon agriculture and natural resource extraction. After the dams, the region has become a major industrial and trading center with millions of residents enjoying one of the highest standards of living in the world.

And yet, not all dams were created equal. The four Lower Snake dams have always been rather poor cousins to the much larger Columbia projects. They have also always been controversial.

In the early years, as Herbert West and the IEWA struggled year after year to persuade Congress to authorize locks and dams on the Lower Snake, their most fierce adversaries, ironically, were representatives of the Army Corps of Engineers, who repeatedly testified before Congress that such a series of dams could never be economically justified based upon navigation alone. Not until the end of World War II could economists (often exaggerating future needs, as it turned out) envision a Pacific Northwest that would boom so dramatically that it could actually use all of the hydropower the great federal dams would produce. Thus, Congress authorized the Lower Snake project because of

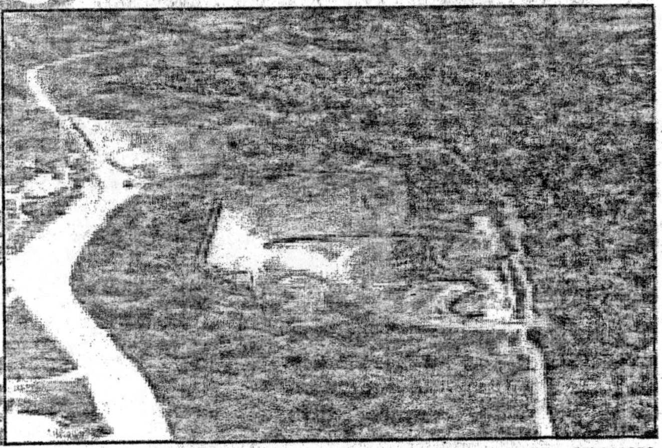

OREGON HISTORICAL SOCIETY CN 019652

Aerial view of construction of Lower Granite Dam, 1968

hydropower: 77 percent of project benefits were to come from hydropower and only 18 percent from navigation. These are still today dams that can justify their existence only because of their hydropower potential. In other words, while inland navigationists have always been the loudest advocates for the dams, these structures were built at taxpayer expense because of their perceived hydropower benefits. Navigation has always been the tail attempting (usually very effectively) to wag the dog. Yet determining whether or not these dams provide true benefits to society is a debate that must be waged largely upon whether or not society needs the power they produce.

While navigation interests were able to eventually woo the Corps to their side of the debate, they were never able to convince fish advocates that these dams would be anything other than fish killers. The contemporary controversy over endangered Snake River fish stocks did not suddenly arise; well over half a century ago fish advocates accurately predicted what would happen with the completion of the Lower Snake system.

As soon as Bonneville Dam went on line in 1938, biologists became very concerned about the impacts of a string of large dams between Bonneville and Lewiston. In the 1930s, 1940s, and 1950s, most public attention focused on the issue of getting adult fish over dams on their return to home waters to spawn. Finally, the Army Corps of Engineers found a good solution – effective fish ladders – that has been fine-tuned since the 1930s but not dramatically altered.

Yet invisible to the public who visited the fish ladders and cheered the adult fish were tiny juveniles trying to find a safe way to pass through the huge dams. As we were to learn, dams can kill these fish in a wide variety of ways—via turbines, via increased predation in warm water reservoirs, via nitrogen supersaturation poisoning, and via timing dysfunctions as tiny fish biologically programmed to rush to sea in a free-flowing river now have to somehow try to swim through warm water pools or catch a ride on a barge, something akin to elk migrating to the highlands via a Greyhound bus: it just doesn't work well, despite the best of intentions.

As early as 1934 the Bureau of Reclamation recognized the difficulty of attempting to get juvenile fish past a major dam. Largely because of this, the Bureau chose to provide no fish passage at Grand Coulee. In 1947 biologist Harlan Homes, working for the Corps, began studying juvenile mortalities at dams and soon discovered how lethal they could be. In 1952, when Holmes accurately estimated that Bonneville Dam killed 15 percent of juveniles passing through, the Corps refused to publicize his report. In 1948 the U.S. Fish and Wildlife Service stated of the proposed Lower Snake dams: "Adequate facilities can be provided for the upstream passage of fish.... The potential loss of downstream-migrating fingerlings presents a more serious problem.... The Lower Snake dams collectively present the greatest threat to the maintenance of the Columbia River salmon population of any project heretofore constructed or authorized." Although later Corps of Engineers employees sometimes conveniently forgot their agency had arrived at this conclusion so early, by 1954 even the Corps came to recognize this position. Walla Walla District Engineer Colonel Fremont Tandy admitted that year, "The basic element of the anadromous fish problem as related to water resource development is the downstream passage of fingerlings .... We are confident ... that we can pass adult migrants upstream over dams of any height, but we have yet to learn how to pass them downstream successfully."

Along the Lower Snake, fish advocates continued their aggressive fight against the dams even after Congress authorized the project. The battle centered on convincing Congress to withhold construction money for Ice Harbor Lock and Dam. They knew if they lost the battle of Ice Harbor, the fish might well be doomed, because if the Corps built that dam, it would surely construct the other three proposed for upstream.

The Washington and Oregon fish and game departments took active roles in attempting to kill Ice Harbor. Although the IEWA wanted the dams constructed because of their navigation potential, once it became clear that these were really authorized only because of their hydropower potential, the fish advocates had grounds for optimism. As the Washington Department of Fisheries pointed out, "There are 387 dam sites that are undeveloped in the Columbia River basin" that could produce power with limited threat to fish runs. Build at these sites and save the Snake River runs, they advocated.

For ten years, the fish and navigation advocates battled each other and for ten years Congress refused to provide funding for Ice Harbor. It might have been that the Lower Snake would today be undammed had it not been for the Korean and Cold Wars. The Ice Harbor dam site is located virtually next door to Hanford. In the early 1950s, the nation clamored for atomic superiority over the Soviet Union. Presidential reports outlined a need for many more kilowatts of power to meet critical national defense programs in atomic energy. What better place to attain some of that energy output than at a dam next door to the Hanford works?

As it turned out the fish advocates could battle river developers to a standstill when the issue was whether or not to create a navigable waterway to Lewiston. But when the issue of atomic power superiority came into play, they had no chance. In 1955 Congress—over the objections of President Dwight Eisenhower who protested the move as being economically unsound— allocated money to construct Ice Harbor Dam. In 1975 the Corps completed Lower Granite and slackwater made its way, after more than a century of political struggle, to Lewiston.

For many, it seemed that the completion of Lower Granite Lock and Dam was the end of the story. But as it turns out, perhaps it is only a mid-way mark. Today, the Lower Snake dams provide less than 5 percent of the Northwest's energy supply. While the Columbia River navigation system is a huge regional economic catalyst, the economic advantages of the Lower Snake navigation system, which almost exclusively ships wheat (full barges going down; empty ones coming back up), as marginal. At the same time, there is no doubt about what is killing our fish. While we should be concerned about ocean conditions, about upstream alterations to habitat, and about overfishing, it is essential that the debate over whether we want continued Snake/Columbia River anadromous fish runs be focused clearly on the dams, for they are fish killers of unprecedented precision.

Can we live without the power the Lower Snake dams produce and without a year round navigable waterway to Lewiston, Idaho? Most certainly the answer to that question is yes. Will removal of the dams cause traumatic disruption to some people's lives — particularly some inland wheat farmers and port employees? The answer to that question is also most certainly yes. Are the greater societal benefits that would come with the salvation of Columbia/Snake anadromous fish runs worth this disruption to the lives of some Northwest families? That is the question upon which this debate must revolve.

OREGON HISTORICAL SOCIETY ORHI 98014

Downstream approach to Ice Harbor navigation lock on Snake River, looking upstream. Ice Harbor Lock and Dam, Snake River, WA; April 16, 1960

Keith Petersen/Pullman, Washington
Author, River of Life, Channel of Death: Fish and Dams on the Lower Snake

INTRODUCTION

Snake River salmon are on the verge of extinction. Snake River coho are extinct. Sockeye, spring and summer Chinook, fall Chinook and steelhead are listed under the Endangered Species Act.*[1] There is a tremendous opportunity to bring this Northwest legacy back to healthy, harvestable levels by retiring the four Lower Snake dams and restoring their long, slow reservoirs back to a healthy, free-flowing river. Taking this step toward the future would restore the river and its salmon. Without even considering the value of a restored fishery, river restoration would create significant economic benefit.

For tens of thousands of years, Snake River salmon returned from the Pacific Ocean to spawn in tributaries as far as 1,000 miles inland. The prolific runs sustained Native American peoples and communities along the river to its far inland reaches. Almost every accessible stream had its own specially-adapted run which evolved to the dynamic natural conditions of that special stream. Even after dying, the salmon played a critical role in their stream ecosystems, as the nutrients they collected in their bodies in the far-off Pacific decomposed in inland streams to nourish a new generation of insects, plants and young salmon.

In the late 1800s, probably over 1.5 million spring/summer Chinook, 70,000 fall Chinook and 100,000 sockeye returned each year to the Snake River basin.[2] About half of the steelhead and spring/summer Chinook in the entire Columbia River basin came from the Snake River and its tributaries.[3] Salmon fishing on the Snake and its tributaries was for decades an enormous economic boon for the region. It is estimated that if Chinook and sockeye fishing were restored to the levels even of the 1950s, it could today generate in Idaho alone $62.5 million extra in economic activity per year and support over 1800 additional jobs. This estimate does not even include likely improvements in the steelhead fishery, which, even in its state of decline, brought Idaho $90 million in the 1992-93 season; nor does it include economic benefits downstream.[4]

~~increased~~ benefits from increased fish stocks

Yet virtually all this has been lost with the decline of these magnificent fish. There has been no general salmon fishing season in Idaho since the 1970s.[5] Tribes that fished for salmon in the Snake River and its tributaries for millenia now must apply for exemptions under the Endangered Species Act in order to fish at all. Stream ecological productivity has begun to decline because of the lack of nutrients formerly supplied by salmon carcasses.[6]

native americans: standing

There is powerful evidence that the four Lower Snake dams and reservoirs in Washington state are the principal cause of the near extinction of the Snake River salmon.[7] Juvenile salmon or smolts face high mortality and loss going through and over dams and the reservoirs created by dams. The problem is cumulative: the historic record shows that the hardy Snake River salmon were able to cope – albeit at reduced numbers – with dams on the Columbia River, but as additional dams were added on the Lower Snake, the runs declined dramatically.[8]

The Army Corps of Engineers (ACOE), which operates the four Lower Snake dams, and other agencies are now seriously considering retiring the dams, removing their earthen sections and allowing the river to flow freely around the concrete portions, which would remain.[9] This river restoration plan would return a natural flow to the river.

ACOE - considering restoration

This report does not analyze the biological arguments for restoring the river, or detail the probable biological effects. The State and Tribal Fisheries Agencies' Analytical Team predicts that if the Lower Snake River is restored, salmon

* Dates of Endangered Species Act listings are:
- coho - declared extinct in 1985;
- sockeye - listed in 1991;
- spring/summer Chinook - listed in 1991;
- fall Chinook - listed in 1991;
- steelhead - listed in 1997.

populations will return. They predict an 80 to 100 percent probability of returning spring/summer Chinook salmon populations to the levels of the 1960s within 24 years.[10] Some of the largest areas of pristine salmon spawning and rearing habitat left in the Northwest are in Idaho, in tributaries of the Snake River.[11] If enough salmon can survive the trip down the Snake and Columbia Rivers and return to this Idaho habitat as adults, they can thrive.

In this report, we are concerned with economics. We assume that restoring the Lower Snake River will recover Snake River salmon to naturally sustainable population levels. We make no predictions of future harvests. Recovery alone would allow removal of these runs from the Endangered Species list, and prevent the need for expensive restoration efforts.

The proposal to restore a free-flowing Lower Snake River has raised considerable controversy. Opponents argue that we cannot afford the economic losses that would result from losing the Lower Snake dams. Two residents of southeast Washington wrote, "[We] rely heavily

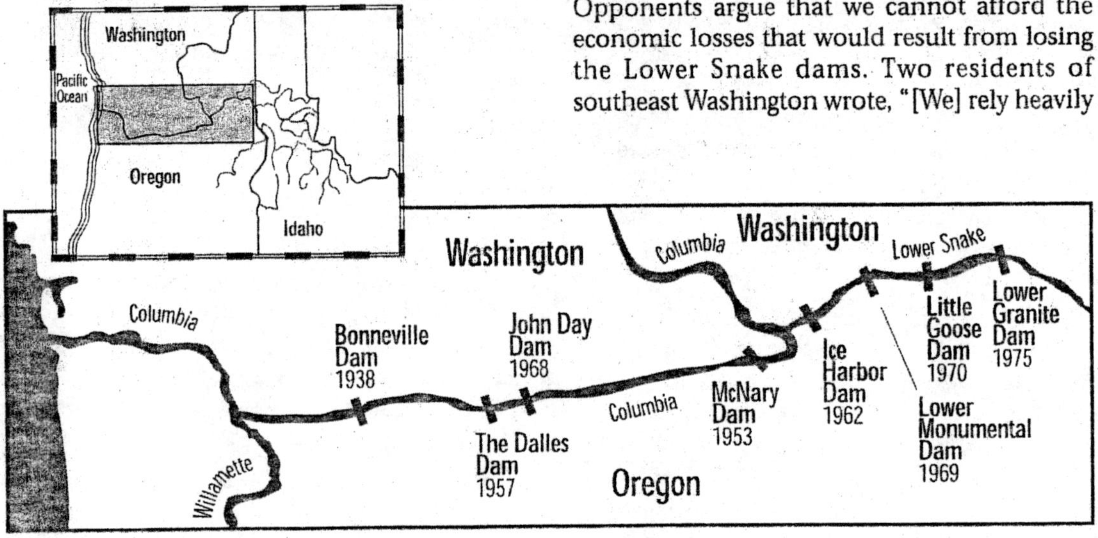

The Lower Columbia and Lower Snake dams, with the year each was built.

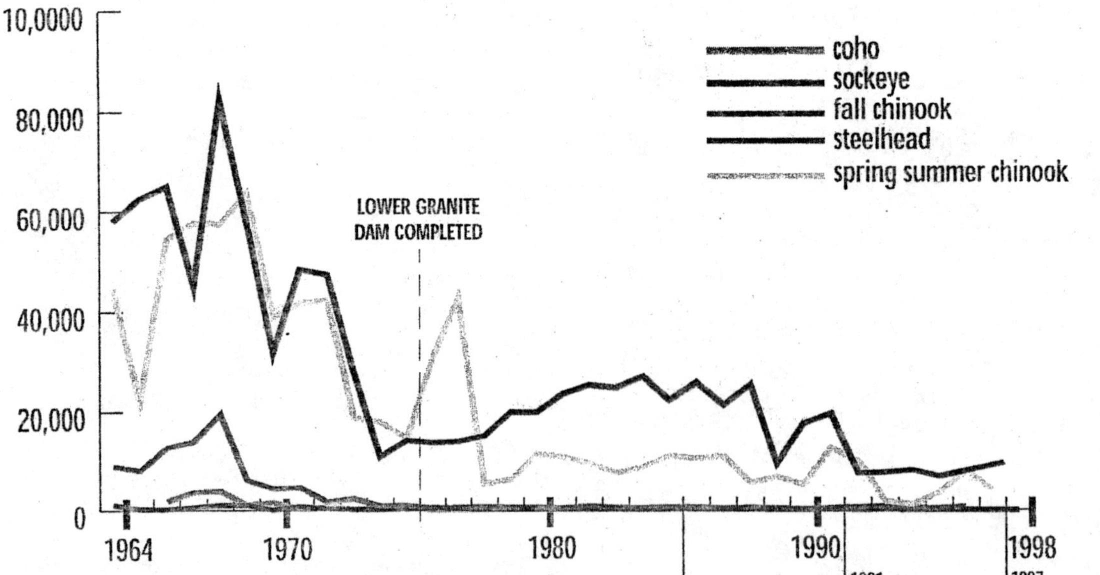

Decline of Snake River salmon over time.
The runs survived the construction of the Lower Columbia dams. All have been listed under the Endangered Species Act (ESA) since the last of the Lower Snake dams was built in 1975.

on water resources for recreational activities, irrigation water and hydroelectric power.... Economically, our community is dependent on river resources.... We cannot go back to the past."[12] Equally adamant that dam retirement should not even be on the table, Washington's Senator Slade Gorton said, "Those that want to make a habit of dam removal should understand this. I will never support their proposals to remove Snake or Columbia River dams. Never."[13]

RESTORING A RIVER

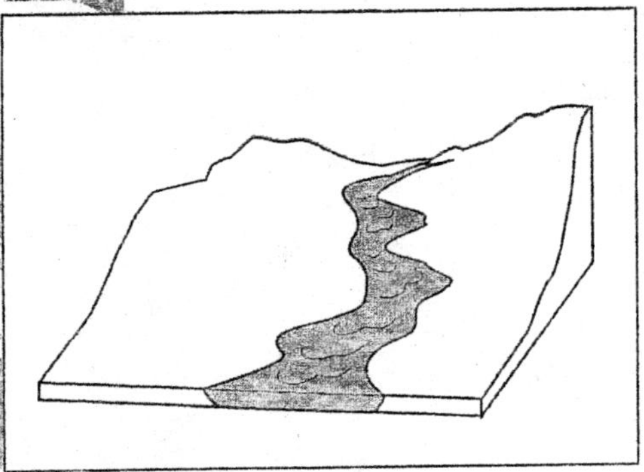

Before the dams were built, the Lower Snake River flowed freely, sustaining millions of salmon.

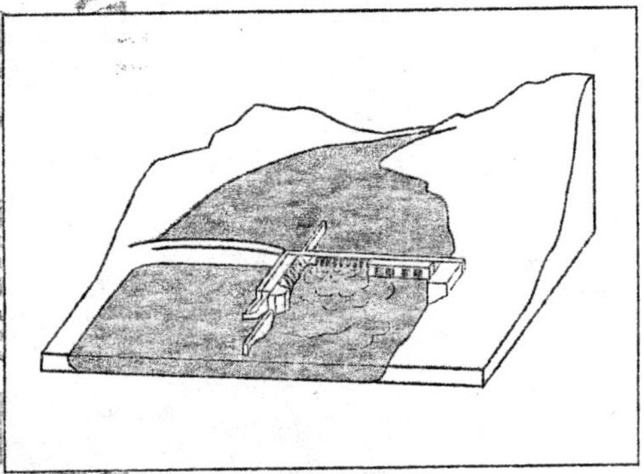

Currently the four dams create a series of long, slow reservoirs. Salmon die both in the reservoirs and at the dams.

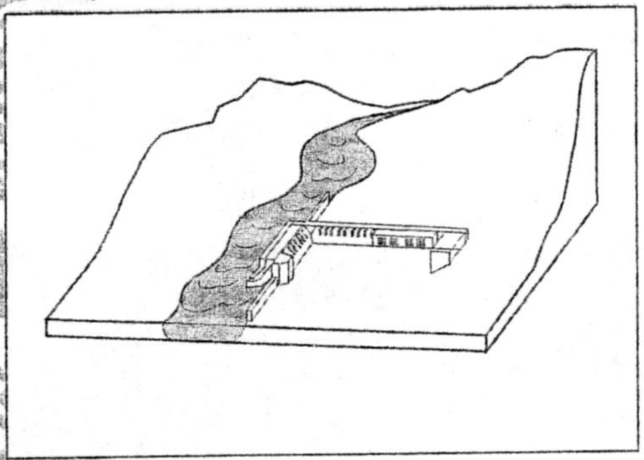

River restoration would require breaching the earthen portion of the dams and allowing the river to flow freely past the concrete structures.

Yet others have endorsed river restoration wholeheartedly. *The Idaho Statesman* ran a three-day Opinion Page series in July, 1997 called "Dollars, Sense & Salmon" that clearly called for breaching the four Lower Snake dams as "a step forward" that could return vital fisheries, benefit the economy, protect Idaho farmers, nourish Idaho forests and free the Northwest from many federal regulations.[14] The extensive salmon restoration plan published in 1996 by the four Columbia basin tribes with treaty fishing rights calls for breaching the four Lower Snake dams.[15] Advocates for river restoration acknowledge that there will be some economic and social impact and pain with dam retirement. They believe, though, that nearly all losses can be alleviated by re-investing the savings that would come from river restoration back into economic development.[16]

There is little doubt that salmon restoration has up until this point been an expensive and largely unsuccessful effort. Recently, it has been widely reported that the Bonneville Power Administration has spent $3 billion in the last 20 years for mostly failed attempts at salmon protection and recovery. These numbers may be exaggerated; a well-founded account could attribute at least $1.7 billion to fish restoration spending in the last 20 years.[17] Present costs include transportation of juvenile salmon around the dams, hatchery production, and the loss of revenue that comes when water is released over or around turbines to help fish. Released water does not generate electric power.

Despite this expense and effort, Snake River stocks have continued their precipitous decline.

This report seeks to answer the question: ***Would restoring the Lower Snake River to free-flowing conditions cost or save money?***

This question can be answered through an economic benefit analysis which accounts for all costs as well as all benefits.

Method of Analysis

Net economic benefit analysis is a method to account for different kinds of spending and receiving, and for putting the analysis in the context of the whole economy.

There are two kinds of net economic benefit: producer and consumer.

Producer benefit is the difference between the cost to create a good and its value to society. In an open market, value to society is reflected accurately by market price. If it costs 10 cents per pound to catch salmon that sells for a dollar a pound, then the producer benefit of that salmon is 90 cents per pound.

In a regulated market like electric power, price does not always reflect value to society. Producer benefit is then the difference between what producing a good costs and what it would cost to produce it somewhere else. If a power dam produces electricity for 2 cents per kilowatt hour (kWh) that could only be replaced by the economy through other means at 3 cents per kWh, then that dam is creating a 1 cent per kWh producer benefit.

Consumer benefit is similar, but it is based not on production costs but rather on people's willingness to pay for goods and services. If a consumer is willing to pay a dollar a pound for salmon but is only charged 75 cents, then that consumer's benefit is 25 cents. If a consumer would be willing to pay $150 to catch a salmon but only needs to spend $60 to do so, then the benefit of that salmon to the consumer is $90.

By comparing net benefits, which puts things in the context of the economy overall, we can tell if a given purchase makes sense or not when compared to other opportunities. Sometimes net benefit is a negative result. This is because of hidden costs, external costs or subsidies that allow the economy to pay more for a good than its value in an open market.

In this study, we analyze the net economic benefit provided by the dams at present. Then we compare that to the net economic benefit that would result from a restored river. The difference between the two is our answer: the savings that would result from restoring the Lower Snake River.

Our analysis is based on the best available data. There are two areas where key data are currently incomplete.

First, Columbia and Snake hydropower generation is constrained by fish recovery efforts at many locations in the system, not just on the Snake River. Up until recently this constraint (which BPA estimates to cost $164 million per year) was fully explained by BPA as a cost of attempting to recover Snake River salmon. Thus, it made sense to treat this entire amount as a cost of the Snake River dams. But recent BPA estimates charge the cost to both Snake and Columbia River fish. It is possible that recovery of the Snake River runs would only allow a partial removal of this power generation constraint.

Without a run-by-run estimate of hydropower costs, we cannot further refine our estimate of the proper amount to charge to the Snake River dams. We here ascribe the entire $164 million pending additional data. Even if this estimate is too high by as much as half ($82 million) our results will continue to show economic savings from Lower Snake River restoration.

Second, there has been no full analysis of the predicted economic value of a restored Snake River salmon fishery. Though these benefits may be large, available data from agencies does not allow a good estimate at this time.

We therefore have chosen to include no economic benefits of restored Snake River salmon fisheries and ecosystems in this analysis.

These two points drive our results in opposite directions -- the first possibly overstating and the second understating the economic benefits of restoring the Lower Snake River.

OUTLINE OF REPORT AND ANALYSIS

SECTION 1: Calculates the annual costs of running the Lower Snake dams and reservoirs. Then it calculates the annual costs of restoring and running a restored free-flowing Lower Snake River.

SECTION 2: Performs the bulk of the net benefit calculations and analysis. It calculates the net benefit that society now derives from the four dams via hydroelectric power generation, river transportation and irrigation. It then estimates the benefits to society after the bypass channels are cut and the river is restored to a free-flowing condition.

SECTION 3: Provides a brief summary and conclusion. The total net benefit of the Lower Snake dams and reservoirs is calculated, as is the total net benefit of a restored Lower Snake River. The difference shows the savings that would result from river restoration.

APPENDICES: Provides details and discussions on our analysis.

SECTION 1
Paying System Costs
Dams and Reservoirs or Restored River

system costs only

THIS SECTION CALCULATES:

- The annual system cost of running the Lower Snake dams and reservoirs;
- The annual system cost of restoring and running the natural river instead of the four dams and reservoirs.

KEY REPORT FINDINGS FOUND IN THIS SECTION:

- The Lower Snake dams and reservoirs require BPA to spend $194.4 million every year on salmon restoration.

OTHER FINDINGS IN THIS SECTION:

- The system cost to run the Lower Snake dams and reservoirs is $228 million each year.
- The system cost to run a restored, free-flowing Lower Snake River is $25.6 million each year.

This section looks at system costs: the cost of running four dams and reservoirs, and the cost of a natural river. These system costs are overall costs that are necessary to have the dams and reservoirs or a natural river in place and functioning. This section does not include the costs of providing particular benefits like electric power or transportation.

Running structures like dams requires on-going spending on operations and maintenance. There are side effects of maintaining dams and reservoirs that cause real costs as well. In the case of the Lower Snake dams, the damage these dams do to salmon result in enormous economic expenditures. These expenditures are costs that society pays to have these dams.

A natural river is a free gift of nature. In the case of the Lower Snake River, it will cost money to breach the dams and physically restore the river. However, once this cost has been paid, there will be no operations or maintenance costs.

Assume no costs after restoration of free flowing river.

Paying for Dams and Reservoirs

ANNUAL LOSS: -$228,000,000

Costs are shown as negative numbers.

salmon restoration is much > than operation costs!!!

PAYING SYSTEM COSTS DAMS AND RESERVOIRS	$ (MILLIONS)
Operations and maintenance	-$33.6
External costs:	
Salmon restoration spending	-$194.4
TOTAL	-$228.0

The four Lower Snake dams have already been built. The physical resources like steel, concrete and labor that were used to create them have already been allocated. These costs cannot be recovered and are called sunk costs. The Bonneville Power Administration (BPA) still owes money to the U.S. treasury for this capital investment. Whether the dams remain in use or the river is restored, BPA will continue to pay off these capital debts – about $62 million per year for both interest and depreciation. We leave sunk costs out of our society-wide benefits analysis because it does not make sense to include costs which the economy already has paid.

BPA Bonneville Power Administ.

exclude sunk costs

For our calculations of the system cost of the Lower Snake dams and reservoirs, we include operations and maintenance costs of the dams and reservoirs, and the tremendous external costs required to reduce the damage these dams and reservoirs have done to the Snake River salmon. We add these numbers to find the total system cost of the dams and reservoirs.

Details on the development of these numbers are provided in the Appendix for Section 1, Paying System Costs, pp. 26-29.

Operations and maintenance of dams and reservoirs

ANNUAL COSTS: -$33,600,000

Operations and maintenance costs for the four Lower Snake dams and reservoirs for 1995 were $33,621,884.[18] We use the 1995 cost as an approximation for annual costs.

Costs per dam and system-wide operations and maintenance costs are presented in a table in the Appendix for Section 1, pp. 26-27.

External costs:* salmon restoration

ANNUAL COSTS: -$194,400,000

BPA divides Columbia-Snake fish and wildlife costs into four broad categories:[19]

- Fish and Wildlife Direct Program Expenses,
- Fish and Wildlife Expenses of other agencies reimbursed by BPA,
- Capital Investments Fixed Expenses for Fish and Wildlife, and
- Power System Operations for Fish and Wildlife

In general, we have ascribed as external costs of the Lower Snake dams those costs that BPA identifies specifically as Snake River fish restoration costs or that BPA identified before 1997 as Endangered Species Act costs. We use Endangered Species Act costs because until 1997, only Snake River fish were listed under the Act. Included in Endangered Species Act costs are costs required of BPA under the 1994 National Marine Fisheries Service Biological Opinion on recovery of listed Snake River salmon species.[20]

other external costs are not calculated by this CBA: only salmon restoration costs. (excludes habitat lost wildlife lost river bottomland)

Thus we ascribe to the dams costs like fish bypass systems and water spill for fish passage that BPA has identified as Snake River fish restoration costs.†

[We find that BPA spends $194.4 million dollars each year attempting to make up for the damage done to threatened and endangered Snake River salmon.]

Details on these numbers and a full discussion of these allocations are in the Appendix for Section 1, Paying System Costs, pp. 27-29, External Costs: Salmon Restoration Costs.

BPA FISH & WILDLIFE BUDGET AND AMOUNTS SPENT BECAUSE OF LOWER SNAKE DAMS:

■ Direct program expenses	
Total	-$100,000,000
Lower Snake dam costs:	-$12,400,000
■ Expenses of other agencies reimbursed by BPA	
Total	-$39,700,000
Lower Snake dam costs:	-$6,300,000
■ Capital investments fixed expenses, 1996-2001, annualized at 3% over 50 years	
Total	-$26,000,000
Lower Snake dam costs:	-$11,700,000
■ Power system operations	
Total	-$164,000,000
Lower Snake dam costs:	-$164,000,000
TOTAL:	
TOTAL	-$329,700,000
LOWER SNAKE DAM COSTS:	-$194,400,000

* External costs are indirect costs that are caused by a project but are not paid for directly by the project. For example, dams commonly result in lost wildlife habitat and lost river bottomland, but dam cost calculations often underestimate the value of these destroyed lands and ecological services. The greatest cost related to the four Lower Snake dams but not included in project costs is the multi-million dollar expense of Snake River salmon restoration. Further details are included in the Appendix for Section 1, pp. 27-29.

† By far the largest portion of this amount, $164 million, is because of power system operations. We recognize that this number may be overstated as a cost of the Snake River dams. See discussion in the Appendix for Section 1, External costs: Power system, pp. 28-29.

Paying for a Restored River

ANNUAL LOSS: -$25,600,000

PAYING SYSTEM COSTS

RESTORED RIVER

	$ (MILLIONS)
River restoration capital costs, annualized at 3%	-$25.6
TOTAL	-$25.6

Retiring the dams and restoring free-flowing river conditions would save considerable amounts of money, but would also add the one-time new capital expense of breaching the earthen parts of the dams and modifying infrastructure like roads and bridges. Operations and maintenance would not be necessary for the restored self-sustaining natural system.* Similarly, external costs associated with combating the deleterious effects to fish of the four Lower Snake dams would disappear.

For details in these calculations see the Appendix for Section 1, Paying for a Restored River, p. 29.

River restoration capital costs

ANNUAL COST: -$25,600,000

To restore the Lower Snake River, the Army Corps of Engineers will need to drain the dam pools, remove the earthen portion of the dams, and re-engineer banks, roads and bridges around the newly freed river. Recent cost estimates range between $500 and $816 million.[21] We use the midpoint, $658 million, to estimate the cost.

To annualize these costs, or spread them out over a number of years like a capital debt or mortgage, we assume a 50-year payment period and three percent real interest. These are standard in analyses of dams.† This comes to $25,573,000 annually. We round to $25,600,000 per year.

Summary:

PAYING SYSTEM COSTS

DAMS AND RESERVOIRS VS. RESTORED RIVER

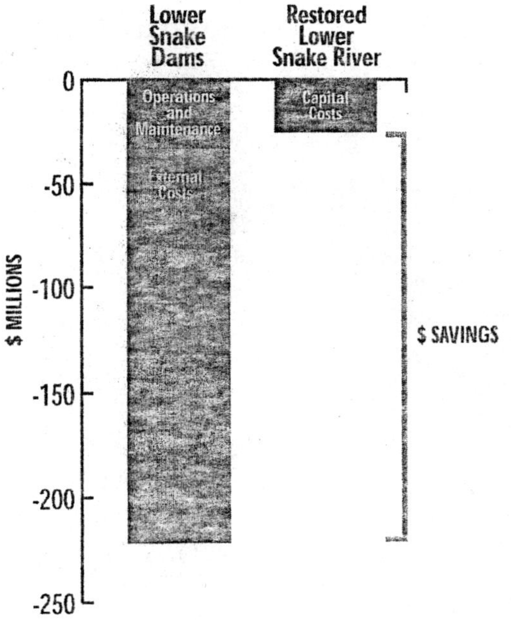

How long to restore the river and destroy dams?

* River restoration will restore a free gift of nature, leaving nothing to maintain. We recognize that the dam carcasses may become an attractive nuisance and require some security or maintenance to protect public safety. Some maintenance may be needed on river banks or new structures. We lack an Army Corps of Engineers estimate of these costs, however, and suspect they will be very low. For this reason we treat the cost of maintenance of a restored river as zero, with the caveat that the issue may need to be revisited and the cost estimate revised upward.

post restoration maintenance costs assumed to be zero. (not true).

† Real (as opposed to nominal) interest is corrected for inflation. Three percent may appear low, but it is close to the real long term interest rate on capital. Consider that three percent real interest plus three percent inflation would give nominal interest of six percent.

SECTION 2

Comparing Net Benefits
Dams and Reservoirs vs. Restored River

THIS SECTION CALCULATES:

- The portions of the Lower Snake dams and Lower Snake River system costs that can be attributed to electric power production, transportation, and irrigation.
- The net economic benefit that society now derives from the four Lower Snake dams and reservoirs via hydroelectric power generation, river transportation and irrigation.
- The net economic benefit to society of power generation, transportation and irrigation after the river is restored to a free-flowing condition.
- The change in economic benefit that will result from river restoration for power generation, transportation and irrigation.

SUBSECTIONS:

KEY REPORT FINDINGS ARE SHOWN IN SUBSECTIONS.

The Lower Snake dams and reservoirs currently produce economic benefit by generating electric power, providing a river transportation system, and helping a few farmers who irrigate their lands to reduce their water pumping costs. Restoring the Lower Snake River would end the production of electricity and the provision of river transportation in the Lower Snake. Also, farmers who now pump water from the high Ice Harbor pool would need to extend their pump intakes to the natural river level.

For our analysis it is easiest to look at each of these benefit areas in turn. For each, we calculate the net benefit with the Lower Snake dams and reservoirs in place and compare it to the net benefit with a restored Lower Snake River. The economic effect of river restoration will be shown by the change in net benefit for electric power generation, transportation and irrigation.

In other words, to judge the full economic effect of restoring the Lower Snake River we need to know:

WHICH IS GREATER:

BENEFIT OF DAMS & RESERVOIRS		BENEFIT OF RESTORED RIVER
■ Electric power net benefit with Lower Snake dams and reservoirs		■ Electric power net benefit with restored Lower Snake River
■ Transportation net benefit with Lower Snake dams and reservoirs	OR	■ Transportation net benefit with restored Lower Snake River
■ Irrigation net benefit with Lower Snake dams and reservoirs		■ Irrigation net benefit with restored Lower Snake River

To answer this question, we begin by allocating a portion of the Lower Snake dams and reservoirs system cost to each of the three main economic benefits of the dams: electric power generation, transportation, and irrigation. We allocate the same cost portions for the restored Lower Snake River system.

Then, we calculate, for electric power generation, river transportation and irrigation:

1) Annual net economic benefit provided by the four Lower Snake dams and reservoirs; and the

2) Annual net economic benefit provided by a restored Lower Snake River;

3) Change in annual economic benefit that will result from river restoration.

A summary table and graph in Section 3 (p. 25) summarizes the net benefit of both the current dam option and the proposed river option, and shows the net economic effect of river restoration.

Dividing Costs by Benefit Area

Here we calculate:

- The portions of the Lower Snake dams and reservoirs system cost that should be attributed to power production, transportation and irrigation;
- The portions of the restored Lower Snake River system cost that should be attributed to power production, transportation and irrigation.

Because the four Lower Snake dams and reservoirs are multi-purpose, providing economic benefit through electricity generation, transportation and irrigation, it is difficult to calculate the cost to provide each benefit. For example, turbine maintenance costs may be ascribed to electric power production, and lock operation to transportation. However, most of the general system costs we calculated in Section 1 are spent in order to provide all three services.

We adopt the allocation system of the original legislation that authorized the four Lower Snake dams. The U.S. Congress authorized the dams based on a 1930s Army Corps of Engineers (ACOE) report on the feasibility of the projects. The ACOE report allocated "cost-carrying abilities," here converted to percentages, of: Power 77.39%, Navigation 18.5%, Irrigation 4.11%.[22] The ACOE report was a full economic review of the dams as multi-purpose projects, and its reasoning and arguments allow for a clear distinction among the main economic benefit areas.

To find the portions of the system costs attributable to electric power generation, transportation and irrigation, we multiply the system costs found in Section 1 (pp. 12 and 14) by these percentages. Thus we find:

ACOE provided cost allocation percentages. This analysis adopts these to calculate individual costs for electric, transport, and irrigation. [77.39, 18.5, 4.11]

PORTIONS OF SYSTEM COSTS ELECTRIC POWER GENERATION, TRANSPORTATION AND IRRIGATION:

HYDROPOWER: 77.39%;
TRANSPORTATION: 18.50%;
IRRIGATION: .... 4.11%.

SYSTEM COST OF LOWER SNAKE DAMS AND RESERVOIRS:

	($MILLIONS)	
Electric power generation portion:	$176.4 million	228 × 0.7739
Transportation portion:	$42.2 million	228 × 0.1850
Irrigation portion:	$9.4 million	228 × 0.0411
TOTAL (p. 12):	$228 million	

SYSTEM COSTS OF RESTORED LOWER SNAKE RIVER:

	($MILLIONS)	
Electric power generation portion:	$19.8 million	25.6 × 0.7739
Transportation portion:	$4.7 million	25.6 × 0.1850
Irrigation portion:	$1.1 million	25.6 × 0.0411
TOTAL (p. 14):	$25.6 million	

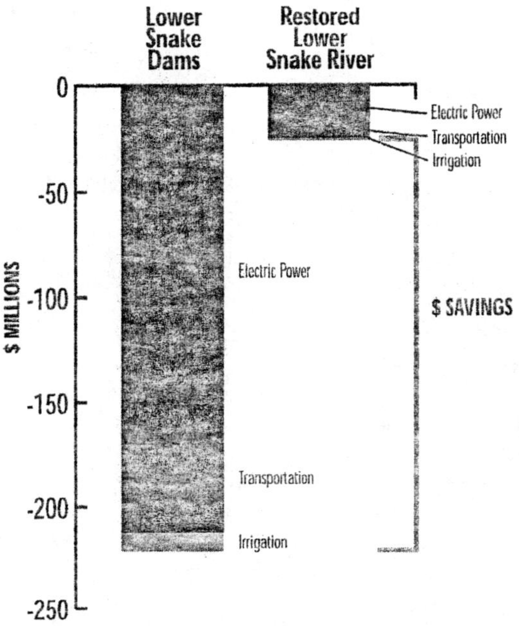

Electric Power Generation Dams And Reservoirs vs. Restored River

THIS SUBSECTION CALCULATES:

- The net economic benefit of power production with the Lower Snake dams and reservoirs.
- The net economic benefit of power production with a free-flowing restored Lower Snake River.
- The economic savings that would result for power production from restoration of the Lower Snake River.

KEY REPORT FINDING FOUND IN THIS SUBSECTION:

Electric power from the Lower Snake dams is not competitive. It costs 2.44 cents per kilowatt-hour. If we restore the Lower Snake River and purchase power elsewhere, we could provide energy for 1.87 cents per kilowatt-hour. These numbers are calculated in the Appendix for Section 2, p. 29, Costs of electric power on a per-kWh basis.

OTHER FINDINGS OF THIS SUBSECTION

- Producing power with the four Lower Snake dams produces an economic benefit *loss* of $60.8 million each year.
- Restoring the Lower Snake River and purchasing power elsewhere would produce a smaller economic benefit loss: only $19.8 million each year.
- Restoring the Lower Snake River and purchasing power elsewhere would save $41 million each year.

The net economic benefit of an energy producing resource is not the cost of the energy subtracted from the sales price of the energy sold, but rather the difference between the full cost of producing that energy and the full cost of replacing it from the next least cost source. To show a positive power benefit, a project must produce power at less than the next least cost source.

COST TO PRODUCE POWER	–	NEXT LEAST COST SOURCE	=	NET BENEFIT OF POWER PRODUCING RESOURCE

In this subsection we calculate first the net economic benefit to society of power production with the Lower Snake dams and reservoirs. Next, we calculate the net economic benefit to society of power production with a free-flowing restored Lower Snake River. In the summary table at the end, we find the difference to show the economic savings that would result for hydropower production from restoration of the Lower Snake River.

Net Economic Benefit with Dams and Reservoirs

ANNUAL LOSS: -$60,800,000

ELECTRIC POWER GENERATION:
NET ECONOMIC BENEFIT WITH DAMS AND RESERVOIRS

	$ (MILLIONS)
Cost to produce power:	
Electric power portion of dam system cost	-$176.4
Total cost to produce power:	**-$176.4**
Subtract next least cost source	
(subtract negative = add value)	+115.6
NET POWER BENEFIT WITH DAMS:	-$60.8

Cost to produce power

ANNUAL COST: -$176,400,000

The cost to produce power from the Lower Snake dams is the electric power generation portion of the Lower Snake dam system cost: $176.4 million.

* A next least cost source is an analytic tool, not an energy plan. Our use of the concept of replacement power to estimate the economic benefit of hydropower from the Lower Snake dams does not constitute an endorsement of any power resource mix, nor does it constitute a suggestion that the power will actually have to be replaced (which is not at all clear given the current power surplus). The use of the next least cost source is simply our best estimate of the cost at which power could be replaced by alternate sources as needed. It should also be noted that this is not a tally of ratepayer or BPA costs and receipts, which would be calculated by a different method and would produce a different result.

Subtract Next Least Cost Source

ANNUAL COST: +$115,600,000

With either the Lower Snake dams and reservoirs or with a restored Lower Snake River the next least cost source will be the same. As of this writing, the Pacific Northwest is enjoying an electric power surplus, and the cost of replacement firm power of the quality produced by the Lower Snake dams is now low, just 1.6 cents per kilowatt hour (kWh).[23] BPA's Pacific Northwest Loads and Resources Study says the four Lower Snake dams produce 7,227,000 megawatt hours, or 7,227,000,000 kilowatt hours, of power.*[24] To find the next least cost source, we multiply:

7,227,000,000 KILOWATT HOURS PRODUCED	X	-$0.016/KWH NEXT LEAST POWER COST	=	**-$115,600,000** TOTAL NEXT LEAST COST SOURCE

Since we subtract this negative number, we add its value to get the net benefit loss of power production with the Lower Snake dams.

Net Economic Benefit with Restored River

ANNUAL LOSS: -$19,800,000

ELECTRIC POWER GENERATION:
NET ECONOMIC BENEFIT WITH RESTORED RIVER

	$ (MILLIONS)
Cost to produce power:	
Electric power portion of the restored river system cost	-$19.8
Replacement power cost	-$115.6
Total cost to produce power:	-$135.4
Subtract next least cost source (subtract negative = add value)	+115.6
NET POWER BENEFIT WITH RESTORED RIVER:	-$19.8

Cost to Produce Power:

With a restored Lower Snake River, the cost to produce power is the electric power portion of the system cost, plus the cost of replacement power.

Electric power generation portion of restored river system cost

ANNUAL COST: -$19,800,000

As shown on p. 16, the electric power portion the restored Lower Snake River system cost is $19,800,000.

Replacement energy costs

ANNUAL COST: -$115,600,000

Unlike the current situation, we can obtain replacement power at a competitive rate. We replace it with power from the next least cost source.

Subtract next least cost source

ANNUAL COST: +$115,600,000

As when calculating current benefit with the Lower Snake dams, we finish by subtracting the next least cost source. Because we subtract a negative number, we add its value.

SUMMARY:
ELECTRIC POWER GENERATION DAMS AND RESERVOIRS VS. RESTORED RIVER

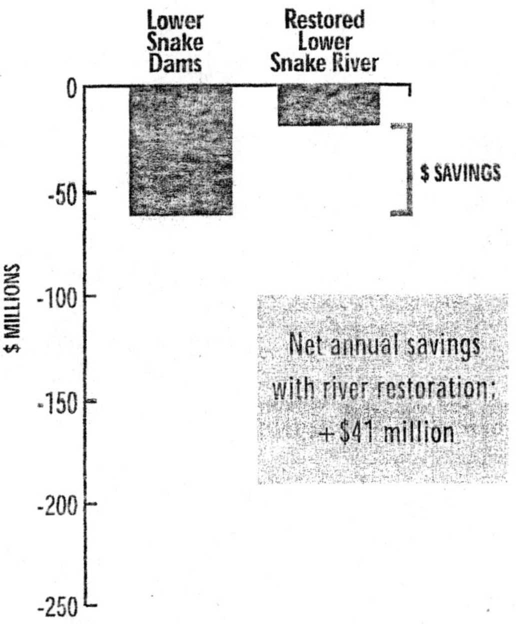

* In some recent years actual power production has been less than this. In 1994, for example, only 6.1 million megawatt hours were actually generated. We accept BPA's figure in this analysis.

Transportation
Dams And Reservoirs vs. Restored River

THIS SUBSECTION CALCULATES:

- The net economic benefit to society of transportation with the Lower Snake dams and reservoirs;
- The new transportation savings and costs that would result from a restored free-flowing river;
- The savings that would result for transportation from river restoration.

KEY REPORT FINDING FOUND IN THIS SUBSECTION:

River transportation on the Lower Snake is expensive and heavily subsidized. Although river shippers pay only $1.23 per ton from Lewiston, Idaho to Kennewick, Washington, taxpayers and electric ratepayers pay an additional $12.66. The total cost to ship one ton of goods on the Lower Snake is $13.89. In comparison, rail costs only $1.26.

Detailed calculations are in Appendix for Section 2, Comparing Net Benefits, p. 32, Costs of transportation on a per-ton basis.

OTHER FINDINGS OF THIS SUBSECTION:

- Providing transportation with the four Lower Snake dams and reservoirs produces an economic loss of $44.2 million each year.
- Taxpayers and electric ratepayers subsidize Lower Snake transportation with $44.3 million each year.
- Providing transportation with a restored Lower Snake River would save all transportation subsidies, and increase private costs by as little as $100,000 per year total.
- Restoring the Lower Snake River would result in a net economic gain of $39.4 million each year for transportation.

next least cost source of transport is rail.

As with electric power production, the net economic benefit of a resource that provides transportation is the difference between the full cost of providing that transportation and the full cost of the next least cost source.* To show a positive transportation benefit, a project must provide transportation at less than the next least cost source.

COST TO PROVIDE TRANS-PORTATION	–	NEXT LEAST COST SOURCE	=	**NET BENEFIT OF TRANS-PORTATION SYSTEM**

In this section we first calculate the current net economic benefit of transportation with the Lower Snake dams and reservoirs. We use the cost of shipping goods by rail from Lewiston, Idaho to Kennewick, Washington as the next least cost source. Like the cost of replacement energy, it is a surrogate for the economy's ability to provide a given service, even though it is highly unlikely that goods would follow a parallel rail route down the Columbia after the barge system is dismantled. They would more likely travel to a variety of alternate seaports and destinations by a variety of modes.

To estimate the net transportation benefit with a restored Lower Snake river, we first subtract from our present benefit the public costs of the dams and locks. Then we add the transportation portion of the restored river system cost. Finally, we add the increase in private costs that would result from a restored river. Private costs are estimated as the market price of comparative rail transport. $100,000

The difference between current benefit and benefit with the restored river shows the net gain that would result for transportation from restoring the Lower Snake River.

*As with power, a next least cost source here is an analytical tool, not a transportation plan. Our use of the concept of alternative transportation does not constitute an endorsement of any particular transportation alternative, nor does it constitute a suggestion that the transportation will all have to be replaced. In any case, new transportation could be acquired via free market choices, making it competitive and flexible.

Net Economic Benefit with Dams and Reservoirs

ANNUAL LOSS: -$44,200,000

TRANSPORTATION:

NET ECONOMIC BENEFIT WITH DAMS AND RESERVOIRS

	$ (MILLIONS)
Cost to provide transportation:	
Public subsidies and supports:	
Transportation portion of dams system cost	-$42.2
Electric power foregone to lock flush	-$0.8
Local property tax support	-$1.3
Private shipping costs	-$4.3
Total cost to provide transportation:	-$48.6
Subtract next least cost source (subtract negative = add value)	+4.4
NET TRANSPORTATION BENEFIT WITH DAMS:	-$44.2

Cost to provide transportation

Transportation is heavily subsidized by taxpayers and electric ratepayers.* Public subsidies and private costs are here shown separately.

Public Costs

Total annual public subsidies: $44,300,000

Transportation portion of dams system cost:

ANNUAL COST: -$42,200,000

As shown on page 16, the transportation portion of the Lower Snake dams system cost is ~~$45,700,000~~ $42,200,000.

Electric power foregone to lock flush

ANNUAL COST: -$800,000

When barges go through the locks at Ice Harbor, Lower Monumental, Little Goose and Lower Granite dams, water is flushed through the locks so the boats can go up or down river. This water is then lost from the reservoir and cannot be used for hydropower generation, and may be counted as a cost of river transportation.

During our study year, approximately 3100 commercial and 1400 recreational lock flushes diverted about 590,000 acre-feet away from power turbines at one of the four Lower Snake dams. Accounting for the different power potentials (power head) at each dam, this comes out to a loss of about 51 million kilowatt hours, or about $800,000.

Details of these calculations are in the Appendix for Section 2, Comparing Net Benefits, pp. 30-31, Electric power foregone to lock flush.

Local property tax support

ANNUAL COST: -$1,300,000

The ports serviced by the Lower Snake dams and reservoirs are supported by $1,293,022 in local property taxes paid by the general public. These are local taxpayer subsidies, not rents paid by port tenants.*

Are prop. taxes really a net economic loss? No

Details and a discussion of these taxes are in the Appendix for Section 2, Comparing Net Benefits, p. 32, Local property tax support.

Private costs

Private shipping costs

ANNUAL COST: -$4,300,000

According to the ACOE, 469,552,000 ton miles of goods were shipped on the Snake in 1994. Since the Snake navigation system is 135 miles long (from Lewiston, Idaho to Kennewick, Washington), there were 3,478,163 ton trips of goods shipped on the Snake in 1994. Shippers pay $1.23 per ton per trip. The total private shipping cost on the Snake navigation system is therefore $4,278,140.

Subtract next least cost source:

ANNUAL COST: +$4,400,00

The next least cost source of transportation may be estimated with the cost of shipping by rail,† about $1.26 per ton/trip[25] instead of $1.23 per ton/trip to ship by barge. With 3,478,163 ton trips of goods shipped, this would cost $4,382,485.

* Commercial navigators pay a tax on fuels to the federal Inland Waterways Trust Fund, but these funds have been used to pay only half the cost of a new lock at Bonneville dam. The rest of the system, including the entire Snake system, is entirely subsidized.

† It may be noted that while commercial rail was once heavily subsidized in this country, that is no longer the case. Land grants and other supports to commercial rail are long since sunk. So no cost other than the actual shipping rate is here ascribed to rail.

New Costs and Saving with Restored River:

ANNUAL LOSS: -$4,800,000

TRANSPORTATION:

NEW COSTS AND SAVINGS WITH RESTORED RIVER

	$ (MILLIONS)
New costs with restored river:	
Public subsidies:	NONE
Transportation portion of restored river system cost	-$4.7
Private shipping costs:	
Additional Shipping Fees	-$0.1
TOTAL NEW COSTS AND SAVINGS WITH RESTORED RIVER	-$4.8

variable maintenance costs are not included (although they are likely insignificant)

Restoration of the Lower Snake River would result in an end to all transportation subsidies. Only private shipping costs would remain, plus the cost to restore and run the free-flowing Lower Snake River.

Transportation share of restored river system cost:

ANNUAL COST: -$4,700,000

As shown on page 16, the transportation portion of the restored river system cost will be $4,700,000.

Replacement Transportation Costs:

ANNUAL COSTS: -$100,000

Restoring the Lower Snake River would end commercial navigation on the river. Shippers would have to pay for alternate transportation. However, they could use economically competitive sources, represented here by the next least cost source of $1.26 per ton. Since the current subsidized rate is $1.23 per ton, per ton costs would increase 3 cents. To ship 3.5 million tons the length of the Snake River navigation channel, shippers would pay an additional $100,000.

shippers pay an additional $100,000 for alt. transport.

SUMMARY:

TRANSPORTATION DAMS AND RESERVOIRS VS. RESTORED RIVER

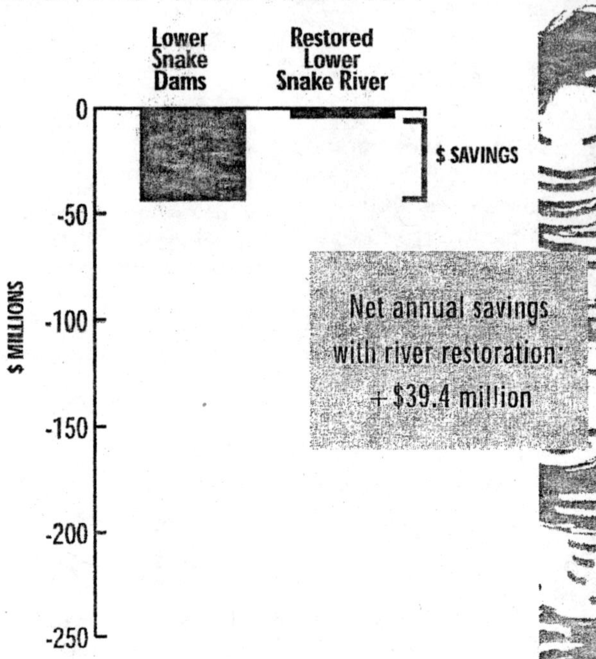

Is railroad transport subsidized? If so, the $1.26 per ton may not be an accurate representation of the 'least cost alternative'.

Irrigated Farming
Dams And Reservoirs vs. Restored River

THIS SUBSECTION CALCULATES:

- The net economic benefit to society of irrigated farming using water from Lower Snake reservoirs.
- The net economic benefit to society with a restored Lower Snake River, where the irrigated farmland has been purchased and farming ended.
- The change in economic benefit of that would result from river restoration.

KEY REPORT FINDING FOUND IN THIS SUBSECTION:

Thirteen agribusinesses pump water from the Ice Harbor reservoir. Together, these farms earn a net $1.9 million per year. But taxpayers and electric ratepayers subsidize these farms with $11.2 million. If the farms paid their full costs, they would lose $9.3 million every year. It would be cheaper to buy these farms outright and end their production altogether.

OTHER FINDINGS OF THIS SUBSECTION:

The annual savings that would result if the Lower Snake River were restored and the irrigated farmlands retired is $6.2 million.

The four Lower Snake dams do not store water for irrigation and are not considered irrigation dams. However, thirteen large irrigators* do take water from the system, all from the Ice Harbor pool, to irrigate about 35,000 acres.[26] The key benefit the dam provides is raising the water level and thus reducing the height these irrigators must lift the water to get it to their fields and orchards.

To find the actual economic net benefit of irrigating these 35,000 acres we find first the private benefit they produce, a small net return to farmers from crop sales after their private costs are spent. Then we find the public cost of support subsidies from ratepayers and taxpayers.

Ratepayers pay for Ice Harbor pool irrigated farming by paying to run the Lower Snake dams and reservoirs, subsidizing electricity for irrigation pumping, and foregoing power revenue because of water lost to irrigation. Taxpayers pay for irrigated farming through crop subsidies and other supports. Subtracting costs from benefit gives the economic net benefit of irrigated farming.†

We can then find the irrigation net benefit with a restored Lower Snake River. Because these irrigated lands are so heavily subsidized, we estimate the new benefit based on purchasing the irrigated lands outright** and ending irrigation. The net benefit of a restored Lower Snake River is calculated by adding the irrigation share of the restored river system cost to the cost of purchasing the land.

The change in net benefit that would come through river restoration is then the difference between these two net benefits. This is shown in a summary table at the end of this subsection.

Poor assumption that farms will be retired!

* These are listed in the Appendix for Section 2, p. 33, Irrigation beneficiaries.

† The Army Corps of Engineers calculates the net benefit of irrigated farming differently. A description of their method and a critique are provided in the Appendix for Section 2, pp. 33-34.

** Our consideration of a farmland buy-out is not a developed policy suggestion. The other alternative for these lands after Snake river restoration would be to provide longer pump in-takes that could reach the water at the natural river level. A low estimate of the cost of extending intakes is $3,236,979 (Army Corps of Engineers, 1991, Investigation of Pumping Facilities, Lower Snake River, 4-14, Table 40-4). We have no data on estimates for how much water consumption or crop prices might change with more expensive in-takes.

Net Economic Benefit with Dams and Reservoirs:

ANNUAL LOSS: -$9,300,000

IRRIGATION

NET ECONOMIC BENEFIT WITH DAMS AND RESERVOIRS

	$ (MILLIONS)
Net returns to farmers	+$1.9
Public costs:	
Irrigation portion of dam system cost	-$9.4
Subsidized electricity for irrigation pumping	-$0.5
Electric power foregone	-$0.5
Taxpayer crop support	-$0.8
IRRIGATION NET BENEFIT WITH DAMS:	-$9.3

Irrigated farming benefit comes from crop sales. Costs come from farmers' production costs and public subsidies or supports. Farmers' production costs are included in the calculation of net return to farmers. All the other listed costs are subsidies.

Net returns to farmers

ANNUAL BENEFIT: +$1,900,000

The agribusinesses irrigated by Lower Snake water create economic benefit by producing crops. The value of crop sales minus farmers' production costs is the net return to farmers.

Net cash return to farming in Washington State is estimated on a countywide basis by the Washington Agricultural Statistics Service. The average net return in the counties adjacent to Ice Harbor pool was $53.93 per acre[27]. Since there are about 35,000 acres irrigated by Ice Harbor pool water, the total net cash return to these acres is approximately $1,900,000.

Public costs:

Total annual public subsidies: -$12,000,000

Irrigation portion of dam system cost:

ANNUAL COST: -$10,200,000

As shown on p. 16, the irrigation portion of the annual costs of running the Lower Snake dam and reservoir system is $10,200,000.

Subsidized electricity for irrigation pumping

ANNUAL COST: -$500,000

Irrigators are given reduced rates for electricity in order to pump water cheaply from the Ice Harbor reservoir to their farmland. This requires other electricity ratepayers to cover the difference. Ratepayers thus provide about $500,000 in subsidies to Ice Harbor irrigators.

A list of the irrigators, their energy use and the estimated subsidies they receive for pumping is provided in the Appendix for Section 2, p. 33, Subsidized electricity for irrigation pumping.

Electric power foregone:

ANNUAL COST: -$500,000

About 101,600 acre feet are lost to the Ice Harbor turbines and 81,300 acre feet to all downstream dams. The total power foregone is about 22 million kWh and, using the replacement power cost of 1.6 cents per kWh, is worth about $500,000.

Details of these calculations are provided in the Appendix for Section 2, p. 34, Electric power foregone to irrigation.

Taxpayer crop support

ANNUAL COST: -$800,000

U.S. taxpayers subsidize production of many agricultural commodities. Assuming 20 percent of the 35,000 acres irrigated with water from Ice Harbor Reservoir is dedicated to subsidized crops, and estimating crop ratios and yields from regional data, we estimated a taxpayer subsidy to these 13 agribusinesses of $830,323.[28]

Details of these calculations are provided in the Appendix for Section 2, p. 35, Taxpayer crop supports.

Net Economic Benefit with River Restoration:

ANNUAL LOSS: -$3,100,000

IRRIGATION COSTS

NET ECONOMIC BENEFIT WITH RESTORED LOWER SNAKE RIVER

	$ (MILLIONS)
Irrigation portion of restored river system cost	-$1.1
Purchase of irrigated land	-$2.0
IRRIGATION NET BENEFIT WITH RESTORED RIVER:	**-$3.1**

Irrigation portion of restored river costs:

ANNUAL COST: -$1,100,000

As shown on p.16, the irrigation portion of the restored Lower Snake River system cost will be $1,100,000.

Purchase of irrigated land

ANNUAL COST: -$2,000,000

If irrigators are bought out at an estimated $1,500 per acre, all 34,924 acres can be bought for approximately $52,400,000. At 3 percent real interest for a 50 year payment period, this would cost about $2,000,000 per year.

SUMMARY:

IRRIGATION: DAMS AND RESERVOIRS VS. RESTORED RIVER

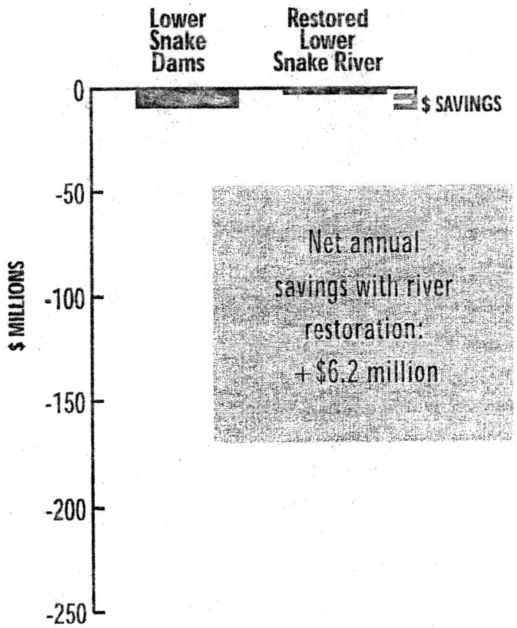

No use of uncertainty testing in calculating costs of buying out all of farmland:

~~$52,400,000~~

$$\$52.4 = A\left[\frac{1-(1.03)^{-50}}{0.03}\right]$$

$$A = \$2.04$$

- Authors should give a range of annual costs by doing sensitivity analysis or using a model for σ uncertainty.

- If r is uncertain and/or ~~higher~~ > 0.03 the Annuity costs will be greater. If n < 50 the Annuity costs will also be greater.

SECTION 3
Summary and Conclusion

THIS SECTION CALCULATES:

- The total net benefit of using the Lower Snake dams and reservoirs to provide electric power, transportation and irrigation.
- The total net benefit that would result from providing power, transportation and irrigation and a restored Lower Snake River.
- The annual savings that would result from restoring the Lower Snake River.

KEY REPORT FINDING FOUND IN THIS SECTION

Taxpayers and electric ratepayers subsidize electric power production, river transportation and irrigation from the Lower Snake dams and reservoirs. With all costs accounted, these three Lower Snake dam benefits actually produce a net benefit loss to the economy of $114 million every year. Restoring the Lower Snake River stands not only to reduce our current losses but, with the value of restored fisheries, create substantial net economic gains.

REPORT CONCLUSION:

Restoring the Lower Snake River would produce an economic benefit of $87 million each year. This includes the costs of replacing Snake River hydropower, ending the barge transportation system, and buying out the thirteen farms that use Lower Snake water for irrigation.

The Lower Snake dams have not been a good investment. They may appear profitable, because they generate hydropower at costs that seem low and because hydropower benefits have tended to obscure the dams' lackluster performance in creating real irrigation and navigation benefits. However, when a proper accounting is performed on the four dams, including the costs of attempting to retain and restore salmon, even their hydropower is no longer competitively priced. The dams actually operate at a substantial economic loss when all costs are reckoned.

It would be expensive to end the economic and ecological damage caused by the four Lower Snake dams and reservoirs. Current capital investment is irretrievably sunk and would be stranded. New capital would have to be invested. Power and transportation now produced by the dams and reservoirs might have to be replaced.

Retaining the dams is more expensive still. The external costs are so high that even with the cost of replacement power included, the economy benefits from river restoration.

The following table summarizes the results found in Section 2 on the net economic benefit of electric power generation, transportation and irrigation, first with the Lower Snake dams and reservoirs in place and then with a restored Lower Snake River.

TOTAL ANNUAL COSTS

LOWER SNAKE DAMS	$ (MILLIONS)
Net Power Benefit:	-$60.8
Net Transportation Benefit:	-$44.2
Net Irrigation Benefit	-$9.3
TOTAL BENEFIT LOSS WITH DAMS	-$114.3

RESTORED LOWER SNAKE RIVER	$ (MILLIONS)
Net Power Benefit	-$19.8
Net Transportation Benefit	-$4.8
Net Irrigation Benefit:	-$3.1
TOTAL BENEFIT LOSS WITH RIVER	- $27.7
TOTAL ECONOMIC GAIN	**$86.6**

SUMMARY:

ELECTRIC POWER, TRANSPORTATION AND IRRIGATED FARMING DAMS AND RESERVOIRS VS. RESTORED RIVER

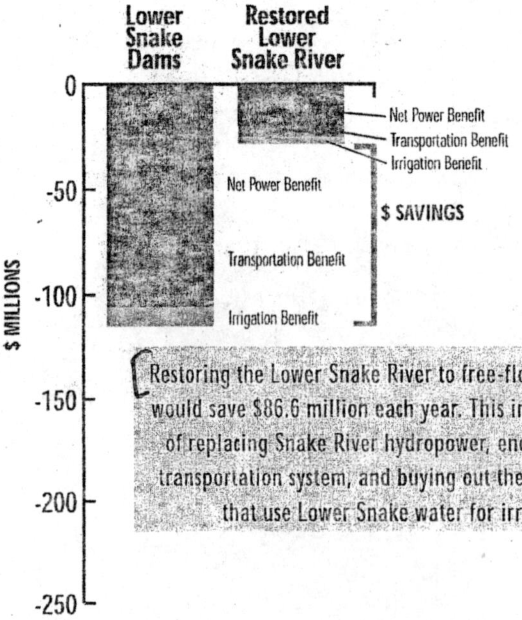

Restoring the Lower Snake River to free-flowing conditions would save $86.6 million each year. This includes the costs of replacing Snake River hydropower, ending the barge transportation system, and buying out the thirteen farms that use Lower Snake water for irrigation.

Benefit Analysis Versus Impacts

It is important to differentiate between economic benefit and economic impact. They are not the same thing. Benefit has to do with value and returns to wealth. Impact has to do with the geographic allocation of wealth. Consider that a subsidized industry may have a negative benefit to the economy as a whole and at the same time have a positive impact in a local geographic area. In this paper we are concerned with benefit, not local geographic impacts unless specifically noted. We are concerned with overall economic impacts in the broader sense, however, in that positive economic benefits tend to have the impact of creating wealth and jobs and negative economic benefits tend to reduce wealth and jobs.

Understating Our Case

There are at least two reasons to believe that our conclusion of an $87 million gain from river restoration is understated.

First, we have not documented all the costs of retaining the Lower Snake dams, nor have we projected how those current costs might increase in the future. For example, we have not discussed limits in the Upper Snake River basin on recreational activities such as float boating, camping and fishing for non-anadramous species caused by the decline in salmon stocks. Nor have we discussed the impacts of possible additional flow augmentation on the Snake. At present under half a million acre feet of Snake River water is allocated to salmon flows. This has not constrained irrigated agriculture on the Snake River plain. But if the dams remain in place, an additional three million acre feet or more of upper Snake River water could be used. This is an undocumented, and potentially uncontrollable expense would be unnecessary with restoration of a free-flowing Lower Snake River.

Second, we have not addressed the economic benefits of restored fisheries, both commercial and recreational. We lack data on the numbers of increased harvestable fish after restoration in the ocean, the Columbia, the Lower Snake and the Upper Snake. We lack data on the present constraints on mixed stock ocean fisheries caused by the decline of Snake River stocks. Even given estimates of fish harvest increases, we lack comprehensive data on the recreational and existence values of the increased harvests. A recent impact analysis of salmon harvest in Idaho estimates that a restored Idaho salmon fishery would produce $60 million in economic activity and 1,000 new jobs.[29] A report by the Sport Fishing Institute values the benefit of recreational fishing for salmon in Washington and Oregon at over $50 per day.[30]

We do not here speculate on even the range of values of restored Snake River stocks, but it appears those values will be of the order of magnitude of the power production of the dams.

Data Sources and Years

This analysis makes use of a wide variety of data from disparate sources. Some of this data is available every year from public sources, such as agency budget reports. But a great deal of information used here is from the System Configuration Study (SCS), performed by the Army Corps of Engineers in 1992, and from the Systems Operations Review (SOR), completed by the Bonneville Power Administration and other agencies in 1995. In some cases values and estimates developed in the SCS and SOR could not be brought forward to today without a significant loss of accuracy. So 1992-1994 data is used throughout this analysis for the sake of consistency, unless otherwise noted. The authors look forward to obtaining updated figures in 1998 and 1999 as the ongoing studies by the ACOE and other agencies progress.

APPENDIX TO SECTION 1: Paying System Costs (pp. 12-14)

In this Appendix section, we detail the sources and calculations used to develop the system costs of the Lower Snake dams and reservoirs and of a restored Lower Snake River. We also detail how we allocated external costs to the Lower Snake dams and reservoirs.

Paying for Dams & Reservoirs

As explained in the main text, benefits analyses do not include sunk costs. We therefore include only on-going and future operations and maintenance costs of the Lower Snake dams and reservoirs, plus the external costs of Snake River salmon restoration spending. These are the costs that will disappear if the river is restored.

Operations and maintenance of the dams & reservoirs

The table below shows the operations and maintenance (O & M) costs of the Lower Snake dams and reservoirs as provided by BPA. The first column, labeled Lower Snake, refers to costs that are not specific to any single dam. Total O & M of $33,600,000 is in the right hand column of the table.

Operations and maintenance Costs of the dams and reservoirs

1995	LOWER SNAKE	ICE HARBOR	LITTLE GOOSE	L. GRANITE	L. MONUMENTAL	TOTAL
Operations	$12,070,540	$1,478,206	$1,362,009	$2,516,632	$902,362	$18,329,749
Maintenance	$635,292	$2,829,873	$2,852,700	$3,780,669	$5,193,601	$15,292,135
Total	$12,705,832	$4,308,079	$4,214,709	$6,297,301	$6,095,963	$33,621,884

Sources: BPA spreadsheets, provided at a public meeting in Boise, Idaho, 22 Feb. 1996.

External costs: Salmon restoration costs

We show here what is meant by 'external costs' in analysis of dams and present an estimate of external costs of the Lower Snake dams. These include money spent on present efforts to recover and restore Snake River salmon.

Defining external costs of the Lower Snake dams & reservoirs

External costs are indirect costs which must be assigned to a project because the presence of the project is what causes society to incur them. Snake River salmon costs which are caused by the presence of the Lower Snake dams and reservoirs should be ascribed as external costs of the Snake River dams. The costs incurred by the Federal Columbia Power System cooperating agencies and by the general economy of attempting to restore those salmon runs are causally linked to the dams, not to the salmon, and not to the Federal Columbia River Power System as a whole, as is a common agency practice.[31] Further, it makes no sense to ascribe salmon restoration costs to laws like the Endangered Species Act or to the Northwest Power Act which express society's desire to restore the salmon; this ignores physical causality and is less than a precise approach.

BPA fish and wildlife budget amounts spent because of Lower Snake dams

The Bonneville Power Administration divides its fish and wildlife costs into 1) Direct BPA fish program expenses, 2) Other agencies' programs that are reimbursed by BPA, 3) Capital investments and 4) Power system costs. We detail these here and identify which portions of these costs are external costs of the Lower Snake dams and not the power system as a whole.

1) DIRECT BPA FISH PROGRAM EXTERNAL COSTS, 1996-2001 AVERAGE

	BPA TOTAL	ASCRIBED IN THIS ANALYSIS
Direct F&W Program	$66,000,000	$12,400,000
New Activities	$30,000,000	$0
BPA Program Overhead	$4,000,000	$0
Total	$100,000,000	$12,400,000

Sources: BPA :Fishcost.xls, 12/11/95, & BPA Table SB31D, 4/13/95, & calculated as described.

The adjacent table summarizes BPA's projected annual average direct Fish and Wildlife Program Expenses for the years 1996 through 2001. We ascribe $12,400,000 of these costs to the four dams because, according to BPA, this amount was spent in 1994 on Endangered Species Act activities. At that time only Snake River salmon were listed under the ESA, so ESA spending was by definition dedicated to Snake River salmon. Our key point here is that with restoration, the salmon could be taken off the Endangered Species List and the need for this spending would disappear.

2) COLUMBIA POWER SYSTEM FISH & WILDLIFE PROGRAM SPENDING, AGENCIES OTHER THAN BPA

	BPA TOTALS	ASCRIBED IN THIS ANALYSIS
USFWS: Lower Snake Hatcheries	$13,600,000	$0
ACOE O&M:		
Hatcheries	$4,200,000	$0
Passage	$8,200,000	$4,100,000
Research	$2,000,000	$0
Hauling	$2,200,000	$2,200,000
Wildlife	$1,600,000	$0
Other	$2,600,000	$0
Bureau of Reclamation:		
Leavenworth Hatchery	$1,200,000	$0
Northwest Power Planning Council:		
Fish & Wildlife budget	$4,100,000	$0
Total	$39,700,000	$6,300,000

Source: BPA: Fishcost.xls, 12/11/95, & calculated as described

The adjacent table, fish and wildlife program spending by other agencies associated with the Federal Columbia River Power System are summarized. The right hand column shows amounts we ascribe to Snake River Salmon. We ascribe one half of passage costs to the four Snake River dams because there are a total of eight dams on the Snake and Columbia Rivers with passage problems, four on the Snake and four on the Columbia. Restoring the Lower Snake River would remove the need for passage facilities on the Snake River dams only. We ascribe all of costs of hauling juvenile salmon, as dam circumvention would obviate the rationale for all juvenile salmon hauling. We believe our approach is conservative and that costs caused by the Lower Snake dams and reservoirs (and savings caused by river restoration) are here understated.*

* We have two concerns with the validity of the estimates presented in this table. First, we may have erred by not ascribing the Lower Snake hatcheries as externals to the dams. It is our assumption that, unlike other major costs we ascribe, hatcheries would be phased out over time. So they are included in this short range analysis. Second, since some upper Columbia River fish are barged we may have ascribed too large a portion of the Passage and Hauling to the Snake dams. We look forward to additional agency data on this topic.

3) EXTERNAL COSTS: CAPITAL INVESTMENTS CAPITAL INVESTMENT IN SNAKE RIVER SALMON, ANNUAL AVERAGE 1996 - 2001

	1996-2001	ASCRIBED IN THIS ANALYSIS
Ice Harbor Juvenile Salmon Bypass	$17,800,000	$17,800,000
Little Goose Salmon Screens	$17,900,000	$17,900,000
Lower Granite Salmon Screens	$23,800,000	$23,800,000
Gas/Turbine Juvenile Survival Study	$76,800,000	$76,800,000
Natural River Design	$30,700,000	$30,700,000
Surface Bypass Salmon Collector	$102,400,000	$102,400,000
Lower Granite Juvenile Salmon Facility	$20,500,000	$20,500,000
Additional Salmon Barges	$11,200,000	$11,200,000
Non-Snake River costs	$367,900,000	$0
Capital TOTAL	$669,000,000	$301,100,000
Annualized at 3% 50 Years	$26,001,015	$11,702,400

Source: BPA :Fishcost.xls, Reference Table 3. 12/11/95, & calculated as described.

In Table 3 projected cooperating agency capital investment 1996-2001, which we ascribe to the Snake River dams, is detailed. $367,000,000 in new capital investment is not ascribed and is shown in the Table as Other. The annualized cost of this new capital is projected using a 3 percent interest rate. The basic expense figures are average projections provided by BPA and projected payments are not discounted. So early year spending may be overstated and late year spending understated. The listed expenditures have to do with getting salmon past the Snake River dams. They are by definition external costs of those dams.

4) EXTERNAL COSTS: POWER SYSTEM

The listing of Snake River salmon under the Endangered Species Act and decisions of the National Marine Fisheries Service under the Act have caused the ACOE and BPA to modify operations on the Snake River, and on the mainstream of the Columbia. There are two main kinds of modification. First, the timing of water releases has been changed to provide higher flows for juvenile salmon during their downstream migration. Second, some water is spilled over dams instead of through electric turbines, in an effort to decrease salmon mortality at the dams.

These modifications are a major, and very expensive, constraint upon the generating capability of the Columbia River system as a whole. As BPA itself explains in a March, 1998 white paper, when electric power cannot be generated, "BPA has to increase its prices or cut its costs to continue to make ends meet. The lost revenue phenomenon has exactly the same impact on BPA as an increase in direct fish and wildlife measure costs."[32]

A key problem is timing; the young salmon need water flows during months when energy demand in the region is low, so even when flows are run through generating turbines rather than spilled the power produced has a low value or even no value. In high power demand months the water is no longer available.

The greatest cost of the power system constraint is not on the Snake River portions of the system but on the Columbia. Columbia flows are increased to help Snake River salmon over the lower four Columbia River dams: John Day, McNary, The Dalles and Bonneville. These are run-of-the-river dams without significant water storage. Water for increased Columbia flows comes from storage dams on the upper end of the system above Grand Coulee dam. Hydropower generation is limited by both volume of water and by power head – the amount of drop in the system. So changes is storage schedules and power operations at the upper end of the Columbia are felt all the way to the ocean and are far more costly than changes affecting only the lower end of the river.

Most recent (March 1998) BPA estimates are that the average annual cost of the power system constraints dedicated to fish is $164 million per year.[33]

Given that this spending grew out of decisions led by Endangered Species Act listings of Snake River salmon, it is reasonable to assume that this spending could stop with the restoration of these runs. However, there are three reasons why, given restoration as described and de-listing of Snake River salmon, the full $164 million cost may not be removed.

First, the estimate of loss may be too high. In 1995 BPA estimated the average annual cost of the power system operations for fish at $183 million.34 Future work by BPA, the Northwest Power Planning Council or other economists may result in additional reductions of this number.

Second, while breaching the Lower Snake dams would plainly remove the need to provide Snake River fish with flow augmentation or power constraints on the Snake River, some Columbia River flows might be needed to help them through the Columbia dams. The historic record suggests this may not be necessary, but it is possible.

Third, even with the recovery of the Snake River stocks, some or all of the present Columbia flows and power system constraints may be needed to help Columbia River salmon, several stocks of which are in serious decline. The costs of these constraints would be external costs of the Columbia dams, not the Lower Snake dams, and would remain even with restoration of a free-flowing Lower Snake River.

If less than the entire $164 million constraint is removed by Lower Snake River restoration, our estimates of external costs would have to be revised downward. For example, if none of it were removed, then our final benefit estimate would change from an $87 million gain to a $77 million loss. If half, $82 million, were removed, our final result would show restoring the river producing a $5 million instead of an $87 million gain.

Since the results of this analysis, or any economic analysis of the Lower Snake dams, turns on this point, it would be very useful to Northwest citizens and policymakers for BPA and/or the Power Council to disaggregate their power system modelling results so that power system constraints could be ascribed to particular power projects and fish stocks rather than generalized to the entire system. It is axiomatic in modelling that one models at the simplest level that yields useful results. Columbia River power system-wide results are adequate for analyses of the whole system. When we begin to look at removing or modifying individual dams, as the region is now doing, we need project- and stock-level analyses which BPA so far has not produced. We look forward to, and urge, further analyses by the agencies which can provide this information.

With this caveat, annual salmon preservation and restoration costs which should properly be ascribed to the Lower Snake dams, are projected at $194,400,000 annually over the next five years. Because lost economic values due to constraints on other watershed resource users are not included in this projection, and because of the conservative estimates noted above, this figure may be low. See discussion in the Appendix: Understating Out Case, p. 26.

Paying for a Restored River

River restoration is now being studied in detail by the Army Corps of Engineers. The basic steps will involve draining the dam pools through the spillways and turbine passageways, then removing the earthen portions of the dams that stand next to the concrete structures. In addition, some ancillary work will need to be completed such as bank stabilization and modification of bridge piers. In 1995 an ACOE representative estimated the cost of the project at around $600,000,000[35]. More recently, a preliminary summary of costs prepared by the ACOE puts the amount in a range of $500,000,000 to $816,000,000[36]. The midpoint of this range is $658,000,000. This is the amount we use for an estimate of breaching costs in this analysis.

The next step is to annualize this capital cost, so that it can be presented in the context of the other costs and benefits in this analysis. Annualizing means spreading the cost out over a number of years, like a capital debt or mortgage. Plainly the number of years and the interest rate used are significant in this process. We use fifty years and three percent real interest* because these are standard in analysis of dams. $658,000,000 paid over fifty years at 3 percent interest amounts to $25,573,000 annually. This is our estimate of the annual capital cost of restoring the Lower Snake River.

APPENDIX TO SECTION 2: Comparing Net Benefits

Electric Power Generation (pp. 17-18)

In this appendix section, we provide additional information on per-kWh costs to provide electric power.

KEY REPORT FINDING:

Electric power from the Lower Snake dams is not competitive. It costs 2.44 cents per kilowatt-hour. If we restore the Lower Snake River and purchase power elsewhere, we could provide energy for 1.87 cents per kilowatt-hour.

Costs of electric power on a per-kWh basis:

Since we know that the four Lower Snake dams produce 7,227,000 megawatt hours (mWh) or 7,227,000,000 kilowatt hours (kWh) of electricity per year,[37] we calculate from the cost of producing power (Section 2, p. 17) what the cost per kilowatt is when it is provided by the Lower Snake dams and and what it would be with a restored river.

With the Lower Snake dams, the cost to produce power is electric power generation's share of the dam-reservoir system cost, $176,400,000.

With a restored river, the cost to produce power is electric power generation's share of the restored river system cost, plus the alternative cost of replacement power. From Section 2, p. 18, this comes to $135,400,000.

We divide: $\frac{\text{Total power costs}}{7{,}227{,}000{,}000 \text{ kWh}} = \$ \text{ per kWh}$

It can be seen that the per-kWh power cost with the restored river more closely approaches the next least cost source. This is another way to explain the improved net economic benefit that would result from restoring the river.

PER KWH POWER COSTS FOR THE LOWER SNAKE DAMS

	COST OF 7,227,000,000 KILOWATT HOURS	COST PER KWH
Power costs with LS dams	$176,400,000	2.44 cents
Power costs with restored LS River	$135,400,000	1.87 cents
Next least cost source power	$115,600,000	1.6 cents

* Real (as opposed to nominal) interest is corrected for inflation. Three percent may appear low, but it is close to the real long term interest rate on capital. Consider that 3 percent real interest plus 3 percent inflation would give nominal interest of 6 percent.

Transportation (pp. 19-21)

In this appendix section, additional information is provided on electric power foregone to lock flush and on local property tax supports for Lower Snake ports.

KEY REPORT RESULT:

River transportation on the Lower Snake is expensive and heavily subsidized. Although river shippers pay only $1.23 per ton from Lewiston, Idaho to Kennewick, Washington, taxpayers and electric ratepayers pay an additional $12.66. The total cost to ship one ton of goods on the Lower Snake is $13.89. In comparison, rail costs only $1.26.

Electric power foregone to lock flush

When water is used to flush or cycle locks on the Columbia and Snake Rivers, the opportunity to use that water to generate electric power is lost.

Foregone power per lock flush

The method for calculating this loss at any given lock is straightforward:

Acre/feet of water diverted x Power head x 0.87 = loss in kWh

For example, given a typical system lock with a volume of 133 acre feet and a power head of 100 feet, the calculation is: 133 x 100 x 0.87 = 11,571 kWh. So the opportunity cost in electric power of operating this lock is 11,571 kWh per flush. This formula is applied in the table below to establish loss in kWh per lock flush for the four Lower Snake River dams.

Foregone hydropower per lock flush at each dam, in kWh

DAM	ACRE/FEET	POWER HEAD	K FACTOR	LOSS/FLUSH
Lower Granite	130.6	98	0.87	11135
Ice Harbor	130.6	98	0.87	11135
Little Goose	130.6	98	0.87	11135
Lower Monumental	133.3	100	0.87	11594

Source: Report of the Secretary of the Army on Civil Works Activities, Walla Walla District, Army Corps of Engineers 1993 & calculated as described.

Total number of lock flushes with lost water

Operating a lock does not always entail losing water. Some lock operations do not require flushing water, and some water would be lost during high flows whether or not the locks were in operation. Taking these into consideration, we calculate for commercial and recreational lock flushes the amount of water lost to power generation.

LOCK OPERATIONS THAT REQUIRE FLUSHING

If the lock is empty and a vessel arrives from downstream then the lock will be filled in operating, not flushed. In such a case the next vessel through in either direction will account for flushing the lock. There are four possible permutations of the relative positions of barges and locks. In three of these, operating the lock involves a flush. So three-fourths of lock operations are counted as lock flushes in developing this estimate.

LOCK/VESSEL CONDITION MATRIX

INITIAL LOCK CONDITION	INITIAL SHIP CONDITION	FLUSH CAUSED
Full	Upriver	Yes
Full	Downriver	Yes
Empty	Upriver	Yes
Empty	Downriver	No

SPRING SPILL

When water is spilled over the dams during spring high water, there is no foregone power generation ascribable to lock flush. So lock flushes during the high-water month of May are not included in our estimate.

Power foregone to lock flush: calculations

Fiscal 1994 monthly commercial and recreational lock flushes data provided by the Corps of Engineers is presented in the two tables below. Several operations are performed on this data: 1) Monthly results are totaled, leaving out May. 2) One half of flushes caused by upriver traffic are removed. 3) The resulting flushes are multiplied by the number of acre-feet per lock flush to get the total number of acre-feet of lost water. 4) The lost acre-feet are multiplied by the power head to get the loss in kWh's. 5) kWh losses are multiplied by 1.6 cents, the replacement cost of power developed in the power section above. The result is the gross value of the power foregone. As with power foregone due to irrigation, this amount is incremental and treated as all benefit.

POWER VALUE LOSSES TO LOCK FLUSH FOR THE FOUR SNAKE RIVER DAMS ARE:

- Recreational lock flushes: $242,795.
- Commercial lock flushes: $566,226.
- Total value of power lost to Lower Snake dam lock flushes: $809,021.

Power Foregone to Lock Flush: Calculations

FOREGONE HYDROPOWER, RECREATIONAL LOCK FLUSH, FISCAL 1994

LOCK FLUSHES

	LOWER GRANITE		ICE HARBOR		LITTLE GOOSE		LWR MONUMENT	
	UP	DOWN	UP	DOWN	UP	DOWN	UP	DOWN
Oct-93	56	53	67	70	60	63	61	64
Nov-93	44	47	64	65	50	51	52	52
Dec-93	39	39	74	77	50	51	52	55
Jan-94	39	38	77	76	50	49	54	50
Feb-94	36	36	62	59	43	43	41	42
Mar-94	25	25	45	50	30	31	31	32
Apr-94	41	40	77	77	55	57	57	59
Jun-94	33	33	56	60	46	48	49	49
Jul-94	26	26	34	38	27	29	28	31
Aug-94	24	27	35	33	31	28	30	30
Sep-94	45	42	68	66	52	55	55	59
TOTAL	408	406	659	671	494	505	510	523
Subtract 1/2 Upstream	204	0	329.5	0	247	0	255	0
# Lock flushes w/lost water	204	406	329.5	671	247	505	255	523
Acre-ft per lock flush	131	131	131	131	131	131	133	133
Acre feet diverted	26,724	53,186	43,165	87,901	32,357	66,155	33,915	69,559
Power Head	98	98	98	98	98	98	100	100
Power Head x 0.87(x acre-ft = kWh)	85.26	85.26	85.26	85.26	85.26	85.26	87	87
Loss in millions of kWh	2.28	4.53	3.68	7.49	2.76	5.64	2.95	6.05
$/kWh	$0.016	$0.016	$0.016	$0.016	$0.016	$0.016	$0.016	$0.016
Foregone Value	$36,456	$72,554	$58,883	$119,911	$44,140	$90,246	$47,210	$96,826

LOWER SNAKE TOTAL/COMMERCIAL LOCK FLUSH

Lock flushes w/lost water: 3140.5
Acre-feet of water diverted: 412,962
Foregone kWh (millions): 35.39
Value of foregone power: $566,226

FOREGONE HYDROPOWER, RECREATIONAL LOCK FLUSH, FISCAL 1994

LOCK FLUSHES

	LOWER GRANITE		ICE HARBOR		LITTLE GOOSE		LWR MONUMENT	
	UP	DOWN	UP	DOWN	UP	DOWN	UP	DOWN
Oct-93	29	24	18	18	5	6	4	5
Nov-93	10	9	3	3	1	2	0	1
Dec-93	12	9	4	1	0	1	0	0
Jan-94	8	9	2	0	0	0	0	0
Feb-94	4	3	1	1	0	0	0	0
Mar-94	0	1	4	4	0	0	1	2
Apr-94	13	14	20	15	4	6	5	7
Jun-94	33	38	11	14	16	13	19	20
Jul-94	57	68	24	24	42	48	37	53
Aug-94	52	550	5	4	23	30	26	20
Sep-94	29	33	0	1	14	11	11	11
TOTAL	247	758	92	85	105	117	103	119
Subtract 1/2 Upstream	123.5	0	46	0	52.5	0	51.5	0
# Lock flushes with lost water	123.5	758	46	85	52.5	117	51.5	119
Acre-feet per lock flush	131	131	131	131	131	131	133	133
Acre-feet diverted	16,179	99,298	6,026	11,135	6,878	15,327	6,850	15,827
Power Head	98	98	98	98	98	98	100	100
Power Head x 0.87(x acre-ft = kW)	85.26	85.26	85.26	85.26	85.26	85.26	87	87
Loss in millions of kWh	1.38	8.47	0.51	0.95	0.59	1.31	0.60	1.38
$/kWh	$0.016	$0.016	$0.016	$0.016	$0.016	$0.016	$0.016	$0.016
Foregone value	$22,070	$135,458	$8,220	$15,190	$9,382	$20,908	$9,535	$22,031

LOWER SNAKE TOTAL, RECREATIONAL LOCK FLUSH

Lock flushes w/lost water: 1,353
Acre-feet of water diverted: 177,519
Foregone kWh (millions): 15.17
Value of foregone power: $242,795

IN TOTAL: LOWER SNAKE TOTAL, COMBINED COMMERCIAL & RECREATION LOCK FLUSH

Total lock flushes with lost water: 4,493
Acre-feet of water diverted: 590,480
Foregone kWh (millions): 50.56
Value of foregone power: $809,021

Sources: Vessel & Lockage Summary, Walla Walla District, Army Corps of Engineers & Calculated

Local property tax support

The adjacent table shows the 1994 local taxes paid in support of Lower Snake ports. These amounts are property taxes paid by local taxpayers, not rents paid by port tenants. We acknowledge the point that the river ports also have a quite separate function as industrial development parks that have nothing to do with navigation. A case could be made that the property tax support to the ports is devoted to that function and not to navigation, or to some combination of the two. So an end to navigation would not necessarily free up this wealth for other purposes. This is really a political matter and unpredictable. For now we assume all property tax support to the ports is support to navigation, which would, by definition, either end or become support for something else if the natural river is restored.

PROPERTY TAX SUPPORT TO PORTS, BY STATE, 1994

Idaho	
Lewiston	$522,000
Washington	
Columbia	$73,482
Whitman County	$517,540
Clarkston	$180,000
Total	$1,293,022

Sources: Port of Lewiston, Washington State Auditor.

Costs of transportation on a per-ton basis:

We know from Section 2 (p. 20) that shippers pay $1.23 per ton to ship goods the length of the Lower Snake navigation system. Similarly, we know that they would pay $1.26 to ship the same quantity by train the same distance. The question is: how much more per ton does it actually cost the economy to send goods by barge on the Lower Snake?

We know the total costs to provide transportation on the Lower Snake: $48.6 million. To calculate per ton costs, we simply divide by the 3,478,163 tons travelling that distance on that route.

Per ton transportation costs for the Lower Snake dams and reservoirs:

	COST TO SHIP 3.5 MILLION TONS 135 MILES	COST PER TON
Transportation fees barge shippers pay	$4.3 million	$1.23
Transportation subsidies	$44.3million	$12.66
Actual costs to ship on Lower Snake	$48.6 million	$13.89
Cost to ship by rail	$4.4 million	$1.26

Irrigated farming (pp. 22-24)

This appendix section provides further information on the thirteen farms that use water from the Ice harbor pool, the Army Corps' approach to irrigation net benefit, electricity ratepayer subsidies for irrigation pumping, electric power foregone to irrigation, and taxpayer crop supports.

IRRIGATION BENEFICIARIES: FARMS THAT USE ICE HARBOR POOL WATER

Today, about 35,000 acres are irrigated for agriculture from the Lower Snake. The average farm size is 3,300 acres.

OWNER OR MANAGEMENT	ACRES	OWNER OR MANAGEMENT	ACRES
Carr/Parker Farms	3400	Snake River Vineyards	2750
Carr Farms	1300	Flat Top Ranch	540
Ice Harbor Farms	4500	Broetge	2100
WSDNR	520	T & R Farms	3200
Agri-Northwest	10000	Darryl Klundt	300
Hilltop Farms	3814	Gordon Brothers	165
Burbank Ranch	3800	Average Farm Size	3308

Source: Investigation of Pumping Facilities. Lower Snake River. Appendix B, User Information Sheets. Walla Walla District Army Corps of Engineers 1991. Table 2-1, pp. 2-6.

Approaches to calculating net benefit of irrigated farming

Army Corps Of Engineers Approach

When Congress authorized the building of the four Lower Snake dams, it accepted and incorporated an Army Corps of Engineers feasibility study that stated that the projects would produce an irrigation benefit. The Corps' reasoning was that raising the level of water in the river and reducing the required lift meant reduced electric power required to irrigate. The Corps projected the irrigation benefit as the reduced cost of pumping.

Pre-dam cost of lifting water - Post-dam cost of lifting water = Irrigation Benefit

The Army Corps knew at the time exactly how many feet it would raise the river and reduce the required lift. They knew the approximate price of electric power for irrigation pumping, and they knew approximately how much water would have to be pumped per acre. A key variable that they could not project accurately at the time was the actual number of acres that would eventually be irrigated. They assumed that all the acreage near the Lower Snake that could be irrigated with water pumped from the river, some 70,000 acres, would be irrigated with water pumped from the river. In their report to Congress the Corps thus calculated $220,000 of irrigation benefit per year from the proposed dams (1938 dollars).[38] In 1994 dollars that is $2,292,000.

In retrospect it is clear that this was not a good method for finding irrigation benefit. It did not address the crucial issues of economic outcomes from the proposed irrigation and whether irrigation, even subsidized irrigation, would be performed to the extent projected by the Corps. More importantly, it was not really an irrigation benefit analysis in the technical sense, but rather an analysis of a kind of producer support or subsidy provided to irrigation. Despite this, the Corps used this line of reasoning to state that 4.11 percent of the costs of the dams could be carried by irrigation[39]. The Corps did not state that irrigators would actually pay this percentage of dam costs. They were specifically referring to economic tradeoffs and outcomes.

Over the years the costs of providing this benefit to irrigators has slipped from the Army Corps of Engineers and BPA books. Costs are allocated to other areas, like power production, even though irrigation benefit is still claimed by the agencies as a rationale for the dams. The agencies still reckon benefit based on the original Army Corps of Engineers reduced lift equals benefit calculation shown above, albeit with updated acreage and power cost figures[40].

Our Approach

Our method for estimating irrigation benefit is a different method than we used in the electric power and transportation sections, but is the best choice given the available data. It may be summarized as follows:

Value of crops produced - Farmers' costs - Farming subsidies = Economic Benefit of Farming

Subsidized electricity for irrigation pumping

The table below shows the amount of electric power used for irrigation pumping by the Ice Harbor irrigators and their power costs of $2,472,055 in 1991. The power rate subsidy to irrigation pumping is estimated at 20 percent of this amount, or $494,411[41].

IRRIGATED ACREAGE AND POWER USE 1991.

IRRIGATOR	ACRES	POWER $	IRRIGATOR	ACRES	POWER $
Carr/Parker Farms	3400	$183,000	Snake River Vineyards	2750	$298,510
Carr Farms	1300	$95,000	Flat Top Ranch	540	$275,000
Ice Harbor Farms	4500	$218,472	Broetge	2100	Included w/Flat Top
WSDNR	520	$30,000	T & R Farms	3200	$134,000
Agri-Northwest	10000	$933,000	Darryl Klundt	300	$8,000
Hilltop Farms	3814	$286,000	Gordon Brothers	165	$3,750
Burbank Ranch	3800	$7,323	Average	3,308	$2,472,055

Source: Army Corps of Engineers Walla Walla District. Investigation of Pumping Facilities, Lower Snake River. 4-13, Table 4-3. 1991.

Electric power foregone to irrigation

When water is removed from the river for irrigation its stored kinetic energy is no longer available for generating electric power. Since the economy foregoes that electric power in order to irrigate, it makes sense to ascribe the value of that foregone energy as a cost of irrigation.

Irrigators divert an average of 2.909 acre/feet per acre at Ice Harbor pool[42], or 101,594 acre feet per year. The power head at Ice Harbor is 98 feet[43]. Using the standard hydropower coefficient of .87 this causes a loss of potential power of 8,661,8976 kWh. Some of the diverted water finds its way back into the river in return flows. But a great deal, some 81,268 acre/feet, does not[44]. It evaporates or transpires through the crops. This amount of water is lost to power generation not just at Ice Harbor but at all downstream power generating stations. The cumulative head of these stations is 316 feet[45]. The power foregone is 22,342,239 kWh. We value this power at 1.6 cents per kWh, the replacement power cost.

CALCULATIONS: POWER FOREGONE TO IRRIGATION DIVERSION AT ICE HARBOR

Total acres farmed: 34,924

Loss at Ice Harbor:

Acre-feet of water lost: 34,924 acres x 2.909 acre-ft water diverted per acre = 101,594 acre-feet diverted per year.

kWh lost:

Acre-feet x Power Head x .87 = lost kWh

101,594 acre-ft x 98 x .87 = 8,661,897 kWh

Loss below Ice Harbor:

Acre-feet lost: 81,268

kWh lost: Acre-feet x Cumulative downriver power head x .87 = lost kWh

81,268 acre-ft x 316 x .87 = 22,342,239 kWh

Total foregone:

kWh: 31,004 ,137 $ (at 1.6 cents/kWh): $496,066

Sources: Norman K. Whittlesey et al. Energy Tradeoffs and Economic Feasibility of Irrigation Development in the Pacific Northwest, College of Agriculture Research Station, Washington State University, Bulletin 0896, 1981. Page 9. A.J. Crook Company. Diversion and Return Flow Patterns, Summation of Depletion Adjustments, Evaporation Adjustments. 1990 Level Modified Streamflow. 1993. Page 164., & calculated as described.

Taxpayer crop supports

The United States Department of Agriculture prepares estimates of overall subsidies to agriculture by commodity. They put dollar values on a wide variety of supports, from the better known like price support loans, to the more obscure and difficult to value supports like storage programs and assistance to farm research. Their estimates do not include support for irrigation, so the amounts presented here are not double counted with other irrigation costs.

The USDA support estimates are by commodity. We do not have commodity production data for the 35,000 acres. So to use the USDA figures we had to estimate both the crop mix and the yield. For the crop mix we used ratios developed from detailed Bureau of Reclamation data on cropping in the nearby Columbia Basin Project. For yields we used county level Washington State Agricultural Statistics Service data.

Using the Columbia Project cropping ratios, it was estimated that less than 20 percent of the 35,000 irrigated acres are devoted to taxpayer-supported commodities (barley, corn, oats, wheat) in any given year. The table below shows the precise estimates of devoted acres, the estimated yields in tons, the support per ton and the estimated total support. This is admittedly a rough methodology. It should be noted that over 80 percent of the acreage is excluded from this support estimate, despite the fact that the crops produced, while not tracked by the USDA, almost inevitably receive a variety of indirect public support. The estimate provided below is thus at the lower end of the range.

PRODUCER SUBSIDY EQUIVALENT SUPPORT TO AGRICULTURAL COMMODITIES ON ICE HARBOR

CROP	ACRES	PRODUCTION/TONS	SUPPORT/TON	SUPPORT
Barley	381	1,117	$47	$52,515
Corn	2543	10,284	$21	$215,966
Oats	12	30	$8	$236
Wheat	3813	11,232	$50	$561,604
Total				$830,323

Sources: Bureau of Reclamation Summary Statistics 1991. Washington Agricultural County Data. United States Department of Agriculture Economic Research Service Statistical Bulletin Number 913. Estimates of Producer and Consumer Subsidy Equivalents.

References

[1] Federal Register: V. 57, 21 Nov. 1991 58619, V. 59, 18 Aug. 1994 42529, 28 Dec. 1994 66784, V. 62, 18 Aug. 1997 43937.

[2] Snake River Recovery Team: Final Recommendations to the National Marine Fisheries Service. May, 1994. p. II-7.

[3] Bert Bowler, Idaho Department of Fish and Game, April 1998, personal communication.

[4] Don Reading, Ben Johnson Associates, Idaho, May 1996. "The Economic Impact of Steelhead Fishing and the Return of the Salmon in Idaho." Study supported by Idaho Fish and Wildlife Foundation.

[5] Ibid.

[6] Bert Bowler, Idaho Department of Fish and Game, April 1998, personal communication.

[7] Idaho Department of Fish and Game Data, 14 February 1997.

[8] Snake River Recovery Team: Final Recommendations to the National Marine Fisheries Service. May, 1994. p. II-13.

[9] ACOE Lower Snake River Juvenile Salmon Migration Feasibility Study Process. Ongoing.

[10] STFA Analytical team. 1995. Preliminary summary of spring/summer Chinook model results for the 1995 Biological Opinion. State and Tribal Fisheries Agencies' Analytical team report submitted to the NMFS Endangered Species Act record.

[11] Bert Bowler, Idaho Department of Fish and Game, April 1998, Personal communication.

[12] Kris Watkins, executive director, Tri-Cities Visitor and Convention Bureau and Sue Delucchi, Rivershore Enhancement Coordinator, Tri-Cities Rivershore Enhancement Council, Tri-Cities, Washington. Statesman Readers Comment. In "Dollars, Sense and Salmon," a reprint of Opinion pages, July 20, 21 and 22, 1997. The Idaho Statesman.

[13] Slade Gorton, Sept. 15, 1997. Press Release.

[14] "Dollars, Sense and Salmon," a reprint of Opinion pages, July 20, 21 and 22, 1997. The Idaho Statesman.

[15] Ted Strong, Executive director, Columbia River Inter-Tribal Fish Commission. Statesman Readers Comment. In "Dollars, Sense and Salmon," a reprint of Opinion pages, July 20, 21 and 22, 1997. The Idaho Statesman.

[16] "Breaching: A natural river saves fish and money." In "Dollars, Sense and Salmon," a reprint of Opinion pages, July 20, 21 and 22, 1997. The Idaho Statesman.

[17] Northwest Energy Coalition Report, December 1997. Seattle: Northwest Energy Coalition.

[18] BPA spreadsheets, provided at a public meeting in Boise, Idaho, 22 Feb 1996.

[19] Bonneville Power Administration: FishCosts.xls, 12/11/95.

[20] Bonneville Power Administration: FishCosts.xls, 12/11/95, Table 4.

[21] Drawdown Implementation Preliminary cost Summary, ACOE, 21 January 1998. The estimates do not include removal of concrete dam carcasses.

[22] House of Representatives Document No. 704. 75th Congress, 3rd Session. Letter from the Secretary of War, p. 41. Ratios calculated from table and text.

[23] Northwest Power Planning Council. Personal Communication with John Fazio, 4 December 1997.

[24] Federal Columbia River Power System Statement of Power Production Costs, FY 1994. Handout distributed by BPA at Boise, ID 22 February 1996.

[25] Army Corps of Engineers, 1992. Flow Measures EIS. Table 4.7-7.

[26] Investigation of Pumping Facilities, Lower Snake River. Appendix B, User Information Sheets. Walla Walla District Army Corps of Engineers 1991, pp. 2-6.

[27] Washington Agricultural Statistics Service. Washington Agricultural County Data. 1994. Pages 26,27,76,77.

[28] For these numbers we used:

- Documented crop ratios from the nearby Columbia Basin irrigation project;
- Yield estimates from the Washington State Agricultural Statistics Service.
- United States Department of Agriculture's subsidy estimates for barley, corn, oats and wheat. USDA numbers do not include any irrigation subsidies so there is no double counting. See Appendix for Section 2 for calculation details.

[29] Don Reading, Ben Johnson Associates, Idaho, May 1996. "The Economic Impact of Steelhead Fishing and the Return of Wild Salmon in Idaho." Study supported by the Idaho Fish and Wildlife Foundation.

[30] Economic Value of Recreational Fishing and Commercial use of Pacific Anadromous Fish in Washington, Oregon and California. Anthony Fedler. Sport Fishing Institute and the USDA Forest Service, page 17.

[31] Columbia River System Operation Review, Final EIS, 11/95 Appendix O, Summary.

[32] "What is BPA spending for fish and wildlife?" BPA White Paper, March 1998.

[33] Ibid.

[34] BPA: Fishcost.xls, Reference Table 4. 12/11/95.

[35] Statement of John McKern, ACOE, Before the Pacific Fisheries Legislative Task Force, Lower Granite Dam, November 1995.

[36] Drawdown Implementation Preliminary Cost Summary, ACOE, 21 January 1998. The estimate is for breaching only and does not include removal of the concrete dam carcasses.

[37] Pacific Loads & Resource Study. BPA 1994 (The White Book).

[38] House of Representatives Document No. 704. 75th Congress, 3rd Session. Letter From the Secretary of War. Page 41. Par. 96.

[39] House of Representatives Document No. 704. 75th Congress, 3rd Session. Letter From the Secretary of War. Page 41. Table & Text, Par. 97.

[40] Columbia River System Operation Review, Final EIS, 11/95 Appendix O, Section 2.3.4.2.

[41] 20% irrigation rate support estimated from BPA power exchange costs, Note 5, Annual Reports 1993-1994. BPA.

[42] A.J. Crook Company. Diversion and Return Flow Patterns, Summation of Depletion Adjustments, Evaporation Adjustments. 1990 Level Modified Streamflow. 1993. Page 164.

[43] Norman K. Whittlesey et al. Energy Tradeoffs and Economic Feasibility of Irrigation Development in the Pacific Northwest, College of Agriculture Research Station, Washington State University, Bulletin 0896, 1981. Page 9.

[44] A.J. Crook Company. Diversion and Return Flow Patterns, Summation of Depletion Adjustments, Evaporation Adjustments. 1990 Level Modified Streamflow. 1993. Page 164.

[45] Norman K. Whittlesey et al. Energy Tradeoffs and Economic Feasibility of Irrigation Development in the Pacific Northwest, College of Agriculture Research Station, Washington State University, Bulletin 0896, 1981. Page 9.

THE ROLE OF RIGHTS IN BENEFIT COST METHODOLOGY: THE EXAMPLE OF SALMON AND HYDROELECTRIC DAMS*

Richard O. Zerbe Jr.† & Linda J. Graham#

Abstract: Benefit cost analysis is a well-established technique for assessing the impacts of proposed actions. Accurate benefit cost analysis is essential to making informed decisions through an understanding of the trade-offs involved in alternative actions. This Article presents a methodology for improving current benefit cost techniques and hence the usefulness of benefit cost analysis to decisionmakers. The proposed methodology is based on recognition of the roles of legal rights and psychological expectations in benefit cost analysis. Proper consideration of these rights and expectations is critical to an accurate determination of how benefits and costs are measured and whose interests are included in the analysis. Addressing these issues will provide more accurate and comprehensive information to decisionmakers. Application of the proposed methodology may significantly affect the outcome of a benefit cost analysis and hence impact the decisionmaking process.

The decision of March 1999 to order new protections for nine threatened salmon[1] populations in the Pacific Northwest, combined with those previously established, will likely result in the largest and most expensive rescue effort in the twenty-six-year history of the Endangered Species Act.[2] Reportedly, significant contributors to Northwest salmon mortality are the numerous hydroelectric dams on the Columbia and Snake Rivers.[3] Fishery experts were concerned about the effect of dams

* The authors would like to thank Ron Conner, Eric Espenhorst, Daniel Huppert, Jacoba Johnson, William Rodgers, Mark Plummer, Jack L. Knetsch, Gary Ellis, John Loomis, The Inter-Tribal Fish Commission, Ed Woodruff, and librarians at the Walla Walla branch of the Army Corps of Engineers. We alone are responsible for analyses and conclusions.

† Professor of Public Affairs, Daniel J. Evans School of Public Affairs, University of Washington; Adjunct Professor of Law, University of Washington School of Law.

J.D. expected 2001, University of Washington School of Law; M.P.A expected 2001, Daniel J. Evans School of Public Affairs, University of Washington.

1. For purposes of this Article, the term "salmon" includes all affected salmonoid species and steelhead trout.

2. *See, e.g.*, Editorial, *Saving a Regional Icon*, N.Y. Times, Mar. 18, 1999, at A24.

3. *See, e.g.*, Henry B. Lacey, *New Hope for Pacific Salmon?* Northwest Resource Information Center v. Northwest Power Planning Council, Idaho Department of Fish & Game v. National Marine Fisheries Service, *and the Aftermath of Judicial Impatience*, 3 Hastings West-Northwest. J. Envtl. L. & Pol'y 19, 21 (1995) (citing Michael C. Blumm & Andy Simrin, *The Unraveling of the Parity Promise: Hydropower, Salmon, and Endangered Species in the Columbia Basin*, 21 Envtl. L. 657, 663–64 (1991); National Marine Fisheries Serv., National Oceanic & Atmospheric Admin., *Factors for Decline: A Supplement to the Notice of Determination for Snake River Spring/Summer Chinook*

on fish as early as 1924. For instance, the 1924 report of the Washington State Supervisor of Fisheries noted, "The damming of our larger streams, the ones most frequented by the anadromous fishes, is rapidly becoming a serious menace to the existence of the latter."[4] In his 1925 report, the Supervisor of Fisheries further stated that "the decline of the runs has been constant, and has approached the danger point."[5] In 1931, the following appeared in the biennial report:

> Practically all established power and irrigation projects have already taken a large toll on fish life. No matter how carefully developed any fish saving device may be[,] . . . any dam or diversion at once changes the natural conditions of any stream and thus to a greater or lesser extent depletes the fish life contained therein.[6]

Snake and Columbia River salmon runs have continued to decline, resulting in listings under the Endangered Species Act.[7]

Current proposals to mitigate the impacts of hydroelectric dams on Northwest salmon include increasing the quantity and flow of river water, constructing bypass channels, and breaching dams. Such mitigation efforts will likely impact hydropower operators, electricity consumers, commercial navigators, irrigators, water consumers, fishing interests, recreational and tourism interests, and the general public. As final decisions are made regarding strategies for salmon protection, it is important that decisionmakers consider and properly measure all consequences faced by these interests. Benefit cost analysis will necessarily be an integral part of the decisionmaking process. The contribution of benefit cost analysis depends, of course, on the quality of

---

Under the Endangered Species Act 8 (1991); Northwest Power Planning Council, *Compilation of Information on Salmon and Steelhead Losses in the Columbia River Basin* 121–72 (1987)).

4. 32–33 *Washington Supervisor of Fisheries Biennial Rep.* 11 (1924).

5. 34–35 *Washington Supervisor of Fisheries Biennial Rep.* 4 (1926).

6. 40–41 *Washington Supervisor of Fisheries Biennial Rep.* 28 (1932).

7. The following species are listed under the Endangered Species Act as threatened or endangered: Snake River sockeye, 50 C.F.R. § 222.23 (1998); Snake River spring/summer and fall chinook, 50 C.F.R. § 227.4(g), (h) (1998); Snake River Basin steelhead, 50 C.F.R. § 227.4(l) (1998); lower Columbia River steelhead, 50 C.F.R. § 227.4(m) (1998); and upper Columbia River steelhead, 50 C.F.R. § 222.23(a) (1998); lower Columbia River chinook, 64 Fed. Reg. 14,308, 14,321 (1998) (to be codified at 50 C.F.R. § 223.102(a)(17)); upper Columbia River chinook, 64 Fed. Reg. 14,308, 14,324 (to be codified at 50 C.F.R. § 224.101(a)); Columbia River chum, 64 Fed. Reg. 14,508, 14,513 (1999) (to be codified at 50 C.F.R. § 223.102(a)(13)); and middle Columbia River steelhead, 64 Fed. Reg. 14,517, 14,525 (1999) (to be codified at 50 C.F.R. § 223.102(a)(15)).

benefit cost analysis performed. Accurate and comprehensive benefit cost analysis is essential both to understanding the trade-offs involved and to making informed decisions.

Benefit cost analysis techniques have evolved over time, prompted by changes in sentiment, technique, and environmental law. Still, further evolution and refinement are needed.[8] This Article suggests how benefit cost analysis can be refined by considering benefits and costs in relation to the legal rights and psychological expectations of parties impacted by salmon recovery efforts.[9] Proper consideration of these factors is important in determining how benefits and costs are measured and whose interests are included in the analysis. Thus, the inclusion of these factors will likely produce a significant effect on the outcome of the analysis and the decisionmaking process.[10]

Part I of this Article outlines the history of hydropower development in the Northwest. Part II discusses the proposed methodology for applying legal rights and psychological expectations to benefit cost analysis in more detail. Part III explores the various interests that may be impacted by proposed alterations to Northwest hydroelectric projects. It also describes the relative certainty of the legal rights and psychological expectations involved and how these factors should be reflected in a benefit cost analysis. Part IV illustrates how a consideration of legal rights and psychological expectations would impact benefit cost analyses currently being conducted. This Article concludes that proper

---

8. *See, e.g.*, Victor B. Flatt, *The Human Environment of the Mind: Correcting NEPA Implementation by Treating Environmental Philosophy and Environmental Risk Allocation as Environmental Values Under NEPA*, 46 Hastings L. Rev. 85 (1994). Further refinement of benefit cost analysis is particularly important for the Army Corps of Engineers, which performs these analyses for hydroelectric projects. The Corps currently relies on the U.S. Water Resources Council's Economic and Environmental Principles and Guidelines for Water and Related Land Resources Implementation Studies. This document has not been modified since 1983 and is in need of significant improvement in a number of areas. For example, there are clear errors in the application of discount rates, and the guidelines fail to consider income distributional effects. Of particular concern, the guidelines also fail to consider the rights of parties impacted by actions and how these rights affect the valuation of benefits and costs.

9. A path for further evolution is suggested in Richard O. Zerbe Jr., *Economic Efficiency in Law and Economics* (Edward Elgar ed., forthcoming 2000) and Richard O. Zerbe Jr., *Is Benefit Cost Analysis Legal? Three Rules for Benefit Cost Analysis*, 17 J. Pol'y Analysis & Mgmt. 419 (1998) [hereinafter Zerbe, *Is Benefit Cost Analysis Legal?*]. This Article expands upon one element of the suggestions made therein.

10. While proposals for dam modification and removal on Northwest rivers resulting from the listing of salmon under the Endangered Species Act provide the vehicle for our analysis, the basic technique is relevant to any benefit cost analysis.

consideration of rights and expectations may significantly impact the outcomes of benefit cost analyses.

I. HISTORICAL BACKGROUND OF HYDROPOWER DEVELOPMENT IN THE NORTHWEST

The U.S. Army Corps of Engineers provided the original analyses of Snake and Columbia River hydroelectric projects.[11] These analyses were simplistic and uncluttered by mention of ecological concerns, free-flowing river benefits, tribal interests, species preservation or habitat concerns, consideration of the winners and losers, or uncertainty of impacts. The primary benefits considered were power generation, flood control, navigation, and recreation. While the Corps noted that the fishery interests sought delay of development of the Columbia and Snake Rivers until the impact of the proposed dams on the fishing industry could be determined,[12] the primary costs considered were limited to dam construction and operating expenses.[13]

These early benefit cost analyses failed to provide sufficient justification for the dams[14] even without considering the impacts on fish, fishermen, tribes, and other interests. The Corps' report to Congress as part of authorization for dam construction noted:

> [T]he direct navigation and irrigation benefits that would accrue to the general public from the proposed improvements are not commensurate with its cost, but it is possible that sufficient surplus power from the dams can be sold within the next 50 years to make

---

11. *See* H.R. Doc. No. 75-704 (1945).

12. *See id.* at 25.

13. Report on Little Goose Lock and Dam concludes typically: "Based on the investigation and analyses presented in this report, it is concluded that locating Little Goose Lock and Dam . . . will most economically develop maximum power here, and will provide satisfactory navigation conditions." U.S. Army Corps of Engineers, *Design Memorandum No. 1: Site Selection and Upper Pool Determination: Little Goose Lock and Dam Lower Snake River Project* 3–46 (1961). This is typical of many analyses. *See* Michael C. Blumm et al., *Saving Snake River Water and Salmon Simultaneously: The Biological, Economic, and Legal Case for Breaching the Lower Snake River Dams, Lowering John Day Reservoir, and Restoring Natural Riverflows*, in *Northwest Water Law and Policy Project* 35 (1998) (on file with authors) ("[T]he perceived benefits of dams are fully quantified and often overstated, while the costs are greatly understated or ignored. Traditional cost-benefit analysis did not calculate true social costs, such as environmental damage. . . . Environmental damages were often dismissed as mere externalities, and systematically excluded from the economic cost-benefit balance sheet because their impacts were dispersed or more difficult to quantify than benefits.").

14. *See* H.R. Doc. No. 75-704, at 42.

> the improvement economically sound. It is not safe to assume, however, that this can be done . . . .[15]

Inclusion and proper measurement of the benefits and costs of all affected interests would have provided more accurate information and allowed for a more thorough consideration of the true long-term effects of the hydroelectric projects. While the results of benefit cost analyses are only one element of the decisionmaking criteria, an accurate and comprehensive analysis has the potential to impact the end result of the decisionmaking process.

II. THE BENEFIT COST APPROACH

Benefit cost analysis is a well-established policy analysis technique used by all levels of government.[16] The technique compares the benefits and costs of alternative actions. The purpose of benefit cost analysis is to provide useful information to the decisionmaker and not to furnish the decision itself.[17] It is one tool in understanding the trade-offs involved in the decisionmaking process. The methodology presented in this Article is intended to improve the usefulness of this tool by considering how legal rights and psychological expectations should be included in the analysis and whose benefits and costs matter.

A. The Relationship of Rights to Benefit Cost Analysis: The Legal and Psychological Nature of Gains and Losses

Benefit cost analysis values benefits and costs in the form of gains and losses experienced by those impacted by a proposed action. Gains and losses are determined or experienced as deviations from a status quo reference point. What people own or feel they own determines the reference point. In other words, what people own or feel they own is a psychological state, a matter of psychological ownership or expectation. A major determinant of psychological ownership is legal rights. Most people feel psychological ownership of what they legally own. Hence, legal rights are important to the calculation of benefits and costs. Where legal rights and psychological perceptions of ownership diverge,

15. *Id.*

16. *See* Jonathan Lesser & Richard O. Zerbe Jr., *A Practitioner's Guide to Benefit Cost Analysis*, in *Handbook of Public Finance* 221–68 (Marcel Dekker ed., 1998).

17. *See id.*

however, psychological perceptions or expectations become important and should form the reference point from which to measure gains and losses.[18] Benefit cost analysis will be most valuable when it is built upon the recognition of these legal rights and psychological expectations, and how these impact the values used to measure benefits and costs and the selection of parties to be included in the analysis.

B. *Benefit Cost Measurements: Willingness to Pay and Willingness to Accept*

Benefits and costs should be measured by the willingness to pay (WTP) and the willingness to accept (WTA) payment.[19] The legal rights and psychological expectations of the parties affected by a proposed action should be used to select between the willingness to pay or the willingness to accept measures. The willingness to pay (WTP) reflects the price that someone who does not have a good or right would be willing to pay to buy it—the maximum amount of money one would give to buy a good or service or to avoid harm. Thus, the WTP value represents benefits in the form of gains, and costs in the form of gains foregone, to those who do not have a good or right. The willingness to accept (WTA) reflects the price that someone who has the good or right would accept to sell it—the minimum amount of money one would accept to forego a good or right or to bear harm. Thus, the WTA value represents benefits in the form of losses restored, and costs in the form of losses, to those who have a good or right. As a result, benefits and costs are the sum of the appropriate WTP and WTA measures:

> Benefits: The sum of the willingness to pay (WTP) for changes that are seen as gains and of the willingness to accept (WTA) for changes that are seen as restoration of losses.
>
> Costs: The sum of the willingness to accept (WTA) for changes that are seen as losses and of the willingness to pay (WTP) for changes that are seen as foregone gains.[20]

---

18. Psychological expectations include the perception of or belief in ownership and the expectation of maintaining a chosen way of life. *See* discussion *infra* Part II.D.

19. *See* Richard O. Zerbe Jr. & Dwight Dively, *Benefit Cost Analysis in Theory and Practice* (1994). WTP and WTA are exact utility indicators that provide a complete ranking of choices for an individual.

20. It is important to note that benefits are not measured exclusively by the WTP, nor are costs by the WTA. Benefits are to be measured by the WTA when they include losses restored, and costs are

C. Divergence Between Willingness to Pay and Willingness to Accept

Until recently, it was thought that characterizing a particular benefit or cost as willingness to pay (WTP) or willingness to accept (WTA) made little difference in the values used in the benefit cost analysis. It is now recognized that the distinction between WTP and WTA can make a great difference.[21] Researchers have demonstrated repeatedly that WTA questionnaires, which ask how much one would accept to sell a good or right, generate values three to nineteen times greater than those elicited by WTP questionnaires, which ask how much one would give to buy a good or right.[22] Thus, recognition of the rights of the affected parties can greatly impact the outcome of a benefit cost analysis, as the value of benefits and costs to those with rights will be properly reflected by the use of the potentially higher value of WTA, not WTP.

There are three factors that affect the extent of the divergence between the willingness to pay and the willingness to accept values: income effect, substitution possibilities, and loss aversion.

1. Income Effect

The more valuable the good or right, the greater the difference between WTP and WTA. This is referred to as the income effect. Consider the value of a pleasant view from your home. Someone wishes to erect a building that will block your view. If you were considered to own the view, WTA would be used as the measure of value in recognition of your ownership—it is the price at which you are willing to sell your view. If you were not considered an owner of the view, WTP would be used to recognize your lack of ownership. It measures your

---

to be measured by the WTP where they include gains foregone. The difference between benefits and costs is simply their sign: positive for benefits and negative for costs. Thus, without loss of accuracy, costs can be counted as negative benefits and vice versa.

21. This has been demonstrated and noted in what is now a voluminous literature. *See, e.g.*, Jack L. Knetsch, *Asymmetric Valuation of Gains and Losses and Preference Order Assumptions*, 33 Econ. Inquiry 134 (1995); Jack L. Knetsch, *Environmental Valuation: Some Problems of Wrong Questions and Misleading Answers*, 3 Envtl. Values 351 (1994); Daniel Levy & David Friedman, *The Revenge of the Redwoods? Reconsidering Property Rights and the Economic Allocation of Natural Resources*, 61 U. Chi. L. Rev. 493 (1994); Murray B. Rutherford et al., *Assessing Environmental Losses: Judgments of Importance and Damage Schedules*, 22 Harv. Envtl. L. Rev. 51 (1998).

22. *See* Levy & Friedman, *supra* note 21, at 506; *see also* Donald Coursey & R.D. Roberts, *Aggregation and the Contingent Valuation Method for Evaluating Environmental Amenities* (1992) (stating that differences for environmental goods may be as much as 142 to 1).

ngness to buy the same view, for example, by paying the builder to a smaller building. The difference between WTA and WTP, as the equence of owning or not owning a good, will be small in the case n object of little worth. In the case of a poor view, ownership is ...nsequential because the view has little value and its ownership does not much change your wealth. Thus, recognition of ownership in a benefit cost analysis through the use of WTA would have little effect on the outcome of the analysis. A great view, on the other hand, would be a different matter. The use of WTA would result in a much higher value than the use of WTP. Thus, proper recognition of your ownership of a great view will significantly impact the outcome of a benefit cost analysis.

2. *Substitution Possibilities*

Recently, it was shown that the poorer the substitutes for a good, the greater the divergence between WTP and WPA.[23] Put another way, the more unique the good, the greater the divergence will be between WTP and WTA. In general, the divergence between WTA and WTP can take any positive value for normal goods.[24] This concept is particularly important for environmental goods such as unique salmon runs, a unique grove of trees, and the Grand Canyon, because these goods have poor substitutes.

3. *Loss Aversion*

The essence of loss aversion—that individuals value losses more highly than they value gains—is well supported by empirical studies. Individuals appear to place a significantly higher value on the units of a good they already have than on getting additional units of the same good. Thus, higher values will result where losses of ownership or rights are properly valued using the WTA, as compared to gains valued using the WTP.

23. *See* W. Michael Hanneman, *Willingness to Pay and Willingness to Accept: How Much Can They Differ?*, 61 Am. Econ. Rev. 635 (1991).

24. Normal goods are those that become more desirable when income increases.

D. *The Application of Legal Rights and Psychological Expectations to Determine the Reference Point*

As discussed above, benefits and costs are measured as gains or losses from a reference point established by legal rights and psychological expectations.[25] Because psychological expectations are often based on having a legal right, the legal right in most cases establishes the reference point. The value of a good to one with a legal right is measured using the willingness to accept (WTA) while the value to one without a legal right is measured using the willingness to pay (WTP). Where legal rights and psychological expectations differ, the psychological expectations should generally be used to define the reference point and hence the use of WTA or WTP.[26]

1. *Where Legal Rights Are Clear and Correspond with Psychological Expectations*

Where legal ownership or rights are clear, well recognized, and not contrary to well-ingrained social norms, they will generally correspond with accepted psychological concepts of ownership or expectation. When this is the case, legal ownership or right establishes a reference point from which losses and gains are measured. The value of goods or rights to owners is to be measured by the willingness to accept (WTA), including the value of previous losses restored. The value to nonowners is to be measured by the willingness to pay (WTP), including the value of gains foregone. For most cases, the legal rights will determine whether WTP or WTA will be used.

2. *Where Legal Rights Are Uncertain or Diverge from Psychological Expectations*

Where legal rights are not clear or diverge dramatically from the psychological precept of ownership, psychological expectations should be considered. This methodology recognizes the validity of psychological ownership or expectation in measuring gains and losses.

25. *See* discussion *supra* Part II.A.

26. See Zerbe, *Is Benefit Cost Analysis Legal?* and Zerbe, *Economic Efficiency in Law and Economics*, *supra* note 9, for an elaboration of the reasons why psychological expectations should be recognized.

A typical case would be one in which the legal rights are uncertain and each party has some incomplete psychological expectation of ownership. In this situation, the benefit cost allocation should be made based not only on the willingness to pay (WTP) but also on the willingness to accept (WTA) to the extent that each party has a subjective sense of psychological ownership. This is equivalent to examining not only WTP but also the divergence between WTP and WTA.[27] This result is interesting because it signifies that both the sense of psychological ownership and the divergence between WTA and WTP are relevant to the decision concerning who should receive the entitlement. While it may be difficult to represent accurately the sense of ownership or expectation, it is important for decisionmakers to understand its significance. Consider, for example, the question of whether or not the dams on the Elwha River should be removed. There is general uncertainty regarding a legal public right, but perhaps a strong psychological sense of entitlement to a free-flowing Elwha. The divergence between WTP and WTA should, therefore, be weighted by this sense of public entitlement (WTA), acknowledging the extent to which restoration of the Elwha is viewed as restoration of a previous loss rather than as a gain. This weight will include the effect of the substitution and income effects.[28]

Consider also the Headwaters Grove in Northern California, the last major privately owned stand of ancient redwoods. Environmental groups have thwarted efforts to log the old-growth forests through a series of lawsuits.[29] In this example, the timber company, unlike the environmental groups, has a recognized legal ownership right. Furthermore, Headwaters Grove is of purely commercial value to the timber company and is measured by WTP. The WTP of the environmental groups is less than the WTP of the timber company, as evidenced by the environmental groups' inability to purchase the forest or pay the timber company to prevent logging. However, under the

---

27. Let P_a and P_b represent the subjective sense of psychological ownership by *A* and *B* respectively. Gains are represented by the WTP weighted by the extent to which the party does not have psychological ownership. Losses are measured using the WTA weighted by the extent to which a party does have psychological ownership. The good or right goes to *A* when the net benefit of having a good is greater to *A* than to *B*. The equation can be expressed as $WTP_a + P_a(WTA_a - WTP_a) > WTP_b + P_b(WTA_b - WTP_b)$, which considers both the WTP and the divergence between the WTA and the WTP.

28. *See* discussion *supra* Part II.C.

29. *See* Environmental Protection Info. Ctr., Inc., *A Headwaters Forest Chronology* (on file with authors).

proposed methodology, which recognizes psychological expectations, the inclusion of WTA will better measure the psychological effect of losing the redwoods on the environmental groups. The resulting value, which incorporates the environmental groups' psychological expectation, is presumably much higher than the WTP of the timber company, due in part to the unique quality of the grove (the substitution effect). In fact, the environmentalists' ability to delay the cutting of this timber appears to suggest that courts have recognized their psychological expectation and have given weight to the willingness to accept (WTA) valuation.[30]

Providing some role for psychological expectations in benefit cost analysis is not entirely original. In some circumstances, the law has also recognized psychological expectations, noting at times the discrepancy between measures of legal and psychological values and wondering whether these values are gains or losses.[31] In these instances, the law has evolved to recognize a psychological basis of valuation.[32]

30. In addition, environmental groups succeeded in compelling the timber company to abandon certain logging rights or claims to rights in exchange for money and other rights, thereby furthering the recognition of the public's psychological ownership. However, some regarded this bargain as a demonstration of inept negotiating by government officials. The contention is that not only was too much money paid but that too many development rights were given to the timber company so that coho salmon in the South Fork of the Elk River, which is surrounded by Headwaters, may be imperiled. *See* Alexander Cockburn, *The Headwaters Deal: Less Than Meets the Eye*, Seattle Times, Mar. 4, 1999; Environmental Protection Info. Ctr., Inc., *EPIC Update and Alert* (1999); *The U.S. Assailed on Redwood Appraisal*, N.Y. Times, Nov. 27, 1998, at A26.

31. *See* Levy & Friedman, *supra* note 21, at 514.

32. Consider: The value calculated for the restoration of environmental health following an environmental harm recognizes a form of psychological expectation on the part of the public—that is, the price the public is willing to accept (WTA) in exchange for environmental health. This is different from a market measure of damages calculated by the diminution in value of the environment, which tends to be based on a lack of ownership—that is, the price the public is willing to pay (WTP) to protect environmental health. The law has recognized the cost of restoration as an appropriate measure of damage if the cost of restoration is reasonable in comparison to the diminution in the value of the land. Since restoration costs that are greater by 50% or more than the market diminution of value may be recognized as reasonable, restoration costs and psychological expectations clearly have been afforded special status. *See* Heninger v. Dunn, 101 Cal. App. 3d 858 (1980); Newsome v. Billips, 671 S.W.2d 252 (Ky. Ct. App. 1984); Trinity Church v. John Hancock Mut. Life Ins., 502 N.E.2d 532 (Mass. 1987). Recently, a number of environmental statutes have been interpreted by the courts and regulatory agencies as stating a preference for evaluating environmental damages in terms of restoration costs (WTA) over diminution of economic value (WTP). *See, e.g.*, Ohio v. United States Dep't of the Interior, 880 F.2d 432 (D.C. Cir. 1989). Moreover, in response to such judicial decisions, both the Department of the Interior (DOI) and the National Oceanographic and Atmospheric Administration (NOAA) adopted new regulations giving greater recognition to restoration costs. *See* 43 C.F.R. § 11.83 (1998).

3. *Valuation of Commercial Goods*

Commercial goods are those goods that are not valued for themselves; rather, they are valued for the monetary income they provide. Commercial goods present a special case in the valuation of benefits and costs. The issue of rights is unimportant for economic evaluation of commercial goods in a benefit cost analysis because the commercial value of an asset is represented by the present value of the income that the good provides, which is the equivalent of the market price of the asset.[33] This dollar value is properly represented by the willingness to pay (WTP).

E. *The Relationship of Rights to Economic Standing:*[34] *Determining Whose Interests to Include in a Benefit Cost Analysis*

Every benefit cost analysis involves two issues: (1) the value of the action being contemplated—in the current case, whether or not to modify the operations of or to breach hydroelectric dams; and (2) whose values are to count in addressing the first question. Economic standing refers to those interests who are counted in a benefit cost analysis.[35] Whether a party has economic standing is part of the fundamental question of the pattern of rights that are assumed extant in performing a benefit cost analysis. Under the proposed methodology, legal rights are one determinant of whose values count, that is, who has economic standing. Where law and public policy are unclear regarding which party is assigned a legal right or where the assignment differs substantially from generally accepted psychological expectations, the proposed methodology dictates that psychological expectations be considered.

---

33. The present value of a stream of earnings is the investment required to produce the stream of earnings at a specified interest rate. For an investment with an infinite time horizon and constant earnings, the present value formula is simply A/r, where A is the periodic earnings and r is the period interest or discount rate. Consider: The value of a machine that produces $100 per year forever has a present value of $1000 at a 10% discount (interest) rate. This should be the value to one who is either buying or selling. There is no divergence between the WTP and the WTA. Where one person can use the machine more effectively than another can, or if the discount rate for one person is less than for another, the machine would have greater value to that person and thus the person with the higher value would "win" the good in an auction.

34. Questions of standing are considered extensively in Richard O. Zerbe Jr., *Comment: Does Benefit Cost Analysis Stand Alone? Rights and Standing*, 10 J. Pol'y Analysis & Mgmt. 96 (1991) and Zerbe, *Is Benefit Cost Analysis Legal?*, *supra* note 9, at 419.

35. *See* Dale Whittington & Duncan MacRae Jr., *The Issue of Standing in Cost Benefit Analysis*, 5 J. Pol'y Analysis & Mgmt. 665 (1986).

Those interests with psychological expectations must necessarily be counted, that is, they must be granted economic standing, as these can significantly impact the outcome of the analysis.

F. Summary of Proposed Methodology

The following chart summarizes the proposed methodology for incorporating rights into benefit cost analyses.

	RIGHTS	SOLUTION
No Divergence Between Legal and Psychological Ownership	Rights are certain. Party A is the owner, party B is not the owner.	Use the WTA for party A and the WTP for party B.
	Rights are certain. Neither party is the owner.	Auction: Use WTP for Both Parties.
	Rights are uncertain. Both parties claim ownership.	Use both WTP and WTA for both parties weighted by the extent of psychological expectations or provide alternative calculations using WTP and WTA.
Divergence Between Legal and Psychological Ownership	Rights are as in categories above.	Solutions as above except weight is given to psychological expectations (WTA).
Commercial Goods	Property is valued as a commercial resource, regardless of rights.	Use market value, typically referred to by WTP, for all parties.
ECONOMIC STANDING		
Count values for all interests not excluded by law or custom. Where the law is unclear, provide alternative calculations.		

III. DEFINING RIGHTS AND THEIR IMPACT ON BENEFIT COST ANALYSIS: THE EXAMPLE OF SALMON AND HYDROELECTRIC DAMS

This section explores the legal rights and psychological expectations of those interests impacted and considered to have economic standing in salmon recovery efforts related to the dams on the Columbia and Snake Rivers.[36] Proposals to mitigate the impact of dams on salmon have

36. The authors have sought to include all of the major interests affected, whether legal or psychological, in their discussion of the proposals to alter Columbia and Snake River dams, but recognize that not every interest may be included in this discussion.

ranged from altering the quantity and flow of river water to constructing bypass channels to breaching dams. These measures would affect hydropower operators, electricity consumers, commercial navigators, irrigators, water consumers, fishing interests (commercial, tribal, and sport), recreational and tourism interests, and the general public. The nature of the legal rights and psychological expectations of these interests is assessed through an interpretation of case law, relevant statutes (principally the Endangered Species Act, the Federal Power Act, and the Pacific Northwest Electric Power Planning and Conservation Act (Northwest Power Act)), and a discussion of the psychological expectations of the affected interests. The proposed methodology is then applied to demonstrate the impact that these rights and expectations have on the measurement of benefits and costs.

A. *Hydropower Licensees*

Salmon recovery proposals related to hydroelectric dams would impact the rights of hydropower licensees. Requiring seasonal changes in river flow, reservoir drawdowns, construction of bypass channels, and the partial breaching of dam structures would reduce the capacity of a hydroelectric project to produce power.[37] Proposals for decommissioning would go further, resulting in the loss of a franchise to produce hydroelectricity.

The property interests and rights of nonfederal hydropower licensees are controlled, in part, by the Federal Power Act.[38] The Act empowers the Federal Energy Regulatory Commission (FERC) to regulate nonfederal hydroelectric projects through the issuance of licenses, and the Act establishes federal control over the operation of hydroelectric projects.[39] An existing license is in essence a contract between the licensee and the federal government, making the contract a property right to the licensee.[40] But once the license expires, the contract ends and the property right is terminated. The licensee may seek to extend its contract

---

37. The amount of energy a hydroelectric facility produces is dependent on the elevation of the reservoir. Several of the proposed scenarios result in changes to reservoir elevations, thereby affecting maximum energy production. *See* Northwest Power Planning Council, *Analysis of the Bonneville Power Administration's Potential Future Costs and Revenues* 33 n.5 (1998).

38. 16 U.S.C. §§ 791–823 (1994).

39. *See* 16 U.S.C. §§ 791–823.

40. *See* Katharine Costenbader, Comment, *Damning Dams: Bearing the Cost of Restoring America's Rivers*, 6 Geo. Mason L. Rev. 635, 657 (1998).

with the government under relicensing proceedings, but the government is under no obligation to renew a contractual relationship with the licensee.[41] Under this analysis, the legal rights of the hydropower licensee are limited to the duration of the contract. United States Supreme Court decisions support the conclusion that licensees do not have a vested property interest in an expired license, the value of the waterpower, the franchise to produce electricity, or the hydropower development site.[42]

The rights of hydropower operators are further limited by the authority of the federal government to control the operations of licensees. Under the Federal Power Act and subsequent amendments, FERC is obligated to give development and nondevelopment values equal consideration in deciding whether to issue a license.[43] New and renewal licenses are to be granted only if the proposed project is found to protect and enhance fish and wildlife, and satisfies other criteria.[44] Through the licensing process, FERC has the authority to impose conditions on the operation of hydroelectric projects to address these environmental and other criteria.[45] The rights of current license holders are also limited by the potential for the license contracts to be reopened and new conditions imposed.[46] FERC, with apparent congressional approval, has also announced that it possesses the authority to order dam decommissioning at relicensing.[47]

41. *See id.*

42. *See* United States v. Grand River Dam Auth., 363 U.S. 229 (1960); United States v. Willow River Power Co., 324 U.S. 499 (1945); United States v. Chandler-Dunbar Water Power Co., 229 U.S. 53 (1913). In addition, these cases demonstrate that compensation for lost water power or lost franchise to produce hydroelectricity is not required under the Fifth Amendment. Nonfederal hydropower owners do acquire property rights associated with the project lands. However, the proposed scenarios for protecting salmon generally will not impact private property. Even a decommissioning order, which extinguishes the value of the property as a hydropower site, does not destroy all rights of the property. By decommissioning, FERC is ordering licensees to stop producing hydropower with existing dams. *See* Costenbader, *supra* note 40, at 657.

43. *See* 16 U.S.C. § 797(e).

44. *See* 16 U.S.C. § 797(e).

45. *See* 16 U.S.C. § 797(e).

46. Some licenses include specific re-opener clauses. FERC has also adopted a policy to use reserved authority in licenses to ameliorate cumulative impacts of projects in the same river basin through a relicensing process. However, FERC appears reluctant to use these devices and the FPA seems to suggest that licenses can be altered only upon mutual agreement. *See* State of Washington, Draft Statewide Salmon Recovery Strategy 10 (1998) (unpublished).

47. *See* Costenbader, *supra* note 40, at 652 ("If State or Federal fish and wildlife agencies report that a project's impacts . . . cannot be mitigated, FERC may have to conclude that issuance of the license, whether original or otherwise, may be inappropriate."); *see also* 60 Fed. Reg. 339 (1995) (codified at 18 C.F.R. pt. 2.24 (1997)); H.R. Rep. No. 99-597, at 32 (1986).

The provisions of the Endangered Species Act (ESA) also apply to the operation of federal dams and federal licensing of privately owned dams insofar as they affect listed species.[48] Therefore, it will likely have a significant impact on the legal rights and psychological expectations of dam licensees. Federal agencies that have control over hydroelectric projects, such as the Bonneville Power Administration, the Army Corps of Engineers, and the Bureau of Reclamation, are required to insure that any action they authorize will not likely jeopardize any endangered species.[49] The application of the ESA to hydroelectric projects is supported by judicial opinions that have upheld conditions placed on the operation of dams, including the requirement that water be released from dams to protect the habitat of endangered species.[50] One court has also mandated action after finding that agency failure to challenge status quo operations violated the ESA.[51] Thus, while it is currently unclear what changes in operations the ESA may require, it is evident that changes to hydroelectric projects are likely to be mandated under the authority of the ESA.

The Northwest Power Act establishes the interstate Pacific Northwest Electric Power and Conservation Planning Council to develop a twenty-year plan, which has the potential to impact the rights of hydropower operators. This plan is required to balance the protection and enhancement of fish and wildlife with an "adequate, efficient, economical, and reliable power supply," essentially placing fish and wildlife concerns on "equal footing" with hydroelectric power generation.[52] The Council theoretically possesses the ability to reject

48. *See* Lacey, *supra* note 3, at 47.

49. *See* 16 U.S.C. § 1536(a)(2) (1994).

50. *See* Riverside Irrigation Dist. v. Andrews, 758 F.2d 508, 513 (10th Cir. 1985).

51. *See* Lacey, *supra* note 3, at 47–48; *see also* Idaho Dep't of Fish & Game v. National Marine Fisheries Serv., 850 F. Supp. 886 (D. Or. 1994). In its 1993 biological opinion, NMFS noted several impacts dams have on salmon and concluded that the Columbia River dams pose the largest single human-induced cause of salmon mortality. *See* National Marine Fisheries Serv., *1993 Draft Biological Opinion on the Operations of the Federal Columbia River Power System* (1993). Despite this, NMFS issued a "no jeopardy" opinion. The Idaho Department of Fish and Game challenged this finding. In 1995, NMFS responded by issuing a revised biological opinion which concluded that status quo operations of the hydroelectric system would jeopardize the listed stocks. *See* National Marine Fisheries Serv., *Endangered Species Act Section 7 Biological Opinion on the Reinitiation of Consultation and 1994–98 Operation of the Federal Columbia River Power System and Juvenile Transportation Program* (1995).

52. 16 U.S.C. § 839(1)(A), (1)(B), (2) (1994). *See also* National Wildlife Fed'n v. FERC, 801 F.2d 1505, 1514–15 (9th Cir. 1986); Confederated Tribes & Bands of the Yakima Indian Nation v. Federal Energy Regulatory Comm'n, 746 F.2d 466, 473 (9th Cir. 1984).

biologically beneficial measures on the basis of "economic" considerations.[53] However, the federal courts have ruled that the Council may not reject recommended measures simply because they reduce power production and impose economic costs on the region.[54] Thus, in order to comply with the equal footing principle, the Council may recommend changes in the operation of federal and nonfederal hydroelectric projects to balance power production with fish and wildlife protection.

No matter what measures are taken to protect salmon, hydroelectric operators will likely experience a loss. The correct measure of value for this loss to hydropower licensees is nevertheless the willingness to pay (WTP). There is two-fold support for this conclusion. First, and definitively, the value of a hydroelectric project is in its commercial value. Thus, the WTP measure is used, as this will not differ from the willingness to accept (WTA).[55] Second, this conclusion is supported as a matter of legal rights. The legal rights of licensees are clearly limited, thus requiring the use of WTP.[56] Hydropower licensees may argue a psychological expectation of a reasonable return on their investment particularly in light of FERC imposed requirements.[57] Acceptance of this argument would warrant the use of WTA as the measure of loss. This psychological expectation, however, is not enough to overcome the necessity of valuing the loss based on commercial value.[58] The potential cost to hydropower licensees should therefore be measured using the willingness to pay (WTP), which reflects the present value of their lost income.

B. Electricity Consumers

Salmon recovery proposals will also impact the rights of electricity consumers. Decreases in power generation are likely to cause increases in electricity rates to commercial and private consumers. In addition, as

53. *See* Lacey, *supra* note 3, at 44.

54. *See id.*; *see also* Northwest Resource Info. Ctr., Inc. v. Northwest Power Planning Council, 35 F.3d 1371, 1395 (9th Cir. 1994).

55. *See* discussion *supra* Part II.D.3.

56. *See* discussion *supra* Part II.D.

57. *See* Costenbader, *supra* note 40, at 656.

58. It is relevant to the discussion of compensation, which is a related issue but is not directly relevant to our discussion here.

mitigation conditions are imposed on hydroelectric projects, the cost of these mitigation actions may be passed on to electricity consumers.

The Northwest Power Planning Council is charged under the Northwest Power Act with providing an "adequate, efficient, economical, and reliable power supply."[59] This suggests some consumer rights to and expectations of a certain level of economical power costs. However, courts have stated that power losses and economic costs should not preclude restoration of the salmon runs as long as the Northwest Power Act's baseline condition of an "adequate, efficient, economical, and reliable power supply" remains in place.[60] Based on the courts' interpretation, the balancing of economic power production with salmon protection appears to allow for some changes in the current rates imposed on consumers.

In general, higher electricity prices will be experienced as a loss to commercial and private consumers. For commercial consumers, the willingness to pay (WTP) should be used to represent the loss because the value of the electricity lies solely in its commercial value. For private consumers, there will likely be some divergence between the willingness to pay and the willingness to accept as a result of the divergence between legal rights and psychological expectations. This divergence between the WTP and WTA for electricity users will depend on how great the increase is in electricity prices. If the increase in price is large enough to have a significant effect on income, the income effect will produce a significant discrepancy.[61] In this case, the willingness to accept (WTA) measure should be used. The WTA should be measured by the additional income the customers would need to buy the same electricity at the new, higher prices.[62]

C. *Commercial Navigation*

Proposals for reservoir drawdowns and changes in river flow have the potential to impact the rights of navigation interests because the navigation locks at one or more dams would become unusable. Insufficient depth in the river and in the locks would prohibit the locks

59. 16 U.S.C. § 839(1)(A), (1)(B), (2) (1994).
60. 16 U.S.C. § 839(1)(A), (1)(B), (2).
61. *See* discussion *supra* Part II.C.
62. This will slightly overvalue the WTA.

from lifting vessels into navigation pools. Breaching dams also has the potential to impact navigation as the level and flow of the resulting river could preclude vessel passage. Thus, commercial navigation interests, including port facilities and the economy in these areas, face the potential for the end of commercial navigation on at least portions of the Columbia and Snake Rivers.

According to legal opinion, the Columbia and Snake River ports, as well as the tug and barge industry, have congressionally granted legal rights in the navigability of these river systems.[63] The right of slack-water navigation was granted by Congress, under its Commerce Clause authority, to a depth of no less than fourteen feet, both in the river channels and through the navigation locks at each of the dams from Bonneville Dam to Lower Granite Dam.[64] Any alteration in the navigability, or slack-water, of the system is unlawful and prohibited unless Congress specifically authorizes such a change.[65] Congress has not granted specific authority to modify this right. Thus, neither the Endangered Species Act nor the Northwest Power Act currently confers any power to bring the navigation channels below the congressionally mandated fourteen-foot level.[66]

Despite this interpretation of legal rights, the measurement of the loss to commercial navigation is a matter of commercial value, thus willingness to pay (WTP) is the correct measure.[67] This measure would apply for navigators as well as port facilities. To the extent economic standing is extended to economic impacts on port communities, the willingness to accept (WTA) should be used to represent the psychological loss of a way of life.

---

63. *See* Memorandum from Schwabe, Williamson & Wyatt, P.C., to Columbia River Tug Ass'n and Port of Morrow 2–3 (Apr. 29, 1997) (on file with authors).

64. *See id.* at 7 (citing 76 Stat. 1173 (1962)).

65. *See id.* at 8 (citing United States v. Arizona, 295 U.S. 174 (1934); Wisconsin v. Duluth, 96 U.S. 379 (1877)). Only Congress can modify what it has previously granted, as the separation of powers prevents the courts and federal agencies from acting unless the power to do so has been specifically delegated by Congress.

66. *See id.* at 9–12. Under section 7 of the Endangered Species Act, the power of federal agencies to enforce ESA's mandate for species preservation is limited to their statutory authorities. Recommendations of the Northwest Power Council plan are only advisory.

67. *See* discussion *supra* Part II.D.3.

D. *Irrigators and Other Water Users*

The rights of water users could be affected through changes in reservoir and river levels resulting from the release of water in order to maintain instream flows or from breaching of hydroelectric dams. Ample water levels, particularly in reservoirs, are crucial to ensure an adequate supply of water for the mid-April through late-September irrigation season in the Columbia River Basin.[68] Requiring changes in reservoir levels or other alterations to dam operations and structures could result in system modifications or the unavailability of water as it is diverted from current users to protect salmon. Impacts will likely include costly irrigation system modifications or the loss of farmland due to the unavailability of water, as well as impacts to municipal and industrial water consumers.

The allocation of water is governed by a state law appropriation system that determines the private rights to the use of water.[69] The system is based on the principle of "first in time, first in right," which governs the priority in water rights and allows water users to divert water from streams for beneficial uses.[70] A crucial question is the extent to which these rights can be abrogated by federal statutes and the impact of this on the assessment of rights.

The Endangered Species Act (ESA) requires federal agencies to cooperate with state agencies to resolve water resource issues.[71] According to judicial interpretation, this cooperation does not preclude the federal government from overriding state water laws to protect a listed species. The ESA has been applied to uphold conditions placed on the operation of hydroelectric projects, such as the diversion of water for the conservation of endangered species at the expense of state water rights.[72]

---

68. *See* Bonneville Power Admin. et al., *The Columbia River System: The Inside Story* 6–8 (1991); Joy Ellis, *Drafting from an Overdrawn Account: Continuing Water Diversions from the Mainstem Columbia and Snake Rivers*, 26 Envtl. L. 299, 303 (1996).

69. *See* Connecticut v. Massachusetts, 282 U.S. 660 (1931); Kansas v. Colorado, 206 U.S. 46 (1907).

70. *See* Ellis, *supra* note 68, at 304.

71. *See* 16 U.S.C. § 1531(c)(2) (1994).

72. *See* Riverside Irrigation Dist. v. Andrews, 758 F.2d 508 (10th Cir. 1985); Carson-Truckee Water Conservancy Dist. v. Watt, 549 F. Supp. 704 (D. Nev. 1982), *aff'd in part and vacated in part sub nom.* Carson-Truckee Water Conservancy Dist. v. Clark, 741 F.2d 257 (9th Cir. 1984).

Congress established federal control over the use of waters for hydropower purposes with the enactment of the Federal Power Act.[73] Courts have interpreted this authority to include the ability to impose conditions when granting hydropower licenses that require maintenance of minimum stream flows to protect salmon runs, even where state-created water rights would be affected.[74] Water rights could be further impacted by the Northwest Power Act's mandate that the twenty-year regional plan include protection and enhancement of salmon.[75] This plan could recommend changes in water levels and water allocation, thereby affecting water rights.

From a legal perspective, it is clear that water users have a legal right to use appropriated water. However, the use of willingness to accept (WTA) is precluded in this case for two reasons. First, statutory authority for abrogation substantially limits these legal rights. Second, the value of water to farmers, municipalities, and industry as a productive resource necessitates the use of willingness to pay (WTP) to represent the loss of commercial value. Neither the income nor the substitution effect would operate here.[76] In the case of farmers, the loss would be reasonably measured by the diminished value of their land as a result of no longer having access to cheaper irrigation water. To the extent that the way of life for farmers is affected, either because they are no longer able to get any water or because equipment modifications are too expensive, the use of willingness to accept (WTA) is appropriate as a reflection of psychological expectation.

E. Commercial Fishing

The anticipated benefit of changes to hydroelectric projects is the restoration of salmon runs resulting in the removal of the species from the Endangered Species list. As a result, strict limitations on commercial fishing for salmon are likely to be reduced or eliminated, thereby increasing the potential of financial benefits to commercial fishermen and associated businesses.

---

73. *See* 16 U.S.C. §§ 791–823 (1994).

74. *See* Nicholas Targ, *Water Law on the Public Lands: Facing a Fork in the River*, 12 Nat. Resources & Env't 14, 18 (1997); *see also* California v. FERC, 495 U.S. 490 (1990); California v. Federal Power Comm'n, 345 F.2d 917 (9th Cir. 1965).

75. *See* 16 U.S.C. § 839(1)(A), (1)(B), (2) (1994).

76. *See* discussion *supra* Part II.C.

It is generally anticipated that in the short run, commercial fishing will experience a loss due to tighter restrictions on fishing as part of the efforts to restore salmon. Should salmon stocks increase in the long run, however, the net result will be a gain. Based on the purely commercial value of the interest, the willingness to pay (WTP) measure should be used. This is also correct from a rights perspective, as fishing licenses and permits are generally considered to confer a privilege, not a right, which is revocable at the discretion of the issuing agency.[77] The WTP measure should reflect the net long-term gain in income.

F. *Tribal Fishing*

Salmon play a central role in Northwest tribal activity, culture, and ceremony. They provide a source of food, commercial income, and a way of life. Thus, to the extent that changes to the operations of hydroelectric projects are successful in restoring the salmon, tribal interests will benefit.

Treaties between the Northwest tribes and the U.S. government contain provisions acknowledging the right of tribal members to "take fish in common with all citizens of the territory at all usual and accustomed places."[78] The tribal rights secured in such treaties have been defined in a long line of judicial decisions. The U.S. Supreme Court has concluded that treaties are a reservation of rights and that this reservation of rights created, in essence, a property right.[79] Lower courts have further interpreted the extent of this property right as "fair share"[80] and as fifty percent of the catch.[81] The Supreme Court has affirmed these definitions[82] and has also stated that tribal fishermen are immune from all federal and

77. *See* Joseph J. Kalo et al., *Coastal and Ocean Law* (photo. reprint of draft Sept. 1998) (3d ed. 1998).

78. Michael C. Blumm & Brett M. Swift, *The Indian Treaty Piscary Profit and Habitat Protection in the Pacific Northwest: A Property Rights Approach*, 69 U. Colo. L. Rev. 407, 409 (1998) (citing Treaty of Medicine Creek, Dec. 26, 1854, U.S.-Nisquallys-Puyallups, art. 3, 10 Stat. 1132, 1133; Treaty with the Nez Perces, June 11, 1855, U.S.-Nez Perces, art. 3, 12 Stat. 957, 958).

79. *See* United States v. Winans, 198 U.S. 371, 380–81 (1905) (citing Jones v. Meehan, 175 U.S. 1 (1899); Choctaw Nation v. United States, 119 U.S. 1 (1886)).

80. *See* Sohappy v. Smith, 302 F. Supp. 899, 911 (D. Or. 1969).

81. *See* United States v. Washington, 384 F. Supp. 312, 343 (W.D. Wash. 1974).

82. *See* Washington v. Washington State Commercial Passenger Fishing Vessel Ass'n, 443 U.S. 658, 686, *modified sub nom.* Washington v. United States, 444 U.S. 816 (1979) (stating that Indian treaty right "secures so much as, but no more than, is necessary to provide the Indians with a livelihood—that is to say, a moderate living").

state regulation of fishing locations and catch limits except that required for conservation.[83]

Courts have also inferred that these treaties include protection for salmon habitat, stating that the tribes are entitled to more than the mere chance to dip their nets into empty waters.[84] One Washington district court reasoned that the treaties implied a right of protection for fish habitat necessary for the survival of the fish that were the primary purpose of the treaty.[85] While the fulfillment of this right to habitat protection has been controversial both in practice and in the courts,[86] lower courts have provided the tribes with relief. The treaty right has been interpreted to entitle tribes (1) to ask for changes in dam operations to maintain streamflows essential for fish habitat and migration,[87] (2) to enjoin dam construction,[88] and (3) to modify plans of the Federal Columbia River Power System for peaking power purposes.[89] In sum, these cases demonstrate that tribal treaty rights include the power to change dam operations to preserve salmon habitat.[90]

The authority of Congress to abrogate treaty rights has been recognized by the U.S. Supreme Court.[91] However, the Court has ruled that federal statutes do not abrogate treaty rights unless there is "clear evidence" that Congress actually considered the conflict and specifically

---

83. *See Washington State Commercial Passenger Fishing Vessel Ass'n*, 443 U.S. at 658; Puyallup Tribe v. Department of Game, 391 U.S. 392 (1968).

84. *See* United States v. Washington, 506 F. Supp. 187 (W.D. Wash. 1980).

85. *See* Blumm & Swift, *supra* note 78, at 415; *see also United States v. Washington*, 506 F. Supp. at 203–04.

86. *See* Blumm & Swift, *supra* note 78, at 415; *see also* United States v. Washington, 759 F.2d 1353, 1357 (9th Cir. 1985) (en banc). Upon appeal, an en banc panel of the Ninth Circuit noted that the legal standards governing the state's habitat protection duties under the treaty "will depend for their definition and articulation upon concrete facts which underlie a dispute in a particular case." The panel thus failed to reach a conclusion on the habitat issue.

87. *See* Michael C. Blumm, *Fulfilling the Parity Promise: A Perspective on Scientific Proof, Economic Cost, and Indian Treaty Rights in the Approval of the Columbia Basin Fish and Wildlife Program*, 13 Envtl. L. 103, 141 (1982).

88. *See id.*

89. *See id.*

90. *See* Blumm & Swift, *supra* note 78, at 467.

91. Because Congress exercises "plenary power" over Indian affairs, it has the power to unilaterally void or abrogate treaty rights. *See* Robert J. Miller, *Speaking with Forked Tongues: Indian Treaties, Salmon, and the Endangered Species Act*, 70 Or. L. Rev. 543, 563–64 (1991); *see also* United States v. Wheeler, 435 U.S. 313, 331 (1978); Lone Wolf v. Hitchcock, 187 U.S. 553, 565 (1903).

chose to abrogate the treaty.[92] The ESA is silent in regards to treaties.[93] However, the protection of treaty fishing rights has been addressed in a 1997 order issued by the Secretaries of the Interior and Commerce on tribal rights, federal trust responsibilities, and the ESA.[94] United States Fish and Wildlife Service and the National Marine Fisheries Service provide further guidance.[95] These reports detail a set of principles which acknowledge tribal rights and define the government's trust obligation to protect treaty fishing rights.[96]

A determination of the nature of tribal rights and their associated value involves two distinct measurements. The above analysis presents a strong argument that restoration of the rivers and larger salmon runs is a restoration of a loss for tribes. Interpretations of treaties as a reservation of legal rights suggest the use of willingness to accept (WTA) to represent the restoration of a loss. In addition, tribes appear to view the restoration of the rivers and salmon as not just a restoration of a treaty right, but a restoration of a right they are entitled to as a part of the earth and creation.[97] Thus, the WTA measurement recognizes not only the legal right but also the importance of this psychological expectation and the restoration of a way of life. The commercial value of the salmon to the tribes would be measured separately, using willingness to pay (WTP).

---

92. *See* United States v. Dion, 476 U.S. 734, 740 (1986).

93. *See* Mary Christina Wood, *Fulfilling the Executive's Trust Responsibility Toward the Native Nations on Environmental Issues: A Partial Critique of the Clinton Administration's Promises and Performance*, 25 Envtl. L. 733, 790 n.274 (1995).

94. *See* Blumm & Swift, *supra* note 78, at 495.

95. *See* Wood, *supra* note 93, at 792 (citing National Marine Fisheries Serv., *Proposed Recovery Plan for Snake River Salmon* (1995); Memorandum from the Director of U.S. Fish & Wildlife Serv. to the Assistant Secretary of Indian Affairs (Aug. 24, 1994)).

96. The principles would allow the government to impose restrictions on tribal activities only when: (1) the restrictions imposed on treaty fishing are "reasonable and necessary" for the conservation of the species; (2) the restrictions are the least restrictive alternative to achieve the benefits of development; (3) the restrictions do not discriminate in any way against treaty fishing; and (4) voluntary tribal conservation measures are not adequate to achieve the conservation purpose. *See* Blumm & Swift, *supra* note 78, at 495. There is disagreement regarding a fifth principle: the extent to which non-Indian activities must be restricted before regulation may be directed at Indian activities. *See* Wood, *supra* note 93, at 793. Blumm and Swift believe that developments should provide tribes with "just compensation" for the loss or diminishment of treaty rights if the proposed developments produce a significant loss of treaty fishing and impair the tribes' moderate living needs, despite efforts to satisfy these principles. *See* Blumm & Swift, *supra* note 78, at 497.

97. Telephone conversation with Randy Settler, Yakima Division of the Inter-Tribal Fish Comm'n (Mar. 30, 1999).

G. *Sport Fishing*

Sports fishermen, as well as associated businesses, would benefit from increased salmon runs, as limitations imposed on sport fishing are likely to be reduced or lifted. The sport fishermen are likely to experience a restoration or increase in a valued and unique way of life, while supporting businesses may realize financial benefits.

As with commercial fishing, sports fishermen and associated businesses are likely to experience an initial loss due to restrictions on fishing, followed by a long-term gain as the numbers of fish increase. For the supporting businesses to which sport fishing has a commercial value, the correct measure would be willingness to pay (WTP). This should reflect the net long-term gain. To the extent that sport fishing is a way of life that is highly valued and fairly unique, the measure should recognize a sense of psychological expectation. Both the income effect and substitution possibilities will result in large discrepancies between the WTA and the WTP.[98] In this case, the use of willingness to accept (WTA) is the appropriate measure.

H. *Recreation and Tourism*

The results of proposed changes in dam operations increase some recreational opportunities and diminish others. Activities related to rivers and riparian habitats include boating, fishing, and picnicking. Operators of existing recreational facilities and related businesses will likely feel the changes as an economic loss; however, opportunities for new recreational businesses will be valued as a gain. Due to the commercial value associated with recreational and tourism businesses, the correct measure is the willingness to pay (WTP). The value experienced by recreational users of the natural environment is not generally accounted for by economic or market values. Despite the challenge of estimating these values, they are an important element in assessing project benefits and costs.[99] Existing recreational users who would lose opportunities would experience a loss that should be valued by the willingness to accept (WTA), which recognizes the importance of their psychological expectation and their loss. Some recreation users will experience gains

---

98. *See* discussion *supra* Part II.C.

99. *See* Daniel D. Huppert et al., *River Economics: Evaluating Trade-Offs in the Columbia River Basin Fish and Wildlife Program* (manuscript at 24, on file with authors).

from new opportunities which should be valued using the WTA that recognizes a psychological expectation and the restoration of a previous loss. Gains experienced by those who simply value a free-flowing river or wild salmon are addressed in the following section.

I. Existence Value to the Public

In addressing the public as an affected party, we are referring to their "existence values," often called "non-use values" or "passive use values". These concepts represent the value people place on the very existence of a good.[100] Existence values are difficult to measure because they are not reflected by market values. Despite the difficulty of determining these nonmarket values, the values can be large, particularly for environmental goods, and may be crucial to rational preservation decisions.[101]

Three crucial questions arise when using existence values. First, what goods represent existence values that are to be included in a benefit cost analysis? That is, which goods are to be given economic standing? Usually, existence values are calculated only for such goods as species or habitat preservation. Many goods, however, have some existence value. In analyses of proposals to protect salmon, some studies do not consider existence values, others consider the existence value of salmon, while others consider both salmon and free-flowing rivers. No rationale is articulated for these choices. The rule should be to count all goods for which existence value is likely to be important.

Second, what are the groups of people for whom existence value should be counted? Analyses reflect differing assessments of the affected population. For example, in the case of the Nestucca oil spill, the populations of Washington and British Columbia were used for estimating damages, while in the case of the Exxon Valdez spill, the population of the entire United States was held to be the potentially affected population.[102]

---

100. Typically, we do not speak in terms of rights of natural resources themselves. Natural resource rights are reflected through statutory protections such as the ESA that impose legal duties enforceable by others. In benefit cost analysis, a resource's right is reflected in both the use and non-use values we place on it. *See* Christopher D. Stone, *Should Trees Have Standing? Revisited: How Far Will Law and Morals Reach? A Pluralist Perspective*, 59 S. Cal. L. Rev. 1 (1985).

101. *See* Huppert et al., *supra* note 99, at 27.

102. *See* Richard W. Dunford et al., *Whose Losses Count in Natural Resources Damages?*, 15 Contemp. Econ. Pol'y 77, 80 (1997).

Related to this second question is the issue of whether or not existence values should be counted when the harm is not known. The argument has been made that without specific knowledge of the injury there can be no loss.[103] This argument fails, however, since it ignores the relation of wealth to value. People who care about salmon runs and free-flowing rivers care about environmental wealth. They care about the Elwha River salmon and the like as belonging to a class of goods that constitute this wealth. Those who put a non-use value on species preservation may not know about a particular species, but may be reasonably said to care about it as part of a genera or class of species they do care about. Thus, existence value should be counted regardless of whether the harm is known.

A thorough discussion of how to resolve these two issues is beyond the scope of this Article. In short, the determination of what goods represent existence values and what groups of people for whom existence value should be counted will involve consideration of the concepts of legal and economic standing. In addition, the proposed rights-based approach requires recognition of psychological expectations in making these determinations.

The third question, which is most relevant to the proposed methodology, is how to determine the correct measurement of existence values—willingness to pay (WTP) or willingness to accept (WTA). Surveys framed from a WTA perspective, asking how much one would be willing to accept to sell his or her right, tend to elicit much higher values than WTP questions, asking how much one would pay to obtain the right or protection.[104] The phrasing of the question reflecting ownership or a lack thereof can thus greatly impact the measurement of existence value. Resolution of these issues will depend in part on the definition of ownership of natural resources. Consider: If the public owns the right to clean air, then the use of WTA is appropriate. If polluters have the right to degrade the air, such as through pollution permits, then the use of WTP for the public reflects the lack of a public right.[105] The common law, statutes, and economic analyses have been inconsistent in regards to the legal rights associated with existence value but appear to be tending toward recognition of public ownership rights, both legal and

---

103. *See id.* at 81 ("[A] . . . criteria for economic standing for nonuse damages is that people must have knowledge of the specific injuries to the natural resources in their utility function.").

104. *See* Levy & Friedman, *supra* note 21, at 496.

105. *See id.* at 514.

psychological.[106] Due to this recognition and the generally strong sense of psychological expectation on the part of the public, the use of both WTP and WTA is appropriate, using a weighted average that accounts for the degree of psychological expectation. In the case of Northwest dam policy, a crucial question in determining the appropriate measure is whether or not the public regards salmon and river restoration as an environmental gain or as loss restored. To the extent the public has always felt ownership, the weight of the willingness to accept (WTA) should reflect the loss restored. The magnitude of existence value will also be influenced by the divergence between the WTP and WTA due to the public sense of value of the salmon and the river (the income effect), and by the uniqueness of these resources (substitution possibilities).[107]

Existence values reflect real values that merit consideration. In addition to the appropriate application of willingness to pay and willingness to accept values, the questions that surround existence value are essentially questions of economic standing: how broadly to define the public for which existence values are measured and how broad is the class of goods for which existence values exist? These questions are matters of law and economics so an appropriate rights-based benefit cost analysis must address them.

---

106. Federal common law has recognized public ownership of natural resources. *See id.* at 515. Current state and federal court decisions tend to support the notion of public ownership rights. *See id.* at 519. Further, under the common law concept of a public trust doctrine, the government is deemed to hold title to natural resources in trust for its citizens. This doctrine has the potential to create enforceable legal rights for private citizens to enforce the public's interest in natural resources. *See* Frona M. Powell, *The Public Trust Doctrine: Implications for Property Owners and the Environment*, 25 Real Est. L.J. 255, 257–58 (1997). Exceptions to the common law recognition of public ownership of natural resources do exist, however, as illustrated by the legal use of "public" resources for private grazing and mining purposes. *See* Levy & Friedman, *supra* note 21, at 521–22. The Endangered Species Act, with its mandate for species protection and citizen suit provisions, appears to suggest some recognition of existence value for the public and a sense of public ownership of natural resources. Regulations related to the Comprehensive Environmental Response, Compensation and Liability Act (CERCLA) originally required the public trustee to select the lesser of either restoration costs or diminution of value of the resources at issue. *See* 42 U.S.C.A. §§ 9601–9675 (West Supp. 1998). New parallel regulations giving greater weight to restoration were, however, adopted by both the Department of the Interior (DOI) and the National Oceanographic Atmospheric Administration in response to judicial decisions. *See, e.g.*, Ohio v. United States Dep't of the Interior, 880 F.2d 432 (D.C. Cir. 1989); 43 C.F.R. § 11.83 (1998). The DOI also appears now to acknowledge the appropriateness of WTA as the measure of public ownership of natural resources. *See* Levy & Friedman, *supra* note 21, at 514–15.

107. *See* discussion *supra* Part II.C.

J. Summary of Application of the Proposed Methodology

The following chart summarizes the application of the proposed methodology to a benefit cost analysis of the major interests impacted by proposals to alter hydroelectric operations and facilities.

INTERESTS	BENEFITS	COSTS
Hydropower Licensee		Use WTP based on commercial value and limited legal rights
Electricity Consumers		For commercial consumers, use WTP based on commercial value; for private consumers, use WTA for significant price increases to represent the loss
Commercial Navigation		Use WTP based on commercial value
Irrigators & Other Water Users		Use WTP to reflect the commercial value of the water; use WTA to reflect any loss of way of life/psychological expectation
Commercial Fishing	Use WTP to reflect net long-term gain in commercial value	
Tribal Fishing	Use WTA to reflect net long-term restoration of legal right and psychological expectation; use WTP for any commercial value	
Sport Fishing	Use WTA to reflect restoration and psychological expectation of a way of life; Use WTP for commercial value of associated businesses	
Recreation and Tourism	Use WTP for commercial value of new business opportunities; for users of new recreational opportunities, use WTA to reflect psychological expectation and restoration of a previous loss	Use WTP for commercial value of lost business opportunities; for existing recreational users, WTA should reflect psychological sense of loss
Existence Value to the Public	Use WTP and consider divergence between WTP and WTA weighted by extent of psychological expectation (which should reflect the sense of a loss restored and the impact of substitution possibilities)	

K. Significant Impacts of the Proposed Methodology

Consideration of legal rights and psychological expectations has significant impacts on the measurement of values in a benefit cost analysis by requiring the application of the willingness to accept (WTA) value for those with rights who suffer loss or experience losses restored. In addition, legal rights and psychological expectations are important to the economic standing issue of whose interests and goods are included in the analysis, particularly the inclusion of tribal rights and existence value. The treatment of these issues can dramatically affect the outcome and reliability of the benefit cost analysis, as values may be miscalculated and relevant interests may be excluded from the analysis. In general, an appropriate rights-based consideration of benefits and costs will lead to an increase in the calculation of the net benefits of dam modifications and other salmon restoration proposals.

IV. ANALYSIS OF CURRENT STUDIES IN LIGHT OF PROPOSED METHODOLOGY

The analyses originally undertaken to evaluate the building of hydroelectric projects on the Lower Snake River showed that the dams did not pass a benefit cost test. As we have noted, these analyses were performed without mention of rights, tribal or otherwise, fishing values, existence values, or species or habitat values.[108] Had consideration been given to any of these sources of value, the arguments for not building the dams would have been all the stronger. But they have been built. Now, as fish preservation and restoration have become important, consideration is being given to breaching dams on the Lower Snake River and modifying operations at other Snake and Columbia River dams.

At least ten studies, in various stages of completion, include elements of benefit cost analysis of salmon recovery efforts on the Snake and

108. *See supra* note 15 and accompanying text; *see also* Asami Miyata, Changes in Valuation of the Environment in Benefit Cost Analysis: A Case of Four Lower Snake Dams (1999) (unpublished M.P.A. thesis, Univ. of Wash.) (on file with authors) (citing Keith C. Peterson & Mary E. Reed, *Controversy, Conflict and Compromise: A History of the Lower Snake River Development* (1995); Mary E. Reed, *A History of North Pacific Division, U.S. Army Corps of Engineers* (1991)). As noted previously, the original analyses also failed to consider issues of uncertainty. According to Gary Ellis of the U.S. Army Corps of Engineers, the ongoing Lower Snake River Feasibility Study includes a section on uncertainty. *See* Comments on a Draft of this Article by Gary Ellis, U.S. Army Corps of Engineers (June 7, 1999) (on file with authors).

Columbia Rivers.[109] One cannot report either comprehensively or definitively on these studies, as most are incomplete. But if past reports, current studies, drafts of forthcoming studies, and the guidelines used by the Army Corps of Engineers are any indication, legal rights and psychological expectations and the distinction between valuing gains and losses in terms of WTP and WTA will be largely ignored. In general, the studies simply use the WTP as the measure of costs and benefits for all interests and ignore key interests, particularly tribal rights and existence value.

These issues are evident in one of the few completed reports, Lansing's analysis of restoring the Lower Snake to a free-flowing river.[110] He concludes that removal of the four Lower Snake River dams is supported by his benefit cost analysis. The study fails to distinguish between the use of WTP and WTA for any of the interests addressed. He focuses only on costs and savings associated with power generation, mitigation of impacts on salmon, navigation, and irrigation. In doing so, he gives no consideration to rights. The study fails to address the effects on tribes or recreation and does not consider the existence value of salmon, a free-flowing river, or the like. On balance, an appropriate rights-based consideration of benefits and costs, incorporating all interests and the using WTA to recognize legal rights and psychological expectations, would likely lead to an increase in the calculation of the net benefits of dam removal, at least as calculated by Lansing.[111]

---

109. *See* Government Accounting Office, *Potential Economic Costs of Further Protection for Columbia River Salmon* (1993); Joel R. Hamilton & Norman K. Whittlesey, Cost of Using Water from the Snake River Basin to Augment Flows for Endangered Salmon, Paper Presented Before the Reg'l Science Ass'n Meeting (Feb. 26, 1996); Harza Northwest, Inc., U.S. Army Corps of Engineers, *Salmon Decision Analysis: Lower Snake River Feasibility Study* (1996); Daniel D. Huppert & David L. Fluharty, Nat'l Marine Fisheries Serv., *Economics of Snake River Salmon Recovery* (1996); Daniel D. Huppert et al., Northwest Power Planning Council, *River Economics: Evaluating Trade-Offs in the Columbia River Basin Fish and Wildlife Program* (1999); Philip S. Lansing, Oregon Natural Resources Council Fund, *Restoring the Lower Snake River: Saving Snake River Salmon and Saving Money* (1999); U.S. Dep't of Energy, *Columbia River System Operating Review Final Environmental Impact Statement* (1995); Gardner M. Brown Jr. et al., Washington State Dep't of Ecology, Estimated Economic Benefits of Regulations to Improve Washington State Fisheries (1999) (unpublished, on file with authors); Daniel D. Huppert, Snake River Salmon Recovery: Quantifying the Costs, (Nov. 2, 1998) (unpublished, on file with authors); John Loomis, U.S. Army Corps of Engineers, Lower Snake River Juvenile Mitigations Feasibility Study (1999) (unpublished, on file with authors).

110. *See* Lansing, *supra* note 110.

111. Concerns have been raised regarding other aspects of Lansing's analysis, a subject that is beyond the scope of this Article.

A notable exception to the tendency to ignore these critical issues appears to be the Corps's ongoing Lower Snake River Feasibility Study. In response to an early draft of this paper, Gary Ellis of the U.S. Army Corps of Engineers indicates that the feasibility study now includes a section on tribal circumstances and covers existence values in a portion of the Recreation Study. While the analyses of these issues are not specifically calculated as part of the benefits and costs, they are discussed in an effort to provide information to decisionmakers.[112] The inclusion of these issues appears to indicate both the continued development of more sophisticated benefit cost methodologies and changes in environmental values.

A. *Distinguishing Between WTP and WTA*

The importance of choosing between the use of willingness to pay (WTP) and willingness to accept (WTA) as the measure for certain interests is demonstrated in Loomis's draft work on recreational benefits. Loomis notes:

> The U.S. Water Resources Council (1983) which governs the conduct of benefit cost analyses by federal agencies such as the U.S. Army Corps of Engineers (COE) requires that benefits to the visitor be measured as the . . . net willingness to pay (WTP). . . . The economics profession also recommends net WTP as the conceptually correct measure of benefits for benefit cost analysis.[113]

This last sentence is incorrect. Current literature on this subject is voluminous and its conclusions are generally quite opposite of the above statement that the WTP is in all cases the correct measure.[114] The main support for the use of the WTP is limited to practical considerations—namely that it is easier to calculate. While calculation of the WTA values may pose practical difficulties, incorporation of these values where appropriate is essential for accurate and comprehensive benefit cost analysis. As noted previously, such calculations have been found to be as

---

112. *See* Comments on a Draft of this Article by Gary Ellis, U.S. Army Corps of Engineers (June 7, 1999) (on file with authors).

113. U.S. Water Resources Council, *Economic and Environmental Principles and Guidelines for Water and Related Land Resources Implementation Studies* (1983). The conclusions of the U.S. Water Resources Council rely on the work of Sassone & Schaeffer and Loomis & Walsh.

114. Loomis's citation is to an outdated textbook that has never been well regarded.

much as nineteen times greater.[115] Thus, the use of WTA in appropriate circumstances to recognize the existence of legal rights or psychological expectations generally leads to much higher calculations of project benefits and costs and can significantly alter the results of the benefit cost analysis.[116]

B. *Recognition of Tribal Rights*

As in Lansing's analysis, few of the current studies address the issue of tribal rights.[117] From a rights perspective, tribal interests should receive economic standing in recognition of their legal rights and psychological expectations. As noted previously, treaties have been interpreted as a reservation of legal right and the tribes have a strong sense of psychological expectation to the existence and harvest of the salmon. Using the WTA value to represent the tribes' legal rights, psychological expectations, and the restoration of these rights and expectations will result in significantly greater benefit calculations of proposals to protect and restore salmon.

C. *Accounting for Existence Values*

As noted previously, important issues arise with existence values:[118] whose existence values should the analyst include, for which goods should the analyst calculate existence values, and when should the willingness to accept (WTA) be used rather than the willingness to pay (WTP)? Determination of which individuals and goods to include in measuring existence values and the appropriate use of WTA for existence values will, in many cases, be determinative of the benefit cost outcome. Resolution of these issues is critical, yet it has been substantially neglected in the various reports. Two studies highlight the challenges associated with measuring existence values and demonstrate

115. *See supra* note 22 and accompanying text.

116. In response to an early draft of this paper, Loomis indicates the potential of revising his work to take into account the appropriate use of WTP and WTA. *See* Comments on a Draft of this Article by John Loomis (June 9, 1999) (on file with authors).

117. The Corps's ongoing Lower Snake River Feasibility Study includes a section on tribal circumstances that includes tribal viewpoints regarding the various alternatives discussed in the study. *See* Comments on a Draft of this Article by Gary Ellis, U.S. Army Corps of Engineers (June 7, 1999) (on file with authors).

118. *See* discussion *supra* Part III.I. In addition, there exists the practical problem of accurate measurement.

the impact of including existence values and resolving these challenges can have on the outcome of the analyses. Clearly there remain issues of standing with respect to existence values: for whom are existence values measured and what goods are considered to have existence value.[119]

Huppert estimates the existence value associated with dam removal on the Lower Snake based on calculations for the Pacific Northwest, speculating that the high value is unlikely to be greater than $204 million per year.[120] Loomis, however, estimates existence value using values for the Pacific Northwest and California, resulting initially in much higher existence value estimates of approximately $1040 million per year.[121]

Loomis's study points to a second issue related to the inclusiveness of existence value. Existence value is calculated for the predicted increase in salmon as well as for returning the Lower Snake to a free-flowing river, independent of any effect on salmon populations.[122] This demonstrates how the inclusion of all potential classes of existence value is likely to further impact the outcome of benefit cost analyses associated with dam modifications.

Existence values also require consideration of the distinction between the use of willingness to pay (WTP) and willingness to accept (WTA). As noted previously, if restoration of salmon and a free-flowing river are properly regarded as the restoration of a loss in recognition of psychological expectations of the public, then the WTA measure should be used. The resulting values will likely be significantly higher than those calculated using a WTP measurement.[123]

The importance of properly accounting for questions of economic standing and correctly measuring existence value using willingness to accept (WTA) can hardly be overestimated. How the issues are resolved will have a significant impact on the results of any benefit cost analysis.

---

119. Any economic argument for dam removal or modification would be made much stronger by the inclusion of existence values. The differences between Huppert's, Loomis's and McKean's analyses are important and are issues of legal and economic standing. *See* discussion *supra* Part II.E.

120. *See* Daniel D. Huppert, Snake River Salmon Recovery: Quantifying the Costs 11 (Nov. 12, 1998) (unpublished, on file with authors).

121. *See* Loomis, *supra* note 110. This figure has been revised by Loomis to $96 million per year. The revision is based on the assumption that without dam removal, salmon numbers will remain stable. If the assumption is made that salmon numbers will continue to decline without dam removal, the revised estimated existence value is $732 million per year. *See* Comments on a Draft of this Article by Gary Ellis, U.S. Army Corps of Engineers (June 7, 1999) (on file with authors).

122. The study calculates $1040 million for salmon and $420 million for a free-flowing river.

123. *See* discussion *supra* Part II.C.

The failure of studies to use the proposed rights-based methodology means the benefit cost analyses will not provide an accurate and comprehensive assessment of the true impacts of the proposed salmon recovery efforts. The analyses will therefore fail to provide accurate and useful information to decisionmakers as they assess the trade-offs of the proposed actions.

V. CONCLUSION

Benefit cost analyses of proposed alterations to hydroelectric projects as part of salmon protection efforts should address both legal rights and psychological expectations in order to result in comprehensive and accurate assessments from which to make informed decisions. Proper consideration of rights affects the measurement of benefits and costs by requiring the distinction between willingness to pay (WTP) and willingness to accept (WTA) values. The generally higher values associated with WTA measurements are warranted in cases where the interests have either legal rights or psychological expectations. In addition, consideration of rights alters the determination of whose interests and what goods are to be included in the analysis. Proper consideration of these issues has the potential to significantly affect the outcome of the analysis and influence the decisionmaking process. In the case of proposals to alter Northwest hydroelectric projects in an effort to restore salmon, the net benefits of such efforts are likely to be significantly higher under a proper rights-based analysis.

These issues are not trivial ones. Insofar as benefit cost analyses do not address them, the analyses contribute less to the appropriate public discussion required as the public and decisionmakers may not have adequate information from which to assess the true trade-offs of alternative actions.

J O I N T   C E N T E R

AEI-BROOKINGS JOINT CENTER FOR REGULATORY STUDIES

A Cost-Benefit Analysis of the New Orleans Flood Protection System

Stéphane Hallegatte*

Regulatory Analysis 06-02
March 2006

---

*Stéphane Hallegatte of the Center for Environmental Sciences and Policy, Stanford University, and Centre International de Recherche sur l'Environnement et le Développement, Ecole Nationale des Ponts-et-Chaussées can be reached at hallegatte@centre-cired.fr. He is grateful to Philippe Ambrosi, Hans-Martin Füssel, François Gusdorf, Minh Ha-Duong, Robert Hahn, Mike Jackson, Mike Mastrandrea and Jonathan Wiener for very useful suggestions and advices on the form and content of this article. This research was supported by the European Commission's Project No. 12975 (NEST) "Extreme events: Causes and consequences (E2-C2)". The views expressed in this paper reflect those of the authors and do not necessarily reflect those of the institutions with which they are affiliated.

JOINT CENTER

AEI-BROOKINGS JOINT CENTER FOR REGULATORY STUDIES

In order to promote public understanding of the impact of regulations on consumers, business, and government, the American Enterprise Institute and the Brookings Institution established the AEI-Brookings Joint Center for Regulatory Studies. The Joint Center's primary purpose is to hold lawmakers and regulators more accountable by providing thoughtful, objective analysis of relevant laws and regulations. Over the past three decades, AEI and Brookings have generated an impressive body of research on regulation. The Joint Center builds on this solid foundation, evaluating the economic impact of laws and regulations and offering constructive suggestions for reforms to enhance productivity and welfare. The views expressed in Joint Center publications are those of the authors and do not necessarily reflect the views of the Joint Center.

All AEI-Brookings Joint Center publications can be found at www.aei-brookings.org

Executive Summary

In the early stages of rebuilding New Orleans, a decision has to be made on the level of flood protection the city should implement. Such decisions are usually based on cost-benefit analyses. But in such an analysis, the results are contingent on a number of underlying assumptions and varying these assumptions can lead to different recommendations. Indeed, though a standard first-order analysis rules out category 5 hurricane protection, taking into account climate change and other human-related disruptions of environment, second-order impacts of large-scale disasters, possible changes in the discount rate, risk aversion and damage heterogeneity may make such a hurricane protection a rational investment, even if countervailing risks and moral hazard issues are included in the analysis. These results stress the high sensitivity of the CBA recommendation to several uncertain assumptions, highlight the importance of second-order costs and damage heterogeneity in welfare losses, and show how climate change creates an additional layer of uncertainty in infrastructure design that increases the probability of either under-adaptation (and increased risk) or over-adaptation (and sunk costs).

A Cost-Benefit Analysis of the New Orleans Flood Protection System

Stéphane Hallegatte

1. Introduction

Six months after the deadly landfall of the category 4 Hurricane Katrina on New Orleans, there is an active debate about the reconstruction of New Orleans and the design of its future flood protection system (*e.g.*, Schwartz, 2005; Bohannon and Enserink, 2005). Although the reconstruction of New Orleans has been questioned by House Speaker Dennis Hastert and is still a debated question (Hahn, 2005), this paper will assume that it will be eventually carried out and focus on an adjacent question, namely the necessity of making the city flood protection system able to cope with category 5 hurricanes.

The design of natural disaster protection systems is based on cost-benefit analyses (CBA; see for instance Arrow *et al.*, 1996), even though other decision-making frameworks have been proposed (*e.g.*, the precautionary principle). In a CBA framework, New Orleans would only benefit from a flood protection system able to cope with category 5 hurricanes, compared to a system able to cope with category 3 or 4 hurricanes, if the additional cost of the upgraded protection was lower than the expected benefits from reduced flood damages. This is not certain to be the case, as surprising as this might appear given Katrina's devastating impact, and this article will show how two evaluations can reach opposite conclusions.

To do so, we will first carry out a simple CBA using available data on the damages caused by Katrina in New Orleans. As we will see, this first CBA clearly rules out any category 5 protection system. Then, we will show how less optimistic assumptions on anthropogenic perturbations of environment and considering additional processes, namely second-order impacts, discount rate choice, countervailing risks and side-effects, risk aversion, and damage heterogeneity, can change the terms of the analysis and potentially justify the implementation of a category 5 system.

2. A first Cost-Benefit Assessment

To carry out a CBA of a category 5 flood protection system in New Orleans, one needs to assess the cost, *C,* of such a system, and its expected benefits, *B*. On the one hand, assessing the cost, *C,* of an upgrade of the protection system is not that complicated, even though it requires a precise definition of the system and an assessment of its construction and maintenance costs. In the very early stages of rebuilding, state officials evaluate the cost of category 5 protection at about $32 billion, compared with a $1 billion cost to restore the initial category 3 protection (Schwartz, 2005). Precise information on the cost of category 4 protection is unavailable but we will assume that it would be about $5 billion, making the additional cost of a category 5 protection $27 billion.

On the other hand, assessing expected benefits is much more problematic, as one needs to take into account benefits of various natures (avoidance of casualties, injuries, economic losses, psychological trauma, etc...) impacting different groups of people and possibly lying far in the future. This aggregation problem has been largely discussed; see, for instance, Adler (2005) or Schneider *et al.* (2000) for aggregation issues between different categories of impacts and Portney and Weyant (1999) for issues concerning inter-temporal aggregation.

Regardless of these important problems, benefits can be defined as the net present value of the expected amount of damages avoided by the protection system upgrade. These benefits can, therefore, be calculated as the discounted sum, for each year from now through the lifetime of the protection system, of the annual probability that a category 5 hurricane hits New Orleans multiplied by the difference between the damages of such a hurricane on a category 4 versus a category 5 protection system. This difference is discounted to take into account the fact that the same benefit is valuated at a higher value when it occurs in the near future rather than further in the future.

The values of three parameters are thus necessary: the discount rate (δ), the probability of occurrence (p), and the amount of avoidable damages in the year n (d_n). From them, expected benefits, B, are easy to calculate[1]:

$$B = \sum_{0}^{+\infty} p \cdot \left(\frac{1}{1+\delta}\right)^n \cdot d_n \,. \tag{1}$$

Assuming that damages are growing over time at the same rate as economic growth, g, which is a conservative hypothesis considering the current growth of economic losses due to natural disasters (Mills *et al.*, 2004; Munich Re, 2005), expected benefits read:

$$B = \sum_{0}^{+\infty} p \cdot \left(\frac{1}{1+\delta}\right)^n \cdot d_0(1+g)^n \approx \frac{pd_0}{\delta - g} \,. \tag{2}$$

[1] It is assumed that protection systems have an infinite lifetime, after having checked that results were only weakly sensitive to the protection system lifetime, chosen in a reasonable range, for the selected values of the parameters. Indeed, as we will see, if $\delta \approx g$, where g is the economic growth rate (see below), the system lifetime becomes an important variable.

where d_0 is the amount of damages a flooding of New Orleans would cause today. If the cost, *C*, of the flood protection system is lower than the expected benefits, *B*, then the system should be implemented. In spite of the difficulties already mentioned, a rough assessment of *B* can be made based on current information. From historical experience (i.e. by observing hurricane frequencies over the last century), one can evaluate the annual probability that a category 5 hurricane hits New Orleans at about $p = 1/500$ (H. Saffir, quoted in Schwartz, 2005).

The Office of Management and Budget (OMB), which carries out CBA of Federal regulations in the U.S., uses two different discount rates to analyze policy decisions (OMB, 2003; see Appendix D, OMB Circular A-4). These two discount rates are used to assess the robustness of findings to the choice of discount rate and to capture two approaches to CBA. First, the discount rate can be calculated as the opportunity cost of capital, especially when strong capital reallocation is involved, yielding a value of 7 percent in the U.S. Second, especially when the project affects consumption patterns (e.g., fiscal changes), the discount rate can be calculated as the "social rate of pure preference" used by the average American saver in his saving decisions, yielding a value of 3 percent. Because the New Orleans flood protection system deals with the optimal allocation of capital, the use of the first value of 7 percent can appear *a priori* more appropriate. Note also that, according to the *Ramsey growth discount rule* (Ramsey, 1928), the discount rate can be evaluated by the relationship $\delta = \rho + \alpha\, g$, where ρ describes value judgments about time preferences and is referred to as the *rate of pure preference for the present;* α is the elasticity of the marginal utility and describes value judgments about the distribution of wealth; and *g* is the growth rate in the considered economy. The 7 percent discount rate used by the U.S. agency is consistent with a rate of pure preference for the present of $\rho = 4$ percent and an elasticity of the marginal utility of $\alpha = 1$, with an expected economic growth of the U.S. economy of $g = 3$ percent. The 3 percent discount rate derived from the social rate of pure preference is consistent with a less optimistic prediction of economic growth, at 2 percent, and a pure preference for the present of $\rho = 1$. It is noteworthy that if damages are growing at the same rate as the economy, then a null pure preference for the present ($\rho = 0$) would imply that the flood protection would yield infinite benefit, provided that this flood protection system has a quasi-infinite lifetime.

Insurance and reinsurance companies (e.g., Munich Re, Swiss Re, etc...) and disaster modeling companies (e.g., RMS, EQECAT, etc...) estimate the direct damages due to any hurricane or flood, and their results are widely used as proxies for the overall economic cost of disasters. These companies estimate the cost of the New Orleans flooding around \$20 billion (RMS, 2005)[2].

[2] Note that the losses due to the New Orleans flooding were only a fraction of the total cost of the Katrina landfall.

Taking into account casualties (about 1,000 people died in the flooding) raises the difficult issue of attributing a cost to a loss of life. Because the expression "*value of the human life*" problematically suggests a market in which one could buy or sell human lives, it is preferable to use the expression "*amount the public is willing to devote to reducing risk in order to save an additional life*", which is a much more acceptable wording. Even though the value depends on the type of risk and the probability of occurrence of the considered event, most estimates lie between $1 million and $10 million in the U.S. We will use here the commonly-used estimation of the U.S. EPA (1997) of $5 million. Given this figure, the public would be willing to pay $5 billion to avoid the human toll of the New Orleans flood. An additional $5 billion will be added to take into account the numerous injuries and trauma. According to these rough estimates, $30 billion seems to be a good approximation of the New Orleans flood cost[3].

Assuming that a category 4 protection system does not reduce the damages yielded by category 5 hurricanes, which is likely since there is little difference between no levees and broken levees, the expected present benefit of a category 5 flood protection system in New Orleans can be calculated with Eq.(2) at $1.5 billion with a 7-percent discount rate and $6 billion with a 3-percent discount rate. Both are one order of magnitude lower than the building cost of such a system. This rough estimate clearly rules out an upgrade of the protection system to make it able to cope with category 5 storms. It might be difficult to believe that the risk of a repetition of the devastation caused by the category 4 hurricane Katrina is not enough to justify the implementation of the best possible protection system. However, our CBA suggests that it is more rational from an economic point-of-view to live the Katrina nightmare again in a more or less remote future[4].

This estimate is, however, not very solidly grounded, as it does not take into account important processes, whose impacts could be significant. In line with OMB requirements when uncertainty is large and economic implications are in excess of $1 billion (OMB, 2003), we will now review the parameters[5] of the CBA, and propose alternative estimates. We will not, however, attribute subjective probabilities to the various hypotheses that will be proposed and conduct a full probabilistic analysis, as can be found, for instance, in Mastrandrea and Schneider (2005) for the

---

[3] In case of a repetition of the Katrina's scenario, a better evacuation would probably be able to avoid a large part of the human losses and reduce this amount of damages. It has to be mentioned, however, (i) that Katrina's track forecasts have been very good and allowed for anticipated decisions before landfall, which is not always possible, and (ii) that an evacuation is always subject to organisational problems and unexpected practical difficulties, making the human part of the damages highly variable and uncertain.

[4] An annual probability of 1/500 means that there is a 20 percent chance of having a category 5 hurricane hitting New Orleans in the next 100 years, and a 33 percent chance in the next 200 years.

[5] Among the necessary assumptions in the CBA, it is often useful to distinguish between the political choices that must arise from a political process (e.g., discounting scheme), and the scientific uncertainties that can be – at least theoretically – solved through additional research (e.g., future probability of occurrence).

climate change issue. Indeed, current knowledge about natural disaster consequences seems still insufficient to assess these probabilities with any confidence, and the following sections will show how much research is still necessary.

3. Probability of Occurrence

In the first CBA, historical evidence was used to assess the probability of occurrence of a category 5 hurricane landfall on New Orleans. This assessment cannot, however, be considered as robust in this CBA. Indeed, a flood protection system has a very long lifetime. Such a long lifetime arises, of course, from the long lifetime of infrastructures (dams, bridges, gates). But, above all, it comes from the fact that the flood protection system will shape the city development over an even longer time horizon. The decisions that will be taken in the next years will, therefore, constrain the flood protection of New Orleans for at least the next century.

During this century, climate is likely to change significantly in response to human emissions of greenhouse gases (GHG), with consequences for hurricane damages. We already detect a trend in hurricane destructiveness: Webster *et al.* (2005) observed that hurricanes in the strongest categories (4 and 5) have almost doubled in number and in proportion in 30 years; over the last 75 years, Emanuel (2005a) detected in the North Atlantic and western North Pacific basins a strong increase in the power-dissipation index (PDI), which is a proxy of the destructiveness of hurricanes. The debate on the significance and persistence of these trends, however, has yet to be solved (e.g., Landsea, 2005; Emanuel, 2005b)

Regardless, experts expect hurricane maximum intensities to increase as temperatures rise during the 21st century. Global climate-model experiments have suggested an increase in the relative risk of occurrence of category-5 hurricanes under high-GHG conditions (Knutson and Tuleya, 2004). A tropical-cyclone model run by Emanuel (2006) found that a 10 percent increase in potential intensity, corresponding approximately to a 2°C-warming, could lead to a 65 percent increase in PDI. Even though uncertainty remains in the amplitude of the change (Trenberth, 2005; Pielke *et al.*, 2005), it is noteworthy that any change in the mean characteristics of hurricanes might easily translate into large changes in the probability of the most powerful hurricanes. As an illustration, if the distribution shape of the hurricane PDI were unchanged, the 65-percent increase in the mean PDI found by Emanuel (2006) would multiply by 3.8 the frequency of the 1-percent most powerful hurricanes (see Appendix A).

Also, sea level rise and other human-induced disruptions to the Mississippi River delta (*e.g.*, sediment deposition reduction) will worsen the floods associated with any hurricane falling on this low-lying area (Burkett *et al.*, 2003). Thus, the probability of floods currently caused only by category 5 hurricanes might increase, as less powerful hurricanes could also produce such devastating floods.

To take into account these two phenomena in the CBA, they will be summarized through the assumption that the annual probability of floods currently caused by category 5 hurricanes will be multiplied by 3.8, to reach p=1/130 years. This higher probability alone would make expected benefits rise from $1.5 to $5.7 billion or from $6 to $22.8 billion, depending on the discount rate.

These results suggest that climate change may have an important impact on long-term hurricane risk, even though changes in population and capital at risk will obviously be the main driver of vulnerability during the next decades. Additionally, the large uncertainty of the future probability of occurrence highlights one mechanism that have been disregarded in the climate change impact literature so far, but through which climate change might be responsible for significant economic damages in the future: climate change increases the uncertainty on parameters that impact the design of long-term infrastructure, making them more likely to be ill-suited in the future climate. In the present case, the risk is either to face a series of avoidable disasters in New Orleans, if the probability of occurrence turns out to be much larger than predicted when the protection system is designed, or to bear the sunk costs of an expensive protection system based on an overestimated probability of occurrence.

4. Avoidable Damages

Another major difficulty remains in the assessment of the actual damages that could be avoided through an upgrade of the protection system. Assuming that New Orleans will be reconstructed and that all displaced households will return to their original city (we will address this issue later in the paper), the damages from the Katrina landfall can be used as a proxy for the damages a future flood may cause. As mentioned earlier, however, several authors suggest that the direct costs, evaluated by insurance companies, may be poor proxies of overall costs, especially concerning large-scale events (Tierney, 1995; Lindell and Prater, 2003; Hallegatte and Hourcade, 2006). Indeed, direct cost can be amplified (i) by spatial or sectoral propagation into the rest of the economic system over the short-term (*e.g.*, through disruptions of lifeline services[6]) and over the

[6] For instance, Tierney (1995) finds that data on the consequences of the 1993 Midwest floods and the 1994 Northridge earthquake suggest that "*business properties may escape direct damage and yet suffer extensive disruption as a result of lifeline service outages*". These short-term costs, however, are most of the time included in the assessments by the insurance industry through "business interruption" costs.

longer term (*e.g.*, sectoral inflation due to demand surge, energy costs, insurance company bankruptcy, larger public deficit, or housing prices that have second-order consequences on consumption); (ii) by responses to the shock (*e.g.*, loss of confidence, change in expectations, indirect consequences of inequality deepening); (iii) by financial constraints impairing reconstruction (*e.g.*, low-income families cannot finance rapidly the reconstruction of their home); and (iv) by technical constraints slowing down reconstruction (*e.g.*, availability of skilled workers, difficulties in equipment and material transportation, difficulties in accommodating workers). To measure the impact of these effects, Hallegatte and Hourcade (2006) introduced in their simple economic model a parameter measuring the ability of the economy to fund and carry out reconstruction, and derived the *Disaster Economic Amplification Ratio* (DEAR), which measures the ratio between the overall economic cost and the direct loss due to a disaster. While this ratio is less than one for small-scale disasters, DEAR is found, using a simple model, to increase dramatically for large-scale disasters like the New Orleans floods. This increase arises mainly from the addition to the capital replacement cost of the production losses during the reconstruction phase. For example, if a $1 million plant was destroyed and immediately rebuilt, the loss would be $1 million; if its reconstruction is delayed by one year, the total loss is the sum of the replacement cost and of the value of one year of production. For housing, the destruction of a house with a one-year delay in reconstruction has a total cost equal to the replacement cost of the house plus the value attributed to inhabiting the house during one year. The value of such production losses, in a broad sense, can be very high in some sectors, especially when basic needs are at stake (housing, health, employment, etc.).

A couple of months after the Katrina landfall, initial analyses of the disaster aftermath unfortunately confirm this intuition; because the "*systemic functioning*" of the whole region is now impaired (both economically and technically), the reconstruction is dramatically slowed down and the total cost of the event will be much larger than its direct cost. In recent publications, the RMS research team (RMS, 2005) and the RAND Corporation (McCarthy *at al.*, 2006) highlight the existence of numerous "loss amplification" effects: demand surge (e.g., a 13-percent increase in cement prices between 2005 and 2008 is forecasted); longer delay in reconstruction due to technical constraints; financial constraints in reconstruction due to insufficient flood-insurance policy coverage. These conclusions probably understate these effects, as they focus primarily on direct costs without considering most of the second-order costs, which are not insured but are supported by the overall community (*e.g.*, the impact of Katrina on tourism in New Orleans and its vicinity during future hurricane seasons, which is still unknown but might turn out to be significant; or the cost of taking in thousands of displaced people in other cities).

Social costs of large-scale disaster also involve other dimensions than direct economic losses and casualties, including psychological factors or political and social destabilization (see a review in Lindell and Prater, 2003). For instance, confidence in the ability of public services to carry out disaster relief in an efficient manner may have been undermined by this event, investors may be reluctant to invest large amounts of money into new businesses in the affected area, and tourists may change their favorite vacation destination if they feel endangered in New Orleans. Of course, a comparable event occurring in the next decades would strongly amplify all these reactions, possibly leading to a withdrawal from New Orleans, the cost of which is difficult to assess[7]. Also, natural disasters have been found in the past to cause strong political and social unrest when they amplified pre-existing tensions (*e.g.*, hurricane Bohla in 1970, which killed almost 300,000 persons in Pakistan without provoking an effective mobilization of the central government to provide relief, worsened social tensions that led to the creation of Bangladesh in 1971). Even though the social and political destabilization arising from a hurricane in the U.S. cannot but remain limited (Lindell and Prater, 2003), the consequences of a near repetition of a Katrina-like event on the social and economic climate of Louisiana are difficult to predict[8]. The cost of two Katrinas would be much larger than twice the cost of one Katrina.

Moreover, even if long-term consequences remain limited when considering a single event, the consequences of a distribution of events on regional economic growth can be significant (Hallegatte and Hourcade, 2006). Indeed, as already stated by Benson and Clay (2004), poor regions or countries affected by repeated natural disasters and suffering from a weak ability to conduct reconstruction may prove unable to maintain the infrastructures necessary for economic development, leading to the creation of "*poverty traps.*" As examples of this phenomenon, we cite Guatemala, whose impressive series of weather catastrophes between 1997 and 2001 prevented any development. Similarly, in Honduras, the single hurricane Michele in 2001 "*put the country's economic development back 20 years*" (Honduran Prime Minister, quoted in IFRCRCS, 2002). Again, it is possible that disasters have, at least in some regions, long-run consequences that are neglected in first-order estimates, through changes in potential economic growth.

---

[7] In particular, a high value might be attributed to the historical and cultural content of New Orleans. In other terms, people can decide to pay an additional price to keep living in New Orleans instead of being relocated. The choice of this value, however, must involve a political process which is beyond the scope of this article.

[8] It may also be necessary to take into account the position of the ruling government. Indeed, the government is likely to be held directly responsible for a repetition of such an event in the same location, that would probably be considered more unacceptable than a comparable disaster in another place (e.g., Sacramento, CA, that runs the same kind of risks than New Orleans). This *private* interest may motivate an over-protection against events that have already occurred, justifying the use of economic analysis to assess risk management projects and avoid under-optimal risk management strategies.

For all these reasons, and given the large vulnerability of New Orleans and its vicinity (important economic activity in sensitive sectors like tourism, transportation or energy production; low reconstruction capacity due to a large proportion of low-income population, etc.), the extent of the damages (80% of the city under water), and the difficulties currently met in the reconstruction process, a conservative estimate of the actual overall cost of the New Orleans floods is at least 50% larger than the insurers' approximation based on direct losses only, to reach $45 billion. It is difficult to assess the cost of a repetition of the Katrina scenario. Of course, the closer from the first hit the larger the additional cost. As a best guess hypothesis, we will assume the cost of a second hit to be, on average over the life-time of the protection system, 25% larger than the first hit, *i.e.* amounting to $56 billion. Using the new values of event probability (p=1/130) and potential damages (d_0=$56 billion), the expected benefit of an upgraded protection system would be $10.7 billion with a 7 percent discount rate and $42.4 billion with a 3 percent discount rate.

5. The Resettlement Issue

We assumed in the previous section that New Orleans will be rebuilt with the same structure it had before Katrina and that all previous inhabitants of New Orleans will return to the city, even if no improvement of the flood protection system is undertaken. This assumption is at odds with what is observed and what is predicted in the coming years. For instance, McCarthy *et al.* (2006) estimate that the New Orleans population will be down to 272,000 in 2008, from 485,000 in 2000. If this new population is maintained, the costs of a new flood would of course be largely reduced compared with the 2005 one, making our assessment of avoidable damages overestimated. But it must be remembered that the flood protection system, the design of which is currently being discussed, will protect New Orleans for at least one century. The pertinent variable is thus the population over the long term, not over the next decade. And the low repopulation rate predicted by McCarthy *et al.* (2006) is mainly explained by the slow reconstruction pace due to short term constraints. It provides, therefore, no estimate of the long-term repopulation of the city.

To assess the long-term repopulation, we assume that, before Katrina, the risk of hurricane was perfectly known and that the New Orleans inhabitants had a rational behavior. We neglect here the potentially important role of social networks (see McCarthy *et al.*, 2006). Within this framework, the large population of New Orleans before the storm can only be explained by comparative advantages of the city's location in some sectors (e.g., tourism, shipping) and by the households' willingness-to-pay (WTP) to live there, because of environmental amenities. Both should have more than compensated the well-known hurricane and flood risk, even in absence of improved flood protection system. If these comparative advantages and this WTP have not been changed by Katrina, and if basic services, infrastructures and social networks can be restored, these assumptions mean that the New Orleans population will eventually return to its pre-Katrina level, even in absence of improved flood protection. They also suggest that the currently observed population reduction is more related to financial and technical constraints than to voluntary choices.

These assumptions, even though questionable, can explain the pre-storm New Orleans and allow us to separate the design of the flood protection system from the reconstruction issue and to justify the use of the 2005 flood data to estimate the cost of a future flood.

6. Countervailing risks, side-effects and reduced

Unfortunately, it is also necessary to take into account the possible side-effects implied by the implementation of a large-scale protection system. These side-effects can yield ancillary benefits like infrastructure improvement, as mentioned by Allenby and Fink (2005), or create or increase other risks, referred to as *countervailing risks*[9] by Wiener (1998), who calls for a broader accounting of them in risk management.

One cannot assess a flood protection system without taking into account moral hazard and equity issues. A flood protection system funded through nationwide taxes, like a uniform insurance premium, can constitute an incentive for people to settle in at-risk areas, as they do not pay for the risk their location choice creates. Indeed, even if they prefer to live in New Orleans rather than anywhere else, it is likely that less people will resettle in New Orleans if they think the Katrina catastrophe can happen again than if a flood protection system makes the probability of such an event negligible. This mechanism is potentially significant, since the large increases in population and investments in hurricane-prone regions are responsible for most of the explosive trend in hurricane damages observed over the last decades (Mills *et al.*, 2004; Munich Re, 2005; Pielke *et al.*, 2005). It should be noticed, however, that the urbanization of vulnerable areas around New Orleans in the past few decades does not seem to have been driven mainly by an over-protection against hurricane floods, but rather by the trade-off carried out by low-income households, who have high rates of preference for the present and poor access to information, between long-term flooding risks and immediate lower housing prices.

These side-effects, however, create a paradox. We would expect an increase in the system benefits from the fact that the protection system would allow a larger number of households to

---

[9] Examples of such countervailing risks in flood management are provided by Glenn *et al.* (1996) or Christensen (1997).

resettle in New Orleans, where they prefer to live. It is not the case. Instead, it reduces the benefits, by lowering the number of persons at-risk if the protection system is not built. This paradox arises from the fact that, again, we do not take into account the comparative advantages of New Orleans and the welfare gain or loss (or WTP) of households who would like to live in this city if they were protected from floods. This paradox suggests that a CBA analysis of the flood protection system taking into account countervailing risks cannot be carried out in a rigorous manner independently of a modeling of individual location choices. Such a modeling, however, is made very difficult by the uncertainty of household WTP, and we will have to rely on other approximations to take into account countervailing risks in our analysis.

The importance of these side-effects will be heavily dependent on the design and practical implementation of the protection system. In particular, huge negative consequences would certainly result from the implementation of an ambitious flood protection system that would not be followed by a careful long-term maintenance. In this worst case scenario, the existence of the protection system would raise investment and population in the so-called protected area, which would not be protected any more after a few decades of negligence, making vulnerability even larger than if no protection was implemented in the first place. As a consequence, the implementation of a protection system must be considered as a long-term commitment.

Also, avoiding negative outcomes from the future flood protection system requires careful design and implementation, in order to protect already urbanized areas without steering additional urbanization toward non-protected flood-prone locations. In this respect, the future flood protection system in New Orleans is certainly not only a system of dams, bridges, and gates. It should also include an important set of new regulations for future urban developments. A wisely designed flood protection system should protect selected areas, with dams and levees, and ensure, through land-use regulations, that investments are not attracted to non-protected areas. Hopefully, increased experience with flood management and the high visibility of the project will foster a flood protection plan that limits the negative effects and promotes positive ones, making the overall consequences of these side-effects positive or, if it reveals impossible, negligible compared with direct costs and benefits.

To be conservative, however, we will take into account the fact that a flood protection system could increase the population and capital at risk compared with an optimal situation. To do so, we will assume that, if no protection system is implemented, the potential damages growth rate will be lower than nationwide economic growth, by an amount Δg=0.5 percent, because of the influence of hurricane risks on housing and investment location choices[10]. We will neglect the fact that, if the protection system is not implemented, there is a loss of welfare for households who would move to New Orleans if the city was protected from flood but who do not move because of the absence of such a protection.

It means that Eq.(2) is changed into:

$$B = \sum_{0}^{+\infty} p \cdot \left(\frac{1}{1+\delta}\right)^n \cdot d_0(1+g-\Delta g)^n \approx \frac{pd_0}{\delta - g + \Delta g} \quad (3)$$

With this new equation, the expected benefit of an upgraded protection system would be $9.5 billion with a 7-percent discount rate and $28.4 with a 3-percent discount rate. With a project cost of $27 billion, the decision would, therefore, be dependent on the discount rate, making it necessary to discuss its value in more detail.

7. Choice of the Discount Rate

As already mentioned, the CBA of a flood protection system has to deal with very long time horizons, making the value of the discount rate controversial. Indeed, there are intense debates (Portney and Weyant, 1999) about the discount rate that should be used for environmental or long-term issues that involve intergenerational issues. When intergenerational equity is strongly involved, OMB suggests that discount rates between 1 and 3 percent are appropriate, since welfare of next generations should not be discounted and only the fact that they are likely to enjoy higher consumption levels should be taken into account. Other governments (e.g., U.K.) favor a decreasing discount rate over time, justified by the uncertainty over future economic situations (The Green Book, U.K. Treasury, 2003; Oxera, 2002).

Another approach is to calculate the discount rate that would make equal costs and benefits and assess its relevance. Using our parameters (probability of occurrence p=1/130 years and potential damages of $56 billion, rising at a growth rate 0.5 percent lower than economic growth), the benefits of the protection system are found equal to its cost if the pure preference for the present is lower than ρ_0 = 1.1 percent. With an expected growth rate of 2 or 3 percent, it would correspond to a discount rate of 3.1 or 4.1 percent, respectively. Since these discount rates are both greater than the largest bound of the OMB's discount rate range for projects involving intergenerational equity

[10] In other terms, the existence of the protection system is assumed to increase economic growth in the protected area by 0.5 percent per year, making it equal to the nationwide economic growth.

issues (3 percent), the last set of hypotheses justifies the implementation of the $27-billion flood protection system.

8. Risk Aversion and Damage Heterogeneity

A society that would use the previous method to assess a protection system is called *risk-neutral.* A risk-neutral agent is indifferent to risk, *i.e.* it does not see any difference between losing $1 with certainty and having a 10% chance of losing $10, because the expected loss is the same in both cases. Theoretically, such an agent would never pay for insurance. Regarding protection against large-scale floods, however, there are good reasons to justify *risk-averse* behavior: people might indeed prefer to pay an additional amount of money (a *risk premium*) to avoid the risk of costly and deadly floods.

To incorporate risk aversion, we change our assessment framework to use a *utility function* that measures the welfare gain or loss that is associated with any financial gain or loss. An utility function with risk aversion assumes that the increase in utility due to a $1 gain is smaller – in absolute value – than the decrease in utility due to a $1 loss. As a consequence, the risk of gaining or losing $1 with equal probability lowers the expected utility and is, therefore, equivalent to a certain financial loss, which is referred to as the *risk premium* or the *equivalent-certain* outcome.

However, if we assume that the damages due to a hurricane landfall are perfectly shared among the whole population of the U.S., the damage per capita is small (a few hundred U.S.$ per capita). In such a situation, the Arrow-Lind (1970) theorem demonstrates formally why risk-aversion can be neglected, supporting the choice of the states that consider self-insurance as a basic principle (e.g., France). Indeed, using an utility function with a constant relative risk aversion of one, as suggested in Arrow (1971) for households in developed countries, the risk-premium amounts only to 0.2% of the damages, *i.e.* $120 million (see appendix B).

The picture is different, however, if a substantial part of the damages impacts only by a small fraction of the population. Indeed, when the utility function is not linear, the utility derived from the consumption of $1 becomes lower as consumption increases. This effect represents the fact that rich people do not gain as much from the consumption of $1 as poor people do. But, it also means that it is not equivalent for a group of 10 people to lose $1 each or to know that one of them will lose $10.

The consequences of these factors on the CBA analysis of a hurricane landfall can be very significant. To assess them, we consider a hurricane landfall on New Orleans, which generates $56 billion of damages, 50 percent of which being equally supported by the whole U.S. population (through government spending in reconstruction[11], increase in insurance premium and other propagation effects into the national economy) and 50 percent being shared only by the *affected population*, which represents 0.4% of the total population, *i.e.* one million people. In this case, individual losses become significant (as large as 90% of annual consumption for the affected population) and risk aversion appears far from negligible. The loss of utility due to such an event is found to be equivalent to the loss of utility of a hurricane that would generate $69 billion of damages shared by the whole U.S. population, without risk-aversion (see appendix C). This value corresponds to a risk premium of $13 billion, *i.e.* 23 percent of the damages. This figure can even be considered as underestimated, because (i) low-income population being more likely to belong to the affected population (Lindell and Prater, 2003), accounting for pre-existing income inequalities would increase utility losses; and (ii) the actual repartition of damages is even more unequal than we assumed, as a few people usually suffer from most of the losses (house, belongings, life environment, but also friends and relatives). Regardless, neglecting the damage heterogeneity in the CBA would lead to a large underestimation of the benefits from an improved protection system.

To carry out a CBA in utility terms, we must compare the utility loss due to the risk of hurricane if no upgraded protection system is implemented with the utility loss due to the reduction of consumption, which is needed to fund the protection system. To do so, we use the *present equivalent-certain cost of the risk of hurricane* (B_c), which is the equivalent of the expected benefit, B, when utility losses are used instead of monetary costs. B_c is such that paying, immediately, the amount B_c to build a protection system would reduce utility by the same amount than supporting the risk of hurricane flooding. As a consequence, the protection system should be built if its cost C is lower than the present equivalent-certain cost of the risk of hurricane (B_c). In this case, the calculation with a pure preference for the present of 1 percent (see Appendix C) leads to a value B_c = $35.3 billion, which makes a category 5 hurricane flood protection system economically efficient.

9. Conclusion

Building a flood protection system able to cope with a category 5 hurricane in New Orleans is a huge investment, and it is wise to precisely assess its benefits before any implementation decision, as other, less-costly projects might be more efficient to improve the population's well-

[11] Federal spending formally related to the Katrina reconstruction might even exceed the amount of damages, because reconstruction can be used to improve regional infrastructures.

being[12]. One must, however, be very careful of the underlying assumptions used in the benefit assessment. Indeed, using probabilities derived from historical experience and direct cost estimates produced by insurance companies lead to low assessments of benefits and rule out any additional flood protection system. Nonetheless, making less optimistic assumptions about possible anthropogenic increases in flood probabilities and taking into account estimates of second-order disaster costs, public risk-aversion, and damage heterogeneity can reverse the conclusion of the CBA, even if countervailing risks and moral hazard issues are accounted for.

These results suggest that a CBA is useful but should encompass the whole set of possible assumptions to check its robustness. In the New Orleans case, the recommendation is highly sensitive to these assumptions, even if the protection system is found worth building only for pessimistic assumptions on climate change.

This analysis also shows that second-order damages and impact heterogeneity are responsible for a large increase in welfare losses. Climate change, even though negligible during the next decades compared to other drivers, might also be an important factor of hurricane risk over the long-term. More generally, climate change creates an additional layer of uncertainty in infrastructure design that increases the probability of either under-adaptation (and increased disaster risk) or over-adaptation (and sunk costs in protection).

[12] This is especially true if improved track forecasts, warning systems and evacuation plans can avoid human losses at low costs.

References

Adler, M.D., 2005. Equity Analysis and Natural Hazards Policy, AEI-Brookings Joint Center for Regulatory Studies, Related Publication 05-30.

Allenby, B. and J. Fink, 2005. Toward Inherently Secure and Resilient Societies, *Science* 309, pp. 1034–1036

Arrow, K.J. and R.C. Lind, 1970. Uncertainty and the evaluation of public investment decisions, *Amer. Econ. Rev.* 60, pp. 364–378

Arrow, K.J.,1971. *Essays in the theory of risk-bearing,* Markham Publishing, Chicago.

Arrow, K.J., M.L. Cropper, G.C. Eads, R.W. Hahn, L.B. Lave, R.G. Noll, P.R. Portney, M. Russel, R.L. Schmalensee, V.K. Smith, R.N. Stavins, 1996. Benefit-Cost Analysis in Environmental, Health, and Safety Regulation, American Enterprise Institute Books and Monographs

Benson, C. and E. Clay , 2004. Understanding the economic and financial impact of natural disasters. The International Bank for Reconstruction and Development. The World Bank, Washington D.C.

Bohannon, J. and M. Enserink, 2005. Scientists Weigh Options for Rebuilding New Orleans, *Science* 309, pp. 1808–1809

Burkett, V. R., Zilkoski, D. B., and Hart, D. A., 2003. Sea-level rise and subsidence: implications for flooding in New Orleans, Louisiana, *in* Prince, K. R., and Galloway, D. L., eds., U.S. Geological Survey Subsidence Interest Group Conference, Proceeding of the Technical Meeting, Galveston, Texas, pp. 63–70

Christensen, J., 1997. California floods change thinking on need to tame rivers, *The New-York Times*, February 4, 1997

Emanuel, K, 2005a. Increasing destructiveness of tropical cyclones over the past 30 years, *Nature* 436, pp.686–688

Emanuel, K., 2005b. Emanuel replies, *Nature* 438, E13

Emanuel, K., 2006. Climate and tropical cyclone activity : A new model downscaling approach, *J. Clim.*, in press

Glenn, E.P., C. Lee, R. Felger an S. Zengel, 1996. Effects of water management on the wetlands of the Colorado River delta, Mexico, *Conservation Biology* 10 (4), pp. 1175–1186.

Hallegatte, S. and J.-C. Hourcade, 2005. Why economic growth matters in assessing climate change damages: illustration on extreme events, accepted by *Ecological Economics*, preprint available on http://www.centre-cired.fr/forum/article77.html?lang=en

Hahn, R.W., 2005. The economics of rebuilding cities: Reflections after Katrina, AEI-Brookings Joint Center for Regulatory Studies, Policy matters 05-24

IFRCRCS, 2002. World disaster report 2002, focusing on reducing risk. International Federation of Red Cross and Red Crescent Societies.

Knutson, T. R. and Tuleya, R. E., 2004. Impact of CO_2-Induced Warming on Simulated Hurricane Intensity and Precipitation: Sensitivity to the Choice of Climate Model and Convective Parameterization, *Journal of Climate* 17, 3477-3495

Landsea, C.W., 2005. Meteorology: Hurricanes and global warming. *Nature* 438, E11-E13

Lecocq, F. and J.C. Hourcade, 2003. Equitable Provision of Long-Term Public Goods: The Role of Negotiation Mandates, *CIRED Working Paper*.

Lindell, M.K. and C. S. Prater, 2003. Assessing Community Impacts of Natural Disasters, Natural Hazards Rev. 4, 176-185

Mastrandrea, M.D. and S.H. Schneider, 2005. Probabilistic integrated assessment of "dangerous" climate change, Science 304, pp.571–575

McCarthy, K., D.J. Peterson, N. Sastry, M. Pollard, 2006. The Repopulation of New Orleans after Hurricane Katrina, *RAND Gulf States Policy Institute*

Mills, E., R.J. Roth and E. Lecomte, 2005. Availability and Affordability of Insurance Under Climate Change: A Growing Challenge for the U.S., CERES, available on http://www.ceres.org

Munich Re, 2005. Annual Review: Natural Catastrophes 2004, Topic Geo

Office of Management and Budget, 2003. Informing regulatory decisions: report to Congress on the costs and benefits of federal regulations and unfunded mandates on state, local, and tribal entities

OXERA, 2002. A Social Time Preference Rate for Use in Long-Term Discounting, A report for ODPM, DFT and DEFRA.

Pielke, R.A. Jr., C. Landea, M. Mayfield, J. Laver and R. Pasch, 2005. Hurricane and Global Warming, *Bulletin of the American Meteorological Society*, November 2005, pp.1571–1575

Portney, P. R. and Weyant, J.P., 1999. Discounting and Intergenerational Equity, Resources for the Future, 202 pp.

Ramsey, F.P., 1928. A mathematical theory of saving, *The Economic Journal* 38 (152), p.543–559

RMS, 2005. Hurricane Katrina: Profile of a Super Cat, Lessons and Implications for Catastrophe Risk Management, available on www.rms.com

Schneider, S.H., K. Kuntz-Duriseti, and C. Azar, 2000. Costing non-linearities, surprises and irreversible events, *Pacific and Asian Journal of Energy*, 10(1):81-106.

Schwartz, J., 2005. Full flood safety in New Orleans could take billions and decades, *The New-York Times*, November 29, 2005

Tierney K. J., 1995. Impacts of Recent U.S. Disasters On Businesses: The 1993 Midwest Floods and the 1994 Northridge Earthquake, Disaster Research Center, University of Delaware

Trenberth K., 2005. Uncertainty in Hurricanes and Global Warming, *Science* 308, pp. 1753–1754

U.K. Treasury, 2003. Green Book, Appraisal and Evaluation in Central Government, available on http://greenbook.treasury.gov.uk/

U.S. Environmental Protection Agency. 1997. The Benefits and Costs of the Clean Air Act: 1970–1990. 410-R-97-002

Webster, P.J., G. J. Holland, J. A. Curry, H.-R. Chang, 2005. Changes in Tropical Cyclone Number, Duration, and Intensity in a Warming Environment, *Science* 309, pp. 1844–1846

Wiener, J. B., 1998. Managing the iatrogenic risks of risk management, Risk: Health, Safety and Environment, 9 (39), pp. 40–82

Appendix A:
The link between mean PDI change and the most powerful hurricane probability

Figure 1 shows in blue the current cumulative distribution function of the hurricane power dissipation index (PDI), as calculated from the NHC/NOAA HURDAT database (www.nhc.noaa.gov) between 1900 and 2004. The horizontal blue line distinguishes the 1-percent most powerful hurricanes, *i.e.*, in the current distribution, the hurricanes with PDI larger than 164 10^9 m^3s^{-2} (vertical black line).

It has been predicted that the mean value of North Atlantic PDI could rise, between now and the end of the century, by 50 percent, according to the predicted rise in sea surface temperature (SST) and the observed correlation between SST and PDI (Emanuel, 2005b), or by 65 percent, according to a hurricane intensity model (Emanuel, 2006).

If climate change increased the mean hurricane PDI by 65 percent through a shift of the distribution to the right, the shape being unchanged, the new cumulative distribution function would be the red line in Fig. 1. With this new distribution, 3.8 percent of the hurricanes would have a PDI larger than 164 10^9 m^3s^{-2}. It means that the frequency of the 1-percent most powerful hurricanes in the present climate would be multiplied by 3.8.

Figure 1

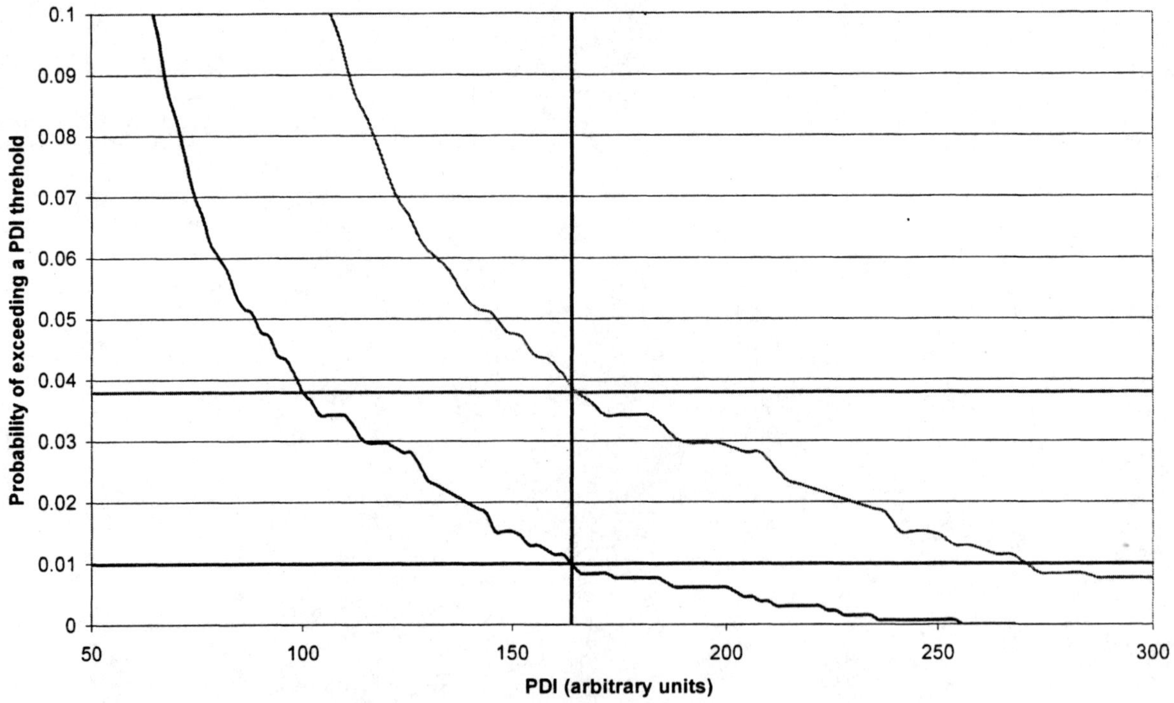

Cumulative distribution function of hurricane PDI in the 1900-2004 climate (in blue) and in a modified climate in which mean PDI would be increased by 65 percent, the shape being unchanged (in red).

Appendix B:
Calculation of the risk-premium

The calculation of the risk-premium is done using the following utility function, with a constant relative risk aversion of one (see Arrow, 1971):

$$u(c) = N\ln(c) \,. \qquad \text{(B-1)}$$

where N is the size of the population and c is the consumption per-capita (about \$31,200 in 2005). Note that we assume here that all citizens have the same consumption and that this utility function aggregates all citizens by summing their individual utility function with the same weight. This method is usually referred to as "*one-man, one-vote*". When income inequalities are taken into account, other aggregation rules are possible, reflecting different moral position with regard to income distribution within a given generation (Lecocq and Hourcade, 2003) (*e.g.*, the "one-dollar, one-vote" aggregation rule, in which weightings are chosen so that the currently observed income distribution is considered socially optimal).

We define the *risk-neutral damages* d_0' by the fact that supporting with certainty an amount of 2005-equivalent damages pd_0' every year would lower utility by the same amount than the risk of having a hurricane that causes an amount d_0 of 2005-equivalent damages with a probability p. Note that all damages are expressed in 2005-equivalent; actual damages are supposed to rise according to economic growth minus Δg=0.5 percent: $d_n = d_0\,(1+g-\Delta g)^n$.

The risk-neutral damages d'_0 can be calculated by the equality[13]:

$$\sum_0^{+\infty}\left(\frac{1}{1+\rho}\right)^n\left[(1-p)u(c_0(1+g)^n)+pu\left(c_0(1+g)^n-\frac{d_0}{N}(1+g-\Delta g)^n\right)\right]$$
$$=\sum_0^{+\infty}\left(\frac{1}{1+\rho}\right)^n u\left(c_0(1+g)^n-\frac{pd'_0}{N}(1+g-\Delta g)^n\right) \qquad \text{(B-2)}$$

This equation states that the expected utility from consumption, every year possibly reduced by hurricane damages $d_0(1+g-\Delta g)^n$, with d_0 = \$56 billion, is equal to the utility from the expected consumption reduced every year by the probability of occurrence p multiplied by the risk-neutral damages d_0', also rising according to economic growth minus Δg. Note that the rate of pure preference for the present ρ is used to discount utility, while the discount rate δ is used to discount monetary values.

For a disaster causing \$56 billion of damages, and using the hypotheses consistent with a discount rate of 3 percent, *i.e.* a growth rate of 2 percent and a pure preference for the present ρ = 1 percent, the resolution of Eq.(B-2) gives the value of the risk-neutral damages d'_0 = \$56,12 billion, corresponding to a risk-premium of \$120 million.

---

[13] Note that population is supposed to be constant.

We now define the *present equivalent-certain cost of the risk of hurricane* (B_c) by the equality of (i) the utility loss due to the risk of hurricane if no upgraded protection system is implemented and (ii) the utility loss due to the immediate payment of an amount B_c. It reads:

$$\sum_0^{+\infty}\left(\frac{1}{1+\rho}\right)^n\left[(1-p)u(c_0(1+g)^n)+pu\left(c_0(1+g)^n-\frac{d_0}{N}(1+g-\Delta g)^n\right)\right]$$
$$=u(c_0-B_c)+\sum_1^{+\infty}\left(\frac{1}{1+\rho}\right)^n u\left(c_0(1+g)^n\right) \quad \text{(B-3)}$$

The protection system should now be implemented if its building costs are lower than the present equivalent-certain cost of the risk of hurricane. Solving (B-3) leads to a value of B_c of \$28.4 billion.

Appendix C:
Calculation of the combined consequences of damage heterogeneity and risk-aversion

The calculation of the impact of the damage heterogeneity is done using the same utility function [Eq.(B-1)]. If a hurricane makes landfall, and if 50% of the damages d_0 are perfectly shared, while 50% of the damages are shared by one million persons, *i.e.* 0.4% of the population, the whole population utility is given by:

$$\begin{aligned} u_n^* &= qNu\left(c_0(1+g)^n - \left(\frac{d_0/2}{N} - \frac{d_0/2}{qN}\right)(1+g-\Delta g)^n\right) \\ &+(1-q)Nu\left(c_0(1+g)^n - \frac{d_0/2}{N}(1+g-\Delta g)^n\right) \end{aligned} \tag{C-1}$$

where q is the proportion of affected population (here q=0.4%).

The *homogenous and risk-neutral equivalent damages* d_0'' are defined by the fact that supporting, every year, with certainty and with perfect sharing among the population, an amount of damages pd_0'', would lower the utility by the same amount than the risk of having, with a probability p, a hurricane that would cause an amount d of damages that would be imperfectly shared among the population.

The *homogenous and risk-neutral equivalent damages* d''_0 is calculated using the relationship:

$$\begin{aligned} &\sum_0^{+\infty}\left(\frac{1}{1+\rho}\right)^n [(1-p)u(c_0(1+g)^n) + pu_n^*] \\ &= \sum_0^{+\infty}\left(\frac{1}{1+\rho}\right)^n u\left(c_0(1+g)^n - \frac{pd_0''}{N}(1+g-\Delta g)^n\right) \end{aligned} \tag{C-2}$$

where the left-hand-side member gives the expected utility under the risk of an amount of 2005-equivalent damages d_0 that would be imperfectly shared; and the right-hand-side member gives the utility of the consumption when an amount of 2005-equivalent damages pd_0'' is perfectly shared every year among the whole population. For a disaster causing \$56 billion of damages, the resolution of Eq.(C-2) gives a value of the homogenous-risk-neutral damages d''_0 = \$69 billion, corresponding to a risk-premium of \$13 billion. In this case, the present equivalent-certain cost of the risk of hurricane B_c is \$35.3 billion.

Robert M.
La Follette School of Public Affa
at the University of Wisconsin-Madison

Working Paper Series
La Follette School Working Paper No. 2006-022
http://www.lafollette.wisc.edu/publications/workingpapers

The Chicago O'Hare Expansion: A Case Study of Administrative Manipulation of Benefit-Cost Principles

Robert Haveman
Professor, La Follette School of Public Affairs and Department of Economics
at the University of Wisconsin-Madison

haveman@lafollette.wisc.edu

THE UNIVERSITY of WISCONSIN MADISON

Robert M. La Follette School of Public Affairs
1225 Observatory Drive, Madison, Wisconsin 53706
Phone: 608.262.3581 / Fax: 608.265-3233
info@lafollette.wisc.edu / http://www.lafollette.wisc.edu

[Conference Draft]

The Chicago O'Hare Expansion: A Case Study of Administrative Manipulation of Benefit-Cost Principles

Robert Haveman*
La Follette School of Public Affairs
University of Wisconsin-Madison

Paper prepared for presentation at conference on

"What We Can Do To Improve The Use Of Benefit-Cost Analysis?"

Thursday, Friday, May 18-19
Talaris Center
Seattle, WA

*The helpful comments of Joseph Karaganis to an earlier version of this paper are gratefully acknowledged. A large number of public documents support the descriptions of the analyses in the paper, and of the critiques of these analyses. References to these documents are not included in this paper; they are available from the author upon request.

The Chicago O'Hare Expansion: A Case Study of Administrative Manipulation of Benefit-Cost Principles

Robert Haveman
University of Wisconsin-Madison

1. Introduction

The principles of benefit-cost analysis have their basis in theoretical welfare economics, and are now well accepted. Application of benefit-cost analysis as a tool for assessing the efficiency effects of public spending and regulatory initiatives is also accepted practice, especially at the Federal government level. However, the gap between the underlying principles and practice is very large, and the subject of concern by many observers. Indeed, the history of benefit-cost applications in the federal funding of public works projects is replete with examples of the failure of analyses to meet minimal accepted standards. Part of the problem stems from the absence of clear statutory and regulatory requirements for sound benefit-cost analysis; agency lack of resources, the limited demand from decision-makers for benefit-cost analysis, and political factors also contribute to this situation.[1]

In this paper, I will describe the application of benefit-cost analysis principles by the Federal Aviation Administration (FAA) to a major infrastructure investment proposal—the expansion of O'Hare International Airport. Chicago O'Hare Airport is one of the most important airports in the National Airspace System. It provides origin and destination service to the nation's third largest metropolitan area, as well as serving as an important connecting hub for American Airlines and United Airlines. O'Hare provides nonstop service to 127 domestic and 48 international destinations.

Most of us have experienced delays as we traveled through O'Hare as connecting passengers. Clearly, the sources of the delays and the dynamics among the variables relevant to understanding these sources are complex. It follows that any effort to alleviate the problem will have to address

[1] See U.S. General Accountability Office, "Economic Performance: Highlights of a Workshop on Economic Performance Measures." GAO-05-796SP, July, 2005.

a wide variety of issues, and consider the benefits and costs of a large number of proposed alternative solutions to the problem.

The City of Chicago is proposing a major expansion of O'Hare Airport, which is but one of the alternatives solutions that have been proposed. The City uses the existing high level of passenger delays at the current airport—and the future expected (and unconstrained) growth in passenger delays—as the primary rationale for its proposal. This proposed expansion to O'Hare involves reconfigured and expanded runways, additional runways, additional air traffic support, redesigned and expanded terminals, and a new Western terminal. The full build-out master plan is currently estimated to cost in the neighborhood of $20 billion.

In order to secure federal government financial support for the expansion, the City of Chicago is required to obtain approval of its funding request by the Federal Aviation Administration (FAA). An important component of the required application for federal funding is a benefit-cost analysis.

Hence, the FAA has the potential to be an exception to the long history of federal benefit-cost analysis applications that fail to meet minimal professional standards. Indeed, Congress has clearly mandated that benefit-cost Analysis be a central decision-making component of FAA's funding decisions.[2] The FAA has responded to that Congressional command by clearly stating that no project will receive funding from FAA's Airport Improvement Program (AIP) discretionary fund unless the project benefits exceed the project costs.[3]

While there are several phases of expansion prior to full build-out, the City is now requesting FAA subsidization and approval for the first phase of expansion, and the benefit-cost analyses that it has presented are pertinent to it. Phase I involves a substantial reconfiguration of runways

---

[2] 49 U.S.C. §47115(d)(1)(B). "In selecting a project for a grant to preserve and improve capacity funded in whole or in part from the fund, the Secretary shall consider… (B) the benefit and cost of the project".

[3] FAA's *Policy for Letter of Intent Approvals Under the Airport Improvement Program* states that the agency must find that a project for which AIP discretionary funds are sought has economic benefits greater than the projects costs. "...[T]he proposed project must have present value benefits that exceed present value costs..." 59 FR 54482 at 54484 (October 31, 1994) (emphasis added).

and associated infrastructure investment. The capital investment cost of this first phase is $2.6 billion, and for planning purposes the expanded facility will be in place in 2007-9.

As this process has evolved, the City has released two, quite different, benefit cost analyses. The first, prepared and released in February, 2005, based its analysis of Phase I project benefits on a 'reduction in delay costs' framework. I will refer to this analysis as BCA-I. This analysis was critically reviewed by opponents of the O'Hare expansion plan (a group of villages and small towns surrounding O'Hare and subject to eminent domain loss of housing and business, and a set of religious groups whose long-standing cemeteries would be removed by the expansion). BCA-I was ultimately rejected by the FAA, largely on the basis of these critiques. In September, 2005, the City submitted a second benefit-cost analysis, designed to meet the critique of the earlier study. This analysis based on a totally different rationale, a 'consumer surplus' rationale. I will refer to this analysis as BCA-II. As expected, City finds positive net benefits attributable to the expansion in both reports.

FAA's recent application of benefit-cost analysis principles to the Chicago proposal provides a useful case study as to whether the agency is able to adhere to a responsible application of those principles to which it has stated allegiance in the case of a politically sensitive project. I will describe the analytic framework and empirical approach of both analyses, and summarize their results. I will also critique the conceptual and empirical approaches of both studies. I conclude that neither study provides an estimate of net national benefits that meets minimal accepted professional standards. In my view, the process is a classic illustration of an administrative 'bob and weave'—if strategy one fails to yield a convincing estimate of positive net benefits, just turn to a totally different justification and see if it flies. It also shows the danger of failing to consider the full range of options for meeting a problem, again a common shortcoming of administrative agencies committed to infrastructure expansion.

2. BCA-I

BCA-I, dated February, 2005, was based on the assertion that the expansion of O'Hare capacity according to the City's plans would generate large savings in travel times for passengers using O'Hare, and that these time savings, when given a value reflecting the time costs that individuals bear, would exceed the costs of the expansion.

The City's analysis of Phase I of the proposed expansion is stated to have a capital cost of $2.6 billion, with the present value of the costs being $1.9 billion. The present value of the benefits is stated to be $4.1 billion (primarily, asserted reductions in the costs associated with travel time), yielding a net benefits estimate of $2.2 billion and a benefit-cost ratio of 2.13.

While important issues arise with the estimates of both the benefits and the costs, it is the estimate of benefits that is the major issue. The City's benefit analysis is based on the standard concave relationship between marginal and average delay times (and delay costs) and levels of demand, in the face of limited capacity—delays and the cost of delays increase exponentially as the number of operations (flights) using the airport expands.

First, a forecast of traffic—the 2002 Terminal Activity Forecast (TAF)—was used to project both operations (flights) and passengers expected to travel to and from O'Hare with no constraint on the level of traffic or delay times. This forecast was taken to be the 'base case' or the no-action scenario. Using this traffic forecast, a standard delay time (delay cost) function was computed using a simulation model (the Total Airspace and Airport Modeler [TAAM] developed by a consulting firm for the purpose of analyzing the aircraft and passenger delays associated with varying levels of airport capacity). TAAM was also used to compute a delay time (delay cost) function for the airport, assuming that the expansion occurred—the 'with project case'.

In the attached Figure 1, the higher curve is the per operation delay cost (in minutes) function for the 'no action' case, and the lower curve is the function for the 'with project case.' The dates attached to curves indicate the times at which forecast traffic is expected to yield the stipulated average minutes of delay, given the existing and proposed (expanded) levels of capacity.

With these two curves in hand, the City made a particular assumption regarding the actual levels of traffic 'without' the project. Instead of allowing delays to build up along the top curve as traffic demand expanded, the City assumed that a particular 'cap' would be imposed on the level of traffic in the 'no action' case. In particular, the City assumed that the number of operations would be capped at 974,000 per year without expansion of capacity, reflecting an average delay of about 15.9 minutes, taken to be the "maximum acceptable" level of delay time. (This is, in fact, about the level of traffic that is currently handled at the airport.)[4]

Third, using this arbitrary assumption, the City calculated the savings in delay time due to the first phase expansion using the two delay functions. Using Figure 2, it can be seen how this is done. The cap (at 15.9 minutes) stops delays at the existing airport from increasing until the expansion comes on line in (say) 2009. Then, with the expanded airfield, delays fall by about 4 minutes per operation.

As a fourth step, the City then calculated for each year the product of this per operation savings in delay time (in hours), the number of operations using the airport, the number of

---

[4] The FAA claims that traffic would cease growing at the airport when delays of this level are experienced. No economic analysis was done regarding this issue, and the level stipulated (15.9 minutes) is substantially greater than prior FAA statements regarding maximum economically acceptable levels of delay. For example, FAA Order 5090.3C FAA *Field Formulation of the National Plan of Integrated Airport Systems* states that an airport reaches annual capacity "when average annual level of delay is 4 minutes." (Section 3-3, page 20) The City of Chicago itself acknowledged that FAA considers that "an airport is at its practical capacity when the average annual delay reaches a range of 4-6 minutes per operation." (City of Chicago Application for an AIP Letter of Intent, March 2004) The Department of Transportation, in a 1995 report to Congress states: "There are no defined criteria that delineate acceptable versus unacceptable delays. FAA has historically regarded up to four minutes of AAAW delay per operation to be an "acceptable" level..." In the absence of specific acceptability criteria for delays, a level-of-service scale has been developed to gauge the extent to which delays *will be tolerated* rather than accepted.

- 0 to 4 minutes of delay per operation: efficient overall operations; delays limited to the most extreme weather conditions.
- 4 to 6 minutes of delay per operation: less *efficient* overall operations; limited peak hour VFR delays along with IFR delays experienced in both moderate and extreme weather conditions.
- 6 to 8 minutes of delay per operation: increasing VFR delays in peak hours; increasing delays and eroding operational reliability in IFR conditions; high sensitivity to operational anomalies.
- 8 to 10 minutes of delay per operation: increasing VFR delays in peak hours with translation to shoulder hours in all but optimum conditions, high delay in IFR with resulting flight cancellations.
- Over 10 minutes of delay per operation: VFR operations experience increasing delays in peak periods and shoulder hours in all but optimum conditions; very high delays in IFR resulting in extensive flight cancellations.

(1995 DOT entitled "*A Study of the High Density Rule*" Report, Technical Supplement # 3) passengers per operation, and a per hour value of time value adapted from FAA guidelines. This yielded the stream of annual savings in time costs. This annual delay reduction effect was then assumed to apply for the remainder of the life of the project (until 2029). The resulting annual delay savings were then discounted using a discount rate mandated by FAA guidelines, to yield the present value of benefits of the expansion of $4.1billion.

Figure 2 illustrates the nature of the "value of time savings" (in minutes) that was developed. The (white and yellow) shaded area beginning in 2009 and extending for 20 years (the life of the project) represents City's estimate of the annual minutes per operation (about 4 minutes) saved because of the Phase I expansion. For each year, the minutes saved per operation was transformed into the number of passenger hours saved, and this value was multiplied by the dollar value of time, yielding the City's estimate of the value of time savings benefits from the proposed expansion. This approach leads to a seriously exaggerated estimate of benefits.

First, the approach assumes that the reduction in average delay time that is estimated to be experienced in the <u>first year</u> after the expansion persists over the lifetime of the investment. As Figure 2 indicates, given the traffic forecasts used, average delay time will increase over time after the expansion. This is shown by the dates placed on the lower of the delay functions in Figure 2. By 2013, average delays are projected to return to the 15.9 minute threshold, using the 2002 traffic forecasts used in the analysis.[5]

This increase in delay times will erode the large per operation savings in delay time (4 minutes) suggested by the City. Indeed, per operation delay savings will be exhausted within a few years after the expansion is in place (2013). In fact, when the increased taxi times experienced at the expanded and reconfigured facility are accounted for in the analysis, delay time is expected to reach the 15.9 minute threshold in 2011.[6] Indeed, if more recent traffic

---

[5] It is likely that average delays of 15.9 minutes will be experienced prior to 2013, when the increased taxi times associated with the Phase I expansion are factored into the analysis.

[6] The City justified the decision to NOT account for the delay costs associated with added operations that could be handled with the expanded airfield by stating that these effects would be 'difficult to quantify.'

forecasts are employed, travel times at O'Hare are likely to reach the assumed 15.9 minute threshold virtually on opening day of the new facility. At best, the savings in delay costs would be represented by the white 'triangle' in Figure 2.

Moreover, this approach neglects the fact that airlines adjust to increased delays (just like they adjust to congestion charges) by shifting some of their flights to less-crowded times (thereby, relieving peak congestion and cutting delays), increasing aircraft size, and shifting some of their through flights to other airports. Hence, delays in the 'no action' case would not build up in real time as the curves in Figure 1 suggest. Failure to account for such adjustments leads to both overstating the reduction in delay times immediately after the expansion comes on line (which reduction was assumed to persist for the subsequent 20 years) and understating the date when the existing facility and the Phase I expansion will be at capacity.

In addition to this basic critique, a number of other assertions in the City analysis appear questionable. These were identified in a report prepared for the set of communities surrounding the existing airport by a research firm that specializes in the analysis of airline industry—The Campbell-Hill Aviation Group (CH). In addition to providing a critique of the basic benefits analysis, the CH study identified numerous other ways in which the City analysis deviates from commonly accepted principles of benefit-cost analysis. These include:

1. Failure to consider alternatives other than infrastructure expansion (e.g., congestion pricing, demand management, increased use of other regional airports, construction of a second Chicago airport) as a means of handling increased air travel demands in the Chicago/Midwest area.

2. Use of the 2002 traffic forecast, when 2003-04 forecasts are available. Use of the more recent forecast yields both lower benefits and higher costs.

3. Failure to consider in the analysis the potential effects of risky or uncertain events (e.g., the possible failure of United, which is the largest hub user at O'Hare), which would lower net benefits.

4. Ignoring the effect on traffic demand of the increased airfares caused by the anticipated charges to be imposed on air carriers using the expanded facility (due to their participation in the financing of the expansion.

5. Use of an arbitrary quantity cap (974,000 operations per year), rather than a minutes-of-delay cap that would reflect actual demand-limiting, cost-based impacts on airport users.

6. Failure to discuss, much less quantify, environmental costs of the expansion.

7. Use of a de minimus contingency allowance for costs.

8. Ignoring interest expense during construction.

9. Failure to assess the additional roadway and terminal costs associated with the proposed expansion.

10. Arbitrary multiplying the estimated reduction in delay costs for passengers using O'Hare by 1.8 to reflect 'downstream' effects of the O'Hare proposed expansion.

The CH study reanalyzed the benefits and costs of the Phase I expansion, using the City's own data, and presented estimates of benefits and costs associated with the Phase I expansion that account for these shortcomings. When the 2002 traffic forecast used by the City is maintained, net benefits fall from the City estimate of $2.2 billion to a negative $4.0 billion, and the benefit-cost ratio falls from 2.1 to –1.1. Even larger reductions in net benefits result when more recent (2003-04) traffic forecasts are used.

3. Between BCA-I and BCA-II

Critiques of BCA-I—including the Campbell-Hill study—were submitted to the FAA on June 6, 2005. Between that date and September, 2005, the FAA provided guidance to the City on how to respond to the criticisms of BCA-I, and "to ensure the correct application of the alternative methodologies." During that period, a decision was made to abandon the 'savings in delay costs' basis of BCA-I, and to move to an entirely different rationale for providing economic justification for the proposed project. In the words of the FAA: "The benefits estimated under the previous approach are artificial and would never have been realized." The City responded to this conclusion and to the FAA guidance, and with the help of a consulting firm, presented a brand new benefit-cost analysis, BCA-II, released on September 27, 2005. According to the FAA, that analysis "utilized a consumer surplus analysis as outlined in … the FAA's Airport Benefit-Cost Analysis Guidance, December 15, 1999."

4. BCA-II

In the City's BCA-II analysis, virtually no "savings in delay costs" are claimed; nearly all of the benefits are attributed to 'Consumer Surplus." The following summarizes the benefit cost results. The relevant analysis is for the Phase I, Master Plan, and as can be seen, the new approach produced a benefit-cost ratio of 4.6.

Summary of Results from Benefit Cost Analysis-II

Scenario	Present Value Benefits (billions)	Present Value Costs (billions)	Net Present Value (billions)	Benefit-Cost Ratio
OMP Phase 1 Airfield	$12.4	$1.9	$10.4	6.3
Master Plan Phase I	**$12.4**	**$2.7**	**$ 9.7**	**4.6**

(Base year: 2001; dollars: 2001)

This new BCA, resting on the conventional consumer surplus concept, sought to evaluate the benefits to demanders (i.e., passengers) from changes in the supply (and related price) of airline services in the Chicago market attributable to the proposed Phase I expansion.[7]

---

[7] Over 90 percent of the $12.4 billion of benefits is attributable to calculated consumer surplus; the remaining 10 percent are attributed to travel cost savings. One would think that after the Phase I project reaches the same level of delay as the base case, and limits on operations (and thereby passenger traffic) are imposed, there would be no savings in the value of travel times. Indeed, the central assumption of Chicago's and FAA's consumer surplus analysis is that both the base case and Phase I would have the same delays. However, the City finds these savings through its reliance on the Total Airspace and Airport Modeler (TAAM). This model suggests that the airlines will simply add numerous short haul flights and change the timing of the flight schedules so that reductions in travel times will result when compared to longer-haul flights. These additional operations are then credited to the proposed airport expansion, and the expansion project is then credited with some savings in the value of travel time.

There are a number of serious errors in this approach. First, the traffic forecasts and the TAAM based savings are justified by asserting that they reflect the continuation of existing trends, and hence unrelated to the expansion of O'Hare. Second, TAF traffic forecast that is used by the City assumes that the passengers represented in the forecast will be paying the same full price of travel (airline fares plus delay times) with both the existing airport and the proposed expansion. However, in calculating the consumer surplus benefits, the City postulates a substantial decrease in the fares airlines will charge their passengers in response to the expansion. These postulated fare decreases will surely have some effect on the traffic that would be forecasted to use O'Hare. Indeed, with lower fares asserted to be generated by the expansion, it follows that forecasted traffic would most likely be larger with the expansion than the City's 2002 TAF-based forecast. In this case, traffic with the expansion would grow faster than is indicated in the with-expansion forecast, and hence the limitations on operations would have to be imposed sooner after the expansion, eroding the asserted with-expansion savings in travel times.

Implementation of the consumer surplus framework in estimating the national economic benefits of a change in capacity to an existing public infrastructure requires careful consideration of a number of issues. In the following, I will describe and then critique the benefits estimate of the City of Chicago resting on this concept. I will conclude that Chicago (and the FAA, who assisted in the analysis) failed to attend to these issues, and that the claims made are deeply flawed.

While the consumer surplus approach and its application to the proposed Phase I expansion can be discussed in both numerical and conceptual terms, Chicago and the FAA use a conceptual graph to visually illustrate the consumer surplus benefits which Chicago claims for Phase I (and later for Total OMP Master Plan). I have labeled this graph Figure 3.

Central to the theoretical consumer surplus economic model envisioned in BCA-II is the assumption that the market for 'operations' into and out of O'Hare is perfectly competitive. In such a market, when a cap is imposed on the amount of the service that can be supplied, the full price is determined by the willingness to pay for the service by the marginal passenger when the cap is just met. Given a downward sloped demand curve, if the cap is expanded, more passengers will be able to be served, and the marginal passenger will have a lower willingness to pay. Hence, the full price of travel (FPT) will fall because of the expanded cap.[8]

This process is depicted in Figure 3, which shows how an expanded cap results in a lower price (FPT), which must be the result so long as the demand curve (a willingness to pay schedule) is sloping downward and to the right. In this situation, the competitive prices shown in the graph, FPT_1 and FPT_2, are determined where the available capacity is equal to the demand curve. These prices reflect the willingness of buyers to pay for the last unit of the available supply.

This money fare reduction benefit which the City attributes to the Phase I project is shown in Figure 3, as the area bounded by FPT_1, FPT_2 and points a and b, which is the full shaded area. In

[8] For example, in the year 2007, a fare decrease of approximately $4 per passenger is calculated, and this value increases over time.

the City's calculation, the discounted present value of these consumer surplus benefits equals 90 percent of the total benefits claimed for Phase I.

This shaded area is, in fact, composed of three components:

1) the consumer surplus benefits for existing buyers (the lined area in Figure 3),

2) an offsetting loss of producer surplus benefits associated with these same buyers, and

3) a consumer surplus benefit for additional buyers who are able to enter the market because of the presumed lower price (the shaded area abc in Figure 3).

Consider these in turn. First, to the extent there is a lower price due to the expansion, existing buyers (passengers) will gain consumer surplus benefits because of this fall in price. However, and second, this lower price will have a fully offsetting effect on the sellers of the service (the airlines). They will lose producers surplus, and their loss will be precisely and exactly equal to the gain in consumer surplus by the passengers. On balance, there is no national benefit that can be claimed from the reduced price affecting existing passengers, as the consumer surplus claimed for these passengers is precisely offset by the loss of producer surplus benefits.[9] Third, the lower full

[9] Chicago apparently recognized that the increase in consumer surplus on existing passengers will be offset by a decrease in producer surplus. In the GRA consultant report that is a part of BCA-II, the existence of this offsetting producer surplus is noted. However, the BCA-II states (without empirical foundation) that carriers will in fact succeed in avoiding this loss of producer surplus:

> "It has been assumed to the extent there is producer surplus in the Base Case, carriers would seek to preserve it in the *OMP Phase I Airfield* case. Because carriers have influence over the approval of the *OMP Phase I Airfield* case, their expectation must be that they can preserve whatever producer surplus exists in the Base Case, otherwise they would not be in favor of the project."

In their discussion, the FAA cites several economic factors that purportedly could explain why the airlines (primarily, United and American) can "preserve" producer surplus, and hence are willing to support the expansion. These factors include an assertion that the expansion will enable the airlines to: 1) experience economies of scope and density, and 2) increase their flight frequency (which is asserted to be more profitable than adding seats to existing flights). These arguments rest on a model of the structure of the market which is dramatically inconsistent with the perfectly competitive model that is the basis of the consumer surplus analysis and for FAA's central conclusion. The FAA cites the following: 1) "O'Hare is the site for two major airline hubs", 2) These hubs are "undersized", 3) Carriers desire to "increase their market share", 4) The two large carriers at O'Hare are concerned that "competitors are adding capacity at their major hubs…", 5) These efficiencies will allow the "two large carriers … to gain [market] shares and compete with their rivals". All of these points suggest that these major carriers have market power, and behave strategically with respect to their rivals. Essentially the FAA argument being made here is that United and American can increase the size of their hubs at O'Hare, and hence increase market share at the expense of their rivals, and hence increase their profits, and that is why they support the expansion.

The FAA has not demonstrated that such economies are available. To offer such a demonstration it would be necessary to have a full network model of the US air traffic system with demands at various markets price will lead to some additional passengers using the airport. For these additional passengers—those represented by moving down the demand curve from the prior higher price—the full price they would be willing to pay will be lower than the pre-expansion full price. As a result, they will experience some consumer surplus benefits.

Now, the core problem with the City's estimate is that it counts both sources of consumer surplus benefit (the lined area and shaded area abc in Figure 3), but ignores the offsetting loss of producer surplus benefits that will be experienced by the airlines. When one accounts for this error, the level of total consumer surplus benefits is limited to those benefits accruing only to the additional buyers (passengers in this case) who are willing to pay more than the lower price but less than the higher price (only area abc in Figure 3). When this is recognized, the consumer surplus benefits claimed by the City fall dramatically.

However, the City's analysis of consumer surplus benefits also has other serious problems. A second serious problem is that the projected fall in the full price of travel calculated by the City is excessive, and hence generates larger consumer surplus benefits for both existing and additional passengers than is warranted. The City's calculated full price decrease derives from an assumed elasticity for the demand curve of passengers for the use of O'Hare. In particular, the City uses an elasticity that is appropriate for use in a national market, but not in a local market where there are a number of very close substitutes to the services provided by the local supplier (in this case,

---

specified and the costs of suppliers and of various flight and craft size (among other things) fully specified. Further, these density gains are the gains to the two major carriers at O'Hare, who would be able to "recapture some lost passengers" from other carriers. These gains to the major O'Hare carriers are losses to the other carriers, and from a national economic perspective the net effect is zero. FAA's claim that the expansion can enable airlines to increase flight frequency, and hence "increase their market shares" and their "returns" is supported by a paper by Wei and Hansen, "Impact of Aircraft Size and Seat Availability on Airlines Demand and Market Share in Duopoly Markets." Importantly, this analysis is for a 'duopoly,' and hence is inconsistent with perfect competition assumption that underlies the consumer surplus framework of Figure 3.

O'Hare airport). For such a local market, the appropriate elasticity value implies a much flatter-shaped demand curve than that suggested by the City.[10]

With a more elastic demand curve, the price reduction associated with the larger cap would be much less than that claimed by the City. With a more appropriate smaller estimated price decrease, the consumer surplus benefits for the additional passengers would be substantially smaller than that estimated in BCA-II.

A third basic problem inheres in the interaction of the claimed price decrease with the traffic forecasts that are used by the City. The City created two new forecasts in doing BCA-II (that for the base case and for the Phase I expansion), neither of which take account of the effect on traffic into and out of O'Hare due to any possible reduction in delay times or any possible reduction in fares. In effect, the City accepted forecasts that were developed for wholly different reasons and on wholly different economic and analytic premises, and applied them to the consumer surplus analysis without regard the effect on traffic of any price (airline fare) decreases that might be associated with the expansion.

Given the City's very large (and exaggerated) projected decrease in price associated with the expansion, it is inconsistent and wrong to continue using a forecast that fails to account for this asserted price decrease. Stated simply, if the primary benefit of the expansion (consumer surplus) claimed by the City depends on traffic forecasts which themselves depend on the asserted price decrease that generates the forecast, the interdependence of the forecast AND the asserted price decrease must be recognized and built into the estimate. In short, any reliable forecast of traffic must reflect the additional traffic generated by the price decrease which the City claims is a result of the expansion. If the forecasts do not reflect these increases in additional traffic generated by

---

[10] The elasticity measure that the City uses (-1.18) implies a substantial decrease in the full price of travel, and hence additional induced traffic. A more appropriate, more elastic demand curve would generate an even larger increment to traffic. Any 'modeled' lower price would increase the projected future traffic, and hence result in the imposition of the cap sooner after the expansion. This revised cap would alter both the estimate of any savings in delay times and any gains in consumer surplus.

the asserted reduction in the cost of travel, they are inconsistent with the consumer surplus model that is relied upon.

Finally, it should be noted that the perfect competition market framework asserted to underlie the analysis has no empirical support. There are a relatively small number of air carriers servicing the Chicago regional market, and a few carriers dominate the supply. It would be more appropriate to classify the market for airline services in the Chicago region as an 'oligopolistic' market, in which producers strategize so as to optimize their own position, given an assumption regarding decisions made by their rivals given the regulatory environment. (This is especially true of that even more limited market—O'Hare airport.) Such suppliers make a wide variety of policy decisions regarding fare structures, flight schedules, flight times, plane sizes, airport usage, etc. in response to a cap or quota or any other institutional arrangement. [11]

It is inconceivable that, in such a market, any expansion of airport capacity could or would, by itself, bring about a fall in fares of the magnitude suggested by the City analysis that was <u>unconnected to the costs of the producers</u> (the airlines). Indeed, in such an oligopolistic market, it

---

[11] Evidence that airline services in the Chicago market are not accurately described by this perfectly competitive market structure model abounds. This market is characterized by a variety of complexities regarding public regulation, the concentration of supply in a limited number of producers, long-term lease agreements, and the strategic considerations weighed by existing (and especially dominant) suppliers regarding market contestability (potential competition from other markets and suppliers). In such a complex market, the strategic decisions of suppliers interact with regulations (quotas, caps) to determine prices, outputs, the composition of outputs (think flight frequency, plane size, origin-destination configurations, etc.), and hence any possible profits or 'rents'. Indeed, the Department of Transportation has issued a study which shows that hub carriers at dominated hubs extract price premiums from consumers: "From a consumer perspective, the primary disadvantage of network hubs is the level of market power that the hub carrier is capable of amassing and the higher prices consumers pay as a result. This stems from the fact that no airline with a similar cost structure can compete effectively at another airline's hub. DOT and others have reported on the prevalence of high fares paid by passengers at hub airports dominated by a network carrier; indeed, no credible study concludes otherwise....It is the view of some, including the Department, that high fares at dominated hub airports are, in large part, a result of the market power exercised by network carriers at their hubs"

Another DOT publication claims: "....Thus, the high fares at hubs are related to an absence of effective price competition, not quality of service." "...to the extent dominant hub carriers have market power, they can not only charge higher prices, but also control capacity, keeping it at a lower level than would prevail in a competitive market. Carriers with market power typically do not add capacity to accommodate low-fare demand." "Clearly, the lack of price competition, not costs, is what drives high prices in hub markets." "...barriers to entry at dominated hubs are most difficult to surmount considering the operational and marketing leverage a network carrier has in its hub markets."

is the costs of the producers that ultimately determine changes in price (fares). Hence, any expansion of O'Hare could only influence the price of travel through O'Hare if it affected the costs of the producers (the airlines) which service O'Hare. A proper economic analysis requires empirical evidence of the anticipated cost reductions experienced by the airlines, which savings could be the basis of a fare reduction.

In fact, the analysis put forth by the City implies that fares will increase and not decrease. BCA-II indicates that the expanded and reconfigured airfield will result in substantial increases in taxi times between terminals and runways. These are cost increases resulting in increases (and not reductions) in the full travel price. Moreover, as part of the City's plan, a share of the financing costs of the airport will be directly borne by the airlines, and these too are cost increases that will result in increases (and not reductions) in the full price of travel. Rather than the expansion of O'Hare leading to decreases in the full travel price of using airport (as the City's inappropriate consumer surplus model posits), the expansion would appear to lead to increases in airline costs, exerting upward pressure on the full price of travel at O'Hare.

In sum, a proper economic analysis cannot use a perfectly competitive short-run model to claim consumer surplus benefits in response to increased airport capacity, when in fact the true market structure bears little resemblance to the theoretical model. In such textbook models, increases in capped supply can result in immediate and short-run price decreases that are not reflected in cost decreases. However, even in such artificial markets such price decreases will not persist over time; over the longer-run any price change will reflect changes in costs. In a real world market with few producers, any increases in infrastructure expansion will result in price decreases only if the expansion results in verifiable and measurable cost decreases. Hence, empirical evidence that there would be actual cost savings (*i.e.*, travel time savings) that would reduce the full price of travel as claimed by the City is essential to assessing their claim. Moreover, any documented cost and anticipated fare reduction would have to be reflected in the forecast of passenger demand used in the analysis.

As in the case of BCA-I, the Campbell-Hill Aviation Group (CH) again reviewed and critiqued this benefit-cost analysis. Again, CH used the City's own data, plus some additional information and forecasts, to present a reanalysis of the proposed Phase I expansion. In addition to the issues discussed above, CH identified several concerns with the BCA-II analysis (in addition to the concerns noted in their earlier report on BCA-I, most of which still persist). These include:

1. The analysis continues to reject alternatives other than infrastructure expansion (e.g., congestion pricing or demand management strategies) as a means of handling increased air travel demands in the Chicago/Midwest area.

2. The analysis continues to attribute savings in delay costs to years when Phase I will be constrained, and when no reductions in delays are possible.

3. The City bases its passenger benefits on phantom fare reductions that are unrelated to its own estimates of airline cost savings, including the cost-increasing effect of financing arrangements, leading to higher fares.

4. The analysis ignores the project's impact on other passenger time factors such as access/egress and terminal facilitation that will certainly increase.

5. The analysis credits the project with time savings that are unrelated to the project, and which are projected to occur whether or not the project is constructed.

As with their analysis of BCA-I, Campbell-Hill adjusted the City's analysis in BCA-II to account for two primary problems—the city's asserted fare savings that are unrelated to the effect of the project and the city's exaggerated changes in flight distances between the base case and Phase I. These adjustments alone reduced the present value of benefits attributable to Phase I from \$12.4 billion to -\$1.5 billion. Since these benefits are <u>negative</u>, without factoring in the cost of the projects; overall net benefits are projected to be -\$4.3 billion.

5. <u>Conclusion</u>

Does this case study contain any general lessons regarding the application of benefit-cost analysis principles by public agencies? Each reader will take away from the discussion their own insights; mine are the following.

First, analytic principles are a weak reed in the face of political pressures and perceptions of agency purpose. The administration of Mayor Richard Daley is committed to this project, and is politically powerful. Moreover, the FAA values public construction to the neglect of nonstructural alternatives such as demand management. No real attention was paid to analyzing the benefits and costs of demand management (and a wide range of other) alternatives, and comparing the results to the benefits and costs of the proposed O'Hare expansion.

Second, embarrassment by public agencies to drastic inter-temporal inconsistency in analytic approach, data, and findings seems nonexistent. The drive to produce positive net benefits easily overwhelms any motivation for consistency and sound evaluation.

Third, the reliance on and misuse of sound basic principles by agencies to justify decisions hinders scrutiny of these choices by courts and the public. The clever use of the travel cost savings and consumer surplus models as a cover for questionable data and assumptions hinders understanding and critical assessment.

This assessment is a pessimistic one; can anything be done to assure that federal decisions will be based on analyses that meet minimum acceptable professional standards? Perhaps this is the time to again consider the proposal for a federal government analytic standards office, staffed by professional analysts committed to accepted standards of analysis, and structured to assess the conformance to accepted analytic principles of analyses supporting public regulation and spending, such as BCA-I and BCA-II.

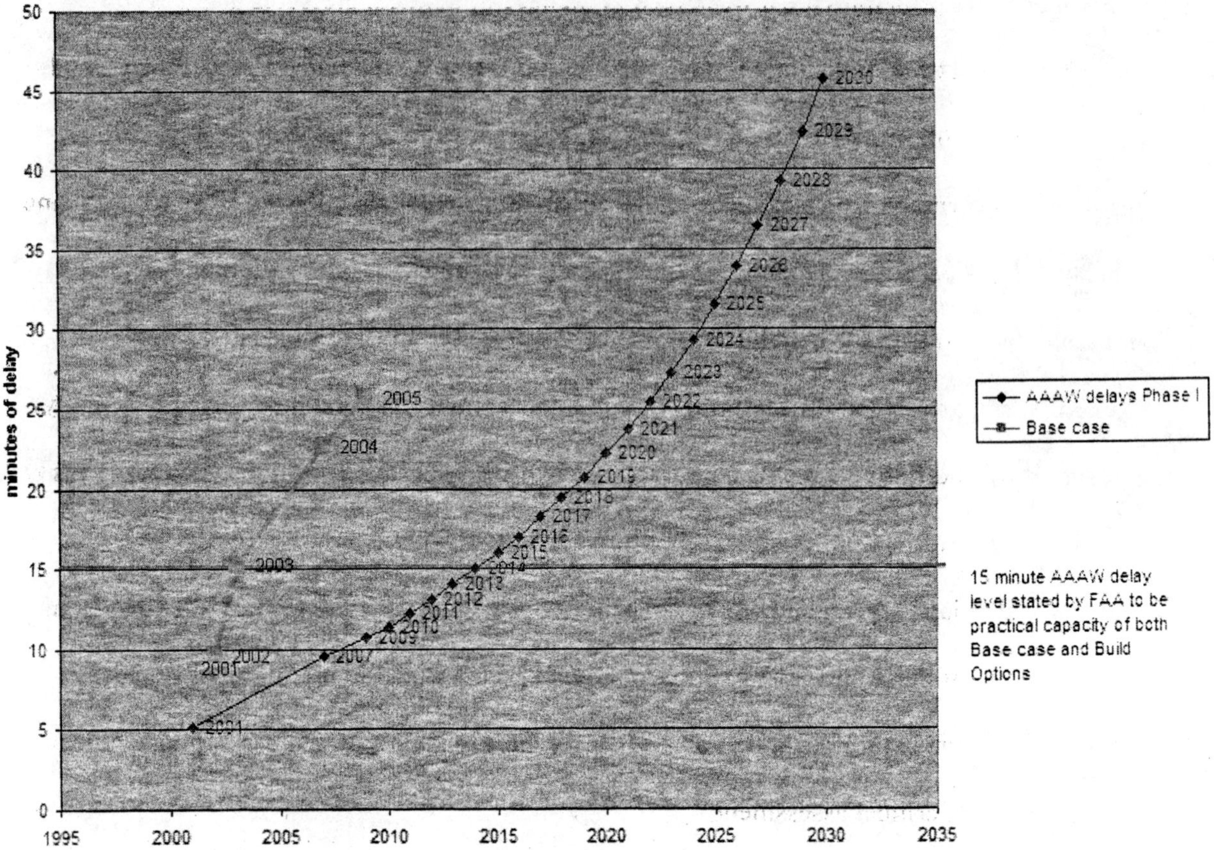

minutes of delay
AAAW delays Phase I
Base case
15 minute AAAW delay level stated by FAA to be practical capacity of both Base case and Build Options

Figure 1

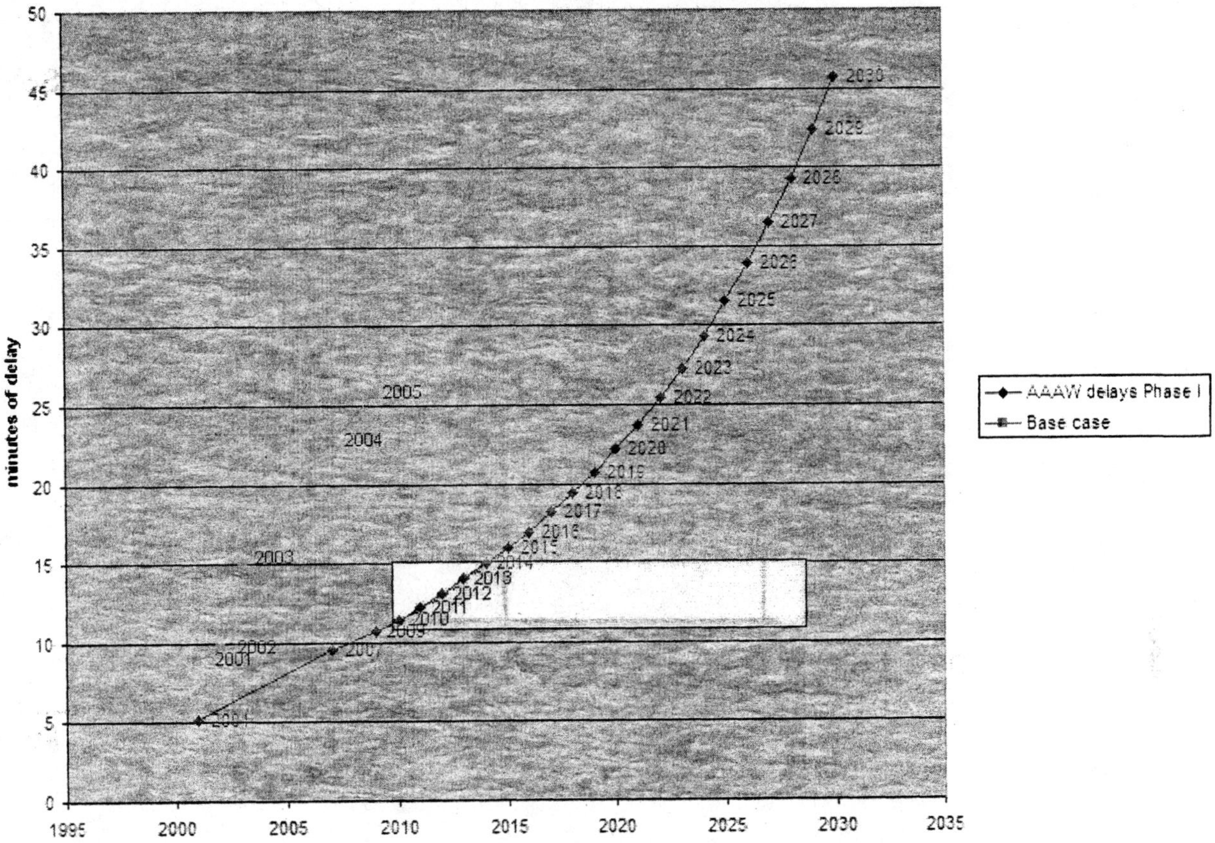
minutes of delay
AAAW delays Phase I
Base case
0
5
10
15
20
25
30
35
40
45
50
1995
2000
2005
2010
2015
2020
2025
2030
2035

Figure 2

Consumer Surplus under 'Base' and 'Phase I' Cases

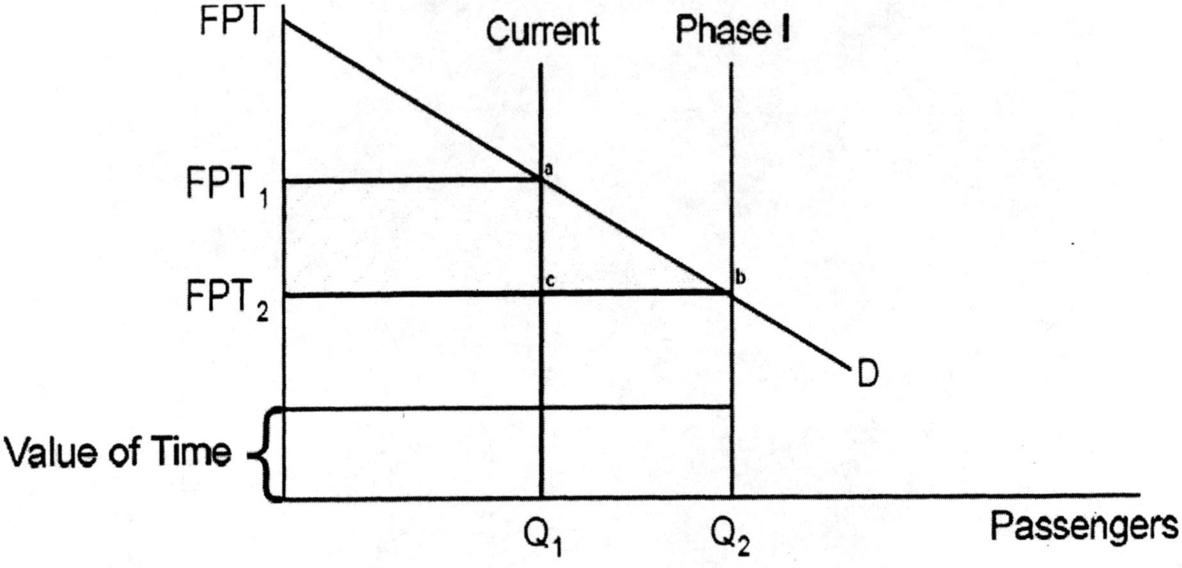

Figure 3

JOINT CENTER
AEI-BROOKINGS JOINT CENTER FOR REGULATORY STUDIES

A Cost-Benefit Analysis of Drug Price Controls in the U.S.

Rexford E. Santerre and John A. Vernon *

Related Publication 04-29
October 2004

*Corresponding author. Please send correspondence to the address above or the email address: jvernon@business.uconn.edu. The authors thank Dennis Heffley, Carmelo Giaccotto, and John M. Vernon for his comments on an earlier draft of this paper.

Executive Summary

This paper uses national data for the period 1960 to 2000 to estimate an aggregate private consumer demand for pharmaceuticals in the U.S. The estimated demand curve is then used to simulate the value of consumer surplus gains from a drug price control regime that holds drug price increases to the same rate of growth as the general consumer price level over the time period from 1981 to 2000. Based upon a 7 percent real interest rate, we find that the future value of consumer surplus gains from this hypothetical policy would have been $319 billion at the end of 2000. According to an earlier study, that same drug price control regime would have led to 198 fewer new drugs being brought to the U.S. market over this period. Therefore, we approximate that the average social opportunity cost per drug developed during this period to be approximately $1.6 billion. Recent research on the value of pharmaceuticals suggests that the social benefits of a new drug may be far greater than this estimated social opportunity cost. Based on empirical findings of the productivity of pharmaceutical R&D over a similar time period, our first approximation of the cost-benefit ratio for this hypothetical price control policy ranges between 62 and 68. This suggests price controls on pharmaceutical prices between 1980 and 2000 would have caused much more harm than good. Society may be better off discovering more efficient ways than price controls to improve access to existing drugs.

A Cost-Benefit Analysis of Drug Price Controls in the U.S.

Rexford E. Santerre and John A. Vernon

1. Introduction

The public debate over prescription drug prices in the U.S. is one of the most contentious in the history of healthcare politics. The commonly held perception that U.S. drug prices are "too high" has been fueled by the fact that real drug prices in the U.S. have been rising steadily, and at a rate faster than that of the general consumer price index for over two decades. As a result, the pharmaceutical industry has come under intense criticism, with both politicians and special interests groups calling for new legislation that will make pharmaceuticals more affordable, either through legalized reimportation from price-regulated markets such as Canada and the European Union, or more directly through government imposed price controls.

While these calls for legislative action are not new, the U.S. does appear to be, for the first time, very close to a major policy change regarding U.S. drug prices.[1] The U.S. government may, like all other industrialized governments around the world, soon begin regulating drug prices[2]. In addition to several reimportation bills currently on the Senate floor, proposed amendments to the recently passed Medicare Modernization Act of 2003 also exist that will allow the U.S. government to negotiate *directly* with drug manufacturers for Medicare prescription drug purchases (the MMA currently has a non-interference clause), which will amount to approximately 60 percent of all U.S. drug purchases (Vernon, Santerre, and Giaccotto, 2004).

While regulated drug prices in the U.S. will undoubtedly improve the public's access to today's medicines, and thus generate both cost savings and improved public health, it will simultaneously reduce firms' incentives to invest in pharmaceutical R&D because of lower levels of pharmaceutical profitability. Less investment in pharmaceutical R&D will have a negative effect on the rate of future pharmaceutical innovation. Recent research has documented

---

[1] Approximately 10 years ago the Clinton Administration's Health Security Act had provisions for directly controlling drug prices. In addition, the drug industry has been under the political microscope since the 1960s (Scherer, 2004)

[2] There are numerous theoretical reasons why reimportation may not generate the desired prescription drug cost savings that the advocates of this and related policies expect. See, for example, the paper by Kanavos et al. (2004).

the considerable benefits of pharmaceutical innovation in terms of improved U.S. longevity (Lichtenberg 2002; Miller and Frech, 2002) as well as the sensitivity of R&D investment to real pharmaceutical prices (Giaccotto, Santerre, and Vernon, 2003, 2005) and profits (Vernon, 2004a). Thus, in addition to the short-run benefits associated with lower, regulated drug prices, there will also be long-run costs. This is precisely the tradeoff the U.S. patent system tries to balance by awarding limited-term patents to new drug products.

Even though a policy of regulated drug prices in the U.S. involves a tradeoff between short-run benefits and long run costs, the former outcome often receives more attention in policy debates (Scherer, 2004). Interestingly, however, efforts to quantify these short-run benefits from a rigorous economic perspective are nonexistent. Therefore, in the current paper, we attempt to do just that. We also compare our findings with the results from an earlier study—one that employed the same data and modeling techniques, but which measured the economic costs of the same U.S. price control policy—in terms of reduced levels of pharmaceutical innovation. Thus, we are able to weigh the benefits of pharmaceutical price controls (in terms of consumer surplus gains) against the costs (measured in terms of forgone drug discoveries). While these studies are retrospective in nature (out of necessity), and consider only one type of U.S. price control policy (one that requires pharmaceutical prices grow no faster than the CPI), the price control policy simulated is, nevertheless, similar to an actual policy enacted in 1992 for drugs purchased by the government for the Veterans Administration (VA) health system. Moreover, and for the first time, a formal cost-benefit analysis of a particular type of drug price control is possible, and this may offer new insights.

Our paper proceeds as follows. In Section II we develop an empirical model of the aggregate consumer demand for pharmaceuticals in the United States. We also outline our empirical strategy and describe the data. Section III reports and discusses our empirical estimates. In Section IV we simulate the consumer surplus gains from a hypothetical price control policy in the U.S.: one that limits the growth rate of pharmaceutical prices to that of the CPI from 1981-2000. We then assess the net benefit of this policy by comparing the gains of consumer surplus to some fairly plausible estimates of the value of the R&D (and drugs) that would be lost had the policy been enacted. Section V provides a summary and offers some conclusions.

If this occurs, direct price regulation will have to follow to procure the cost savings that such reimportation policies were intended to achieve.

2. Conceptual And Empirical Models Of The Aggregate Consumer Demand For Pharmaceutical Products

We begin by assuming a one-period model in which a representative consumer, given her exogenous tastes and preferences, *T*, derives utility from consuming the units of "health services", *H*, that flow from her health capital, and some composite good, *X*. Stated mathematically:

$$U = U(H, X; T). \quad (1)$$

We also make the following standard assumptions about the individual's utility function:

$$\frac{\partial U}{\partial H} > 0; \quad \frac{\partial U}{\partial X} > 0; \quad \frac{\partial^2 U}{\partial H^2} < 0; \quad \frac{\partial^2 U}{\partial X^2} < 0; \quad \frac{\partial^2 U}{\partial H \partial X} > 0. \quad (2)$$

That is, utility is assumed to increase at a decreasing rate with respect to both health services and the composite good. We further assume that health services are produced with various combinations of prescription drugs, *Q* (e.g., dosages), and medical services, *M* (such as office visits or inpatient days), conditioned on the representative consumer's initial endowment of health capital, H_0. Thus, for ease of exposition, we ignore a set of other healthcare "goods" and "bads" such as exercise, diet, alcohol and tobacco use, etc. and the consumer's time involved in producing these healthcare activities.[3] A production function for units of health services can thus be written as follows:

$$H = H(Q, M; H_0), \quad (3)$$

where H is assumed to be concave with respect to both *Q* and *M*.

Substituting equation (3) into equation (1), allows utility to be expressed in terms of the production function for health services and the composite good. It is assumed that expenditures on the two inputs that produce health services, and spending on the composite good, fully exhaust the consumer's income. The consumer's optimization problem is therefore to select the amounts of prescription drugs, medical services, and the composite good that maximize her

[3] For instance, Miller and Frech (2002) examine empirically the effect of pharmaceuticals, medical care, and various lifestyle factors on measures of the quality and quantity of life using a sample of OECD countries. Among other results, they find that pharmaceutical consumption extends and improves life.

utility subject to the constraints of income, Y, and the out-of-pocket prices for drugs, P_O, medical services, P_M, and the composite good, P_X. Stated more formally we have:[4]

MAX $U = U[H(Q,M;H_0),X;T]$ Subject to: $QP_O + MP_M + XP_X = Y$. (4)

Using the method of Lagrange Multipliers to find the solution to this constrained optimization problem generates the familiar first-order conditions. Using the first-order conditions, we can solve for the marginal rate of substitution between drugs and the composite good. This yields:

$$\left[\frac{\partial U}{\partial H}\cdot\frac{\partial H}{\partial Q}\right]\left[\frac{\partial U}{\partial X}\right]^{-1} = \frac{P_O}{P_X}. \quad (5)$$

The first partial derivative in the left-most bracket captures the marginal utility of good health while the second reflects the marginal productivity of drugs on good health. Equation (5) implies that, in equilibrium, the representative consumer equates the marginal benefit of the last drug consumed with its marginal cost, as reflected by the relative out-of-pocket price of an additional drug.

For purposes later in the paper, it is important to consider here that the marginal benefit of an additional drug dosage is influenced by both the value that the consumer places on being in a state of good health and the marginal product of an additional drug on good health. As a result, the actual price paid for an additional drug in the marketplace captures the consumer's willingness to pay for a small reduction in the probability of dying and/or a marginal improvement in her quality of life. This notion becomes particularly important when we use the inverse demand curve to estimate the consumer surplus from a drug price control regime. That is, consumer surplus, the area under the inverse demand curve, captures the value of life and the marginal contribution of an additional drug to good health.

Defining *X* as the numeraire, it also follows from the utility maximization process that the representative consumer's quantity demanded of prescription drugs can be derived as a function of the relative out-of-pocket drug price, relative out-of-pocket medical price, and her real income. Expressed generally, the demand function takes the following form:

---

[4] For simplicity, it is assumed that the decision to purchase pharmaceutical and medical expense insurance coverage has already been made.

$$Q = Q\left(\frac{P_O}{P_X}, \frac{P_M}{P_X}, \frac{Y}{P_X}; T, H_0\right). \tag{6}$$

Lastly, for purposes of empirical estimation, it is assumed that the representative consumer's demand for prescription drugs takes the following specific log-log form:

$$\ln(Q) = \beta_0 + \beta_1 \ln\left(\frac{P_O}{P_X}\right) + \beta_2 \ln\left(\frac{P_M}{P_X}\right) + \beta_3 \ln\left(\frac{Y}{P_X}\right). \tag{7}$$

Therefore, the coefficients in equation (7) may be interpreted as elasticities. According to the law of demand, the quantity demanded of prescription drugs should be inversely related to its relative out-of pocket market price ($\beta_1 < 0$). The relationship between the quantity demanded of prescription drugs and the relative out-of-pocket price for medical services depends on whether pharmaceuticals and medical services are substitutes ($\beta_2 > 0$) or complements ($\beta_2 < 0$). Finally, if prescription drugs can be classified a normal good, real income will have a direct impact on the quantity demanded of prescription drugs ($\beta_3 > 0$). Obviously, an inverse relation holds if prescription drugs are inferior goods.

Time series data for the variables in equation (7) were obtained on-line either at the Center for Medicare and Medicaid Services, the Bureau of Labor Statistics, or the Bureau of Economic Analysis for the period 1960-2000. The quantity of drugs consumed by the average consumer is measured by real drug expenditures per capita. Dividing nominal drug expenditures by the pharmaceutical consumer price index and by the population produces a measure of real drug expenditures per capita.[5]

The out-of-pocket price of drugs is calculated in the following manner:

$$P_0 = cP. \tag{8}$$

Thus, the out-of-pocket price is determined by multiplying the consumer's out-of-pocket share, *c*, by the pharmaceutical consumer price index, *P*, our measure of market price. The expression

[5] Note that real pharmaceutical expenditures per capita capture purchases of both existing and new drugs but a demand curve assumes a standardized product. Technical change over time obviously changes the mix of old and new drugs and thus might present a problem when estimating long-run elasticities. However, variables are first differenced in our multiple regression model. Thus, we are estimating short-run elasticities and technical change therefore presents less of a problem.

in equation (8) is then divided by the general consumer price index, P_X, to derive a real or relative out-of-pocket price of drugs for each year.

As noted by some researchers, consumer price indices are not measured without error because substitution effects and quality changes over time are not fully incorporated (e.g., Hausman, 2003). Several authors have also pointed out the biases that previously existed in pharmaceutical price indices because of (1); the undersampling of new drugs, (2); the failure to treat generic drugs as lower-priced substitutes for branded drugs rather than new drugs, and (3); the use of list instead of transaction prices (Berndt, Griliches, and Rosett, 1993; Scherer, 1993). Nevertheless, the pharmaceutical price index represents the best available time series indicator of drug price swings in the U.S. (Beginning in 1995, the Bureau of Labor Statistics has taken steps to correct some of these biases in the pharmaceutical price index.) Moreover, since we are examining changes in the ratio of the pharmaceutical and general CPI measures over time, some of the substitution and quality bias in the numerator and denominator may tend to cancel out. In addition, average year-to-year parameter estimates are obtained in the multiple regression analysis. These short-run estimates may avoid some of this bias because sufficient time does not pass for substitution effects and quality changes to fully work themselves out. It should be kept in mind, however, that any remaining measurement error biases the parameter estimates towards zero if the rest of the model is properly specified.

Similarly, the out-of-pocket real price of medical care is obtained by multiplying the ratio of the medical care consumer price index and the general price index by the percent of medical care expenditures that were out-of-pocket expenses. Real income is measured by real GDP per capita. Before presenting our multiple regression results, we first discuss how the dependent variable and the two out-of-pocket prices in equation (7) changed over time. This information is provided in Exhibit 1. Notice that real drug expenditures per capita increased rapidly from 1960 to 1975, continued to increase but at a diminishing rate from 1976 to 1994, and then began increasing at an increasing rate once again from 1995 to 2000. It may not be coincidental, but instead reflective of the law of demand, that out-of-pocket real prescription drug prices inversely mirrored these movements in per capita real drug expenditures during this time period. For instance, the out-of-pocket real price of drugs declined rapidly from 1960 to 1975 and from 1993 to 2000, the two time periods when real drug expenditures per capita were rising quickly.

Attention should also be drawn to the fact that the out-of-pocket real price for medical services generally declined over the entire time period, but at a relatively slow rate.

3. Empirical Results

A high degree of serial correlation necessitated first differencing of the data (after taking logarithms). First differencing of the data seems particularly appropriate because diagnostic tests revealed the presence of unit roots in several of the time series data (i.e., real drug spending per capita and real GDP per capita) before they were first differenced. Unit roots can result in spurious correlations among variables. We also included in our empirical model a lagged measure of real drug expenditures per capita as an additional independent variable (after first differencing). The lagged measure was included to control to for unobserved demand factors like tastes and preferences, T, and the initial endowment of health, H_0, as specified in equation (6). Estimation of the first-differenced model by ordinary least squares produced the coefficient estimates and corresponding t-statistics reported in the second column of Exhibit 2[6,7] We note that the adjusted R^2 of 0.58 is quite high for this type of time-series model (i.e., models using first-differenced data).[8]

As anticipated, the estimated own-price elasticity of demand is negative and statistically significant. Our relatively price-inelastic estimate of –0.48 suggests that a 10 percent decrease (increase) in the real out-of-pocket price of prescription drugs increases (decreases) the quantity demanded of prescription drugs by about 4.8 percent, *ceteris paribus*. This estimate is very close to Coulson and Stuart's (1995) estimate of –0.34 and also falls within previous estimates ranging

---

[6] Mathematically, the intercept term in equation (7) falls out after first differencing of the variables. Statistically, an intercept term proved to be no different from zero.

[7] As noted in the text, a one-period lagged value of Q (in logs) was also included in the specification to control for changing tastes and preferences. Because a lagged value of the dependent variable is specified on the right hand side of the equation, the typical Durbin Watson statistic cannot be used to detect serial correlation. We remind the reader, however, that our specification contains first differences of the variables and not levels so we report the Durbin Watson statistic. We also experimented with other diagnostic tests such as the Q-statistic and Durbin's alternative test (Maddala, 1992). These tests failed to detect the presence of serial correlation.

[8] The specification of equation (7) assumes that the market price of drugs, which helps to make up the out-of-pocket real price of drugs, is independent of the amount of existing drugs produced. An assumption of independence or constant returns to scale in production is not unreasonable, particularly in the short run. For example, Schwartzman (1976) finds no evidence to support economies in manufacturing pharmaceuticals. While the market price of pharmaceuticals may be independent of consumption at a point in time, market price may change over time given varying supply conditions, allowing us to identify a demand curve for pharmaceuticals.

from –0.06 to –0.64 as noted by these authors. Earlier research focused on the demand for pharmaceuticals by elderly individuals. Our own-price elasticity is most likely higher because it captures the demand of the representative consumer, rather than the representative elderly individual. Because of their relatively more depreciated health capital, elderly individuals are likely to face fewer health-related choices than the general population, and thus may possess less price-elastic demands for pharmaceuticals.

The positive and statistically significant cross-price elasticity estimate suggests that medical care and prescription drugs are substitute products. For example, based upon our cross-price elasticity estimate of 0.56, a 10 percent increase in the price of medical care is associated with a 5.6 percent increase in the quantity of prescription drugs demanded. The direct relation between the price of medical care and the quantity of prescription drugs demanded suggests that decision-makers have some ability to substitute one good for the other in the production of good health when relative price changes. This finding is consistent with Lichtenberg's (1996) research, which found that increased expenditures on pharmaceuticals leads to reduced expenditures on hospitalizations, ambulatory care, and physician services.

The income elasticity estimate is also positive and statistically significant, indicating that pharmaceutical products can, on average, be treated as normal goods. The income elasticity is fairly sizable suggesting that a 10 percent increase in real income per capita produces a 5.1 percentage increase in the quantity of drugs demanded. Studies tend to suggest that health care is a normal good (Santerre and Neun, 2004). The estimated coefficient on the lagged measure of real pharmaceutical spending per capita is positive and statistically different from zero. This coefficient estimate can be used in conjunction with the short-run estimates to calculate long-run elasticity estimates.[9] According to the calculations, the long run own-price, cross-price, and income elasticities are –0.89, 1.03, and 0.94 respectively.

Although predominately influenced by private demand (because public health insurance for pharmaceuticals was largely absent on an outpatient basis during the sample period), public financing may also influence real drug expenditures per capita, the dependent variable in equation (7). During the time period under investigation, the government paid for drugs

---

[9] For example, the long run price elasticity estimate is calculated by dividing the short run elasticity by one minus the coefficient estimate on the lagged dependent variable. The other long-run estimates are determined in a similar fashion.

administered to inpatients if they were covered by one of the various public health insurance programs. The government also paid for prescription drugs for outpatient care under the Veterans Administration and Medicaid programs. Reimbursement for pharmaceutical is fairly restrictive under the latter two programs, but the programs do provide some of the population with financial access to pharmaceuticals. In any case, a control variable should be included in the multiple regression equation for the percentage of pharmaceutical expenditures paid by government. The ratio of government expenditures on pharmaceutical to total pharmaceutical expenditures ranged from a little under 3 percent in 1960 to slightly under 22 percent in 2000.

Inclusion of this additional independent variable (after taking first differences in logarithms), results in the multiple regression findings reported in the third column of Exhibit 2. Notice that the multiple regression findings remain virtually the same as those reported in column 2, and the coefficient estimate on the public financing variable is not statistically different from zero. Public financing may have had no independent impact on pharmaceutical consumption because of its relatively low percentage over time, at least until very recently, or because our public financing variable captures a host of widely diverse government reimbursement schemes.

4. Simulating Consumer Gains From A Drug Price Control Regime

We use the multiple regression results in column 2 of Exhibit 2 to estimate the future value of the consumer surplus from a drug price control policy that holds drug price increases to the same rate of growth as the general price level over the period from the beginning of 1981 through the end of 2000. To measure the consumer surplus for each year, we estimate the area under the inverse demand curve over the range between actual real drug expenditures for that year and the real drug expenditures that would result from a lower controlled price.

We pick the years between 1981 and 2000 to conduct the experiment because real drug prices increased throughout that period, as depicted in Exhibit 1. Moreover, in a recent study, Giaccotto, Santerre, and Vernon (2003, 2005) used that same period to estimate the number of new drugs that would have been lost from the same drug price control regime. These authors assumed Congress enacted a law in 1980 requiring pharmaceutical prices in the U.S. to grow no faster than the general price level. This approach mirrors one of the actual mandates in the

Veteran's Health Care Act of 1992: namely, that drug prices paid by federal agencies cannot grow at a rate faster than the urban consumer price index. Thus, while our experiment is couched within a hypothetical and historical context, it will nevertheless reflect an actual approach employed by the Federal Government to control pharmaceutical prices (albeit on a relatively small scale). By combining the results from these two studies, some insight may be gained into the *net* consumer benefits arising from a drug price control system that holds the rate of growth of drug prices to the same rate of growth as the overall CPI.

Retrieving the elasticities from the multiple regression results in Exhibit 2, we can express a representative consumer's constant elasticity of demand curve for drugs as the following:

$$Q = A\left(\frac{P_O}{P_X}\right)^{-0.483}\left(\frac{P_M}{P_X}\right)^{0.560}\left(\frac{Y}{P_X}\right)^{0.512} Q_{t-1}^{0.456} \qquad (9)$$

Or more simply, we can write:

$$Q = K\left(\frac{P_O}{P_X}\right)^{-0.483} \qquad (10)$$

and define,

$$K = A\left(\frac{P_M}{P_X}\right)^{0.560}\left(\frac{Y}{P_X}\right)^{0.512} Q_{t-1}^{0.456} \qquad (11)$$

It follows that K, the amount of drug consumption that results from all factors other than the real out-of-pocket price, can be determined by dividing Q, real pharmaceutical expenditures per capita, by $P_O^{-0.483}$ for each year between 1981 and 2000. K changes over time in response to adjustments in the relative out-of-pocket price for medical care, real income and the lagged measure of the dependent variable.

To estimate the consumer surplus associated with the representative consumer's additional drug purchases under our price ceiling program, we have to invert equation (10) and solve for the market price of pharmaceutical products by employing the expression for the out-of-pocket price depicted by equation (8), which gives:

$$P = \frac{P_x}{c}\left(\frac{K}{Q}\right)^{\frac{1}{0.483}} \qquad (12)$$

Using standard integration techniques, the area under the inverse demand curve can be measured over the range between the actual real drug expenditures observed and the real drug expenditures that would have resulted from a price control regime that held the rate of growth in pharmaceutical prices to that of the general consumer price index. For the purposes of our simulation, the price control policy holds the ratio of the market price of pharmaceutical goods to all other goods at the same level observed in 1980 (but not necessarily the relative out-of-pocket price because c, the out-of-pocket share, changes over time).

Some disagreement exists in the literature regarding the appropriate measure of consumer surplus when health care is involved because of the presence of third-party payers. Health economists typically argue that the uninsured demand curve when people are healthy should be used to estimate consumer surplus to remove the distortion caused by moral hazard. Nyman (2003) insists on the insured demand curve when people are ill because insurance provides access to health care that many could not otherwise afford and because the amount of utility received from medical care depends on health status. Because our demand equation is specified on a per capita basis, it reflects the aggregated demands of the insured (both partially and fully) and the uninsured as well as the sick and the healthy (zero consumption). Thus, following Nyman, the resulting estimate of consumer surplus may be biased downward because it implicitly incorporates the demands of the uninsured and healthy. On the other hand, the estimate of consumer surplus may be biased upward because it incorporates the inefficiencies of moral hazard through c, the out-of-pocket fraction. To remove the potential inefficiencies caused by moral hazard, estimates for consumer surplus are also reported assuming that $c = 1$. However, we are unable to correct for the possible lower bound nature of the consumer surplus estimate because of the inclusion of the healthy and uninsured into the demand specification.

Theory suggests that willingness to pay should be measured by the compensated demand curve because a price change also typically triggers an income effect. However in this particular case the income effect is very tiny because of both a small drug expenditure share (about 1 percent on average for the sample) and an income elasticity of demand less than one. Applying the Slutsky equation, the uncompensated and compensated price elasticities of demands differ by only .005 (i.e., -0.483 versus –0.478). Given this minor discrepancy, we measure consumer surplus with the uncompensated demand curve.

The results of the consumer surplus simulation are shown in Exhibit 3 assuming an insured demand based upon the actual figures for the out-of-pocket fraction in each period. The second column shows the consumer surplus resulting from the drug price ceiling for the representative consumer during each of the years. Notice how individual consumer surplus increases throughout the period as actual drug prices continue to increase relative to the controlled drug prices.

By multiplying the total population in the U.S. by the representative consumer's surplus figures, *aggregate* consumer surplus can be derived. Aggregate consumer surplus for each of the years is shown in column 3. Assuming no interest and compounding of earnings, these yearly figures are summed, and result in a total of $206 billion by the end of 2000. Finally, the fourth column lists the future value of the aggregate consumer surplus that would have been earned over 20 years at a 7 percent real rate of return. Over the last few decades, the average rate of return in the stock market has exceeded general price inflation by about 7 percent. According to the figure shown at the bottom of column 4, the total future value of the aggregate consumer surplus would equal roughly $319 billion if the entire savings from the drug price control regime were invested at a 7 percent annual real rate of return. The future value of the consumer surplus for the uninsured demand (found by setting c equal to 1) amounts to $149 billion. For purposes of comparison, we also report in Exhibit 4 the future value of the consumer surplus for the insured and uninsured demands at different rates of return.[10]

Over this same time period, Giaccotto, Santerre, and Vernon (2003, 2005) estimated that this same price control regimen would have caused firms to reduce pharmaceutical R&D expenditures (in $2000) by between $264.5 and $293.1 billion, because of lower profit expectations and possibly reduced levels of internal funds (which are the primary source of R&D finance)[11]. This reduced investment in R&D would have led to approximately 38 percent fewer new drugs being brought to market in the global economy. If this 38 percent figure is applied to the total number of new chemical entities approved for marketing during this period in the U.S., we can use our simulation results to calculate the average social opportunity cost per new drug.

[10] Over the 1980 to 2000 period, the rate of return in the stock market averaged roughly 17 percent and the general price inflation rate averaged 4 percent.
[11] The latter would be the case if capital market imperfections imparted a cost advantage to internal funds over external debt and equity (see Vernon, 2004a).

During the period from 1980 to 2000, 520 new chemical entities were approved for marketing in the U.S.[12] This figure suggests that 198 drugs would have been "lost" if the assumed price control regime was imposed. Dividing the $319 billion consumer surplus gains from price controls over the period from 1980-2000 by the number of new drugs "lost" due to price controls, we estimate that, on average, consumers (in the aggregate) gave up $1.6 billion in consumer surplus per new drug developed.

This raises the question of whether or not the benefit of a new drug brought to market during this period was greater than or less than $1.6 billion. If the former is the case, then the fact that price controls were not imposed (in the manner we describe and model) was, on net, good for the U.S. If, however, the latter is the case, then not imposing price controls had a net social cost for Americans. While recent research has documented the significant benefits associated with medical and pharmaceutical research, and even suggested that U.S. may be currently underinvesting in R&D (Murphy and Topel, 2003), very few studies have documented the value (in dollar terms) of new drugs or pharmaceutical R&D. A notable exception is the econometric study by Lichtenberg (2002). In his study, which covered a similar time period in the U.S. (1960-1997), he approximated that, on average, every $1,345 spent on pharmaceutical R&D "produced" an additional U.S. life year.

While speculative, we can use this average productivity measure of R&D to compare the benefits of price controls (as modeled in this study) and the costs in terms of "lost" R&D and drugs[13]. To do this we divide Giaccotto and colleague's estimated range of forgone capitalized pharmaceutical R&D, by $1,345 and multiply this by $100,000, which is one measure of the value of a U.S. life year (Cutler and McClellan, 2001). Of course, both higher and lower estimates exist. When this first approximation of the cost of price controls is compared with the $319 billion gain in consumer surplus, the resulting cost-benefit ratio ranges from about 62 to 68. This suggests that, from a social welfare perspective, price controls would have done much more harm than good.

---

[12] Federal Drug Administration at http://www.FDA.gov.

[13] See the papers by Vernon, Santerre, and Giaccotto (2004), and Vernon (2004b) for a discussion of the caveats involved.

5. Conclusion

Rising drug prices have captured the attention of the media, various public interest groups, and politicians. Some have pointed to price controls as a way of reining in what are perceived by many to be "runaway" drug prices. But as economists have known for centuries, price controls simply represent "bad economics". Economic theory suggests that price controls often create shortages, reduce quality, lead to price discrimination, and can harm incentives for innovation. The only benefit to price controls is that some individuals gain, at the expense of others, through an increase in their consumer surplus as a result of the lower controlled prices.

In this paper, we estimate the consumer surplus, or benefit, resulting from a hypothetical price control regime in the U.S. To accomplish this objective, we use national data from 1960 to 2000 to estimate the aggregate private demand for pharmaceuticals. Based upon our empirical results, the demand for pharmaceuticals is shown to be inversely related to its own-price and directly related to the both medical prices and real income. Moreover, the empirical estimation generates elasticity estimates with plausible magnitudes that are in general agreement with previous research findings.

We then use the estimated demand curve to simulate the consumer surplus gains associated with an assumed price control policy that holds the increase in pharmaceutical prices to the rate of growth of the general consumer price index. Giaccotto, Santerre, and Vernon (2003, 2005) have conducted this same experiment, and found that this same price control regime would have reduced the number of new drug innovations by about 38 percent. For the nation as a whole, we estimate that the future value of the consumer surplus from the assumed price control regime would equal approximately $319 billion in 2000. On a per drug basis, we estimate that the social opportunity cost of not imposing this price control policy was approximately $1.6 billion. However, when compared to the estimated benefits of the additional pharmaceutical R&D that was undertaken because these hypothetical price controls were not implemented, these costs appear to be very small. Given our results, and those reported in prior research, society may be better off discovering more efficient ways than price controls to improve access to existing drugs.

Exhibit 1:

Real Drug Expenditures per capita, Out-of-Pocket Real Price of Drugs and Out-of-Pocket Real Price of Medical Care Over Time in the U.S.

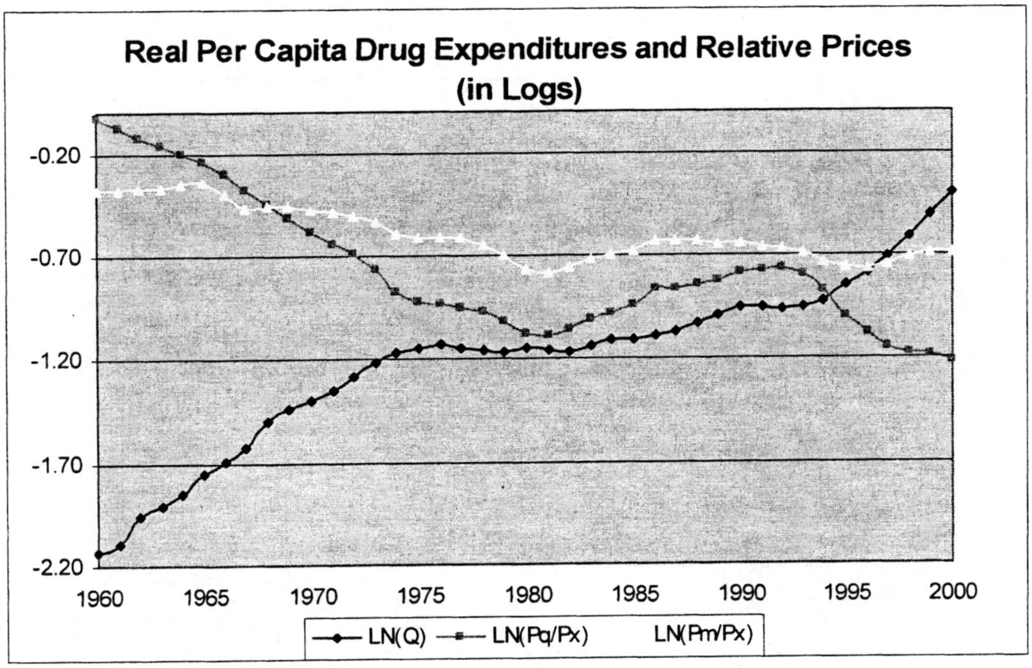

Exhibit 2:

Multiple Regression Results (dependent variable is the first difference of the log of real pharmaceutical expenditures per capita)

Variable	Basic Results	Extended Results
Log of out-of-pocket real price of drugs (P_Q/P_X)	-0.483 (3.73)	-0.469 (3.51)
Log of out-of-pocket real price of medical care (P_M/P_X)	0.560 (3.04)	0.506 (2.38)
Log of real GDP per capita (Y/P_X)	0.512 (2.99)	0.528 (3.00)
One-year lagged measure of real pharmaceutical expenditures per capita	0.456 (4.06)	0.492 (3.70)
Log of percent of total pharmaceutical expenditures paid by government		-0.039 (0.52)
Adjusted R^2	0.584	0.575
Durbin Watson Statistic	1.81	1.84
Observations	39	39

Exhibit 3:

Determination of the Aggregate Consumer Surplus From a Drug Price Control Regime

Year	Money value of the consumer surplus from one individual	Money Value of Aggregate Consumer Surplus (i.e., the second column times population)	Future value of consumer surplus (invested at 7 percent until the end of the year 2000)
1981	$0.26	$60,472,360	$234,008,952
1982	$1.84	$426,554,876	$1,542,647,455
1983	$4.57	$1,069,482,312	$3,614,777,785
1984	$6.96	$1,642,217,474	$5,187,461,537
1985	$9.88	$2,350,009,621	$6,937,613,212
1986	$13.63	$3,271,366,127	$9,025,802,326
1987	$16.80	$4,071,236,379	$10,497,822,037
1988	$20.79	$5,082,849,457	$12,248,879,350
1989	$25.37	$6,260,541,229	$14,099,938,298
1990	$31.74	$7,918,736,937	$16,667,768,902
1991	$38.55	$9,722,865,584	$19,126,348,231
1992	$43.93	$11,201,883,372	$20,594,205,681
1993	$46.79	$12,061,384,335	$20,723,703,874
1994	$50.03	$13,021,977,945	$20,910,450,971
1995	$54.36	$14,286,584,751	$21,440,311,361
1996	$59.89	$15,881,839,547	$22,275,101,543
1997	$67.23	$18,003,459,448	$23,598,862,810
1998	$79.11	$21,375,526,811	$26,185,939,492
1999	$97.97	$26,716,982,518	$30,588,273,285
2000	$115.32	$31,747,355,082	$33,969,669,938
TOTAL		**$206,173,326,166**	**$319,469,587,040**

Exhibit 4

Future Value of the Consumer Surplus for Various Rates of Return and Insured versus Uninsured Demands

Real Rate of Return	Uninsured Demand	Insured Demand
5%	$128 Billion	$280 Billion
9%	$174 Billion	$366 Billion
13%	$241 Billion	$488 Billion

References

Berndt, Ernst R., Zvi Griliches, and Joshua G. Rosett. (1993) "Auditing the Producer Price Index: Micro Evidence From Prescription Pharmaceutical Preparations." *Journal of Business and Economic Statistics* (July), pp. 251-64.

Coulson, N. Edward and Bruce C. Stuart (1995) "Insurance Choice and the Demand for Prescription Drugs" *Southern Economic Journ*al, 61, pp. 1146-57.

Congressional Budget Office (http://www.cbo.gov/): Cost Estimate for H.R. 1 Medicare Prescription Drug, Improvement and Modernization Act of 2003 (and personal conversation with W. Philip Ellis from the CBO on December 3, 2003)

Cutler DM and McClellan M (2001) Is technological change in medicine worth it? *Health Affairs*. Sept/Oct; pp. 11-29.

Giaccotto, Carmelo, Rexford E. Santerre, and John A. Vernon. (2005). "Pharmaceutical Pricing and R&D Growth Rates," *Journal of Law and Economics*, forthcoming.

Giaccotto, Carmelo, Rexford E. Santerre, and John A. Vernon. (2003) "Explaining Pharmaceutical R&D Growth Rates at the Industry Level: New Perspectives and Insights" AEI-Brookings Joint Center, Related Publication 3-31, December 2003, http://www.aei.brookings.org/publications/index.php?tab=author&authorid=368.

Hausman, Jerry. (2003) "Sources of Bias and Solutions to Bias in the Consumer Price Index" *Journal of Economic Perspectives*, 17 (Winter), 23-44.

Kanavos P., Costa-i-Font J., Merkur S., and M. Gemmill (2004) "The Economic Impact of Pharmaceutical Parallel Trade in European Union Member States: A Stakeholders Analysis," London School of Economics and Political Science working paper

Lichtenberg, Frank (1996)"Do (More and Better) Drugs Keep People Out of Hospitals?," *American Economic Review* 86, May, 384-8.

Lichtenberg, Frank (2000) "The Effect of Pharmaceutical Utilisation and Innovation on Hospitalisation and Mortality," in *Productivity, Technology, and Economic Growth*, ed. by B. van Ark, S. K. Kuipers and G. Kuper (Kluwer Academic Publishers)

Lichtenberg FR (2002) Sources of U.S. longevity increase, 1960-1997. National Bureau of Economic Research, working paper 8755, Cambridge, MA.

Maddala, G.S. (1992) *Introduction to Econometrics*, New York: Macmillian Publishing Company.

Miller, Richard D. Jr. and H.E. Frech III. (2002) "The Productivity of Health Care and Pharmaceuticals: Quality of Life, Cause of Death, and the Role of Obesity." *Mimeo*, University of California at Santa Barbara.

Murphy KM and Topel RH (2003) The economic value of medical research; in Measuring the gains from medical research; edited by Kevin M. Murphy and Robert H. Topel, The University of Chicago Press.

Nyman, John A. (2003) *The Theory of Demand for Health Insurance*, Stanford, CA: Stanford University Press.

Santerre, Rexford E. and Stephen P. Neun (2004) *Health Economics: Theories, Insights, and Industry Studies*, Thomson Learning.

Scherer, F.M. (2001) "The link between gross profitability and pharmaceutical R&D spending" *Health Affairs*, 20: 216-220.

Scherer, F.M. (2004) "The Pharmaceutical Industry—Prices and Progress," *The New England Journal of Medicine*. 351:9.

Schwartzman, David (1976). *Innovation in the Pharmaceutical Industry: The Declining Profitability of Drug Innovation*, Baltimore: John Hopkins Press.

Vernon, J.A. (2004a) "Examining the Link Between Price Regulation and Pharmaceutical R&D Investment," *Health Economics*, forthcoming.

Vernon, J.A. (2004b) "New Evidence on Drug Price Controls" *Regulation*, Fall p. 13-15.

Vernon, J.A., Santerre, R.E., and Giaccotto, C. (2004) "Are Drug Price Controls Good for Your Health" University of Connecticut, Department of Finance Working Paper.

Research Papers in Management Studies

UNIVERSITY OF CAMBRIDGE
Judge Institute of Management
cambridge's business school

APPLYING A CBA MODEL TO THE THREE GORGES PROJECT IN CHINA

R Morimoto & C Hope

WP 01/2003

The Judge Institute of Management
University of Cambridge
Trumpington Street
Cambridge CB2 1AG, UK

APPLYING A CBA MODEL TO THE THREE GORGES PROJECT IN CHINA

R Morimoto & C Hope

WP 01/2003

Risako Morimoto
Judge Institute of Management
University of Cambridge
Tel: +44 (0) 1223 339700
Fax: +44 (0) 1223 339701
Email: r.morimoto@jims.cam.ac.uk

Dr Chris Hope
Judge Institute of Management
University of Cambridge
Tel: +44 (0) 1223 338194
Fax: +44 (0) 1223 339701
Email: c.hope@jims.cam.ac.uk

Please address enquiries about the series to:

Research Support Manager
Judge Institute of Management
Trumpington Street
Cambridge CB2 1AG, UK
Tel: 01223 339611 Fax: 01223 339701
E-mail: research-support@jims.cam.ac.uk

Applying a CBA model to the Three Gorges Project in China

Risako Morimoto and Chris Hope

Judge Institute of Management Studies

University of Cambridge[1]

Abstract

The world's largest hydro project, the Three Gorges Dam in China is currently under construction. The project is controversial as large environmental and social impacts are expected despite the fact that the project is supposed to control the region's severe floods, to generate 18.2 GW of hydropower, and to improve river navigation. This paper uses the cost benefit analysis (CBA) model developed in Morimoto and Hope (2001) to examine all the major economic, environmental and social impacts of this massive project. Probabilistic analysis allows the distribution of the net present value to be calculated, and the most significant impacts to be identified. The mean and the 95th percentile of the cumulative net present value at the 5% discount rate were positive, whereas the 5th percentile was negative. The variables with the largest contribution towards cumulative net present value were benefits of power generation, associated economic growth, and clean hydropower; and costs of construction resettlement and lost archaeological sites. The project seems to be promising as the benefits of power generation, flood control, and navigation improvement are expected to be large. Nevertheless, the analysis in this paper has illustrated that the uncertainty associated with the project is huge and cannot be ignored.

[1] Judge Institute of Management Studies, Trumpington Street Cambridge CB2 1AG UK; Tel: + 44 (1223) 339700; Fax: + 44 (1223) 339701; Email: RM253@cam.ac.uk

1. Introduction

The Three Gorges Project (TGP) is the world's largest hydro project. It is currently under construction and is expected to be completed in 2009. The project involves about 20,000 workers of whom 40% are women, according to the China Yangtze Three Gorges Project Development Corporation (CTGPC)[2]. The dam site is surrounded by scenic landscape with beautiful gorges and many important cultural sites. The area to be submerged is fertile and densely populated. Opposition around the world argues that the project would be a social and environmental disaster, having seen the tragedies of large dams elsewhere in the world[3]. This paper uses the cost benefit analysis (CBA) model developed in Morimoto and Hope (2001) to examine all the major economic, environmental and social impacts of this massive project. Probabilistic analysis allows the distribution of the Net Present Value to be calculated, and the most significant impacts to be identified.

2.1. The Three Gorges Project

China's rapid economic growth results in both dramatic improvements in living standards and serious damage to its environment. China's real GDP grew by 8% in 2000 and is forecast to grow by 7.5% in 2001 (EIA 2001). More than 70% of electricity in China is generated by coal; in total, 80% is thermal (coal, gas, and crude oil); 19% hydro; and 1% nuclear (Zeng and Song 1998)[4]. Such high dominance of coal use in China creates serious environmental problems such as air, land and water pollution[5]. Burning coal produces greenhouse gases, and emission levels of CO_2 in China are increasing continuously. According to Chinese officials, electricity supply would have to increase

[2] This information was collected during the fieldwork conducted in China in March 2001.

[3] For example, serious negative impacts on agriculture in the case of Aswan High Dam in Egypt, or large resettlement problems in the case of Narmada Valley project in India.

[4] See also http://www.pnl.gov/china/outmix.htm

[5] See Simbeck et al (1994) for a detailed discussion on coal induced environmental problems.

by 20-30% to eliminate present power shortages; the economic cost of these power shortages is very high (Wu & Li 1995). The installed hydro capacity in China is less than 15% of its exploitable hydro potential (Zeng and Song 1998). The Chinese government is intending to obtain 40% of its power from clean hydroelectric sources[6] (WCD 2000).

As a result of an economic slow down and demand reductions from closures of inefficient state owned industrial units, China's electric power industry experienced oversupply in 1998-1999 (EIA 2001). However, this was a short-term event and growth in electricity consumption is projected at 5.5% per year through 2020 (EIA 2001). More electricity is required in order to boost the economy, including still underdeveloped regions, to meet expected future economic growth, and to meet future increases in household electricity consumption as a result of increased use of electric appliances due to improvements in the standard of living. Currently, the electricity transmission capacity is limited. However, once this distribution problem is solved, a huge increase in electricity consumption in remote areas will be expected[7].

The most environmentally controversial project in China today is the construction of the Three Gorges Dam (TGD) on the Yangtze River in western Hubei province. Dr Sun Yat-Sen, the forerunner of China's democratic reform, first proposed to dam the Three Gorges in 1919. The dam is intended to raise flood control capacity from the present 10-year frequency to 100-year frequency, to provide one tenth of China's existing energy

[6] Today, China has the world's largest number of dams (85000 dams including 20000 large dams, most of which have been built since 1949).
[7] 70 million of Chinese population had no access to electricity in 1996 compared to 120 million in 1994 (Buczek 1996; Sharman 1994)

needs, and to improve navigation along the river (CTGPC 1995) [8]. In order to generate the same amount of electricity, 50 million tons per year of coal, 25 million tons per year of crude oil or 18 nuclear-power plants would be required (Thurston 1996; National Geographic 1997 September). The plan of the project has been interrupted over the years by war, the Cultural Revolution, economic troubles and other events.

In 1989, the 70m high Gazhouba Dam (40km downstream of the TGP) opened after nearly 20 years of construction in response to the increasing demand for electric power in the region. In August 1996, two major projects to improve transportation in the Three Gorges area, the Xiling Bridge and the airport, were completed and went into service. Construction of the TGD is divided into three stages. The river was blocked at the end of Stage I (1993-1997), then the hydro power station will start operating at the end of the Stage II (1998-2003), and the project will be completed at the end of the Stage III (2004-2009).

The world's third largest river, the Yangtze, carves its route through the mountains of southwestern China, springing from the glacial mountains of northern Tibet. It heads North East to surge through a spectacular 200km reach of deep, narrow canyons known as the Three Gorges. From there, the river widens and meanders across southern China's vast fertile plains to the East China Sea at Shanghai. The Yangtze River valley is China's agricultural and industrial heartland. It is supporting one third of China's population, producing 40% of the nation's grain, 70% of its rice, and 40% of China's total industrial output (Morrish 1997).

---

[8] The hydroelectric power generated from the TGP is to be used in eastern and central China regions and the eastern part of southwest China's Sichuan province.

The river possesses 300 species of fish (of which one third are endemic) and its annual aquatic production output accounts for 50% of the whole nation's gross output (CTGPC 1995). Fish resources in the river are declining due to human activities. After the completion of the dam, the change may benefit some species and adversely affect some others since different fish species have different living habits (CTGPC 1995).

The project area is a great tourist attraction, which has scenic natural landscapes as well as cultural relics and sites with high aesthetic value. Construction of the dam will result in not only the loss of a large number of artifacts from this area, but also the destruction of an important link in understanding China's civilization. Only some of the relics can be removed or reproduced (CTGPC 1995).

The Yangtze River has produced some of China's worst natural flood disasters. In 1954, the Yangtze floods killed 30,000 people (Fung 1999). The heavy rains and flooding along the Yangtze River damaged 100,000 houses, toppled 34,000 houses, inundated 1.13 million hectares of farmland causing a grain output loss of 880,000 tons, forced more than 2,000 companies to limit production, killed 36 people and 5,200 livestock, and induced economic losses of more than 4.6 billion yuan in less than one month[9]. In Hubei province alone, the 1998 flood resulted in total economic losses of 30 billion yuan. Agricultural production in this region accounts for about 22% of GDP and the flood inundated about 1.7 million hectares of crops (Saywell 1998).

[9] http://www.irn.org/programs/threeg/991029.central.html

The project would displace about 1.98 million people; submerge approximately 150,000 acres, including 160 towns, 13 cities, 1352 villages, 1500 factories, 12000 cultural antiquities and 16 archaeological sites[10]. There is a fear of depriving downstream fisheries due to a decline in water quality (Thirston 1996; ASCE 1997). Over 3000 factories and mines are in the reservoir area; they currently produce 10 billion tons of waste annually containing 50 different toxins (Topping 1996). Topping (1996) argues that if we assume the waste water level remains unchanged, the waste content will increase 11 times in some areas due to the dam. There is also a possibility of dam failures and earthquake (Thurston 1996)[11]. Large dams can be a prime military target; for example, Kajaki dam in southern Afghanistan was bombed by the American air force on the 1st November 2001.

The water of the Yangtze River carries the fifth largest sediment discharge in the world, most of which is conveyed during floods[12]. The Three Gorges area has been intensively cultivated so that soil erosion has become a very serious problem due to a loss of a forest cover (CTGPC 1995). Sedimentation problems are likely to reduce power generation capacity[13].

---

[10] See Topping (1996); Goldstein (1998); Ren (1998); Childs-Johnson and Sullivan (1998); Caufield (1997)

[11] On average, there are 110 dam collapses per year and the official deaths toll shows 9937 deaths due to dam failures (Fu 1998). See WCD (2000); Topping (1996); Si(1998) for the details of dam failures in China. Many Scientists argue that the pressure from the reservoir and the dam to fragile geological structures may cause earthquakes. The first record was in the late 1930s when seismic activity started after the building of the Hoover dam in the US. See also New Scientist 2 Nov 1991 p.13 for the article on dam and earthquake in the Hymalayas.

[12] The Yangtze river discharges 486 Mt of sediment into the sea annually (CTGPC 1995).

[13] About 230 dams in China have a significant problem of sediment deposition, leading to a combined loss of 14 % of the total storage capacity (Leopold 1998). The Three Gate Gorge dam on the Yellow River produces less than 1/3 of the power that was promised due to heavy sedimentation (Qing 1998). Some dams have lost more than 50 % of the storage capacity (Chunhong 1995). The Sanmexia Reservoir was decommissioned because of sedimentation in 1964 four years after completion. The Laoying reservoir silted up before the dam was completed (Sullivan 1995).

2.2. Modifications to the CBA model

Since the characteristics of the TGP are different from the previous application of the model to Sri Lanka, five new variables are added to the model as shown in Table I: NI (navigation improvement), FC (flood control benefit), FI (negative impact on downstream fishery), DE (mitigation cost of downstream water pollution) and AS (loss in archaeological sites). The size of the dam is massive; therefore an expression of the possibility of dam collapse due to special circumstances (earthquake, technical failures and being a military target) is also added to the evaluation of the variable AC (accident cost). Descriptions of the main parameters in the model and their distributions are presented in Table II and Table III respectively. The rest of the parameters are found in Table A-I in the Appendix. Some of these data may not be very accurate or precise. However, this is inevitable, as many variables are not readily quantifiable and some data have a limited availability because of the project complexity. Hence, the data are given as ranges representing our best attempts to extract as much up-to-date information as possible from various sources. Repeated runs of the model obtain a probability distribution of possible outcomes, which is a more defensible procedure than just using single values for inputs that are in reality not well known.

Table I **New variables added to the model**

Variable	Description
FC (flood control)	The monetary value of flood control benefits. Reductions in flood control benefit due to sedimentation problems are also considered.
NI (navigation improvement)	The benefit from navigation improvements is expressed by reduction in shipping costs (improvement in river transportation). Changes in transportation costs and reduced navigation improvement benefit due to sedimentation problems are also considered.
DE (downstream effects)	The cost for dealing with downstream pollution caused by the dam construction
FI (impacts on downstream fishery)	The impacts on fishery are expressed by a decline in fish catches.
AS (value of the lost archaeological sites)[14]	The value of the lost archaeological sites is approximated by the proportion of the budget for the preservation of cultural antiquities under the international standards and the budget to rescue those cultural sites.

[14] How archaeology is perceived is different from place to place and generation to generation (Carver 1996). Although there are many studies on how to place values on archaeological sites, there is no simple conclusion for this argument. See Carman et al (1999); Carver (1996); Darvil, Saunders, and Startin (1987); Lipe (1984); Schaafsma (1989). Hence, the proxy is used as an approximation in this analysis.

Table II **Main input parameters**

Parameter	Units	Description
P0		Initial proportion of time during which an alternative power generation technology is not available
φ		Parameter which describes the rate of decrease in P over time
E0	Yuan/MWh	Initial expected increase in economic output due to increased power supply
a		Annual rate of decline in power generation due to sedimentation[15]
GC	GW	Generation capacity
AL	GYuan	Archaeological loss

Table III **Main parameter values and descriptions**

Parameter	Minimum value	Most likely value	Maximum value
P0	0.17[a]	0.2[b]	1[c]
φ	0[d]	0.018[e]	0.085[f]
E0[g]	3200	7800	12500
A	0.001[h]	0.005[i]	0.03[j]
GC	12.6[k]	16.4[l]	18.2[m]
AL	1.5[n]	4.9[o]	33[p]

Notes: PERT distribution (a special form of Beta distribution) is used for all the parameters except E0; [a] About 40 million rural households out of 232 million have no access to electricity. 40/232=0.17 (*China's Energy: a forecast to 2015*); [b] The State development and planning Commission estimated that about 20% of China's area suffered power shortages in 1998 (*South China Morning Post 10 December 1998* 'Obstacles block path to reform of industry' China Business Review: Power and Infrastructure). See also Sinton and Fridley (2000); [c] The projected rate of China's total energy requirement is increasing continuously in the next 20 years (US Department of Energy 1996); [d] According to WCD (2000b), coal cannot be considered as an alternative to hydropower as a source of peaking power due to its inefficiency. Gas turbines could be an alternative, but would offer fewer benefits. Hence, assume that alternative

[15] Experiences of dams worldwide in the past show that sedimentation problem is a common issue. See e.g., WCD (2000); Smith (1999); Dixon (2000); Leopold (1998); Chunhong (1995). However, there is little data avaialble on loss of live storage capacity (WCD 2000b).

techniques would not be available in a feasible period; [e] Electricity generated by coal and gas fired thermal power plants increased by 1.8% in 1998 (China Energy Efficiency Information Bulletin March 1999); [f] Electricity generated by coal and gas fired thermal power plants increased by 8.5% in 1995 (China Energy Efficiency Information Bulletin March 1997); [g] In China, each kWh of power shortage results in a loss of economic output of $0.38-1.5 (MOF 1990); [h] The samples examining rates of loss of active storage due to sedimentation in WCD Cross-Check Survey are clustering around a line of 0.1% annual loss[16] (WCD 2000); [i] It is estimated that after 100 years, 50% of the reservoir will be filled due to sedimentation. Thus, the annual rate will be 50/100 = 0.005 (Ryder and Barber 1993); [j] The maximum annual rate of loss of active storage due to sedimentation in WCD Cross-Check Survey. A relatively high rate is set in order to challenge project optimism (WCD 2000); [k] The energy output of Victoria Dam in Sri Lanka is about 31% lower than the planned figure (WCD 2000); [l] The WCD Cross-Check Survey shows that over half of the projects in the sample generate power less than the planned figure. The most likely case is 10% below the target (WCD 2000); [m] The current planned installed capacity (CEB 1994); [n] The estimated cost of the necessary excavations in the proposed reservoir area is $180 million (Topping 1995); [o] The estimated cost of salvage work for the TGP area is $590 million (The Associated Press News 29th January 1995); [p] The maximum value for TCC above is 660 Gyuan. The budget for the preservation of historical relics and cultural antiquities should be about 3-5% of the total budget according to the international standards (Qing, 1998 Chapter 9). Thus 660Gyuan*5%=33Gyuan.

2.3. Mean present value results

A simulation with 10000 iterations was run. There are three large positive impacts, EG (economic growth), PG (power generation), and CP (clean power); three large negative impacts, CC (construction cost), AS (archaeological loss), and RE (resettlement cost) as shown in Table IV. Figure 1 gives a visual presentation of the mean present values by year; the areas under the lines in Figure 1 are the cumulative net present values in Table IV. The scale of resettlement for the TGP is extremely large compared to most dams since the area is densely populated.

[16] A sample of 47 dams are chosen, and the age of dams against the % active storage loss is plotted. See Figure 2.14 in WCD (2000) p.65. Assuming storage volumes and power generations have a positive linear relationship.

Table IV Cumulative net present value for the fourteen variables at t=100 in billion yuan.

Benefits		(Billion Yuan)	Costs		(Billion yuan)
PVEG	Economic growth	744	PVCC	Construction cost	417
PVPG	Power generation	263	PVAS	Archaeological loss	120
PVCP	Clean power	141	PVRE	Resettlement	93
PVFC	Flood control	43	PVOM	O & M cost	39
PVNI	Navigation improvement	26	PVAC	Accident cost	29
			PVDE	Downstream effect	29
			PVFI	Fishery loss	27
			PVLT	Tourism loss	14
			PVIN	Land inundation loss	2

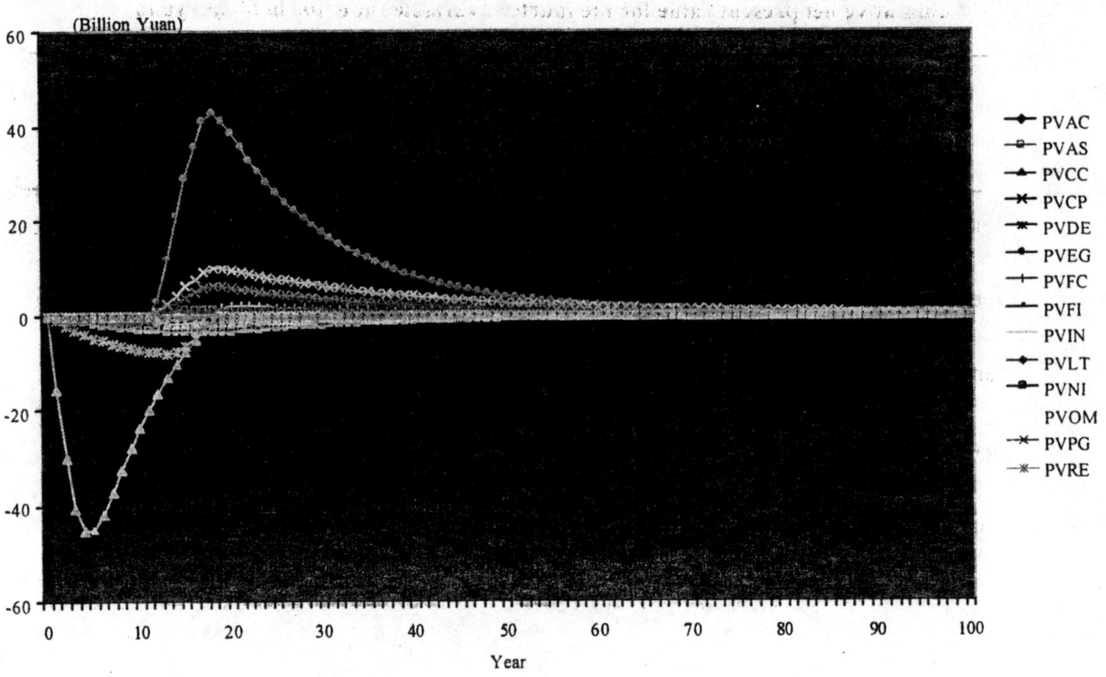

Figure 1 Mean present values for the fourteen variables in the model by year

2.4. Ranges of the six most influential variables

According to Table IV and Figure1, the variables EG (economic growth), PG (power generation), CP (clean power), CC (construction cost), RE (resettlement cost), and AS (archaeological loss) are likely to have the largest impact on the NPV. Figure 2 plots the 90% ranges of these six most influential variables over time in present value form. The variable PG (power generation) seems to have a long-lasting positive impact. Although both capital costs and resettlement costs are huge, they are required only during construction period. The variable CP (clean power) has a very similar trend to the one for PG (power generation), however with a smaller magnitude. This gives support to the view of hydropower as one of the cleanest energy generation techniques. The magnitude of the impact of EG (economic growth) is much higher than the other variables, though it ceases more rapidly, mainly because gradually alternative power generation techniques would be more readily available, and also the country's energy scarcity is likely to reduce as time passes.

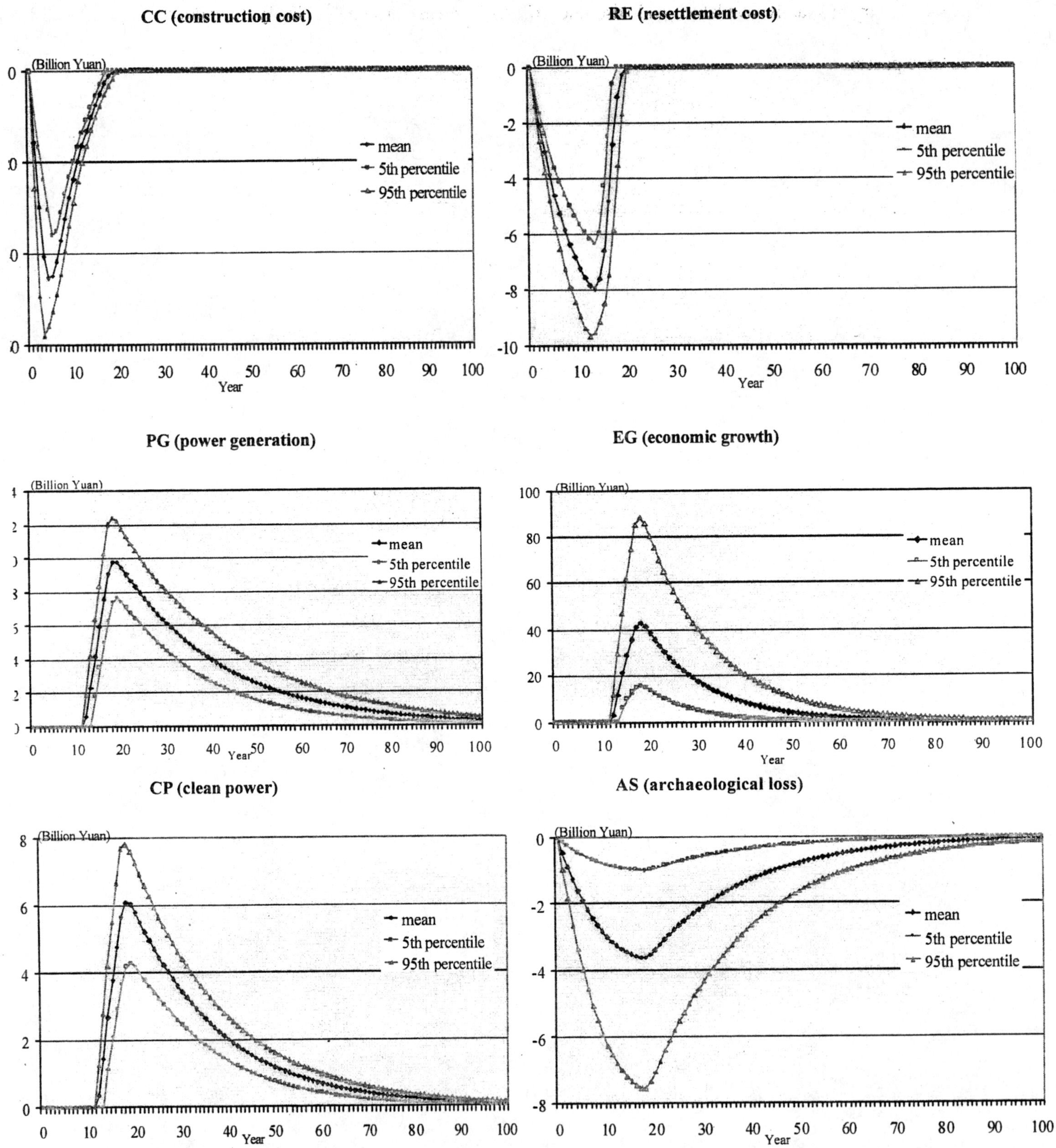

Figure 2 Present value ranges of the six most influential variables

2.5. Cumulative net present value

The evolution of the 5th percentile, mean, and the 95th percentile of the cumulative NPV with a 5% discount rate are shown in Figure 3. The final values are −114, 424, and 1321 billion Yuan respectively. The cumulative NPV is initially negative due to the large construction and resettlement costs as discussed above. However, a rapid upward movement follows as a result of increased clean electricity sale and stimulated economic growth. The benefit never outweighs the cost for the 5th percentile of the cumulative NPV, due to the reduction in electricity generation because of sedimentation problems, low prices for electricity, ongoing costly operation & maintenance cost, and the loss of important archaeological sites. The model includes a premature closure option, where if the ongoing costs outweigh the benefits, the dam is closed down rather than keep making an increasing loss. In practice for the TGP, the possibility of premature closure does not affect the result, even at the 5th percentile since the possibly recoverable costs (after premature closure) of OM (O&M cost), AC (accident cost), DE (downstream effect), and FI (fishery loss) are not very significant. Therefore, premature decommissioning would be highly unlikely to take place.

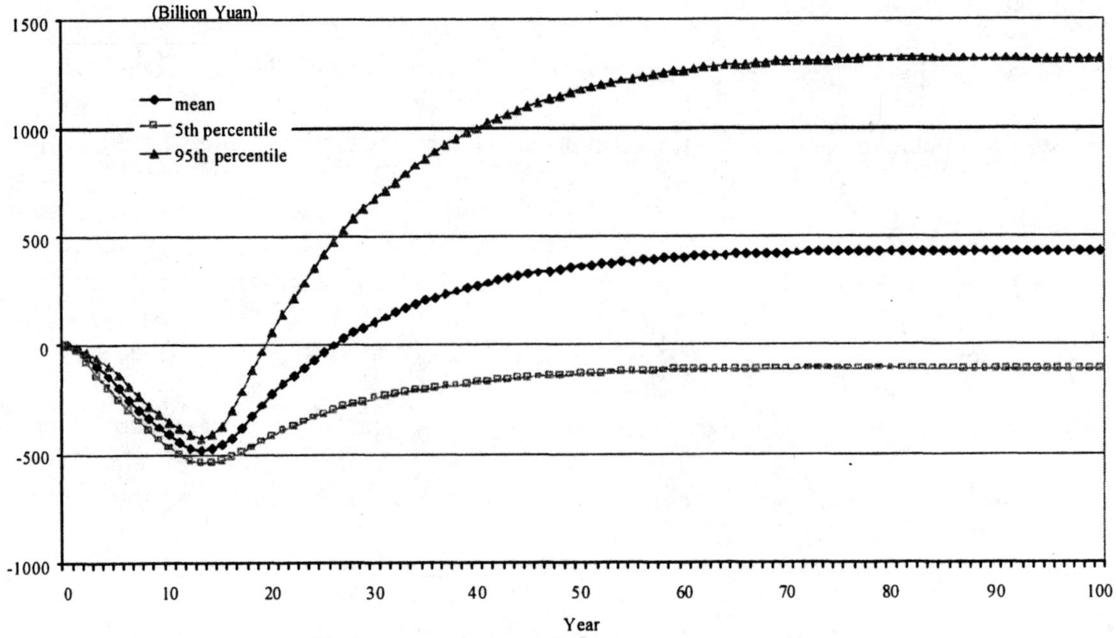

Figure 3 **Range of cumulative NPV with a 5% discount rate by year**

2.6. Sensitivity analysis

Table V shows that the following input parameters have the most significant impact on the cumulative NPV: P0 (Initial proportion of time during which an alternative power generation is not available.), φ (Parameter which describes the annual rate of decrease in P (proportion of time during which an alternative power generation is not available)), EO (Initial expected increase in economic output due to increased power supply), a (annual rate of decline in power generation due to sedimentation), GC (power generation capacity), and AL (Archaeological loss). Each parameter has a correct sign and is therefore consistent with the model. Although this massive project demands a huge cost, it seems not to have a large impact on the NPV. This may be due to the fact that a fairy small range of data (470-660 billion Yuan) is used for the variable TCC (construction cost), as it is thought that this parameter is fairy well known.

Table V **Statistically significant parameters**

Parameter	Description	Student b coefficient
P0	Initial proportion of time during which an alternative power generation is not available.	+ 0.58
φ	Parameter which describes the annual rate of decrease in P (proportion of time during which an alternative power generation is not available)	- 0.54
EO	Initial expected increase in economic output due to increased power supply	+ 0.39
A	Annual rate of decline in power generation due to sedimentation	- 0.19
GC	Power generation capacity	+ 0.15
AL	Archaeological loss	- 0.14

Note: The input parameter values are regressed against the output (NPV). The student b coefficient is a coefficient calculated for each input parameter in the regression equation.

Several variable discount rates were used to see the effect of different rates of pure time preference[17]. Figure 10 shows that choice of pure time preference rate (p) has a strong effect on the value of the cumulative NPV. The fixed discount rate of 5% used for the basic analysis lies in between p=1% and p=2%. The mean value of the cumulative NPV becomes negative when the pure rate of time preference is above about 5%.

[17] These discount rates are calculated in the same manner as the ones in Morimoto and Hope (2001). r(t)=g(t)+p, where r(t)=variable discount rate, g=annual growth rate and p=pure rate of time preference. The estimated growth rates in China are 4% (1999-2000); 3.5% (2000-2020); 3.3% (2020-2040); 3.1% (2040-2060); 3% (2060-2100); 2% (2100-2120), according to EME (1994).

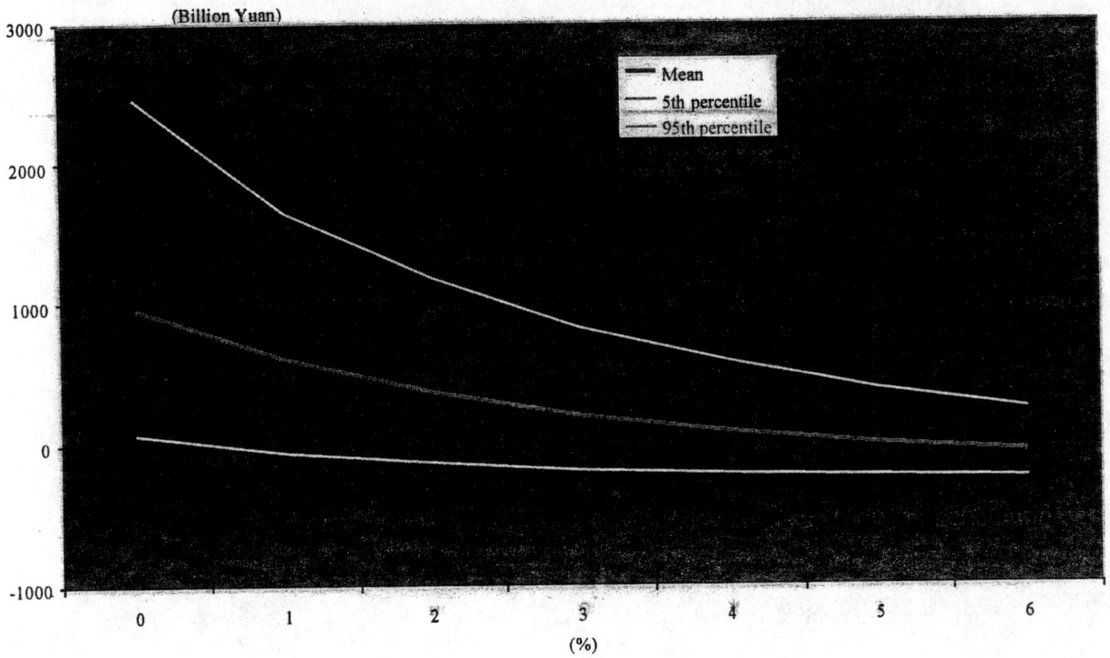

Figure 4 **The cumulative NPV against the pure rate of time reference**

3. Conclusion

This paper has illustrated the use of a CBA model of hydropower projects, slightly modified from the model presented in Morimoto and Hope (2001), using China's massive Three Gorges Project (TGP) as a case study. Five new variables were added, namely FC (flood control), NI (navigation improvement), DE (downstream effect), FI (impacts on downstream fishery), and AS (lost archaeological sites). The variables with the largest contribution towards the cumulative net present value were PG (power generation), EG (economic growth), CC (construction cost), CP (clean power), RE (resettlement cost), and AS (lost archaeological sites). These impacts are widely discussed in newspapers, related books and literature. The sensitivity analysis showed that the parameters P0 (Initial proportion of time during which an alternative power generation is not available) and φ (Parameter which describes the annual rate of decrease in P (proportion of time during which an alternative power generation is not available)) have particularly

IV. Cost Benefit Model
    a. Net Benefits & NPV
    b. Other options:
        i. Thermal generations
        ii. Smaller series of dams
        iii. Nuclear

Model used (based on analysis Sri Lanka dams):

14 variables

PG = non-environmental cost savings on incremental power

EG = willingness to pay for incremental power

CP = cost of environmental damage saved for building TGC instead of thermal power

Probability multiplies:

P: proportion of time clean power not available -- EG x P

(1-P) → CP x (1-P) – this is obtained only when dam is functioning

New Variables:

NI – navigation

FC – flood control

FI – negative effect on downstream fisheries

DE – mitigation of downstream pollution

AS – value of lost archeological sites

Largest impact variables – have the largest PV impacts:

Positive: EG, PG & CP

Negative: CC (construction costs), AS & RE (resettlement)

Monte Carlo analysis was used to determine outcome

Sensitivity analysis based on different discount rates.

The analysis was sensitive to the different rates. See Figs 3 & 4

This also brought to light the two most impactful variables:

P0 – initial portion of time alternative power not available

φ- Describes annual rate of decrease in P (see multipliers above)

Thoughts/Issues/Questions

- Should the project TGD been built?
- What isn't taken into consideration?
- Take into consideration the environmental impact of construction alone? LCA of concrete? Environmental impact of relocating industry and people?
- NPV for 100 year - this just meets current demand – what will the demand for electricity be in 20 years?

Probabilistic CBA – Appling a cost-benefit analysis model to the Three Gorges project in China

I. Objectives
   a. Perform an analysis on the Three Gorges Dam (TGD) that incorporates the economic, environmental and social impacts of the project using a probabilistic Cost-Benefit analysis
   b. Build on previous one-dimensional studies performed on the TGD by adapting a model used to analysis large dam project in Sri Lanka

II. Background
   a. China's current needs
      i. Currently: 80% of electricity is generated by thermal means (70 % coal, rest crude oil and natural gas), 19% hydro power, 1% nuclear generated
      ii. To just eliminate the current electrical shortage China needs to increase electrical generation by 20-30%
   b. Goals & Challenges
      i. Goal to have 40% of electricity come from clean hydro power
      ii. Currently a distribution problem so the use of electricity doesn't represent the actual demand.
      iii. Consumerism

III. Impacts (positive and negative)
   a. Positive
      i. Provide 1/10 of current electrical needs (equivalent to 50 million tons coal or 24 million tons of crude oil or 18 nuclear plants)
      ii. Flood control – this region has history of devastating floods
      iii. Navigation improvements
   b. Negative
      i. Agricultural & industrial sector
         1. the area supports 1/3 of the population
         2. produces 40% of nation's grain, 70% of nation's rice and is responsible for 40% of the total industrial output
      ii. Social aspects
         1. Project is displacing 1.98 million people
         2. 100,000 hectares of farmland (1 hectare = 2.4 acres)
         3. 13 cities,160 towns, 1352 villages, and 1500 factories
         4. chance of dam failure due to earthquake or military target
         5. Archeological & cultural sites/history
      iii. Biodiversity loss
         1. Negative impact to hundreds of fish species, some only found in the Yangtze River.
         2. Sediment accumulation
         3. Toxic pollution from current factories

amount / int rate

value of information

significant impacts on the project cost. The possibility of premature decommissioning was also added to the previous model, though its inclusion did not give a noticeable change to the outcome for the TGP. The improvements of the results could be seen only if sedimentation problems of the TGP were assumed to be even larger than expected, when premature decommissioning would take place.

The mean and the 95th percentile of the cumulative NPV at the 5% discount rate were positive, whereas the 5th percentile was negative. The project seems to be promising as the benefits of power generation, flood control, and navigation improvement are expected to be large. Nevertheless, the analysis in this paper has illustrated that the uncertainty associated with the project is huge and cannot be ignored.

Acknowledgement

We would like to thank Mr Tang Jie and the China Three Gorges Project Corporation (CTGPC) who provided us useful data/information. The interesting tour of the dam site and the visit to the research institute of Yangtze sturgeon, organized by the CTGPC should also be greatly acknowledged.

Appendix

I. Additional equations to the previous model in Morimoto and Hope (2001)

$$FIt=FB*(1-b*t) \qquad \text{for } t>Tc \qquad \text{Gyuan/year}$$

where FI=benefit from flood control in Gyuan/year, FB = mean annual benefits from flood control in billion Yuan and b=annual rate of decline in flood control benefit due to sedimentation.

$$NIt=[SC*(1-c*t)]*e*TRt \qquad \text{for } t=TS \qquad \text{Gyuan/year,}$$
$$TRt=TRo \qquad \text{for } t=0$$
$$=(1+g)TRt\text{-}1 \qquad \text{for } t>0 \qquad \text{yuan/ton}$$

where NI=benefit from navigation improvement in Gyuan/year (it starts functioning in TS), SC= annual shipping capacity in Gtons/yr, e= annual rate of reduction in shipping costs, c=annual rate of decline in navigation control benefit due to sedimentation, TRt= shipping costs in yuan/ ton, TRo= shipping costs at t=0 in yuan/ton, g= annual rate of change in transportation costs

$$CPt=(1-Pt)*\sum_{i=1,2}[CLi*CMi] \qquad \text{Gyuan/year}^{18}$$
$$CLi=(Ci*QEt)/10^9 \qquad \text{Gtons/year}$$
$$Pt=P0*\exp[-\varphi t]$$

where CP=benefit from replacing coal use, CL1= annual decreased CO_2 level due to a decrease in coal use as a result of the TGP in Gtons/yr, P0=initial proportion of time during which an alternative power generation technology is unavailable, φ=parameter which explains the rate of decrease in P over time, CL2= annual decreased SO_2 level due to a decrease in coal use as a result of the TGP in Gtons/yr, C1= annual decreased CO_2 level due to a decrease in coal use as a result of the TGP in tons/GWh/yr, C2= annual decreased SO_2 level due to a decrease in coal use as a result of the TGP in tons/GWh/yr, CM1= benefits of CO_2 reduction in yuan per ton of CO_2, CM2= benefits of SO_2 reduction in yuan per ton of SO_2

$$FIt=(FP*t)/Tc, \qquad \text{for } t\leq Tc$$
$$=FP \qquad \text{for } t>Tc,$$

where FP= annual lost profits from fishery in billion yuan/year.

$$DEt=0 \qquad \text{for } t\leq Tc$$
$$=ADE \qquad \text{for } t>Tc \qquad \text{GYuan/year,}$$

where ADE= annual investment costs to deal with downstream effects in billion yuan/yr (clean-up costs and water pollution mitigation costs).

$$ASt=AL*t/Tc \qquad \text{for } t\leq Tc$$
$$=AL \qquad \text{for } t>Tc \qquad \text{GYuan/year,}$$

AS= value of lost archaeological sites in billion yuan, AL= archaeological loss in billion yuan,

Due to the scale of the dam and the geographical characteristic of its location, significant economic damage and deaths/injuries would be expected if the dam collapsed due to technical failures, being a target of terrorism and earthquake. Hence,

$$ACt=\sum_{j=1,2}ACCjt+DMt \qquad \text{GYuan/year,}$$
$$ACC1t=VD*[DCt+DOMt+DDt] \qquad \text{GYuan/year}$$
$$ACC2t=VM*[INCt+IOMt+IDt] \qquad \text{GYuan/year}$$

[18] The equation is slightly changed due to data abailablity.

where ACC1t= estimated annual costs of deaths due to accidents in billion yuan, ACC2t= estimated annual costs of injuries due to accidents in billion yuan, DMt= estimated annual damage costs due to special events (costs of economic loss) in billion yuan, VD= value estimate for deaths in Myuan/death, VM= value estimate for injuries in Myuan/illness, DCt= annual no of deaths during construction, INCt= annual no of injuries during construction, DOMt= annual no of deaths during O&M, IOMt= annual no of injuries during O&M, DDt= annual no of deaths due to dam technical failures/terrorism/earthquake, IDt= annual no of injuries due to dam technical failures/terrorism/earthquake,

Special events such as dam technical failures, terrorism, and earthquake are very rare cases so that each estimated accident costs will be multiplied by probability of occurrence of these events.

$$DDt = (GC*DCR'')*(P+P'+P'') \quad \text{for } t>Tc$$
$$= 0 \quad \text{for } t \leq Tc \qquad GYuan/year$$

where DCR''= annual number of deaths due to special circumstances in deaths/GW/yr, P= probability of occurrence of technical failures per year, P'= probability of occurrence of terrorism per year, P''= probability of occurrence of earthquake per year,

$$IDt = (GC*MCR'')*(P+P'+P'') \quad \text{for } t>Tc$$
$$= 0 \quad \text{for } t \leq Tc \qquad GYuan/year$$

where MCR''= annual number of injuries due to special circumstances in injuries/GW/yr

$$DMt = ECL*(P+P'+P'') \quad \text{for } t>Tc \qquad GYuan/year$$

where ECL= economic loss in Gyuan/yr

Decommissioning costs are presently difficult to predict due to the uncertainty surrounding the various parameters affecting the costs and the limited practical experiences with decommissioning (WCD, 2000). Decommissioning costs vary from project to project, though they are usually large[19].

$$DCCt = \pi * TCC \quad \text{if } t=TTDC$$
$$= 0 \quad \text{otherwise} \qquad Gyuan/year$$

where DCCt= costs of decommissioning the TGP in Gyuan./year, π=proportion of decommissioning costs in the construction cost, TDC=time of decommissioning. If policy makers choose premature closure as the cost outweighs the benefit, TDC=time of premature closure. If the costs start outweighing the benefits, it would be better to close down the dam prematurely. Policy makers have an option to close down if

$$TBt-(OMt+DEt+FIt+ACt)+DCCt-DCCt+1<0$$

Where DCCt+1=DCCt/(1+d)=the NPV this year of paying DCC next year.

Policy makers have a choice each year, either close down or stay open one more year. If they decide to close down, decommissioning costs have to be paid this year, otherwise they pay decommissioning cost next year. The costs of CC, RE, AS, IN and LT are not included in the above equation. This is because CC and RE have already been paid during construction; lost archaeological sites and inundated land may not recover; and the negative impact on tourism may remain since the aesthetic of the Three Gorges once lost cannot be recovered.

---

[19] For example, it is approved to spend $225000 to remove the Chair Factory Dam in the US (IRN's *River Revival Bulletin* No 22 November 29 2000). Total removel cost for the Matilija dam in the US could be $22-200 million (IRN's *River Revival Bulletin* No21 October 17 2000).

$$NPVt = \sum_{t=0}^{T} (1+dt)^{-t}(TBt-TCt) \qquad for\ t = Tc+Tcl \qquad GYuan/year$$

$$NPVt = \sum_{t=0}^{T} (1+dt)^{-t}(TBt-TCt) \quad if\ TBt-(OMt+DEt+FIt+ACt)+DCCt-DCCt+1 \geq 0$$

$$= -\sum_{t=0}^{T} (1+dt)^{-t}(CCt+REt+ASt+INt+LTt+DCCt)\ if\ TBt-(OMt+DEt+FIt+ACt)+DCCt-DCCt+1<0$$

$$for\ t > Tc+Tcl \qquad GYuan/year$$

where TB=total benefits, TC=total costs, dt=discount rate (fixed/variable), and NPV_T= net present value at time T, Tc=construction period, and Tcl=time to close down the dam (time until which policy makers allow NPV to be negative after construction.

II. Data

Table A-I **Parameters in the CBA model and descriptions**[20]

Parameters	Units	Distribution[21] (min, most likely, max)	Description of each value
Tc (construction period)	Years	Pert(17, 18, 22)	The minimum value is the original plan. According to the WCD Cross-Check Survey, about 40% of the delayed projects shows 1-year delay of project schedule is the most common case among the delayed projects (WCD 2000). Similarly, about 5% show 5 years delay (WCD 2000).
PEo (initial price of electricity)	Yuan/MWh	Pert (290, 300, 330)	The minimum value is 5% lower than the most likely value. The most likely value is the price of electricity generated by the TGP based on the CTGPC calculation. The maximum value is 10% higher than the most likely value.

[20] \$1= 8.3 Yuan. This is a market rate end of the year period 1998. Source: IMF IFS 1999 Sept. Hereafter, this exchange rate will be used unless otherwise stated.

[21] Δ(.) refers to a trianguler distribution and Pert (.) refers to a PERT distribution (a special form of beta distributions).

ε (proportional reduction in annual number of tourists in the dam site)		Pert (0.1, 0.6, 0.9)	For the minimum value, assuming the loss of the Three Gorges aesthetics does not affect tourism in the area very much since tourists can visit other attractions in the area. Also tourists may visit the TGP itself. The rate of decrease in number of tourists after the terrorist attack in Sri Lanka during the 1st quarter of 1998 is used for the most likely value (CBSL 2000). For the maximum value, assuming majority of tourists only visit the dam site to see the Three Gorges
NT (annual number of tourists visiting the dam site in absence of the dam)	Persons	Δ(330000,370000,740000)	For the minimum value, assuming 10% less than the most likely value. The most likely value is the number of tourists in Wuhan and Chongqing (the base place to visit the Three Gorges area) in 1996 (China Statistic Year Book 1997). The project area is one of the most popular places for tourists, both domestic and foreign. Hence, assuming twice as much as the most likely value for the maximum value.
f20 (expected annual rate of change in electricity prices during 2000-2020)		Δ(0, 0.011, 0.03)	According to China Energy Efficiency Information Bulletin March 1997, China will not increase electricity prices largely in short term. Thus, assume zero rate of changes for the minimum value. Electricity prices were stable until 1986. A rate of increase in electricity prices from 1986 and 1987 was 0.011 (China Electric Power Industry Year Book 1995). This is used for the most likely value. The same source shows a reasonable rate of increase in electricity prices of 0.03 between 1994 and 1995, which is used for the maximum value[22].
α (parameter which describes the location of the peak of the distribution for the construction cost)		Pert(0.1, 0.2, 0.5)	The official forecast of the distribution of CC skewed to the left (Li 1994 p34 Graph1; Sumi 1971).

[22] Assume the minimum and maximum values are the same, however every 20 years-period

TCC (total construction cost)	GYuan	Pert(470, 610, 660)	The minimum value is the planned figure (CTGPC 1995). 70 hydropower projects commissioned between 1915 and 1986 financed by the World Bank show average cost overruns of about 30% (Bacon and Besant-Jones 1998). Average cost overruns for large dams excluding extreme cases are 40% (WCD 2000).
β (parameter which describes the location of the peak of the distribution for the resettlement cost)		Pert(0.6, 0.8, 0.9)	The official forecast of the distribution of CC skewed to the right (Li 1994 p34 Graph1; Sumi 1971).
σ (parameter which describes the location of the peak of the distribution for number of workers' death/injuries)		Pert(0.1, 0.5, 0.8)	For the minimum value, assuming the peak of the distribution is at the beginning while completing fundamental work. For the most likely value, assuming more complicated and large scale-dangerous work is carried out in the middle of the construction period. For the maximum value, assuming the peak of the distribution is towards the end of the construction period.
C1 (annual decreased CO2 level due to a decrease in coal use as a result of the TGP)	Tons/GWh/yr	Pert(1250, 1390, 1670)	The minimum value is 10% lower than the most likely value. The TGP is expected to reduce 50 million tons of coal-use per year, which may reduce 100 million tons of CO2 (Beijing Review July 8-14 1996). The maximum value is 20% higher than the most likely value.
C2 (annual decreased SO2 level due to a decrease in coal use as a result of the TGP)	Tons/GWh/yr	Pert(25, 28, 34)	The minimum value is 10% lower than the most likely value. The TGP is expected to reduce 50 million tons of coal-use per year, which may reduce 2 million tons of SO2 (Beijing Review July 8-14 1996). The maximum value is 20% higher than the most likely value.
CM1 (benefits of CO2 reduction as a result of the TGP)	Yuan/tons of CO2	Pert(120, 130, 160)	The minimum value is 10% lower than the most likely value. The most likely value is the estimated value (Battelle 198). The maximum value is 20% more than the most likely value.
CM2 (benefits of SO2 reduction as a result of the TGP)	Yuan/tons of SO2	Pert(3440, 3820, 4580)	The minimum value is 10% lower than the most likely value. The most likely value is the estimated value (Battelle 1998). The maximum value is 20% higher than the most likely value.

FB (mean annual benefits from flood control for the dam height of 180m scheme)	Gyuan/yr	Pert(0.76, 0.97, 35)	The minimum value is the estimated value (Luk & Whitney 1993). The most likely value is measured solely by economic criteria in 1986 prices (Rulan et al 1997). 'If an exceptionally huge flood similar to that of 1870 should occur, the project would reduce losses caused by inundation by 35 billion Yuan, and also prevent a great number of casualties caused by burst dikes' (Rulan et al 1997).
SC (annual shipping capacity of the TGP)	Gtons/yr	Pert(0.04, 0.05, 0.06)	He minimum value is 20% lower than the most likely value. The most likely value is the estimated value (Beijing Review March 1992). The maximum value is 10% more than the most likely value.
e (annual rate of reduction in shipping costs)		Pert (0.3, 0.36, 0.37)	According to Youmei (1997), 0.3 (min) -0.37 (max). According to Beijing Review March (1992); EAAU (1997); Edmonds (1999), 0.36.
TRo (initial shipping costs)	Yuan/ton	Pert(110, 120, 140)	The minimum value is 10% lower than the most likely value. The most likely value is the forecasted transport costs of goods from Central to East on Yangtze River of $15 per ton in 2005.Source: Energy Research Institute staff estimates in Table 5.4 Battlle (1998). The maximum value is 20% higher than the most likely value.
g (annual rate of change in transportation costs)		Pert(0, 0.01, 0.011)	Assuming no change for the minimum value. The most likely value is the estimated figure (Energy Research Institute stuff estimates in Table 5.4 Battlle 1998). The maximum value is 10% more than the most likely value.
EL (annual economic losses due to inundation of land in the project area)	GYuan/yr	Pert(0.12, 0.13, 0.26)	The minimum value is 10% lower than the most likely value. The project will submerge 31000 ha of farmland and 4933 ha of citrus orchards (Furedi 1999). The value for farmlands and orchards are assumed to be $380/ha/year, and $760/ha/year respectively[23]. Assuming twice as much as the most likely value for the maximum value.

[23] These values are the lost values of the submerged land for coconuts fields and paddy in monetary terms respectively. Source:CEB (1987).

FP (annual lost profit from fishery)	Gyuan/yr	Pert(0.04, 2.4, 2.7)	US Fish and Wildlife Service studies show that Savage Rapids Dam in Oregon has destroyed at least $5 million/year in fisheries benefits (The pacific Coast Federation of Fisherman's Associations 'From Fisherman's News may 1998). The most likely value is 10% less than the maximum value below. 'The National Marine Fisheries Service estimated the cost of Salmon fishery losses due to dams in the Colombia basin to be $6.5 billion fro the period 1960-80 alone' (McCulley 1997).
TRE (total resettlement cost)	Gyuan	Pert(120, 160, 180)	The minimum value is the planned figure (http: www.china.embassy.org / issues / gorges.htm). The most likely value is based on the actual number of resettled, people is 35% higher than the estimated figure according to the WCD Cross-Check Survey (WCD 2000). Similarly, the actual number is 47% higher than the estimated figure among the projects financed by the World Bank (World Bank 1996).
RS (per capita tourists recipients in the Dam site)	Yuan/yr	Pert(1490, 1660, 2490)	The minimum value is 10% less than the most likely value. The most likely value is per capita international tourist recipients in China in 1996 (China Statistic Year Book 1997). The maximum value is 50% more than the most likely value.
OMC (operation & maintenance cost)	Yuan/KW/yr	Pert(170, 220, 240)	O&M cost for large hydro dams is US$20/kW/year (Battelle 1998 Table 5.11). The same rates for TCC are used, that is 30% and 40% more than the planned figure for the most likely and maximum values respectively.
ADE (annual investment costs to deal with downstream negative impacts)	Gyuan/yr	Pert(3.2, 3.5, 4.2)	The minimum value is 10% lower than the most likely value. The most likely value is the estimated figure (Hui 1998). The maximum value is 20% higher than the most likely value.

VD (value estimate for deaths)	MYuan/death	Pert(33, 60, 550)	A wife of worker for the TGP, who was killed by a construction accident claimed $418,116 for compensation (China News Service 13 October 2000). The most likely value is the estimated value of a statistical life obtained from regression analysis using data from India (Shanmugam 2000). The maximum value of the range of the recent estimate of a statistical life in developed countries is 550 million Yuan per death (Viscusi 1993).
VM (value estimate for injuries)	MYuan/injury	Pert(0.009, 0.03, 3.30)	The minimum value of the estimated range of the statistical injury values obtained from regression analysis using data from India is 0.009 million Yuan per injury (Shanmugam 2000). The maximum value of the estimated range of the statistical injury values obtained from regression analysis using data from India is 0.03 million Yuan/injury (Shanmugam 2000). The average estimated value of injury from developed countries in the past studies is 3.3 million Yuan/injury (Shanmugan 2000).
DCR (estimated annual number of deaths during the construction period)	Deaths/GW/yr[24]	Δ(0.3, 0.8, 1.9)	The minimum value is the estimated value for the Hoover Dam in US (Inhaber 1982; Easton Express 1979). The most likely value is the estimated value for in the Canadian Ontario (Inhaber 1982; Morison 1977). The maximum value is the estimated value for the French hydropower. (Inhaber 1982; Potier 1969).
MCR (estimated annual number of injuries during the construction period)	Injuries/GW/yr	Δ(170, 310, 340)	The minimum value is a half of Inhaber's estimate below. The most likely value is 10% less than the Inhaber's estimate below since technology has improved. The maximum value is the estimated value for past projects. (Inhaber 1982; Potier 1969).
DCR' (estimated annual number of deaths during the O&M period)	Deaths/GW/yr	Δ(0.32, 0.57, 0.63)	The minimum value is a half of Inhaber's estimate below. The most likely value is 10% less than the Inhaber's estimate below since technology has improved. The maximum value is the estimated value for past projects. (Inhaber 1982; Potier 1969).

[24] Number of accidents (deaths/injuries) is likely to increase as construction period becomes longer.

MCR' (estimated annual number of injuries during the O&M period)	Injuries/GW/yr	Δ(7, 12, 13)	The minimum value is a half of Inhaber's estimate below. The most likely value is 10% less than the Inhaber's estimate below since technology has improved. The maximum value is the estimated value for past projects. (Inhaber 1982; Bertoletta and Fox 1974).
DCR'' (annual number of deaths due to special circumstances)	Deaths/GWh/yr	Δ (6750,12150, 13500)	The minimum value is a half of Inhaber's estimate below. The most likely value is 10% less than the Inhaber's estimate below since technology has improved. The maximum value is the estimated value for past projects (Inhaber 1982)[25].
MCR'' (annual number of injuries due to special circumstances)	Injuries/GWh/yr	Δ(34750,62550,69500)	The minimum value is a half of Inhaber's estimate below. The most likely value is 10% less than the Inhaber's estimate below since technology has improved. The maximum value is the estimated value for past projects (Inhaber 1982)[26].
ECL (economic loss due to special circumstances)	Gyuan/yr	Pert(17, 30, 45)	Honduras would need $US 2 billion to meet expected direct and indirect losses after a 1-in-100-year storm (Freeman 2000). The 1998 floods have cost about 30 billion yuan in total economic losses in Hubei province alone (Saywell 1998). The maximum value is 50% higher than the most likely value.
b (annual rate of decline in flood control benefit due to sedimentation)		Pert(0.0001,0.001,0.03)	Assume the rate is same as the annual rate of decline in power generation due to sedimentation.
c (annual rate of decline in navigation improvement benefit due to sedimentation)		Pert(0.0001,0.001,0.03)	Assume the rate is same as the annual rate of decline in power generation due to sedimentation.

[25] According to Inhaber (1982), the estimated deaths per unit energy is 0.0011-0.0016 deaths/Mw. Assuming that the figures calculated by Inhaber are multiplied by probability of occurrence of such dam failures. Thus, DCR''= (1.1-1.6 deaths/Gw)/P= 13500 deaths/Gw/yr. P=10^{-4} according to IRN.

[26] According to Inhaber (1982), the estimated injuries per unit energy is 0.0011-0.0128 injuries/Mw. Similar to the calculation for death, MCR''= (1.1-12.8 injuries/Gw)/P= 69500 injuries/Gw.

π (proportion of decommissioning costs in the construction cost)	Pert(0.025,0.08, 0.25)	The minimum and the most likely values value are one tenth and one third of the maximum value below respectively. Dam decommissioning costs hugely vary from project to project. The removal of the Marmot and Little Sandy dams which generate 22 MW is estimated to be $22 million. Based on this figure, the TGP needs 18.2 GW*8.3 Yuan / (mean TCC = 610) = 0.25.
TDC (time of decommissioning)	Pert(50, 75, 100)	The expected life of a dam is 50 years. About 5000 large dams in the world are now more than 50 years old (McCully 1997; Wade 1999). Assume 50% more than the above minimum value for the most likely value. The maximum value is T=100.
P (probability of occurrence of technical failures per year)	10^{-4}	According to IRN, average risk of dam breaking in given year is 1 in 10,000. Bacher et al (1980) also assume the rate to be 10^{-4}.
P' (probability of occurrence of terrorism per year)	10^{-5}	Large cities, nuclear power plants, and hydro projects are routinely considered prime military targets[27]. From historical experience the probability of its occurrence is assumed to be low. Hence, the probability of terrorism is assumed to be much lower than those for technical failures. P'= 10^{-5} shall be used.
P'' (probability of occurrence of earthquake per year)	10^{-5}	Assume that the probability of earthquake occurrence is the same as that for terrorism

III. Photographs taken by the author during the Three Gorges Dam site visit in March 2001

[27] For example, The British bombed Germany's Mohne and Eder dams during World War II, the US bombed North Korean dams during the Korean War and Vietnamese dams and dikes during the Vietnam War. (See Bing 1998 for more detail).

Town near the dam site on the Yangtze River to be submerged completely after the project completion

The sign shows the water level to be raised, initially up to 135m and then to 175m after the project completion. This fertile agricultural land will be completely under the water.

The TGP construction site in March 2001: massive scale of the world's largest hydropower project.

References

ASCE (1997) *Journal of the Boston Society of Civil Engineering Section* **12** (1) Spring/Summer

Bacher.GB, Pate.ME, and De Neuville.R (1980) 'Risk of Dam Failure in Benefit-Cost Analysis' *Water Resources Research* **16** (3) 449-456 June

Bacon. RW and Besant-Jones. JE (1998) 'Estimating Construction Costs and Schedules: Experiences with Power generation Projects in Developing Countries' *Energy Policy* **26** (4) 317-333

Battelle (1998) *China's Electric Power options: An analysis of economic and environmental costs*, Battelle Memorial Institute

Bentkover. JD, Covello. VT and Mumpower. J (1986) 'Risk of dam failure in Benefit Cost Analysis' *Water Resources Research*

Bertoletta. AD and Fox. RJ (1974) 'Accident rate sample favors Nuclear' *Electrical World* 15 40-43

Bing. D (1998) 'Military Perspectives on the TGP' in Qing (1998)

Buczek, M (1996) 'Fueling China's growth' *The China Business Review*, Washington Sept-Oct

Carman. J, Garnegie. GD, and Wolnizer. PW (1999) 'Is archeological valuation an accounting matter?' *Antiquity* 73 143-8

Carver. M (1996) 'On archaeological value' *Antiquity* **70** 45-56CTGPC (1995) *Environmental Impact Statement for the Yangtze Three Gorges Project* (A Brief Edition) Science Press

Caufield. C (1997) 'Rough sailing at Three Gorges dam' *World Rivers Review* 12 (6) December

CEB (1987) *Master Plan for electricity supply in Sri Lanka*, 1st July

CEB (1994) *Environmental Impact assessment for the UKHP*

Childjonson. E and Sullivan. LR (1998) 'The Three Gorges dam and the fate of China's southern heritage' in Qing (1998)

Chunhong. H (1995) 'Controlling reservoir sedimentation in China' *Hydropower & Dams*, March 50-52

Cleere. HF (1984) *Archaeological Heritage Management I the Modern World*

CTGPC (1995) *Environmental Impact Statement for the Yangtze Three Gorges Project*

CTGPC (2000) *Proceedings of China Yangtze Three Gorges Project* for 2000 ICOLD 68th Annual Meeting & 20th Congress

Dervil. T, Saunders, A, and Sartin, B (1987) 'A question of national importance: approaches to the evaluation of ancient monuments for the monuments protection programme in England' *Antiquity* **61** 393-408

Dixson. DA (2000) 'A Growing Problem' *International Water Power and Dam Construction,* May 23-25

EAAU (1997) *China embraces the market*

Easton Express (1979) Pennsylvania October 28 p. F-13

Edmonds. RL (1999) 'China's environmental problems' Chapter 9 in Gamer (1999)

EIA (2001) *China Country Analysis Brief,* April

FMF (1994) *Final First Round Study Design for EMF 14: Integrated Assessment of Climate Change Energy Modelling Forum (EMF),* Terman Engineering Center, Stanford University

Freeman, PK (2000) 'Estimating chronic risk from natural disasters in developing countries: A case study on Honduras' *paper for* the *Annual Bank Conference on Development Economics-Europe Development Thinking at the Millennium June 26-28*, Paris

Fu. S (1998) 'A profile of dams in China' in Qing (1998)

Fung. S (1999) 'That dam project!' *Across the board,* New York May

Furedi. F (1999) 'Power to the People', *KLW*

Gamer. RE (1999) (ed.) *Understanding contemporary China* Lynn Rienner Publishers London

Goldstein. S (1998) 'The Three Gorges Saga: The high price of modernisation' *Columbia East Asian Review,* Spring

Hansson.L and J.Marckham (1992) 'Internalising External Effects in Transportation' *IRU,* Paris

Hui. H (1998) 'Water pollution in the Three Gorges Reservoirs' Chapter 11 in Qing (1998)

Inhaber. H (1982) *Energy Risk Assessment* Gordon & Breach Science Publishers

Le Net.M (1992) 'Le prix de la vie humaine', *Report for the General Commission for the Plan*, Paris

Leone. MP and Potter. Jr. PB (1992) 'Forum: Legitimation and the classification of archaeological sites' *American Antiquity* **57** (1) 137-145

Leopold. L (1998) 'Sediment problems at the TGD' in Qing (1998)

Li, B and Dorian JP (1995) 'Change in China's power sector' *Energy Policy* **23** (7) 619-626

Li, Y (1994) 'On the overall strategy of the Three Gorges Project fund raising' *Construction of China's Three Gorges,* London Routledge 38-51

Lipe,WD (1984) 'Value and meaning in cultural resources' in Cleere. HF (1984) (ed.) Approaches to the Archaeological Heritages, Cambridge University Press 1-11

Luk. SH and Whitney. J (1993) (ed.) *Megaproject: A case study of China's Three Gorges Project,* M.E Sharpe

McCulley, P (1997) 'Taking Down Bad Dams' *World Rivers Review* **12** (4) August

MFO (1990) *Energy in China* The Ministry of Energy Press Beijing

Morimoto. R and Hope. C (2001), 'A cost benefit analysis of hydro projects in Sri Lanka', *Judge Institute Working Paper Series 15,* University of Cambridge

Morison. WG (1977) 'Director, Design, and Development' *Ontario Hydro Toronto personal communication*

Morrish. M (1997) 'The living geography of China' Geography **83** (354) Junuary

Potier. M (1969) *Energie et Securite* Mouton & Cie Paris

Qing D (1998) 'The danger to historical relics and cultural antiquities in and around the Three Gorges area' in Qing (1998a) (ed) *The River Dragon Has Come!* , IRN

Quinet.E (1994) 'Internalising the social costs of transport' Chapter 2: the social costs of transport: Evaluation and links with internalization polices' *ECMT seminar* 1993

Ren. Q (1998) 'Discussing population resettlement with Li Pong' in Qing (1998)

Rulan *et al* (1997) 'The Three Gorges project: key to the Development of the Yangtze River' in *Civil Engineering Practice: Journal of the Boston Society of Civil Engineers Section/ASCE* (1997), Spring/Summer **12** (1)

Ryder. G and Barber. M (1993) (2nd ed.) (ed.) *Damming the Three Gorges: 1920-1993,* Probe International

Sanghvi. AP (1991) 'Power shortages in developing countries: impacts and policy implications' *Energy Policy,* June

Saywell. T (1998) 'A river run wild' *Far Eastern Economic Review,* April

Schaafsma. CF (1989) 'Significant unit proven otherwise: problems versus representative samples' in Cleere (1984)

Shanmugam. KR (2000) 'Valuations of Life and Injury Risks: Empirical Evidence from India' *Environmental and Resource Economics*

Sharman. RT Jr (1994) 'Power in the PRC' *Independent Energy,* October

Si. Y (1998) 'The World's most catastrophic dam failures in Qing (1998)

Simbek. DR, Dickenson, RL, and Carter, LD (1994) 'China's coal use' *Independent Energy*, Milaca, Jul/August

Sinton, JE and Fridley, DG (2000) 'What goes up: Recen Trends in China's Energy Consumption' *Energy Policy* March

Smith. VK (1999) 'A controversial overview of the foundations of BCA' in Bentkover *et al* (1986)

Sullivan. ME (1995) 'The Three Gorges Dam Project: The need for a comprehensive assessment' *The Georgetown International Environmental law Review* **8** (109) 109-140

Sumi. K (1997) *Three Gorges Dam and Japan*

Tainter. JA and Lucas. GJ (1983) 'Epistemology of the significance concept' in *American Antiquity* **48** (4) 707-719

Thurston. K (1996) 'Rebuilding China' *The Newsletter of Environmental Geology: Environmental focus*, Miami University

Topping AR (1995) 'Ecological roulette: Damming the Yangtze' *Foreign Affairs,* New York September

Topping. AB (1996) 'Dai Qing, voice of the Yangtze River Gorges' The Earth Times http://weber.cusd.edu/-dmccubbi/chinadaiqingjan11_97.htm

US Department of Energy (1996) *China's Energy: A forecast to 2015*

Viscusi. WK (1993) 'The value of Risks to Life and Limb' *Journal of Economic Literature* **31** 1912-1946

Wade, B (1999) 'Brining down the dams' *The Ameican City & County,* Pittsfield, June

WCD (2000a) *Dams and Development: A New framework for decision making,* Earthscan London

WCD(2000b) *China Country Review Paper*

World Bank (1996) 'Resettlement and Development: The Bankwide Review of projects involving involuntary resettlement 1986-1993' *Environment Department paper* **32** The World Bank, Washington DC

Wu.K and Li.B (1995) 'Energy development in China: National policies and regional strategies' *Energy Policy* **23** (2) 167-178

Youmei, L (1997) 'China's Economic Development and the Construction of the Three Gorges Project' *Hot Talks About TGP* CTGPC

Zeng, QY and Song, YH (1998) 'Electricity market develops in China' *Transmission & Distribution*, World Overland Park, May

Do Speed Cameras Produce Net Benefits? Evidence from British Columbia, Canada

Greg Chen
Rebecca N. Warburton

Abstract

Traffic collisions kill about 43,000 Americans a year. Worldwide, road traffic injuries are the leading cause of death by injury and the ninth leading cause of all deaths. Photo Radar speed enforcement has been implemented in the United States and many other industrialized countries, yet its cost-effectiveness from a societal viewpoint, taking all significant impacts into account, has not been reported. This paper fills this gap, reporting on a Photo Radar traffic safety program introduced in 1996 in British Columbia, Canada, and incorporating the results of rigorous statistical analyses on speed and crash impacts into a comprehensive cost-benefit analysis from both societal and sponsoring-agency perspectives. The study reveals that the Rhoto Radar Program cost C\$27 million per year in 2001 Canadian dollars (≈US\$21 million) and generated benefits valued at \$142 million per year (≈US\$109 million), for net societal benefits of C\$115 million per year (≈US\$88 million). It was estimated that the sponsoring agency saved C\$38 million (≈US\$29 million) annually in claim costs. These results are robust to plausible alternate assumptions. Societal net benefits become negative only if the reduction in injuries and fatalities is one standard error below the expected value, or if private travel time is valued at or above C\$15 per hour. Agency claim cost savings are greater than program costs under all scenarios tested. These results are likely applicable to jurisdictions in developed countries with similar traffic infrastructure: Greater use of highway photo radar speed enforcement would be good public policy. © 2006 by the Association for Public Policy Analysis and Management

INTRODUCTION

The World Health Organization reports that road traffic injuries are the leading cause of death by injury and the ninth leading cause of all deaths worldwide. Road safety was the theme of World Health Day 2004 (WHO, 2004a, 2004b). Traffic collisions kill about 43,000 Americans a year, and are increasing; in 2003, the estimated number of persons killed in motor vehicle crashes increased to the highest level since 1990 (National Highway Traffic Safety Administration, 2004).

Based on estimates by the National Highway Traffic Safety Administration, two-thirds of fatal collisions in the United States in recent years can be attributed to aggressive driving, including speeding, running red lights, and tailgating (Turner & Polk, 1998). In 2003, unsafe speed contributed to 31% of all fatal crashes in the

Journal of Policy Analysis and Management, Vol. 25, No. 3, 661–678 (2006)

Published by Wiley Periodicals, Inc. Published online in Wiley InterScience (www.interscience.wiley.com)
DOI: 10.1002/pam.20196

United States, causing 13,380 deaths; and according to the National Highway Traffic Safety Agency, the cost of speed-related collisions to American society is over $40 billion per year (Runge, 2005).

Unsafe speed is also a significant contributing factor to traffic collisions in British Columbia (B.C.), Canada (current population 4.2 million, 1.4% of current US population of 296 million). In 1995, "unsafe speed," as judged by police attending traffic collisions, was involved in 37% of all fatal collisions, 15% of all personal injury collisions, and 9% of all property-damage-only collisions; and more than 8,000 people were injured and 184 people killed in 10,564 speed-related daytime collisions.

Finding the best response to road safety is an important public policy issue for governments around the globe. Increased conventional police enforcement is one potential solution, but budgetary constraints limit its application. Automated speed enforcement methods, such as Photo Radar and Red Light Cameras, are seen as attractive alternatives to conventional enforcement. In the last 30 years, automated enforcement programs have been tested and implemented in the United States and many other industrialized countries (Coleman et al., 1996; ICF Consulting and Imperial College Centre for Transport Studies, 2003; Lynn et al., 1992; Retting, 2003; Retting & Farmer, 2003; Retting, Ferguson, & Hakkert, 2003; Retting & Kyrychenko, 2002; Rogerson, Newstead, & Cameron, 1994). In the past decade, many U.S. states (and the District of Columbia) have introduced red light cameras, photo radar, or both (Photocop, 2003). Proponents argue that photo enforcement improves safety (IIHS, 2002); opponents focus on loss of privacy, revenue-driven (rather than safety-driven) enforcement, and the potential for "accident migration" (where enforcement in one location leads to increased speed and crashes elsewhere; SENSE, 1995).

Because of the similarity of developed-country traffic infrastructure and regulations, traffic safety agencies generally acknowledge the value of experience elsewhere in predicting the effects of particular traffic safety improvements if implemented locally (Federal Highway Administration, 1996; ICBC, 1996; IIHS, 2005; Metropolitan Police Department, 2005; Stuster, Coffman, & Warren, 1998). Before expanding automated speed enforcement, therefore, policymakers should ask whether these programs are effective elsewhere, and how costs compare to benefits for society as a whole. However, rigorous impact assessment in combination with cost-benefit analysis from a societal view has not been reported for photo radar speed enforcement. This paper fills that gap, reporting societal costs and benefits for photo radar as implemented in British Columbia, Canada. This study incorporates the results of rigorous statistical analyses on speed and crash impacts of the Photo Radar Program into a comprehensive cost-benefit analysis, assessing the economic impact of the program from both the societal and sponsoring-agency perspectives. This report reviews the available literature, describes the BC Photo Radar Program, reviews B.C. speed and safety impacts, conducts a base case cost-benefit analysis and a sensitivity analysis, discusses study limitations, and concludes by summarizing results and policy implications of the research.

LITERATURE REVIEW

There are few reported studies on the costs and benefits of photo radar programs. Elvik (1997) conducted an evaluation of the photo radar program in Norway. The study assessed traffic safety effects on 64 road sections where photo radar devices were installed. He found a statistically significant reduction in collisions and injuries at these sites, and estimated that the program reduced injury collisions by

20% at program treatment sites. He also produced a brief cost-benefit analysis. The investment cost for each of the 64 road sections was estimated to be US$49,000; annual operating costs were estimated at US$2.45 million. The investment cost was amortized assuming a 10-year service life and a 7% annual real interest rate. Elvik reported annual savings of US$19.5 million in collision cost, and claimed a benefit-cost ratio of about 8 (19.5/2.45). However, the study overestimated net program benefits by not counting the value of travel time lost due to speed reduction, and no sensitivity analysis was performed.

The U.K. introduced speed cameras in 1992, and several reviews of the program's costs and effects have been reported (DETR, 1999; Gains, Heydecker, Shrewsbury, & Robertson, 2004; Hooke, Knox, & Portas, 1996). Data collection focuses on camera locations, examining speed, crashes, and injuries. Costs considered include purchasing, installing, operating, and maintaining the cameras; court costs; and associated publicity campaigns. The benefits include savings in human lives and injuries; property damage; savings experienced by the police and by emergency and health services as a result of fewer road accidents; fine income; improved traffic flow; reduced travel times; and an "improved environment." The 1996 study revealed a 28% reduction in collisions at the speed camera sites, generating net present value benefits of £462 million (US$874 million) over the ten years studied. All of the ten areas assessed achieved a positive return after one year and, in nine out of ten cases, fine income covered the direct cost of operations. Modeling with more pessimistic assumptions (for example, a decline in incident reductions; reductions in fine income) still produced a substantial net social benefit for speed cameras. The 2004 review also found significant reductions in speed and crashes at camera sites. Average speeds dropped by about 7 percent (or 2.4 miles per hour), and (adjusted for trend and other changes) there was an estimated 33 percent reduction in injury/fatality collisions (4,030 fewer) and a 40 percent reduction in deaths (100 fewer). Following the U.K. Department of Transportation valuation method, which assigns £55,000 to each casualty collision, the annual value of avoided deaths and injuries was estimated at £221 million (US$419 million), while annual enforcement costs amounted to only £54 million (US$102 million). There are several shortcomings to the U.K. research, however. First, these studies potentially understate the value of safety benefits, as using arbitrary casualty valuation probably results in lower values than more methodologically rigorous methods, such as willingness-to-pay or willingness-to-avoid valuations (for example, see Bein, Miller, & Waters, 1994). Second, the U.K. studies also overstate benefits both by failing to consider the value of travel time lost due to speed reductions and by including traffic fines, which are a transfer from the ticketed to government, and hence have no net impact at the societal level. Finally, the potential for accident migration has not been assessed. Together, these limitations probably overstate program net benefits, and greatly reduce the usefulness of the results to inform policy.

In summary, the literature review shows that unsafe speed is a significant problem and that photo radar can be effective in reducing speed and crashes at program sites. However, the literature does not show whether or not such programs produce net societal benefits, nor does it demonstrate whether or not accident migration is a significant problem. The research we report here provides this important missing information.

BC PHOTO RADAR PROGRAM BACKGROUND

The BC Photo Radar Program was jointly initiated in June 1996 by the B.C. provincial government and the (public) Insurance Corporation of British Columbia

(ICBC). The aim of the program was to reduce speed-related crashes; ICBC's rationale for involvement was the expected claim savings. (ICBC is a government-owned provincial Crown corporation, established in 1973 to provide universal auto insurance to B.C. motorists. ICBC currently provides mandatory minimum liability insurance to all motorists, and offers optional coverages as well.)

The BC Photo Radar Program consisted of a number of components: a province-wide deployment of 30 mobile speed-monitoring units; a central unit to process traffic violation tickets; additional support from the provincial judicial system to handle ticket disputes; and a major communications effort to publicize the program.

The program began with a five-month warning phase, during which violators received warning letters rather than tickets. Fines ranging from C$115 to C$173 were imposed starting August 2, 1996, with the highest fines in school and construction zones. From November 1997 to the end of the program in 2001, fines were C$115 to C$460 per incident. Photo radar tickets were issued to the vehicle's registered owner, though owners who were not driving the vehicle at the time of the alleged infraction could nominate another person (with his or her consent) to pay the fine.

The B.C. program used the AutoPatrol PR-100, made by American Traffic Systems. Each unit included a cross-the-road Doppler radar, a camera with a flash, and a laptop computer, all mounted in an unmarked mini van. The vans were various colors but the same model and body style (1996 GMC Safari or Chevrolet Astro). The vans were often parked in easily visible locations, although they had no police markings. The equipment could be set up to monitor either front or rear license plates. Triggered by a vehicle exceeding the posted speed limit by a specified margin, the camera and computer system would record the license plate and speed. The monitoring device had a margin of error of 1 km per hour. The equipment was operated at all times by police officers; there were no fully automated or civilian-operated units as seen in some other jurisdictions (Hooke et al., 1996).

Consistent with the program's stated goal of improving traffic safety, it was initially announced that the BC Photo Radar Program would operate primarily on highways and only at sites meeting stringent safety-related criteria developed by the Integrated Traffic Camera Unit (ITCU, 1996). Sites suggested by municipalities and regional authorities were surveyed to determine their suitability for photo radar operation and (if appropriate) to set the trigger speed. It was announced that trigger speeds would be based on the 85th percentile speed (only 15% of vehicles traveling faster) or 11 km over the posted limit, at the discretion of the police officers.

Figure 1 shows the program logic model, explaining the connections between program inputs and program outcomes. Program resources were used to increase speed enforcement and to publicize the program. It was intended that increased awareness and the threat of fines would change driver behavior, reducing both average speed and speed variance, hence reducing crashes and crash-associated deaths, injuries, and property damage.

The original site selection criteria are summarized below. Photo radar was to be deployed only at sites meeting *all* of the following requirements:

- having a history of speed-related collisions; or having a documented record of local community concern over unsafe vehicle speed, and public support for use of photo radar;
- not within a speed transition zone;
- not within 150 meters of a speed zone change as posted by a sign;
- not within 150 meters of a curve with an advisory speed;

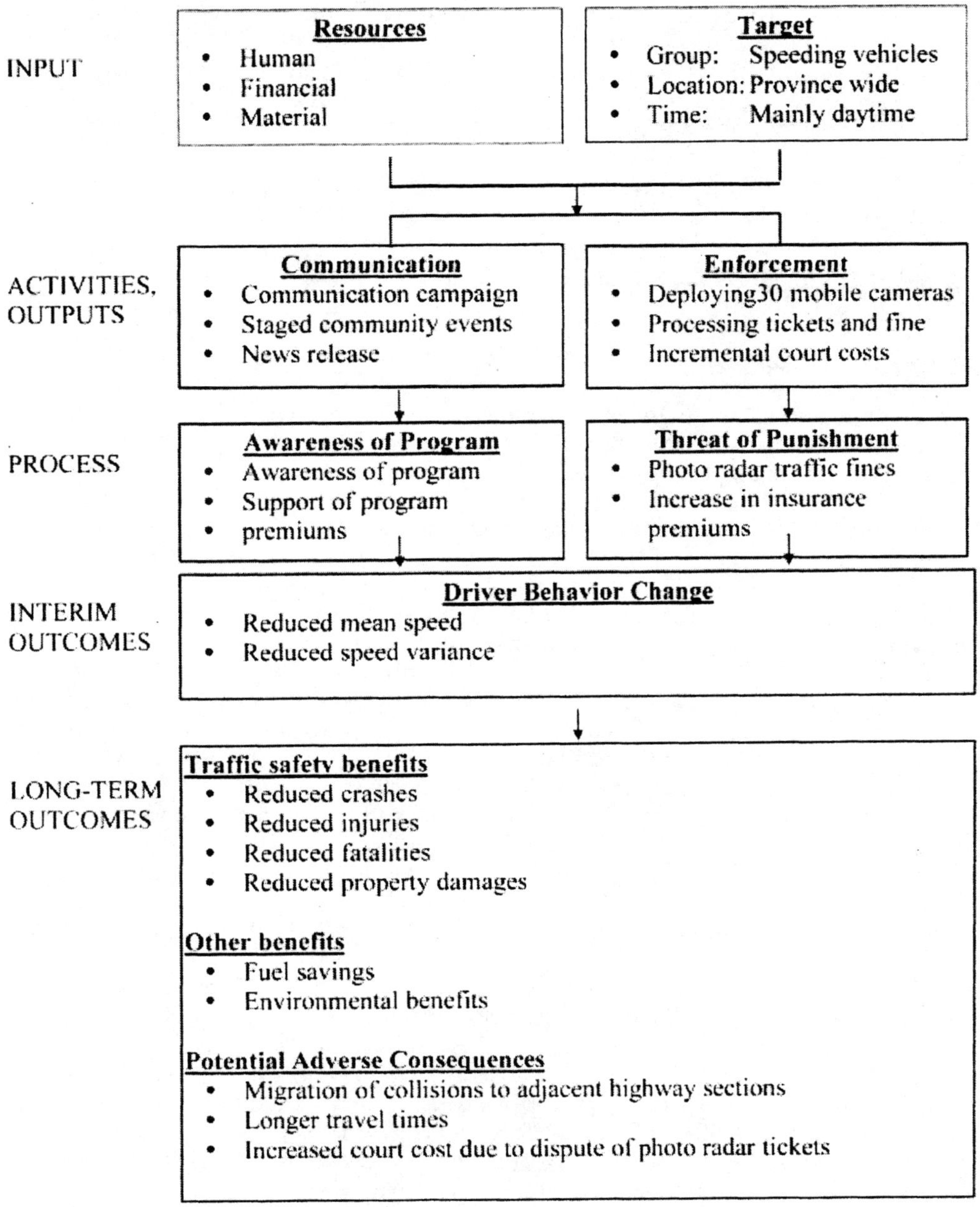

Figure 1. BC Photo Radar Program logic model.

- not containing more than one speed limit;
- where the posted speed limit was appropriate from a safety perspective;
- in a safe area for police to operate; and
- posing no hazard to the public from enforcement activities (for instance, from drivers slowing down suddenly on sighting the photo radar van).

When enacted, the program had reasonable public support, with two-thirds of British Columbians saying they supported photo radar (ICBC, 1996, 1998). However, the site selection criteria were never made part of the legislation governing photo radar. The guidelines were weakened and then violated with increasing frequency as the program continued, allowing opponents to charge that the program was motivated more by finance (collecting fines) than safety (SENSE, 1997a, 1997b). For example, significant enforcement activity occurred on residential city streets with speeds at or below 50 km/hour. The program became an election issue, with the opposition Liberal party promising to cancel it if elected. They won the subsequent election, and kept their promise; the BC Photo Radar Program ended at midnight June 27, 2001.

BC PHOTO RADAR SPEED AND SAFETY IMPACTS

Two studies were conducted to assess the speed and safety effects of the Photo Radar Program: a province-wide impact assessment and a site-specific study. These studies have been reported previously (Chen, 2003; Chen, Wilson, Meckle, & Cooper, 2000; Chen, Meckle, & Wilson, 2002) but are summarized here because they demonstrate the program effectiveness on which the valuations in the cost-benefit analysis depend. The province-wide impact study used time series analysis to assess the overall effect of the program. The study controlled for trend, seasonality, and key traffic safety related variables, including amount of driving, alcohol consumption, economic conditions, and other concurrent traffic safety programs. On an annual basis, photo radar was associated with approximately 2,220 (14%) fewer traffic collision injuries and up to 79 (26%) fewer collision fatalities, including pedestrians. These results indicate that accident migration is unlikely; overall, a reduction of 1,542 injury collisions and 72 fatal collisions can be attributed to photo radar, using the victim/collision ratio of 1.13 for injury and 1.44 for fatal collisions respectively, based on actual B.C. traffic collision and injury statistics (Chen, 2003, Chen et al., 2002).

The site-specific study compared photo radar sites to non-photo radar highway sections in order to control for trend and assess traffic and collision migration. Empirical Bayesian methods were used to improve the efficiency and precision of the estimates. Results showed that mean speed at non-photo radar monitoring sites decreased by approximately 2.4 km/h, a 3% reduction in speed. The standard deviation of speed decreased by 0.5 km/h, a 6% reduction in speed variance (Chen, 2003, Chen et al., 2002). The site-specific study estimated that the program reduced collisions significantly at both photo radar sites (–14% ±11%) and non-photo radar sites (–19% ±10%). These results corroborated the safety impact assessment from the province-wide study. The BC Photo Radar Program reduced traffic speeds at enforcement and non-enforcement sites, and reduced crashes, injuries, and deaths. Accident migration was not observed.

COST-BENEFIT ANALYSIS—BASE CASE

Cost-benefit analysis has been conducted from the perspective of all residents of the province of B.C. This societal perspective was supplemented with a funding agency (ICBC) perspective. The analysis compares the program as operated with a no-program, status quo alternative. All calculations and results are shown in real 2001 Canadian dollars. Cost and effect categories count in both the societal and ICBC perspectives, unless otherwise stated. The analysis is based on two years of program data (from start-up through 1998), with all quantities and values projected at typical levels for a continuing program. Base-case estimates reflect the most likely estimates.

Table 1 shows the categories of costs and effects assessed, summarizes data sources, and notes which costs count from the societal and ICBC perspectives. Program costs were composed of capital equipment and other program start-up costs, ongoing operating costs at ICBC, and police and court costs. Actual program costs were collected by ICBC as the program proceeded.

The included effect categories were safety improvements; travel time and emergency response costs saved due to fewer collisions; time lost due to slower average speeds; and private citizen time spent disputing photo radar tickets.

Actual program expenditures represent the best available measure of the opportunity cost of the Photo Radar Program. Total program costs, as measured here, include some provincial and federal taxes, overstating provincial costs by the amount of tax revenue recovered provincially. The real value of the resources foregone in order to run the program could also be slightly overstated if (for instance) policing or court services were priced (in B.C.) higher than their fair market value. However, the program's capital equipment was all purchased in competitive markets, hence is accurately priced, and no plausible variation in tax recoveries or non-market-priced inputs (policing, courts, ticketing) would materially affect the study results. B.C. program costs are likely similar to those that other developed-country jurisdictions would incur for similar programs.

Some categories of impact were not included in the formal analysis. Photo radar fines (apparently \$40 million to \$160 million annually over the course of the program; SENSE, 1995) are not reflected in the societal perspective because they are simply a transfer from ticketed drivers to government; fines are not included in the ICBC perspective because revenues were collected by the province, not by ICBC. The value of lost privacy is not included because of the difficulty of assigning a credible value to it, and because initial public support for the program in British Columbia appears to indicate that privacy concerns were not paramount or overriding with the public, as compared with safety effects. Based on initial public support for

Table 1. Cost and effect categories.

Category	Description	Data Source	Societal?	ICBC?
Cost	Capital & start-up costs	ICBC, SENSE	X	X
	ICBC operating costs	ICBC, SENSE	X	X
	Police costs	AG, SENSE	X	X
	Court costs	AG, SENSE	X	X
Effect	Reduced deaths, injuries, and property damage	Police, ambulance	X Economic value	X Claim cost
	Collision response savings	Police, ambulance	X	
	Time saved – collisions	MoTH	X	
	Time lost – travel	MoTH, NRC	X	
	Time lost – disputing tickets	BC Stats	X	

Note: SENSE is a private organization opposed to photo radar; AG is the B.C. Ministry of Attorney General; MoTH is the B.C. Ministry of Transportation and Highways; NRC is Natural Resources Canada; B.C. Stats is the B.C. government's statistical service.

the program, we assume that the value of perceived privacy effects would not be large enough to materially affect our results, if net societal benefits due to safety improvements can be demonstrated.

Capital Costs

Program start-up costs included photo radar equipment purchases, software development, and education and publicity campaign costs. Cost data are from ICBC and B.C. government sources, including data obtained and released by SENSE (1998,

Table 2. Societal perspective, costs, and effects of BC Photo Radar Program.

Description	2001 Canadian Dollars Annualized Cost/ Benefit, C$000
Capital	4,745
Police	11,746
Court	1,954
Ticket/photo processing	7,141
Process serving	1,557
Equipment maintenance	147
Total cost	27,290
Safety improvement	513,930
Collision response savings	136
Time lost – travel	–371,643
Time saved – travel	691
Time lost – dispute tickets	–1,041
Total effects	142,072
Net benefit	114,782

Table 3. ICBC perspective, costs, and savings of BC Photo Radar Program.

Description	2001 Canadian Dollars Annualized Cost/ Benefit, C$000
Capital	4,745
Police	11,746
Court	1,954
Ticket processing	7,141
Process serving	1,557
Equipment maintenance	147
Total cost	27,290
Claim cost savings	65,554
Total savings	54,554
Net savings	38,264

2003). Total capital expenditure for the program was approximately C$33 million (US$26 million), based on official accounting records. These costs were amortized over a 10-year period, corresponding to the estimated economic life of the equipment (Elvik, 2001), using a real discount rate of 6% (BC Ministry of Transportation and Highways, 1997), yielding an annualized expenditure of C$4.7 million (US$3.7 million), shown in Tables 2 and 3.

Police and Court Costs

A stand-alone police force was established for the Photo Radar Program. The police force was composed of 102 full-time equivalent (FTE) uniformed police officers operating photo radar vans, 13.5 FTE charging officers (reviewing the photographs of violating vehicles), and four FTE management and administrative staff. The standard annual costing rate for each of the groups is $85,000 for RCMP, $73,690 for local police, $43,101 for charging officers, and $71,681 for managers and administrative staff. Police costs were calculated by summing up the number of people in each category multiplied by their respective standard costing rate, and adding 20% for benefits and other overheads. The typical yearly police cost for the Photo Radar Program thus calculated was C$11.7 million, shown in Tables 2 and 3.

Photo radar also created extra workload for the court system. This included the services of prosecutors, support staff, justices of the peace, sheriffs, and court/registry clerks. The standard annual cost rate for each of these groups was C$106,844, C$52,919, C$90,252, C$47,920, and C$46,796, respectively. The time spent on photo radar tickets for each group was calculated by multiplying the number of tickets disputed (16,388 per year, on average) by the average time spent handling a typical ticket dispute. Adding 20% for benefits and other overhead and additional court costs were estimated at C$2.0 million, shown in Tables 2 and 3.

Ticket Processing Costs

Ticket processing costs included photograph processing, data management, equipment maintenance, and ticket mailing or delivery. Costs were obtained from ICBC accounting records. Process serving (C$1.6 million) was used if registered mail failed to reach the owner of the offending vehicle; ticket processing cost C$7.1 million annually, and equipment maintenance required C$0.15 million, shown in Tables 2 and 3.

Total Program Costs

Overall, Tables 2 and 3 shows that in both the societal and ICBC perspectives, direct annual Photo Radar Program costs were an estimated C$27.3 million.

Benefit from Reduction in Collisions, Injuries, Deaths, and Property Damage

Previous assessments showed that the BC Photo Radar Program was effective in reducing traffic speed and collisions (Chen, 2001, 2003; Chen et al., 2000, 2002). As described above, it was estimated that the program prevented 1,542 injury collisions and 72 fatal collisions annually (causing 2,220 injuries and 79 deaths). The estimated reduction in property-damage-only collisions is small and unreliable, hence was not included in this analysis.

In the societal perspective, lives and injuries were valued using estimated economic values of C$120,000 per injury collision and C$4.58 million per fatal collision (Bein et al., 1994). In the ICBC perspective, all valuations were based on average claim costs of C$40,000 for each injury collision and C$50,000 for each fatal collision.

The total safety benefit for a typical photo radar year is calculated by multiplying the number of fatal and injury collisions prevented by their corresponding estimated costs. From a societal perspective (Table 2), the annual value of these safety benefits was estimated at C$514 million. ICBC accrued estimated annual claim savings (Table 3) of C$66 million. The majority of ICBC's claim cost savings (C$62 million) resulted from the reduction in injury collisions (as opposed to fatal collisions). This contrasts with the societal perspective, where the majority of the benefits (C$329 million) derived from the reduction in fatal collisions.

Benefit from Reduced Collision Response by Emergency Services

Reduced collisions mean fewer responses by police, ambulance, and other emergency services. For the base case, emergency response costs were estimated conservatively based on the number and type of collisions avoided; the delay avoided per type of collision (estimated at 2 hours/fatal collision and 0.5 hour/serious injury collision), and the minimum number and type of personnel responding (2 local police and one 2-person ambulance/advanced life support crew per fatal collision; 1 local police officer and one 2-person ambulance/advanced life support unit per injury collision). The estimated cost of these resources was $40.33/hour for local police ($73,690 ÷ 1,827 hours per year) and $33.50/hour (median of wage scale; BCAS, 2005a) for paramedics; minimum ambulance call $54 as per BCAS, 2005b). The base case estimate was that emergency response worth C$0.14 million annually was avoided by photo radar.

Valuation of Travel Time

For the societal perspective (Table 2), travel effects were shadow-priced using standard economic evaluation methods (Elvik, 2001; Fuguitt & Wilcox, 1999; Layard, 1972; Mishan, 1988) and available B.C. data. Based on BC Ministry of Transportation and Highways (1997) guidelines, a value of C$10 per person per hour was used for passenger vehicles and C$28 for truck drivers in 1998 dollars, inflated to 2001 values ($10.47 and $29.32, respectively) using the BC Consumer Price Index. Travel time is not included in the ICBC perspective (Table 3).

Cost of Travel Time Lost Due to Slower Traffic Speed

The objective of the BC Photo Radar Program was to reduce traffic speed in order to reduce traffic collisions. However, the reduction in traffic speed leads to increased travel time. For the base case, the value of lost travel time was estimated using Natural Resources Canada data (1997) on total vehicle travel distance by passenger vehicles and commercial trucks; the estimated mean speed reduction of 2.4 km/hour due to photo radar; the estimated number of travelers per non-delayed vehicle; and the estimated value of traveler time. The time lost due to reduction in speed was estimated by calculating how many more hours of travel would have been required, in the aggregate, if all travel speeds were reduced by 2.4 km/hour (Chen, 2003). Using this method, the estimated value of lost travel time from photo radar is $372 million, much more than direct program costs.

- People arguing court cases

VII. **Sensitivity Analysis**

- Discount rates
- Reduction in speed
- Collision reduction
- Injury fatality estimations
- Passenger vehicle travel time values
- Equipment life

VIII. **Conclusion**

- BC Photo Radar Program created C$115 million in savings
  - C$22 million in least favorable conditions

XI. **Questions**

1. Should we adopt the Photo Radar Program?
2. How would the public view this project?
3. Are there any additional cost or benefits that were overlooked?

Do Speed Cameras Produce Net Benefits?

I. **Objectives**

- To understand the impact of the Photo Radar Program
- Photo Radar has been used, but it's cost-effectiveness is questionable
- Decide if it's worth using

II. **Background**

- 9th leading cause of death by injury in the world
- British Columbia was one of the first cities to use
- Insurance groups wanted to lower speed-related accidents.
- Drivers were warned, and then later ticketed.
- Citizens complain that the program was use to collect revenue for the govt.

III. **Impact of Photo Radar**

- Traffic Safety
  - Reduced crashes (2,220) 14% less collisions, with 79 less fatal
- Speed reduction
  - 2.4 km/h 3% reduction in speed
  - .5km/h 6% reduction in speed variance

IV. **Cost for the program**

• Capital cost	C$33 mill
• ICBC Operating cost	C$4.7 mill
• Police Costs	C$11.7 mill
• Court Costs	C$7.1 mill

V. **Benefits from the program**

- Reduced collisions, Injuries, deaths, and property damage.
  - C$120,000 per collision
  - C$40,000 each injury collision
  - C$50,000 each fatal collision
- Fewer Responses from emergency services
  - C$40.33/hour police
  - C$33.50/hour paramedics
  - C$54 per call for ambulance
- Timed save from fewer Collisions
  - 2 additional hours for fatal collisions
  - 0.5 hour for non fatal collisions
  - C$0.7 million per year. (assuming an hour of a persons time is =10/person 28/truck driver
- Fuel saving
- Environmental benefits

VI. **Negative effects from the program**

- Lost time by driving slower. Totals C$372 million.

Benefit of Travel Time Saved Due to Fewer Collisions

In fatal and other severe collisions, highway cleanup and police investigation can take many hours, hence reducing major collisions should save time for motorists. For the base case, time saved was estimated based on the number and type of collisions avoided; the delay avoided per type of collision (estimated at 2 hours/fatal collision and 0.5 hour/serious injury collision); the number of non-delayed vehicles per type of collision; the number of travelers per non-delayed vehicle (from Natural Resources Canada, 1997); and the estimated value of traveler time (Chen, 2003). The calculation reveals time saved worth C$0.7 million per year.

Cost of Time Lost Disputing Tickets

Registered owners of ticketed vehicles had the right to dispute tickets in court. The time and expense used disputing tickets is lost for productive activities, hence should be accounted for in cost-benefit analysis. We have not included any estimate for legal counsel costs, assuming that for most ticketed drivers, photo radar fines were not large enough to justify the cost of retaining counsel. Time lost disputing photo radar tickets was estimated by multiplying the average number of disputes (16,388/year on average, fewer than 10% of tickets; Chen, 2003) by the estimated average time spent to attend a court hearing (three hours), and the average hourly wage of B.C. workers (C$17, BC Stats, 2000, adjusted to C$17.87 in 2001). Overall, it is estimated that private time worth $1 million annually was lost disputing tickets.

Summary of Base Case Study

As shown in Table 2, on an annualized basis the program generated C$115 million dollars of net social benefit. The largest single benefit is the value of injuries, deaths, and property damage prevented (C$514 million per year), while the largest single cost is the value of lost travel time (C$372 million per year). By comparison, direct program costs (C$27 million) are small.

For ICBC, Table 3 indicates that on an annualized basis the program produced net savings of C$38 million per year. Claim savings (C$66 million) were more than double program costs.

SENSITIVITY ANALYSIS

Many assumptions were made in the base case analysis, and there was significant uncertainty about some assumptions. It is therefore important to test whether plausible variation in key variables might change the base case results. Table 4 shows the alternate values investigated in the sensitivity analysis:

- Discount rates of 3% and 10% were tested in the sensitivity analysis, to reflect the recommendations of the U.S. panel on cost-effectiveness and the B.C. government official discount rate, respectively.
- Speed reduction was varied $\pm 1\sigma$ (from 2.4 km/hour in the base case) to 2.0 km/hour and 2.8 km/hour, and injuries and fatalities adjusted proportionately.
- Injury and fatality collision reductions were varied by one standard deviation (see Table 4 for alternate values).
- The unit value of injuries and fatalities was varied by ±10%.

- The value of vehicle passenger time (C$10.47 per hour in the base case) was increased to C$15.71 and C$20.95 in 2001 dollars, reflecting the possibility that drivers who speed have higher than average time valuations.
- Equipment life was varied from the expected 10 years to reflect premature cancellation of the B.C. program (after 5 years). This shorter equipment life could affect actual results for B.C., but would not affect expected results elsewhere.

Sensitivity Analysis Results

Table 5 shows sensitivity analysis results from a societal perspective, with base case results in the first column. Base case results are robust to all plausible alternate assumptions except greatly reduced collision reduction (one standard deviation less than estimated) or greatly increased value of private passenger time. The results become strongly negative (C$190 million per year) if passenger time is valued at C$20.95 per hour. Table 6 shows that from ICBC's perspective, photo radar creates net savings under all plausible assumptions.

DISCUSSION AND LIMITATIONS

Although our study includes the known major factors that affect the costs and benefits of radar speed enforcement and tries to value costs and benefits following economic principles, the study cannot answer all questions about all possible automated speed enforcement programs. We are confident, however, that B.C.'s results are broadly generalizable to similar traffic safety programs in developed nations; the speed and collision impacts are similar to those observed elsewhere, and our study demonstrates convincingly that collision migration does not occur. If anything, the benefit valuations may be somewhat conservative, as the U.S. National

Table 4. Sensitivity analysis—alternate values.

Variable	Base Case	Alternate Values	Description
Discount rate	6%	3% 10%	U.S. Panel (Phillips & Chen, 2002) and B.C. government official discount rate
Reduction in speed	2.4 km/hr	+1Û: 2.0 km/hr -1Û: 2.8 km/hr	Estimates with error
Collision reduction	Injury coll.: 1,542 Fatality coll.: 72	+1Û: Injury 1,929; Fatality 87 -1Û: Injury 1,154; Fatality 54	Estimates with error
Injury/fatality valuation	Injury = C$0.12 M Fatality = C$4.58 M	+10%: $0.132 M, $5.035 M -10%: $0.108 M, $4.12 M	Estimates with error
Passenger vehicle travel time valuation	C$10.47	C$15.71 C$20.95	Speeders may give higher value to time
Equipment life	10 years (expected equipment life)	5 years (actual program duration in B.C.)	Program cancellation could affect net benefits for B.C.

Table 5. Sensitivity analysis—societal perspective.

Thousands of 2001 Canadian dollars

Description	Base Case	Discount Rate		Speed reduction (km/hr)		Death/Injury Reduction		Death/Injury Valuation		Private Travel Time Value		5 Year Program
		3%	10%	2.8	2.0	+1 SD	-1 SD	+10%	-10%	$15.71	$20.95	
Cost												
Capital	4,745	4,094	5,684	4,745	4,745	4,745	4,745	4,745	4,745	4,745	4,745	8,291
Police	11,746	11,746	11,746	11,746	11,746	11,746	11,746	11,746	11,746	11,746	11,746	11,746
Court	1,954	1,954	1,954	1,954	1,954	1,954	1,954	1,954	1,954	1,954	1,954	1,954
Ticket/photo Processing	7,141	7,141	7,141	7,141	7,141	7,141	7,141	7,141	7,141	7,141	7,141	7,141
Process Serving	1,557	1,557	1,557	1,557	1,557	1,557	1,557	1,557	1,557	1,557	1,557	1,557
Equipment Maintenance	147	147	147	147	147	147	147	147	147	147	147	147
Total Costs	27,290	26,639	28,229	27,290	27,290	27,290	27,290	27,290	27,290	27,290	27,290	30,836
Effect												
Safety Improvement	513,930	513,930	513,930	599,585	428,275	628,946	384,584	565,323	462,537	513,930	513,930	513,930
Collision Response Savings	136	136	136	158	113	101	169	136	136	136	136	136
Time lost - travel	-371,643	-371,643	-371,643	-436,165	-307,881	-371,643	-371,643	-371,643	-371,643	-524,839	-678,034	-371,643
Time saved	691	691	691	806	576	782	517	691	691	974	1,257	691
Time lost - dispute tickets	-1,041	-1,041	-1,041	-1,041	-1,041	-1,041	-1,041	-1,041	-1,041	-1,041	-1,041	-1,041
Total Effects	142,072	142,072	142,072	163,343	120,042	257,146	12,586	193,465	90,679	-10,840	-163,753	142,072
Net Benefit	114,782	115,433	113,843	136,053	92,751	229,855	-14,704	166,175	63,389	-38,131	-191,043	111,236

Table 6. Sensitivity analysis—ICBC perspective.

Thousands of 2001 Canadian dollars

Description	Base Case	Discount Rate (%)		Speed reduction (km/hr)		Death/Injury Reduction		Death/Injury Valuation		5 Year Program
		3%	10%	2.8	2.0	+1 SD	-1 SD	+10%	-10%	
Cost										
Capital	4,745	4,094	5,684	4,745	4,745	4,745	4,745	4,745	4,745	8,291
Police	11,746	11,746	11,746	11,746	11,746	11,746	11,746	11,746	11,746	11,746
Court	1,954	1,954	1,954	1,954	1,954	1,954	1,954	1,954	1,954	1,954
Ticket/photo Processing	7,141	7,141	7,141	7,141	7,141	7,141	7,141	7,141	7,141	7,141
Process Serving	1,557	1,557	1,557	1,557	1,557	1,557	1,557	1,557	1,557	1,557
Equipment Maintenance	147	147	147	147	147	147	147	147	147	147
Total Cost	27,290	26,639	28,229	27,290	27,290	27,290	27,290	27,290	27,290	30,836
Savings										
Claim Cost Savings	65,554	65,554	65,554	76,480	54,629	81,880	49,073	72,110	58,999	65,554
Total Savings	65,554	65,554	65,554	76,480	54,629	81,880	49,073	72,110	58,999	65,554
Net Savings	38,264	38,915	37,325	49,190	27,338	54,589	21,783	44,819	31,708	34,718

Highway Traffic Safety Administration (Blincoe et al., 2002) reports that speed-related crashes have above-average costs, but increasing estimated crash costs would not alter our results. Overall, comparable results to those seen in B.C. could be expected for similar programs implemented elsewhere.

As mentioned earlier, the program was cancelled after a change of the provincial government. This may seem paradoxical, as the program appears to have been successful in its stated aims of reducing traffic speed, improving traffic safety, and saving lives. The paradox may be partly explained by an asymmetry in the ability of private citizens to perceive benefits and costs in this situation, however. Traffic collisions are relatively infrequent, and drivers generally would not be aware of having avoided a collision; the safety benefit of reduced speed is therefore difficult for motorists to recognize. Radar enforcement and resulting slower traffic, however, affect all motorists and are relatively easy to notice. In addition, traffic fines represent a cost to citizens. Any speed enforcement program can therefore be vulnerable to a public perception that it imposes harm (delay and fines) without creating offsetting benefits. The best remedy is honest use of information. Every effort must be made to publicize the seriousness of speed-related collisions, before introduction and throughout the duration of any such program. The success of speed enforcement in reducing crashes should be rigorously evaluated and the results made public. Finally, and perhaps most vitally, speed enforcement must be restricted to collision-prone areas; suspicions that a program is more about speed traps and revenue than about safety can seriously undermine public support (SENSE, 1997a, 1997b; Escort, 2005).

The present study evaluates the BC Photo Radar Program as it was implemented from 1996 to 2001. Should the necessary data become available, it would be very informative to conduct a retrospective study separating the traffic safety effects of the program on highways and city streets; it would also be interesting to assess whether highway speeds and crashes have rebounded since cancellation of the program.

CONCLUSIONS

Our results show that the BC Photo Radar Program created C$115 million in net benefits annually for society as a whole. These results are robust to all alternate assumptions except greatly reduced collision reductions or greatly increased value of private passenger time. From the sponsoring agency's perspective, photo radar created base case net savings of C$38 million per year and net savings of at least C$22 million per year under even the least favorable assumptions. Comparable results would be expected for analogous programs in developed-country jurisdictions with similar traffic infrastructure: greater use of highway photo radar speed enforcement would be good public policy.

GREG CHEN is Associate Professor at the School of Public Affairs, Baruch College, City University of New York.

REBECCA N. WARBURTON is a health economist and Assistant Professor, School of Public Administration, University of Victoria, British Columbia, Canada.

REFERENCES

Bein, P., Miller, T., & Waters, W. (1994). British Columbia road-user unit costs. Proceedings of the Canadian Transportation Research Forum Annual Meeting, University of Saskatchewan, 714–727.

Blincoe, L. J., Seay, A. G., Zaloshnja, E., Miller, T. R., Romano, E. O., Luchter, S., & Spicer, R. S. (2002). The economic impact of motor vehicle crashes, 2000 (Report DOT HS 809 446). Washington, DC: National Highway Traffic Safety Administration.

BCAS (British Columbia Ambulance Service). (2005a). British Columbia is recruiting ACP/ALS paramedics. Retrieved May 2005 from http://www.healthservices.gov.bc.ca/bcas/pdf/paramedicflyer.pdf.

BCAS (British Columbia Ambulance Service). (2005b). Fees for ambulance service in British Columbia. Retrieved May 2005 from http://www.healthservices.gov.bc.ca/bcas/bcasfees.html.

BC (British Columbia) Ministry of Transportation and Highways. (1997). MicroBencost guidebook: Defaults and standardized economic analysis for highway improvement projects in British Columbia. Victoria, BC, Canada: Author.

BC STATS. Infoline July 2000; Issue 00-30. Retrieved December 2005 from http://www.bcstats.gov.bc.ca.

Chen, G. (2001). Using eEmpirical-Bayesian method to assess traffic safety programs. Paper presented at the Canadian Multi-disciplinary traffic safety conference XII, London, Ontario.

Chen, G. (2003). Evaluation of the British Columbia Photo Radar Program, Ph.D. Thesis, University of Victoria, Victoria, British Columbia, Canada.

Chen, G., Meckle, W., & Wilson, R. J. (2002). Speed and safety effect of photo radar enforcement on a highway corridor in British Columbia. Accident Analysis and Prevention, 34(2), 129–138.

Chen, G., Wilson, R. J., Meckle, W., & Cooper, P. (2000). Evaluation of BC Photo Radar Program in British Columbia. Accident Analysis and Prevention, 32(4), 517–526.

Coleman, J. A., Paniati, J. F., Cotton, R. D., Parker, M. R., Jr., Covey, R., Pena, H. E., Jr., Graham, D., Robinson, M. L., MaClauley, J., Taylor, W. C., & Morford, G. (1996). FHWA study tour for speed management and enforcement technology. Washington, DC: U.S. Department of Transportation.

DETR (Department of the Environment, Transport and the Regions). (1999). The effects of speed cameras: How drivers respond. Road Safety Research Report No. 11, London.

Elvik, R. (1997). Effects on accidents of automatic speed enforcement in Norway. Transportation Research Record, 1595, 14–19.

Elvik, R. (2001). Cost-benefit analysis of road safety measures: Applicability and controversies. Accident Analysis and Prevention, 33, 9–17.

Escort. (2005). Radar detector news: Recent radar detector and traffic enforcement news. Retrieved September 2005 from http://www.escortradar.com/detector-news.htm.

Federal Highway Administration, United States Department of Transportation. (1996). FHWA study tour for speed management and enforcement technology. Washington, DC: Author. Retrieved September 2005 from http://safety.fhwa.dot.gov/media/pdf/tour_spdmngmt.pdf.

Fuguitt, D., & Wilcox, S. J. (1999). Cost-benefit analysis for public sector decision makers. Westport, Connecticut: Quorum Books.

Gains, A., Heydecker, B., Shrewsbury, J., & Robertson, S. (2004). National safety camera programme: Three-year evaluation report. London: PA Consulting Group, 2004. Retrieved April 2005 from http://www.paconsulting.com/industries/government_services/publications/reports_and_surveys/safety_camera_report.htm.

Hooke, A., Knox , J., & Portas, D. (1996). Cost-benefit analysis of traffic light and speed cameras. Police research series, paper 20. London, UK: Police Research Group.

ICBC (Insurance Corporation of British Columbia). (1996). Fair enforcement. Recovery, 7(2). Victoria, BC. Retrieved January 2004 from http://www.icbc.com/Library/.

ICBC (Insurance Corporation of British Columbia). (1998). Interim evaluation report on Photo Radar Program. Victoria, BC: Author.

ICF Consulting and Imperial College Centre for Transport Studies. (2003). Cost-benefit analysis of road safety improvements—final report. London, UK: Author.

IIHS (Insurance Institute for Highway Safety. (2005). Statement of Stephen L. Oesch before the District of Columbia Public Roundtable on Automated Enforcement. Retrieved September 2005 from http://www.iihs.org/laws/testimony/pdf/testimony_slo_022305.pdf.

IIHS (Insurance Institute for Highway Safety). (2002). Automated Enforcement. Status Report, 37(5), 1–7.

ITCU (Integrated Traffic Camera Unit). (1996). Guidelines for photo radar deployment. Vancouver, BC.

Layard, R. (1972). Cost-benefit analysis. Middlesex, England: Penguin Books.

Lynn, C. W., Garber, N. J., Ferguson, T. K., Lau, R., Alcee, J. V., Black, J. C., & Wndzel, P. M. (1992). Automated speed enforcement pilot project for the capital beltway: Feasibility of photo radar—final report. Charlottesville, VA: Virginia Transportation Research Council.

Metropolitan Police Department, Government of the District of Columbia. (2005). Results from other jurisdictions. Washington, DC. Retrieved September 2005 from http://mpdc.dc.gov/mpdc/cwp/view,a,1240,q,548026,mpdcNav_GID,1552,mpdcNav,%7C31886%7C.asp.

Mishan, E. J. (1988). Cost-benefit analysis (5th ed.). London, UK: Unwin Hyman.

National Highway Traffic Safety Administration. (2004). Presentation—2003 early assessment. Retrieved April 28, 2004, from http://www-nrd.nhtsa.dot.gov/pdf/nrd-30/NCSA/PPT/2003EARelease.pdf.

Natural Resources Canada. (1997). Canada's energy outlook: 1996–2020. Table BC-12A, Determinants of transportation demand. Ottawa, Ontario: Author.

Phillips, K. A., & Chen, J. L. (2002). Impact of the U.S. panel on cost-effectiveness in health and medicine. American Journal of Preventive Medicine, 22(2), 98–105.

Photocop. Locations. (2003). Retrieved April 2005 from http://www.photocop.com/locations.htm.

Retting, R. A. (2003). Speed cameras—public perceptions in the US. Traffic Engineering and Control, 44, 100–101.

Retting, R. A., & Farmer, C. M. (2003). Evaluation of speed camera enforcement in the District of Columbia. Transportation Research Record, 1830, 34–37. Washington, DC: Transportation Research Board.

Retting, R. A., Ferguson, S. A., & Hakkert, A. S. (2003). Effects of red light cameras on violations and crashes: A review of the international literature. Traffic Injury Prevention, 4(1), 17–23.

Retting, R. A., & Kyrychenko, S. Y. (2002). Reductions in injury crashes associated with red light camera enforcement in Oxnard, California. American Journal of Public Health, 92(11), 1822–1825.

Rogerson, P., Newstead, S., & Cameron, M. (1994). Evaluation of the speed camera program in Victoria 1990–1991, phase 3. Victoria, Australia: Monash University, Accident Research Centre.

Runge, J. W. (2005). Remarks prepared for Runge MD. Administrator of HSTSA, on Lifesaver 23, HSTSA Reward Luncheon. Victoria, Australia.

SENSE. (1995). Press release: Photo radar, the wrong tool for the wrong problem. Retrieved December 2003 from http://www.sense.bc.ca/news/sen_pr02.txt.

SENSE. (1997a). Truth in advertising, archived news. Retrieved December 2003 from http://www.sense.bc.ca/t-in-a.htm and http://www.sense.bc.ca/news2.htm#97_oct_17.

SENSE. (1997b). "Fairness Code" gutted to make way for increase in ticket volumes. Retrieved September 2005 from http://www.sense.bc.ca/news2.

SENSE. (1998). Photo radar costs and equipment contracts. Retrieved December 2003 from http://www.sense.bc.ca/contract.htm.

SENSE. (2003). Photo radar equipment. Retrieved December 2003 from http://www.sense.bc.ca/equipmnt.htm.

Stuster, J., Coffman Z., & Warren D. (1998). Synthesis of safety research related to speed and speed management. Publication No. FHWA-RD-98-154. Washington, DC: Federal Highway Administration and National Highway Traffic Safety Administration.

Turner, S., & Polk, A. (1998). Overview of automated enforcement in transportation. Retrieved April 2004 from http://safety.fhwa.dot.gov/fourthlevel/pdf/turner.pdf.

WHO (World Heath Organization). (2004a). Road traffic injury prevention. Retrieved May 2004 from http://www.who.int/violence_injury_prevention/unintentional_injuries/road_traffic/rtip1/en/.

WHO (World Heath Organization). (2004b). World Health Day 2004: Road safety. Retrieved May 2004 from http://www.who.int/world-health-day/2004/en/.

Longer-Term Effects of Head Start

By ELIANA GARCES, DUNCAN THOMAS, AND JANET CURRIE*

Specially collected data on adults in the Panel Study of Income Dynamics are used to provide evidence on the longer-term effects of Head Start, an early intervention program for poor preschool-age children. Whites who attended Head Start are, relative to their siblings who did not, significantly more likely to complete high school, attend college, and possibly have higher earnings in their early twenties. African-Americans who participated in Head Start are less likely to have been booked or charged with a crime. There is some evidence of positive spillovers from older Head Start children to their younger siblings. (*JEL* J24, I38)

Head Start, a public preschool program for disadvantaged children, is designed to close the gaps between these children and their more advantaged peers. Begun in 1965 as part of the "War on Poverty," Head Start has enjoyed widespread bipartisan support along with increasing budgets. It is now a $4.7 billion program serving more than 800,000 children and it is a model for separate state-funded programs.

Head Start is an investment in children that is intended to help them through the rest of their lives. Although there is evidence suggesting significant short-term benefits associated with participation in the program, critics point out there is no evidence that the program has lasting benefits. Studies suggest short-term gains in test scores "fade out" for many Head Start children. Evidence cited in support of the long-term effectiveness of early interventions comes from analyses of other programs, such as the famous Perry Preschool intervention, most of which bear little resemblance to the Head Start model.

This paper addresses the important question of whether the Head Start program confers longer-term benefits on participants. We use questions from a supplement to the Panel Survey of Income Dynamics (PSID) which were specifically designed for this study. There are three features of these unique data that are key for our purposes. First, in 1995, questions about participation in Head Start and other preschools were included in the interviews and asked about all adult household members age 18 through 30. These questions make it feasible, for the first time in population-based survey data, to measure the economic and social success of Head Start participants when they have reached adulthood. Second, because the PSID is a panel which stretches back over a quarter century, we are able to control for family background and the environment in which each respondent grew up in great detail. Third, the PSID provides a nationally representative sample of children who participated in actual Head Start programs rather than experimental model programs.

We examine four indicators of economic and social success in adulthood. We find that, for whites, participation in Head Start is associated with a significantly increased probability of completing high school and attending college as well as elevated earnings in one's early twenties. African-Americans who participated in Head Start are less likely to have been booked for or charged with a crime. We also find suggestive evidence that African-American males who attended Head Start are more likely than their siblings to have completed high school.

* Garces: Economic Analysis LLC, 2049 Century Park East, Suite 2310, Los Angeles, CA 90067 (e-mail: egarces@econanalysis.com); Thomas: Department of Economics, UCLA, Box 951477, Los Angeles, CA 90095 (e-mail: dt@ucla.edu); Currie: Department of Economics, UCLA, and National Bureau of Economic Research, Box 951477, Los Angeles, CA 90095 (e-mail: currie@simba.sscnet.ucla.edu). Currie and Thomas thank the National Science Foundation (SBR-9512670) and National Institute for Child Health and Human Development (R01-HD3101A2) for financial support. Greg Duncan, Peter Germanis, Judith Seltzer, Jeanne Brooks-Gunn, and anonymous referees provided very helpful comments. The authors are solely responsible for the contents of the paper. We are grateful to Greg Duncan, Sandra Hofferth, and the Advisory Board of the Panel Survey of Income Dynamics for including the questions used in this study.

Finally, we uncover some evidence of positive spillovers from older children who attended Head Start to younger siblings, particularly with regard to being booked or charged with a crime.

While an experiment in which children were randomly assigned to the program or to a control and then tracked for 30 years might be the ideal way to evaluate the long-term effects of Head Start, such experimental evaluations of the program do not exist. We view our analysis of these nonexperimental data as an important complement to random assignment evaluations. The results presented below provide a first step toward establishing whether Head Start confers long-term benefits on participants. For reasons spelled out in detail below, our methods likely provide lower bound estimates of any positive effects of Head Start.

I. Background

Head Start began as a summer program in 1965 with 561,000 predominantly African-American children. It expanded to serve almost three-quarters of a million African-American and white children in the summer of 1966 at which time about $1,000 (in 1999 prices) was spent on each child. By the early 1970's, Head Start had become an all-year program that served considerably fewer children at a higher annual cost per child. For example, in 1971, the program served slightly less than 400,000 children at an annual cost of about $4,000 per child. Children living in poor families are eligible to enroll in the program and, today, it serves more than 800,000 children at a cost of around $5,400 per child. Most of the children in the program are three or four years old (Administration for Children and Families, 1999). While large, the program serves only about two-thirds of eligible children. This reflects the fact that the program, which is funded by appropriation, has never been fully funded. The program is administered at the local level (there are over 1,400 local programs) and is subject to federal guidelines. The guidelines specify that, in addition to providing a nurturing learning environment, Head Start should provide a wide range of services. These include, for example, facilitating and monitoring utilization of preventive medical care by participants, as well as providing nutritious meals and snacks.

Studies have shown that participation in Head Start is associated with short-term benefits, as indicated by improved test scores. These benefits appear to "fade out" by around the third grade so that Head Start children are no better off than controls at that point (see Steven Barnett [1995] and Lynn A. Karoly et al. [1998] for reviews of this literature). Dissipation of test-score gains does not necessarily imply that Head Start children do not benefit from starting school "on the right foot." For example, avoidance of grade repetition and special education early in life may be associated with higher eventual schooling attainment. Head Start may also be associated with lasting improvements in non-cognitive skills that are important for future success in life (cf. James J. Heckman et al., 2000). These questions have not been directly addressed in the literature. Moreover, many of the studies have been criticized because they use ad hoc control groups, are subject to substantial attrition, or because sample sizes are small resulting in statistical tests that have limited power.

Most of the evidence on longer-term benefits of early intervention is drawn from three studies: The Carolina Abecedarian Project; the Perry Preschool Project; and the Chicago Child-Parent Centers (CPC). A more detailed summary of these studies is available in Currie (2001). For our purposes, the important point is that these programs were quite different from Head Start. For example, the Carolina Abecedarian Project randomly assigned children to the treatment or to nothing. Treatments were provided with an intensive center-based full-day, full-year child care program from three months through age 5. Then, all of the children were again randomly assigned to a follow-up program of support in school for an additional three years. Evaluations report positive effects on schooling attainment at age 21 among children who received the preschool treatment (Frances A. Campbell et al., 2001; 2002). The Perry Preschool intervention was more similar to Head Start in that it involved a half-day preschool every weekday and a weekly 90-minute home visit for eight months of each year for two years while the child was age three and four years old. However, the preschool component was of much higher quality than the average Head Start program in existence during our study period. This intervention had positive effects on achievement test scores, grades, graduation from high school and earnings, as well as negative effects on crime and welfare use (as of age 27).

Both the Carolina Abecedarian Project and Perry Preschool intervention were funded at higher levels than Head Start. For example, in 1998 it cost slightly over $5,000 to keep a child in a part-day Head Start program for 34 weeks a year. The two-year, part-day Perry Preschool intervention cost nearly $13,000 per child (in 1998 dollars) (Karoly et al., 1998).[1] The preschool component of the Abecedarian intervention (which was full-day) cost about $15,000 per child, per year, and this part of the intervention lasted five years.[2] Thus, the results of these programs probably provide an upper limit on what one could reasonably expect from Head Start. These two programs also involved small, localized interventions, and thus their findings may not generalize.

Arthur J. Reynolds (1998), Reynolds (2000), and Judy Temple et al. (2000) study the Chicago CPC program. Unlike Carolina Abecedarian and Perry Preschool, this is a large scale publicly funded intervention. All of the children in this study attended an enriched preschool program for two years starting at age 3. The treatment children then received an additional enriched program up to age 9 while the control children did not. Thus, while these evaluations deal with a public early intervention program, the actual intervention being evaluated is for school-aged rather than preschool children. Still, it is worth noting that the CPC program has been shown to reduce the incidence of high-school dropout, delinquency, and crime.

The methodology used in this study follows Currie and Thomas (1995), who use nonexperimental data drawn from the National Longitudinal Survey's Child-Mother files (NLS-CM) to evaluate Head Start. They attempt to control for unobserved characteristics of children by comparing siblings who participated in Head Start with those who did not. The idea is that by using siblings as the controls, any shared characteristics of family background will be controlled as long as they affect the outcomes examined in a linear and additive way. The Currie and Thomas study is one of a handful that includes a substantial number of Head Start children who are not African-American. This is important for two reasons. First, participants in experimental evaluations have been largely African-American and it has not been possible to separately identify program effects by race. This turns out to be a key distinction. Second, although African-Americans participate at higher rates than whites, the majority of Head Start children are not African-American.

Currie and Thomas report that for children of all racial and ethnic backgrounds, there are substantial and significant gains in test scores associated with attending Head Start. For African-American Head Start children, these gains "fade out" while they are still in elementary grades. For whites, the gains persist into adolescence and participation in Head Start is also associated with reduced grade repetition. It is worth emphasizing that since the initial gains in test scores are the same for whites and African-Americans, the racial differences in fade-out may have less to do with the Head Start program and more to do with the child's experiences after finishing the program.[3] Moreover, the Currie and Thomas findings regarding fade-out for African-Americans closely mirror those of experimental studies which have generally been conducted using primarily African-American subjects. This lends additional weight to both sets of results as well as the methodologies underlying them.

In sum, there do appear to be short-term positive effects of participation in Head Start on outcomes such as grade repetition. That fact, in combination with evidence regarding positive longer-term effects of model early interventions

[1] Twenty percent of the children participated in the program for only one year. The cost figure given by Karoly et al. (1998) is a weighted average that takes this into account. These figures imply that the cost per year was about $7,000 in 1999 dollars.

[2] Craig Ramey et al. (1998) state that on average the preschool component of the program cost about $6,000 per year. Children entered the preschool component between 1972 and 1983. Six thousand 1978 dollars are worth approximately 15,000 1999 dollars.

[3] Currie and Thomas (2000) find that African-American children who attended Head Start continue to schools of lower quality than other African-American children. However, the same is not true among whites. Thus, poor school quality offers a potential explanation for fade-out of Head Start benefits among African-American children but not among whites. The CPC results discussed above also suggest that improved school quality may help prevent fade-out.

make it reasonable to suppose that there may be lasting benefits associated with participation in Head Start programs. Whether there are any long-term benefits remains an open question and is the subject of this paper.

II. Data

The PSID began in 1968 with a survey of 4,802 households composed of 18,000 individuals. These households, and new households formed by the original head, spouse, and their children have been followed ever since. In 1995, special questions on early childhood education experiences were included in the interview on a one-time basis. Information was collected on all adult household members age 30 or below about whether they had ever been enrolled in Head Start and whether they had attended any other preschool or daycare program. Since our interest is in the longer-term effects of participation in Head Start, we focus on slightly less than 4,000 adults (age 18 and older in 1995) for whom this information is reported.

Some of the advantages associated with using PSID were noted above. They come at a price. First, because we are using nonexperimental data, we need to address the fact that children are not randomly assigned to Head Start. Second, because we are measuring the longer-term effects of Head Start participation, and that information was not collected prospectively, the questions on early childhood education are asked retrospectively and may be contaminated by recall error. We have conducted several experiments to evaluate the quality of the data and we describe these experiments before discussing the issue of nonrandom assignment. Sample summary statistics are reported in Table 1.

Overall, 10 percent of the 1964–1977 birth cohort sample in the PSID report having attended Head Start and 28 percent report having attended some other type of preschool program.[4] If we take the same birth cohorts and assume that the average child who participated was in the program for one year, then the numbers of participants reported by the Head Start Bureau for each year imply a national participation rate of slightly over 12 percent.[5] National participation rates were high for those born in 1964–1965 (17 percent), fell to 13 percent for the 1966 cohort, to 11 percent for the 1967 cohort, and then declined slowly to 10 percent for the 1970 birth cohort. Enrollment rates subsequently rose for those born during the decade of the 1970's to slightly over 12 perçent (among the 1977 birth cohort).

This pattern is replicated remarkably closely in the PSID sample with one important exception. Among the earliest two birth cohorts in our sample (1964–1965), reported participation rates are much lower than the national rates (6 percent in the PSID). Participation in the 1966 cohort is higher but still below the national rate (8 percent in PSID). The PSID and national

[4] Our sample includes all white and African-American household members in the 1995 wave of PSID who were born between 1965 and 1977. The SEO ("poverty") sample is not included. Immigrants are underrepresented in the PSID. From the perspective of this study, the missing immigrants are people who had parents who were not living in the United States in 1968 but who were: (1) born between 1965 and 1977; (2) living in the United States at age 3, 4, or 5; and (3) living in the United States in 1995. Thus, in order to be relevant for our sample, someone born outside the United States in 1965 would have had to immigrate to the United States by 1970, while someone born abroad in 1977 would have had to immigrate before 1982. Since immigration was at a much lower level in the 1960's, 1970's, and much of the 1980's than it has been in the 1990's, missing immigrants would pose a greater problem if we were looking at shorter-term effects of Head Start with more recent cohorts of Head Start children. Specifically, between 1969 and 1975, there were approximately 380,000 legal immigrants into the United States each year whereas by 1990 the number of legal immigrants had reached 1,000,000 per year. The majority of the people that are missed because they are eligible immigrants are Hispanic and so we have excluded Hispanics from this study. (See Currie and Thomas, 1999, for a discussion of how the shorter-term effects of Head Start on Hispanics differ from the effects on whites and African-Americans.)

The data have been weighted so that our sample is representative of the 1995 white and African-American populations. Specifically, we have constructed weights so that the joint distribution of race, sex, and year of birth in our sample matches the joint distribution in the 1995 Current Population Survey. We prefer these weights to the PSID longitudinal weights because some new entrants into the PSID sample are assigned a zero PSID longitudinal weight; many of the adults in our sample are new entrants to PSID and so would contribute no information.

[5] This estimate is based on data reported by the Administration for Children and Families on enrollments in each year of the program and the number of births, reported by the National Center for Health Statistics (Administration for Children and Families, 1999; National Center for Health Statistics, 2000).

TABLE 1—SAMPLE SUMMARY STATISTICS: MEANS (AND STANDARD ERRORS)

Measure	All sample (1)	Head Start (2)	Not in Head Start (3)	Sibling sample (4)
Program participation[a]				
Head Start	10.57	100.00	0.00	10.89
	(0.53)			(0.73)
Other preschool	28.34	13.33	30.11	27.71
	(0.77)	(1.51)	(0.85)	(1.05)
Outcomes				
Percentage completed high school	76.60	64.65	78.03	77.21
	(0.74)	(2.16)	(0.79)	(1.01)
Percentage attended some college	37.14	25.08	38.59	38.80
	(0.85)	(1.96)	(0.93)	(1.17)
Earnings (average when age 23–25)	17.29	12.10	17.81	17.31
($1,000's, 1999 prices)	(0.69)	(0.67)	(0.76)	(1.00)
Percent booked/charged with crime	9.69	11.04	9.53	10.04
	(0.51)	(1.39)	(0.54)	(0.70)
Demographic characteristics				
Percentage African-American	25.17	75.32	19.24	22.85
	(0.74)	(1.92)	(0.73)	(0.98)
Percentage female	51.49	56.41	50.91	50.75
	(0.85)	(2.20)	(0.93)	(1.17)
Age (years) in 1995	23.66	23.35	23.70	23.65
	(0.06)	(0.15)	(0.06)	(0.08)
Percentage eldest child in family	53.11	50.89	53.37	50.57
	(0.56)	(1.41)	(0.61)	(0.76)
Percentage low-birth-weight baby	6.99	10.40	6.59	6.69
	(0.37)	(1.24)	(0.38)	(0.56)
Background				
Mother's years of education	12.14	11.33	12.24	12.30
	(0.04)	(0.09)	(0.04)	(0.05)
Percentage whose mother completed high school	70.37	55.52	72.12	78.15
	(0.78)	(2.21)	(0.83)	(0.97)
Father's years of education	11.60	10.19	11.76	12.23
	(0.06)	(0.14)	(0.06)	(0.07)
Percentage whose father completed high school	56.12	26.38	59.64	63.30
	(0.85)	(1.96)	(0.91)	(1.13)
Family income (when respondent age 3–6)	46.23	26.62	48.54	47.33
($1,000's, 1999 prices)	(0.46)	(0.58)	(0.50)	(0.67)
Percentage whose mother single	16.42	40.35	13.59	13.06
(when respondent age 4)	(0.61)	(2.16)	(0.61)	(0.79)
Household size (when respondent age 4)	4.59	4.97	4.55	4.84
	(0.03)	(0.09)	(0.03)	(0.04)
Sample size	3,255	489	2,766	1,742

Note: See footnote 4 regarding sample weights.
[a] Percentage of respondents reporting participation in program.

rates are very close in the 1967 birth cohort (11 percent) and for all other birth cohorts, the PSID mimics the national numbers. (Reported participation in the PSID declines to 9 percent in the early 1970's and then rises to 12 percent by the 1977 birth cohort, the last cohort in our sample.)

Recall that for the oldest birth cohorts, Head Start was primarily a summer program. It is not surprising that the reported rate of participation in Head Start among these birth cohorts in the PSID is much lower than the national rate. First, there is abundant evidence in the survey research literature that the more salient a life event, the more likely it is to be recalled;[6] participation in a summer Head Start program is

[6] See Seymour Sudman et al. (1996).

not likely to be as salient to a respondent as full-year participation in one's first school-oriented program. Second, many of the children who participated in Head Start during the summer are likely to have attended some other preschool during the rest of the year and PSID respondents are more likely to have reported their preschool experience during the school year rather than in the summer. By the early 1970's, Head Start had become a full-year program. Respondents born in the late 1960's would have participated in this full-year program rather than the summer one. Since the summer program is substantially different from the full-year program, we exclude the oldest birth cohorts from the analyses presented below.[7] Among those born between 1966 and 1977, the national enrollment rate is 11.1 percent according to the Head Start Bureau; of PSID respondents, 10.7 percent (standard error = 0.6 percent) report having attended Head Start.

The racial composition of Head Start children is not reported for every year by the Head Start Bureau. Taking 1980 as an example, 42 percent of Head Start participants were African-American. Since about 14 percent of the nation's children were African-American, this implies that about 33 percent of those children participated in Head Start and that the enrollment rate was around 7 percent among white children. The implied enrollment rates in the PSID are very close: for the 1975 birth cohort, 36 percent of African-Americans and 5 percent of whites report participation in Head Start.

Seminal work by Hermann Ebbinghaus (1894) and many subsequent studies in the survey research literature have shown that recall error tends to increase as a respondent is asked to stretch further back in time. If recall error seriously contaminates responses in the PSID, then we would expect the gap between the national enrollment rates and those reported in the PSID to be greater among the earlier birth cohorts. However, once we exclude the 1964–1965 birth cohort who participated in a summer program, enrollment rates implied by the PSID mimic the temporal pattern of the national rates. We also find no pattern of differences by birth year of the respondent in a regression of enrollment rates on year of birth.

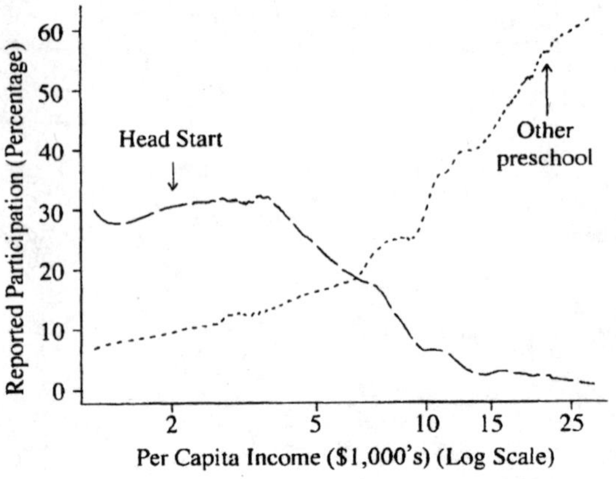

FIGURE 1. REPORTED PARTICIPATION RATES IN HEAD START AND OTHER PRESCHOOLS

Our third assessment of the quality of the recall data on Head Start participation exploits the fact that because the PSID is a long-term panel, we know family income when the person was a child. We have calculated average per capita family income (in 1999 prices) at the time the person was age 3, 4, 5, and 6, and as shown in Table 1, Head Start children tend to be drawn from lower-income families. Figure 1 presents the fraction of respondents who report attending Head Start and other preschools by per capita family income. Of respondents whose families were in the bottom quartile of the income distribution, about 30 percent report attending Head Start. The fraction declines with income and is close to zero for all respondents whose families were above median income.[8]

[7] The 1964 and 1965 birth cohorts have been excluded. Some of the 1966 cohort will have participated in the full-year program and some in the summer program. Assuming that full-year participation is more salient, it is likely that those respondents in this birth cohort who report participation in Head Start were full-year participants. (One in ten participants report participation in another preschool which is slightly lower than the rate for later birth cohorts.) We have experimented with dropping the 1966 birth cohort from our analytical sample. The regression results discussed below are little impacted by this restriction and none of the significant or important results is affected.

[8] Given that Head Start has long enjoyed widespread public support, it is possible that some people who attended other types of preschools erroneously label them "Head

The fraction of respondents who attended other preschools rises monotonically with income. The shapes of the relationships between income and participation in Head Start and other preschool programs are remarkably similar to those reported in Currie and Thomas (1995), which are based on prospective reports in the NLSY-CM. Respondents who report participation in Head Start as children were clearly disadvantaged when young, relative to other respondents. They are also more likely to have been living with a single mother at that time, their mothers are less educated, and they are more likely to have been low weight at birth (see Table 1).[9]

In sum, among the 1966–1977 birth cohorts in the PSID, retrospectively reported rates of participation in Head Start match the national enrollment rates very closely; Head Start participants were clearly disadvantaged around the time of preschool; and the link between participation and family income mimics the associations observed in other data sources. On balance, the PSID data on Head Start participation seem to be of high quality. While there is likely to be some classification error by respondents, we find no evidence of systematic reporting bias. Random classification error will tend to obscure positive benefits of Head Start in which case our estimates are likely to provide a lower bound.

Start." If reported Head Start children had family incomes greater than 150 percent of the poverty line in every preschool year, and never received any form of welfare then we reclassified them as "other preschool." About 5 percent of the reported Head Start participants in each year fell into this category.

[9] There are however, some differences in characteristics of families of Head Start children by race. Mothers of white Head Start children tend to be less educated than those of African-American Head Start children, although when they were eligible for the program, white Head Start children were less likely to be living with a single mother than African-Americans. White Head Start children in the PSID are almost twice as likely to have been low birth weight than African-American Head Start children (14 percent and 8 percent, respectively) although in the general population, African-American children are substantially more likely to suffer from low birth weight than whites. These differences suggest that the mechanisms underlying participation in Head Start are different for African-Americans and whites, and suggest that it may be fruitful to examine the two groups separately.

III. Empirical Methods

The aim of this study is to ask whether participation in Head Start results in greater economic or social success later in life. We focus on four adult outcomes: completion of high school, attendance at some college, ln(earnings) if the household member worked, and whether the household member ever reported being booked or charged with a crime.

A natural starting point would be to estimate a model in which each outcome of an individual respondent, Y_i, is assumed to depend on participation in Head Start, HDST, some other preschool, OPRE, and a set of individual-specific controls, $\mathbf{X}$:

$$(1)\qquad Y_i = \alpha_0 + \alpha_1 \mathrm{HDST}_i + \alpha_2 \mathrm{OPRE}_i + \boldsymbol{\alpha}_3 \mathbf{X}_i + \varepsilon_i$$

where HDST and OPRE are indicator variables and ε captures unobserved heterogeneity. The vector $\mathbf{X}$ includes observable exogenous variables that are likely to be correlated with outcomes such as the respondent's year of birth, and indicators equal to one if the respondent is female or African-American. It is important to include a control for whether the respondent attended a preschool other than Head Start for two reasons. First, we do not want to erroneously attribute the effects of other preschools to Head Start. Second, it is useful to compare the effects of Head Start to those of other preschools, as is discussed further below.

As noted above, the key problem with interpretation of (1) is that participation in Head Start (or other preschools) is not randomly assigned and covariates may be correlated with unobservables, ε. In that case, estimates of the effect of Head Start will be biased. Head Start is targeted toward disadvantaged children and children who are perceived to be "at risk" because of learning disabilities, or a negative home environment are often referred to Head Start by social agencies. Failure to control for these intervening characteristics will result in their being included in ε_i.

To the extent that these characteristics are correlated with HDST, estimates of α_1, the long-run "effect" of Head Start, will be biased. Because disadvantaged children are more likely to participate in Head Start, α_1 will probably be biased downward. Children who attend other preschools are likely to come from more advantaged backgrounds and so α_2 is likely to be biased upward. One approach to addressing this concern is to include measures of the relevant intervening characteristics in the vector **X**.

The PSID is a good data source for taking this approach since extensive information on the child's family background has been collected on an annual basis since 1968. Hence, we augment the vector **X** by including: maternal and paternal education of the respondent; a spline in family income when the child was of preschool age; family size measured at age 4; whether the respondent lived with both parents at age 4; an indicator for whether the respondent was the oldest child, and birth weight.[10] We have also experimented with adding controls for whether the mother worked or was on welfare when the child was age 4. (The addition of these variables had little impact on the results reported below.)

Despite the richness of the PSID, there may well be other unmeasured characteristics that distinguish Head Start children from their peers and which cannot be controlled in the regression model. If, conditional on the controls, these other characteristics are correlated with observable differences between Head Start children and other children then the estimated effects of Head Start will be biased. For example, if parents who send their children to Head Start (or other preschools) place a higher value on building human capital at an early age than other parents, and if that human-capital accumulation is associated with better outcomes later in life, then this unobserved difference will result in an upward bias in the Head Start "effect," α_1. In this case, it will be the (unobserved) parental emphasis on education that leads to better outcomes in adulthood rather than Head Start (or other preschool) attendance per se.

To the extent that parental taste for human capital accumulation does not differ between siblings, then it can be absorbed in a family-specific fixed effect, μ_f:

$$(2) \quad Y_{if} = \beta_0 + \beta_1 \mathrm{HDST}_{if} + \beta_2 \mathrm{OPRE}_{if} + \beta_3 \mathbf{X}_{if} + \mu_f + \xi_i.$$

This design controls for any unobserved family characteristics that have the same linear and additive effect on the adult outcomes of all siblings. As a practical matter, μ_f is specified as a mother-specific fixed effect in the empirical models below.

The fixed-effects method is not without its own limitations. First, the effective sample includes only those respondents with at least one sibling in the sample (which is slightly over half of the total sample). In these models, the effect of Head Start, β_1, is identified by comparing the outcomes of adults who participated in Head Start as children with the outcomes of the siblings who did not (255 adult household members from 100 families).[11]

Second, the effects of random measurement errors may be exacerbated in a fixed-effects framework. That is, by focusing on differences between siblings within a family, we may difference out much of the true signal in the data, and result in an underestimate of the positive effects of Head Start. On the other hand, fixed effects can mitigate the effects of some forms of nonrandom measurement error. Suppose for example, that all siblings in a family erroneously report that they did not attend Head Start but some other form of preschool. This will have no impact on the estimated effect of Head Start in the fixed-effects framework.

The third problem arises when μ_f is not fixed within a family. This would arise if parents treat siblings differently. Say, for example, parents invest more in the human capital of one sibling; if they also send that child to Head Start, β_1 will

[10] Missing values were handled by first determining whether a value could be assigned using information from other waves of the PSID. For example, in some cases, father's education could be assigned to one sibling by looking at reported values for the other sibling. Using the average of household income available at age 3, 4, 5, and 6 resulted in few instances of missing data for this variable (less than 1 percent of the sample). This average income measure is what we loosely refer to as income at preschool age. When data remained missing, we assigned the mean value from the sample and included a dummy variable in the regression which indicated that a value had been assigned.

[11] While small, this sample is larger than many of the experimental samples discussed in Barnett's (1995) summary of the literature. Our small sample should not affect the magnitude of effects but will affect the precision with which they are estimated. It is worth noting as well that given the low Head Start participation rates among whites, there are more African-American than white families with differences in the Head Start participation of siblings.

TABLE 2—RELATIONSHIP BETWEEN PARTICIPATION IN HEAD START AND OUTCOMES AS AN ADULT

					Mother fixed effects		If mother ≤ high school	
Outcome	All respondents (1)	Sibling sample (2)	Control observables (3)	Mother fixed effects (4)	African-American (5)	White (6)	African-American (7)	White (8)
A) Completed high school								
Head Start	−0.089	−0.075	0.006	0.037	−0.025	0.203	0.000	0.283
	(0.026)	(0.035)	(0.034)	(0.053)	(0.065)	(0.098)	(0.071)	(0.119)
Other preschool	0.085	0.073	0.003	−0.032	−0.056	−0.014	−0.080	−0.019
	(0.016)	(0.022)	(0.021)	(0.038)	(0.064)	(0.048)	(0.077)	(0.067)
Difference[a]	−0.174	−0.148	0.003	0.069	0.031	0.217	0.081	0.302
	(0.028)	(0.037)	(0.039)	(0.062)	(0.085)	(0.105)	(0.097)	(0.126)
B) Attended some college								
Head Start	−0.038	−0.016	0.075	0.092	0.023	0.281	0.031	0.276
	(0.023)	(0.033)	(0.033)	(0.056)	(0.066)	(0.108)	(0.067)	(0.120)
Other preschool	0.142	0.149	0.023	0.050	−0.007	0.095	0.022	0.103
	(0.019)	(0.027)	(0.026)	(0.040)	(0.064)	(0.052)	(0.072)	(0.068)
Difference[a]	−0.180	−0.165	0.052	0.042	0.030	0.186	0.009	0.173
	(0.028)	(0.040)	(0.041)	(0.065)	(0.085)	(0.115)	(0.092)	(0.127)
C) ln(Earnings at age 23–25)								
Head Start	−0.034	0.053	0.170	0.194	0.073	0.566	0.051	1.004
	(0.090)	(0.116)	(0.117)	(0.257)	(0.321)	(0.459)	(0.357)	(0.516)
Other preschool	0.173	0.174	0.002	0.079	−0.087	0.146	0.124	0.136
	(0.063)	(0.086)	(0.082)	(0.171)	(0.287)	(0.219)	(0.341)	(0.306)
Difference[a]	−0.207	−0.122	0.167	0.115	0.160	0.420	−0.073	0.868
	(0.104)	(0.138)	(0.144)	(0.302)	(0.420)	(0.504)	(0.482)	(0.548)
D) Booked or charged with crime								
Head Start	0.023	0.041	0.012	−0.053	−0.116	0.122	−0.126	0.058
	(0.018)	(0.026)	(0.026)	(0.039)	(0.045)	(0.077)	(0.050)	(0.095)
Other preschool	−0.017	−0.022	−0.001	0.032	0.000	0.063	−0.023	0.147
	(0.011)	(0.016)	(0.017)	(0.028)	(0.045)	(0.036)	(0.056)	(0.054)
Difference[a]	0.040	0.063	0.013	−0.085	−0.117	0.059	−0.103	−0.089
	(0.020)	(0.028)	(0.030)	(0.045)	(0.059)	(0.082)	(0.070)	(0.100)
Mother fixed effects	no	no	no	yes	yes	yes	yes	yes
Sample sizes:								
Panels A, B, and D	3,255	1,742	1,742	1,742	706	1,036	554	677
Panel C	1,383	728	728	728	272	456	216	320

Notes: Standard errors (in parentheses) permit family clustering and heteroscedasticity in OLS models. Columns (1) and (2) control for year of birth, gender, and race. Column (3) adds controls for maternal and paternal education, whether the mother was the head of household when the respondent was age 4, a spline in the log of family income at age 3–6 (with knots at each quartile), family size at age 4, birth order, whether respondent is oldest child, and whether respondent was low-birth-weight baby. All covariates that vary between siblings are included in columns (4)–(8) along with a mother fixed effect.

[a] (Head Start) − (other preschool).

be biased upward. It is more likely, however, that parents who want to invest in the human capital of a child send that child to another preschool since Head Start is targeted at disadvantaged children. So it is, in fact, β_2 that is more likely to be biased upward. In this case, the difference $B_1 - \beta_2$ could be considered a lower-bound estimate of the effect of Head Start where the estimate takes into account systematic differences in the treatment of siblings which result in one of them attending Head Start or another preschool while the other does not. Hence, we report this difference in Table 2.

Another reason μ_f may not be fixed within a family is that siblings experience different environments while growing up. For example, one child may participate in Head Start because family resources are low when the child is age 4 or 5 but siblings may attend other preschools (or no preschool) because resources are less constrained when the siblings are age 4 or 5. For this reason, we include a control for family income averaged over the period that the respondent was age 3, 4, 5, and 6 in all our regression models.

A special case in which the family effect is not fixed arises when benefits associated with Head Start spill over from one sibling to the other. The Head Start program emphasizes parent participation and teaches parenting skills which might affect all children. Moreover, it is possible that what one child learns may "spill over" to siblings. In general, in the fixed-effects framework, spillovers will tend to result in downward-biased estimates of the effect of Head Start because they reduce the differences in outcomes between siblings who did and did not attend the program. We will explore evidence that spillovers are important below.

IV. Results

Table 2 presents our empirical results. For each of the four adult outcomes, we present a set of estimates following the empirical strategy outlined above. In each panel, we report the correlation of the outcome with participation in Head Start and with participation in other preschools as well as the difference between these correlations. Standard errors below the estimates take into account correlations within families (and are robust to arbitrary forms of heteroscedasticity). For simplicity of interpretation of the coefficients, we present results based on ordinary least squares (OLS); logit (and Chamberlain fixed-effects logit) estimates provide substantively the same results.

We begin with the probability that a child completed high school. About three-quarters of the sample completed high school. The first column is based on OLS estimates of model (1). In addition to HDST and OPRE, the model includes year of birth, gender of the respondent, and whether the respondent is African-American. These OLS estimates indicate that relative to those who attended no preschool, respondents who reported attending Head Start were about 9 percent less likely to complete high school, while those who attended other preschools were about 9 percent more likely to complete high school.[12] In the second column, the sample is restricted to respondents with at least one sibling: the estimates are essentially the same as with the full sample. The results demonstrate once again that adults who attended Head Start are significantly less likely than other children to have completed high school, which is not surprising given their disadvantaged backgrounds.

Column (3) shows that, when we control for observable characteristics, high-school graduation rates are independent of reported preschool experience.[13] Estimates that include maternal fixed effects are reported in column (4). As discussed above, these estimates show the effects of controlling for both observed and unobserved characteristics of mothers that are fixed over time and have a linear and additive influence on high-school graduation. These estimates are consistent with those shown in column (3) in that they suggest that the negative effects of Head Start shown in column (1) are an artifact of the disadvantages of Head Start children. Columns (5) and (6) of Table 2 show estimates stratified by race. The estimates suggest that whites who attended Head Start are 20 percentage points more likely to complete high school than siblings who did not attend. However, there is no statistically significant effect for African-Americans.

In the final two columns of the table, the sample is restricted to respondents whose mother had no more than a high-school education. We examine this subsample for two reasons. First, the probability that a respondent

[12] A small fraction (8 percent) of respondents report attending both Head Start and also other preschools. For these respondents, both indicator variables are turned on. The Head Start effect is, therefore, the marginal effect of attending Head Start over and above the effect of participating in other preschools. We have experimented with including an additional indicator that isolate this group who attended both. The estimates suggest that the effects of other preschools are dominant: in all models that include family controls, there are no significant differences between other preschoolers and those who attended both Head Start and other preschools.

[13] In addition to those in columns (1) and (2), the controls are maternal education, paternal education, whether the mother was the head of the household, family income at age 4–6 (a spline in log income with knots at each quartile), family size at age 4, birth order, whether the respondent is the oldest child in the family, and whether the respondent was a low-birth-weight baby.

attended Head Start rises as socioeconomic status declines and so the percentage of reported Head Starters who are false positives is likely to be lower in this group. Second, since Head Start is targeted toward the most disadvantaged, it is of interest to know whether any long-term benefits associated with the program accrue to those from the poorest backgrounds. (We have also stratified on family income at age 3–6; the results are substantively the same but estimated with less precision in a few cases; these results are not shown.) We find that the long-term benefits of Head Start are even greater for whites in this group: those who attended Head Start are nearly 30 percent more likely to have completed high school than their siblings.

Panel B of Table 2 focuses on the next step in education: attendance at college. In the absence of controls for family background, those who attended Head Start are less likely to go to college relative to those who went to other preschools and, to a lesser extent, relative to those who attended no preschool. However, column (3) shows that after controlling observable differences in family background, those who attended Head Start are more likely to attend college. Column (4) shows that this is also true when unobserved fixed differences between families are controlled using mother fixed effects (although significance is marginal presumably because of the sample size). Columns (5) and (6) suggest that this effect is driven by white children who attended Head Start. These children are 28 percent more likely to attend college than siblings who attended no preschool and nearly 20 percent more likely than those who attended other preschools.[14]

Higher educational achievement is associated with many indicators of social and economic success in adulthood. In Panel C, we focus on one dimension of that success: annual earnings conditional on working.[15] To smooth out year-to-year fluctuations (and fill in some missing values), we examine the logarithm of average earnings in each year the respondent reported working between the ages of 23 and 25. There is little evidence that Head Start is associated with higher earnings at this age except in the case of white children of high-school dropouts [see column (8)]. In this group, children who attended Head Start earn significantly more than their siblings who did not attend preschool and also more than those who attended other preschools (although this latter difference is not significant). It is reasonable to suppose that earnings benefits associated with Head Start may emerge more clearly as these people move through their working lives given the findings for schooling attainment above and the well-documented association between schooling and earnings. (We have also examined whether Head Start is associated with elevated rates of labor-force participation among young adults but we find no statistically significant effects.)

The final panel examines the incidence of reported brushes with the law. Each respondent is asked whether he or she has ever been booked for or charged with a crime. Slightly less than 15 percent of the sample respondents report some brush with the law. Column (1) suggests that people who attended Head Start are significantly more likely than those who attended other preschools to have been booked or charged, although the point estimates for HDST and OPRE are not individually statistically significant. However, column (3) indicates that this gap disappears when observable characteristics are controlled, and column (4) shows that when both observed and unobserved characteristics are controlled the gap turns negative. That is, people who attended Head Start are significantly less likely to report being booked for or charged with a crime than siblings who attended another preschool.

In contrast to the results for educational attainment, this estimate appears to be driven by African-Americans. Columns (5) and (6) show that African-American children who attended Head Start are 12 percentage points less likely to report being booked or charged than siblings who did not. The effect is slightly larger among African-Americans whose mothers have only a high-school education, as shown in column (7). Reynolds et al. (2001) report a similar gap between treatments and controls in juvenile and violent crime rates among poor black children who participated in the Chicago CPC study.

[14] This racial difference is also evident in OLS models that control for observable but not unobservable differences. The point estimate on Head Start is 0.141 for whites with a standard error of 0.073, but the corresponding coefficient is not statistically significant for African-Americans.

[15] Since not all young adults work, the sample available for these models is smaller. There are 1,383 observations in total and 728 for people with siblings in the sample. Of these, 272 are African-American and 456 are white.

There is little evidence that children who attend preschools other than Head Start perform better later in life than children who do not attend preschool. [Of the 20 estimates in columns (4)–(8), one is significant at the 5-percent level which is the number to be expected if the estimates were independent.] This results suggests that the positive outcomes associated with attending preschool in columns (1) and (2) largely reflect selection into these programs.

We have also explored the question of whether the effects of Head Start differ with other demographic characteristics of the respondent, such as gender and birth order. While we find no significant differences in the effect of Head Start on males relative to females, there is one instance in which large differences in the point estimates for males and females emerge. Relative to their siblings, males who attended Head Start are between 15 and 20 percentage points more likely to complete high school than female respondents. This is true for both whites and African-Americans. The gap disappears when we examine college attendance and there are no gender differences with respect to earnings or brushes with the law.[16]

Turning to birth order, we asked whether there were any significant differences between firstborn children and others. Again, we found no statistically significant differences in the effects of Head Start between firstborn children and their siblings. However, once again, the point estimates are suggestive. Among African-Americans, higher birth-order children appear to benefit more from Head Start than their older siblings, particularly with regard to schooling outcomes.

As discussed above, larger effects for younger siblings could reflect the presence of spillovers of Head Start benefits from older to younger children. It is plausible to assume that spillovers flow in this direction rather than from younger to older siblings for two reasons. First, older siblings are more likely to teach (or be a role model) for younger siblings. Second, the Head Start program requires parent participation and some of the skills that parents learn are likely to benefit younger children more than older siblings. For example, if a parent of a five-year-old Head Starter and a one-year-old learns that it is important to read to children from infancy, the one-year-old is likely to benefit more than the five-year-old from this new knowledge regardless of whether the one-year-old goes on to attend Head Start.

In order to assess whether these sorts of spillovers are important, we have estimated models which allow the effects of Head Start (and other preschools) to differ if an older sibling participated in the program. For the two schooling outcomes, the spillover effects of Head Start tend to be positive but they are relatively small and not significant. There is no evidence of spillover effects on earnings. There do, however, appear to be spillover effects for being booked or charged: adults with an older sibling who attended Head Start are considerably less likely to have been booked or charged with a crime, and this effect reinforces the benefits associated with the index adult's participation in Head Start. For example, among African-Americans whose mothers only have a high-school education, the respondent is 11 percent less likely to have had a brush with the law if an older sibling attended Head Start (t statistic = 2.0) and 27 percent less likely if the respondent him or herself also attended Head Start (t statistic = 3.2).

In sum, there is evidence that Head Start attendance is associated with significant improvements in educational outcomes and possibly with higher earnings among whites, while among African-Americans, we find evidence that past Head Start attendance reduces reported

[16] The relationship between Head Start and teenage or out-of-wedlock childbearing has received considerable attention in the literature. Whereas graduating from high school is generally regarded as a positive outcome, there is debate in the literature regarding the welfare interpretation that should be placed on a woman who has children during her teen years or outside of marriage. Moreover, the empirical strategy used in this study is not well suited to analyze the issue since the analytical sample is, by design, restricted to those women who have a female sibling. This results in a sample of 467 women of whom 10 percent attended Head Start and 16 percent had a child out of wedlock (or while a teenager). The effective sample size for these analyses is small. With these caveats in mind, we have investigated the relationship between Head Start and childbearing. Women who attended Head Start are about 10 percent more likely to have a child out of wedlock than other women. However, when selection is taken into account, the differences among siblings are reduced to 5 percent (and the standard error is 6 percent). Among white women, those who attended Head Start are 2 percent *less* likely to have a child out of wedlock relative to their siblings. None of the differences is significant. The differences in teenage childbearing are smaller in magnitude, and none is significant.

criminal activity. We also find some suggestive evidence that Head Start participation improved rates of high-school completion among African-American males (though these estimates were not statistically significant), and that there are spillover effects of Head Start attendance from older to younger siblings.

V. Conclusions

Very little is known about the longer-term effects of participation in Head Start, although previous research showing "fade-out" in effects on test scores raises legitimate questions about whether early gains translate into benefits later in life. This paper uses nonexperimental data on young adults in the PSID to ask whether participation in Head Start is associated with benefits in adulthood. We exploit the panel dimension of the PSID and control for observable differences between respondents when they were young children. We also exploit the family-based sampling frame of the PSID by including maternal fixed effects and comparing adult outcomes of siblings.

Participation in Head Start has positive effects on the probability of attending college. However, these positive effects are driven by whites. Whites also see large increases in the probability of graduating from high school, and possibly in earnings as young adults. We did not find statistically significant effects for African-Americans, though we did find some suggestive evidence that Head Start may increase the probability of graduating from high school among African-American males. We also find that African-Americans who participated in Head Start are significantly less likely to have been booked or charged with a crime than siblings who did not. Head Start did not appear to have any significant effect on reports of being booked or charged among whites. Finally, we find some evidence suggesting that there are positive spillovers from older children who attended Head Start to their younger siblings, particularly with regard to brushes with the law.

We have sought to carefully describe the limitations as well as the strengths of our study sample and methods. With those limitations in mind, we conclude that the results are supportive of the view that Head Start participants gain social and economic benefits that persist into adulthood. Moreover, as we have argued above, our methods are likely to provide lower-bound estimates on the positive effects of Head Start. However, it would be foolhardy to leap to conclusions about the long-term efficacy of a large program like Head Start on the basis of a single study. Much remains to be discovered about the nature and distribution of longer-term benefits from early childhood interventions.

REFERENCES

Administration for Children and Families. *Head Start 1998 fact sheet.* Washington, DC: U.S. Department of Health and Human Services, 1999.

Barnett, Steven. "Long-Term Effects of Early Childhood Programs on Cognitive and School Outcomes." *The Future of Children,* 1995, *5*(3), pp. 25–50.

Campbell, Frances A.; Pungello, Elizabeth P.; Miller-Johnson, Shari; Burchinal, Margaret and Ramey, Craig T. "The Development of Cognitive and Academic Abilities: Growth Curves from an Early Childhood Educational Experiment." *Developmental Psychology,* March 2001, *37*(2), pp. 231–42.

Campbell, Frances A.; Ramey, Craig T.; Pungello, Elizabeth P.; Sparling, Joseph and Miller-Johnson, Shari. "Early Childhood Education: Young Adult Outcomes from the Abecedarian Project." *Applied Developmental Science,* 2002, *6*(1), pp. 42–57.

Currie, Janet. "Early Childhood Education Programs." *Journal of Economic Perspectives,* Spring 2001, *15*(2), pp. 213–38.

Currie, Janet and Thomas, Duncan. "Does Head Start Make a Difference?" *American Economic Review,* June 1995, *85*(3), pp. 341–64.

______. "Does Head Start Help Hispanic Children?" *Journal of Public Economics,* November 1999, *74*(2), pp. 235–62.

______. "School Quality and the Long-term Effects of Head Start." *Journal of Human Resources,* Fall 2000, *35*(4), pp. 755–74.

Ebbinghaus, Hermann. *Memory: A contribution to experimental psychology.* New York: Dover, 1894.

Heckman, James J.; Hsse, Jing Jing and Rubinstein, Yona. "The GED is a Mixed Signal: The Effect of Cognitive and Non-Cognitive Skills on Human Capital and Labor Market Outcomes." Mimeo, University of Chicago, 2000.

Karoly, Lynn A.; Greenwood, Peter W.; Everingham, Susan S.; Hoube, Jill; Kilburn, M. Rebecca; Rydell, Peter C.; Sanders, Matthew and Chiesa, James. *Investing in our children: What we know and don't know about the costs and benefits of early childhood interventions.* Santa Monica: RAND MR-898, 1998.

National Center for Health Statistics. *Vital statistics of the United States, 1997. Volume 1: Natality.* Hyattsville, MD: National Center for Health Statistics, 2000.

Ramey, Craig; Campbell, Frances A. and Blair, Clancy. "Enhancing the Life Course for High-Risk Children," in Jonathon Crane, ed., *Social programs that work.* New York: Russell Sage, 1998, pp. 184–99.

Reynolds, Arthur J. "Extended Early Childhood Intervention and School Achievement: Age Thirteen Findings from the Chicago Longitudinal Study." *Child Development,* February 1998, *69*(1), pp. 231–46.

______. *Success in early intervention: The Chicago Child-Parent Centers.* Lincoln, NE: University of Nebraska Press, 2000.

Reynolds, Arthur J.; Temple, Judy A.; Robertson, Dylan L. and Mann, Emily A. "Long-Term Effects of an Early Childhood Intervention on Educational Achievement and Juvenile Arrest: A 15-Year Follow-up of Low-Income Children in Public School." *Journal of American Medical Association,* 2001, *285*(18), pp. 2339–46.

Sudman, Seymour; Bradburn, Norman M. and Schwarz, Norbert. *Thinking about answers: The application of cognitive processes to survey methodology.* San Francisco, CA: Jossey-Bass Press, 1996.

Temple, Judy A.; Reynolds, Arthur and Miedel, Wendy. "Can Early Intervention Prevent High School Dropout? Evidence from the Chicago Child-Parent Centers." *Urban Education,* March 2000, *35*(1), pp. 31–56.